# BOOKS TO BUILD AN EMPIRE

# BOOKS TO BUILD
# AN EMPIRE

*A Bibliographical History
of English Overseas Interests to 1620*

by

## JOHN PARKER

1965
N. ISRAEL / AMSTERDAM

PRINTED IN THE NETHERLANDS
BY THIEME - NIJMEGEN

For Pat, Jackie,
and Sarah Jane

# TABLE OF CONTENTS

# PREFACE

The major political, economic, and intellectual movements that have influenced Western Europe since the invention of printing have left traces at least, but more often quantities, of literature describing, praising, analysing, condemning what was of current interest at a given place and time. The origins and growth of English interest in those parts of the world that would one day make up the British Empire can be followed in the books that came from English presses between 1481 and 1620. This book is an attempt to record and describe these publications, and to show the part they played as England moved toward her great overseas adventure.

A subject bibliography of this type is by nature subjective in its inclusiveness, and the titles I have chosen to show the growth of English interests abroad probably will not satisfy all who use this book. I have deliberately omitted works on the science of navigation and closely related subjects, since Commander David W. Waters is preparing a book dealing specifically in those areas. Where navigation books have been included it is because they contain material of major geographic interest. I have also omitted travel narratives and geographies relating solely to Europe, as these did not seem to be a part of the novel experience of travel to new and little-known lands. I have attempted to include all English books published between 1481 and 1620 which are of geographic interest, omitting unpublished manuscripts which could have had only a limited circulation and thereby do not represent the state of public interest or knowledge. I have also tried to include all published works of this period which reflect an attitude for or against the idea of establishing an English empire abroad, the promotion of English overseas commerce or missionary activity among distant peoples.

In assembling these 267 titles and editions I have had assistance from many libraries in this country and in Great Britain. Those in Great Britain include libraries of the British Museum; the Public Record Office; Corpus Christi College, Oxford; Emmanuel College, Cambridge; Lambeth Palace; Lincoln Cathedral; and the Bodleian Library. Among libraries in the United States, I have drawn upon the resources of the Folger, Newberry, Henry E. Huntington, William L. Clements, John Carter Brown, New York Public and Boston Public Libraries, the Library of Congress and the libraries of Harvard, Yale and Princeton Universities, the Universities of Michigan, Wisconsin, and Minnesota, particularly the James Ford Bell Collection at the latter institution. I appreciate the assistance I have had from all of these libraries, and am especially grateful for cooperation from the Reference Department of the University of Minnesota Library.

I also wish to acknowledge the guidance of Professor Raymond L. Kilgour who directed the writing of an earlier version of this book as a doctoral dissertation at the University of Michigan. The late William Jackson, Librarian of the Houghton Library, gave me advice frequently. Boies Penrose has been helpful with advice and the loan of a very rare book from his library. Mrs. Martha Bray has made many helpful editorial suggestions, and Professor David B. Quinn's reading of the manuscript has been extremely helpful.

Minneapolis, Minnesota                                    JOHN PARKER

*Chapter I*

## INTRODUCTION

The rise of the British Empire has been attributed to a variety of causes, including domestic economic pressures, ambitious and wise rulers, clever merchants, adventurous seamen, and the zeal to carry Christianity abroad. Yet these forces could not have their ultimate effect until Englishmen had developed a knowledge of distant lands—and the means of sailing there—as well as an enthusiasm for national overseas expansion sufficiently widespread to supply people to hold and settle territories abroad.

In transmitting both knowledge and enthusiasm among the literate public, the printed book was of fundamental importance. If authors, translators, patrons, and publishers cannot be made to overshadow statesmen and adventurers, their contribution was nevertheless significant in that it was they who gave the idea of empire to the English people and supplied England with books on geography and travel which spread to the reading public information essential to the beginnings of empire.

The printing press came to England in the hands of William Caxton in 1477. There were no European empires to publicize at that time. The Portuguese were inching down the coast of Africa and had just crossed the equator. Christopher Columbus, in his mid-twenties, had just been introduced to the Atlantic Ocean. But the invention of the printing press and the voyages of exploration which followed within the next half century were of the same Renaissance, and even in its incunabular age the press was employed on occasion to give out news of distant lands visited by European sailors and merchants. Even before the Portuguese reached India or Columbus found islands in the western ocean, publishers in Europe had responded to the public interest in the distant and little-known lands of the Near East, Asia, and Africa. Geographers from antiquity such as Ptolemy, Strabo, and Solinus were being read from printed books before the art of printing came to England. The story of Marco Polo's remarkable travels came into print in Nuremberg while Caxton was setting up his press in Westminster.

The wonderful, if fictitious, tales of Sir John Mandeville's eastern journeys had by that time begun to catch the fancy of Europeans eager for accounts of strange lands.

European civilization was by the end of the fifteenth century no longer content with its continental boundaries, and it was natural that Englishmen should ultimately find a share in rolling back the horizon. The extent to which Englishmen found it possible to become interested in the opening up of the outer world to European influences is best measured by the publication of books on travel, geography, navigation, and exploration in England; for the publisher, then as now, was a merchant with his output tuned to popular interest. In an age free of the restraints of international copyright, the publisher had a wide choice, and the variety of books that came from English presses between the beginnings of Caxton and the landing at Plymouth Rock show that England's few publishers were not unduly narrow in their selection of titles to offer the public. Indeed they had a manifold opportunity, for the Renaissance in England as elsewhere brought together writings from the classical traditions and the modern world and spread them before minds steeped in medieval ways of thought, and the press served all of these intellectual interests.

As we seek the origins and early development of travel literature in England, we must bear in mind that it could come only from an interest in distant lands, and that interest could develop only in a society where travel books filled a literary need, whether that need was emotional, recreational, or instructive. In addition we must consider briefly the development of the English language as a vehicle for travel narratives in the fifteenth century, the state of the printing technology, and the other reading interests of Englishmen with which travel literature would have to compete.

In the later Middle Ages there were two major reasons for an Englishman to undertake travels beyond his island—commerce and religious pilgrimages. In both of these pursuits Englishmen were under some limitations.

England's commerce was largely based on two commodities—fish and wool—of which the latter was the more important. Three routes served the country's overseas trade, two running east-west, the other north-south. England was at the western end of the east-west routes, one of which led to Italy and the Levant toward India, the other through the Baltic to Muscovy and inner Asia. In payment for spices and furs from the East, Europe's major export was cloth, and in supplying raw wool to Flanders and Germany, England was tied to this international trade. As a supplier of raw materials, however, England had little opportunity to participate in actual trade to distant countries, for the Baltic route was dominated by the Hanseatic merchants and the wool trade of Italy was controlled by Florence and Venice.[1] This relationship to Europe's commerce was long a source of discontent in England, and as early as 1258 a movement to stimulate the native woolen manufacturing industry was begun, but the demand for raw wool in Flanders was strong and English technology was weak, so the plan failed. The next century produced better results. Edward III, in 1331, invited Flemish craftsmen who were beset with various political and economic troubles in their homeland to settle in England, and the result was a substantial migration of weavers, dyers and fullers.[2] It was this immigration, plus an understanding of the use of water power in fulling mills, that started England on her way to becoming an exporter of finished goods and thus an active seeker after new markets. This development did much to encourage the formation of a capitalist class in England, which shortly expressed itself in the Merchant Adventurer type of organization in which English overseas commerce finds its true beginnings.[3] Edward's reign also marked the decline of the influence of foreign moneylenders in England's court as improved trade reduced the King's dependence on Bardi of Florence and Tidemann of Limberg who had been the principal creditors of the crown.[4] This gave England increased opportunity to formulate trade policies without the influence of other commercial interests.

The rise in woolen manufacturing in England, however, did not mean immediate decline for her competitors. Even the moneylenders stayed on as agents of foreign exporters who continued to dominate the export of English wool. But the opportunity for sale of wool at home produced a change in England's agriculture, as it was found that sheep were 'the most profitablest cattle any man can have.' Arable land was frequently converted to pasture, and landholders, realizing their position as suppliers of a key commodity in international trade, developed an increased interest in the overseas commerce of their country. Many men of rank actually became owners of ships in the fifteenth century.[5] While sheep increased, the export of raw wool declined from 35,000 sacks in 1310 to 8,000 sacks in 1450. In the meantime the export of cloths increased from 5,000 per year in the middle of the fourteenth century to twenty times that number in the reign of Henry VIII. In the last decade of the fourteenth century alone, there was nearly a three-fold increase in the number of broadcloths exported per year over the average of the previous decade.[6]

These figures indicate the increasing pressure in England for export markets, and that pressure was confronted by the entrenched interests of the Hanse and the Italian merchants, for in the fifteenth century there was no known outlet for goods except Europe and northern Africa, the commerce of which had long been dominated by these groups. The resulting hostility between England and the Hanse had the effect of improving London's position among her English competitors, for by discriminating against the Hanse, London was able to develop more fully her markets in Holland, which the London Merchant Adventurers came to dominate, whereas the other English cities reaped the hostility of the Hanse and little more. By the beginning of the fifteenth century, this situation had given London one-third of England's woolen exports, and had established her Merchants of the Staple and Merchant Adventurers as the dominant commercial organizations of England. The simultaneous decline of many other ports was to prove a factor in the tardiness of England's later overseas development, for London's dominance in a foreign market, near at hand and centered in a small area, called for little skill in navigation and provided little stimulus in the way of new opportunities to expand sales abroad. It was a safe, conservative and profitable trade.

While London overshadowed the other ports facing the continent, England's best hope for an overseas trade that could reach into new markets lay in the vigorous southern and western ports whose maritime activity had developed skill in seamanship and knowledge of distant regions. Whereas London was the western terminus of the east-west trade, Bristol was the focal point in the north-south route which linked Iceland and the Mediterranean through commerce in fish, grain, cloth and wine—a commerce which incidentally took Englishmen from Bristol to Ireland, Iceland, Norway, Prussia, Rouen, Cherbourg, Bayonne, Lisbon, Seville, Pisa, Jaffa and Jerusalem.[7] No city in fifteenth-century Europe could boast a more far-flung trade than this. Nor was Bristol, though it became the leader, the only participant in the northern trade; several ports in eastern England, including Hull, Newcastle, Berwick and Lynn were also actively engaged in Iceland fishing and trading enterprises early in the fifteenth century.[8]

Meanwhile, southern England was developing a commerce also oriented to distant countries. Records at Southampton clearly indicate that the state fleets of Venice which called there after 1319 brought exotic products for the aristocracy of England, and the city was noted for the hospitality it showed to alien merchants. While these legitimate activities were bringing Southampton into prominence as a major port, which reached its zenith during the reign of Edward IV,[9] the southwestern coastal towns in Devon and Cornwall were growing on an active piracy which produced seamen of great daring and ability. These ports gave fifteenth-century England a tradition of bold enterprise which was to inspire later captains to like achievements in more distant waters.

The pressure to export, the familiarity of some English ports with distant trade, and the competence of her seamen gave England the components of an interest in travel and exploration, but limiting factors were also present. Chief among these was London's position of dominance in English overseas trade.

London was the commercial as well as the political capital of England, and in the fifteenth century London was dominated by her merchants in their guilds, the power shifting from the fishmongers and vintners to the mercers, drapers, and grocers as command of shipping shifted to the latter guilds. These groups which controlled London were oriented toward the nearer ports of the Continent by long tradition.[10] The Merchant Adventurers organization, through which the merchants worked, was capable of exerting strong influence at the seat of England's government, since it was an organization with a government of its own, a policy of its own, and a set of restrictions upon membership which limited the opportunity for new members to alter established policies. So long as its trade to the Continent was satisfactory, it could be counted on to oppose any serious deviation in the direction of English overseas trade.

Bristol had no such influential a group of merchants as had London. Its leaders desired no part in national affairs but concentrated rather upon avoiding the notice of the central government, particularly the Exchequer, as the Atlantic trade developed.[11] If this attitude prevented unwanted influence by the central government in Bristol's affairs, it also removed Bristol's overseas commercial interests from the royal attention.

While London was dominant among English ports, she was herself dominated by the Hanseatic and Italian cities that largely controlled English trade in the fifteenth century. This greatly limited the freedom of the English sailors and merchants to travel abroad. Despite the attempt begun by the Navigation Act of 1381 to keep English goods in English ships, by 1468 English shipping was barely adequate to the nation's needs, and it was necessary to cater to the Hanse as a supplementary source of cargo space.[12] The Baltic trade continued under the control of the Hanse merchants, while Venice and Florence dominated the wool trade to Italy. The cloth trade to Flanders was shared with the Hanseatic and Flemish merchants, and only in the wine and fish trades of the north-south route were the English strong competitors.

Discontented with her commercial captivity, and feeling the need for new markets, England made attempts to break out of it. The last quarter of the century saw numerous instances of hostility between London and the Hanse merchants stationed there, and the reign of Edward IV is punctuated with evidence that England was seeking new markets for its products. Fees were paid out to men listed as 'explorators' who were dispatched to 'extra partes marinas.' The King himself was engaged in commerce in the Mediterranean which would gain for him information on the trade of North Africa. It is apparent that English ships were also making the voyage to the west coast of Africa, for protests from Lisbon in 1482 portray the English along with Spanish as a menace to the Portuguese trade to Guinea.[13] Yet these were mere feelers for new overseas commerce, and there is no sign that they were followed up by a consistent flow of trade, or that they had any effect upon the tendency of English goods to find markets in the convenient Low Countries.

English businessmen did, of course, get established on the Continent in the fifteenth century in places other than the Netherlands. They were to be found in Venice, Rome, Milan, Genoa and Lucca, but they were not numerous, and they were chiefly Londoners participating in well-established channels of trade.[14]

The religious motive must have taken more Englishmen away from their homeland than did commerce in the later Middle Ages. The number of persons who took part in pilgrimages is unknown, but it is certain that the appeal of pilgrimages penetrated to all classes of society, and the destinations of these seekers after holy places extended from Cologne to Jerusalem. France, Spain and Italy all had numerous shrines to which Englishmen traveled in such numbers that Richard II in 1388 sought to regulate the traffic by requiring passports and by designating London, Sandwich, Dover, Southampton, Plymouth, Dartmouth, Bristol, Yarmouth, Boston, Kingston-upon-Hull, Newcastle-upon-Tyne, and the nearer ports of Ireland as the only places at which passports would be available. The acceptability of pilgrimages in England during this period is shown by the fact that some guilds required members to give assistance to those of the guild who proposed to go abroad for this purpose.[15]

Again, however, there were limitations upon this type of travel. Voyages by sea were uncomfortable, dangerous and expensive, while land travel was tedious and slow. A more telling limitation in the fourteenth and fifteenth centuries was the fact that they were not periods of deep piety in England. Churchmen as well as laymen ridiculed the actions of the overly pious, an attitude which sometimes reflected unfavorably on pilgrimages. The fourteenth century was also one of budding nationalism in England, in which the attachment to Rome, always more tenuous than that of France, Italy, and Spain, became even less firm. England's ties with Rome showed a decided weakening in this and the following century, as archbishops and cardinals ceased to visit Rome. The appointment of bishops was, by the fifteenth century, a royal function, with papal consent generally taken for granted. 'It is not the Pope, but the King of England who governs the Church in his dominions,' said Martin V.[16] With this loosening of ecclesiastical bonds, it might be expected that English members of the church should show less interest in the capital of their faith.

In spite of these limitations, English pilgrims in Rome were numerous enough in the late fourteenth century to justify the maintenance of a hospice for them there. While statistics are scarce, it has been estimated that two hundred English pilgrims went to Rome in 1300 and twice that number in 1350. That the taste for pilgrimages did not die out in the following century is indicated by William Wey, an English traveler who, in 1456, noted thirty-two English ships in the harbor at Corunna, bringing English pilgrims to their favorite shrine at St. James of Compostela. In a single year 2,400 licenses were issued to visit that shrine. It is doubtful that the pilgrimage attracted many of the truly devout among the English of the fifteenth century, for other virtues were taking the place of these 'adventures after holiness', but for the adventurous they did give an excuse for travel which had at least the nominal approval of church and society.[17]

Whether owing to commerce, curiosity, or religion, Englishmen had motives for travel before they had a press to print their accounts of distant places. Indeed, there were English travelers before the English language was in general use. As England acquired a degree of commercial and religious independence in the fourteenth century, an English language and literature also began to develop. In 1307 Edward II took his oath in French, Henry IV in 1399 took his in English. This represents less a repudiation of French than its union with Anglo-Saxon. The fusion began at the level of the common people, but it became the language of the courts also in the fourteenth century; and by 1363 the Chancellor opened a session of Parliament with a speech in English. Latin and French remained the languages of learned people, but a national English literature began to take shape with Chaucer and the poets of his period.[18] In the next century, while Latin held its own among scholars, prose writers came forth to dominate the scene with rude but useful works. There were instructive books on medical procedure, the influence of planets, hunting, hawking and making pilgrimages; merchants, servants, and women who were learning to read found utilitarian prose readily available.

The appearance of documents in English frequently, after 1416, gave the new language a sanction which provided further literary stimulus. This, in turn, made it easier for people to become educated, and the fifteenth century was one of constantly expanding educational opportunity.[20] What people chose to read were primarily books of spiritual and emotional appeal, with religious literature clearly dominant. The increased use of English was part of the emerging English nationalism which found emotional expression in the ballad literature inspired by the English victory over the French at Agincourt in 1415 and the defense of Calais in 1436. In such verses as the following, English patriotic feeling found early literary expression:

> *Agincourt! Agincourt!*
> *Know ye not Agincourt?*
> *English of every sort,*
> *    High men and low men*
> *Fought that day wondrous well,*
> *As our old stories tell,*
> *    Thanks to our bowmen.*[21]

Along with such inspirational works there developed secular prose, some of it being concerned with domestic problems of health, crops and etiquette; other literary pieces were devoted to problems of state, such as *The libelle of Englyshe polycye* with its concern for maritime and commercial affairs of the nation and its description of the economies of other states.[22]

By the time printing came to England, therefore, a prose literature in popular language was already well developed, expressing the interest of English readers in a wide range of subjects. This literature, and its audience as well, grew larger in the fifteenth century, and as translations into English increased, a truly national audience was available. A printer would know that his book in English could have an appeal to all but the lowest classes of English society.

England learned from the Continent in printing as she had done in weaving, and as she was to do in navigation. The tardiness of the pupil in the book trade is shown by the large numbers of bookmen from the Continent who came to England to provide both instruction and competition for the native artisans. Undoubtedly, the demand for books far exceeded the supply, and this imbalance was recognized in a law of 1484 which encouraged aliens to participate in England's book trade.[23]

Not only printers but books also came to England from Europe. A brisk literary trade was well established by 1483, and European printers were issuing books with the English market specifically in mind by that time. Customs rolls of the late fifteenth and early sixteenth centuries record that both English and alien booksellers were engaged in this international traffic in books. Primers and histories were major items in this trade which acquainted readers in England with such prominent publishers as Gerard Leeu of Gouda, John Treschel of Lyons, Aldus Manutius of Venice and Francis Birckman of Cologne. Certain of a market, booksellers from France and the Low Countries attended the major fairs on the Continent to buy stock for export to England, and the extent of their success in England can be judged by the fact that in 1479–80 the three major book importers brought about fourteen hundred books into England in one year. The dependability of the English book purchases induced one Dutch printer, Jan van Doesborch, to give one-third of his production to English works.[24]

The comparative backwardness of printing in England in the fifteenth century can be seen when we compare the output of Dutch presses, some 1,900 to 2,000 books published before 1500 to England's production of about 360 books.[25]. No less than 266 European towns had printing presses by 1500, whereas in England only London, St. Albans and Oxford had presses by that date.[26] Of these, London was clearly dominant, an the spread of printing to the provinces was very slow, with probably not more than a dozen master printers working outside of London down to 1557.

In view of England's tardiness in developing native printing industry, it is remarkable to find a law of 1534 protecting English printers against competition. The earlier law of 1484 had encouraged alien craftsmen to bring their knowledge of printing to England, but now it was believed that the English printing industry had grown until 'at this day there be within this realme a great number of connyng and experte in the said science or craft of printing, as able to exercise the said crafte in all pointes as any stranger in any other realme or country.' 27 This law made it illegal for persons in England to trade in books produced outside of the country, and when it is considered in the light of a law of 1523 insisting on English apprentices in the trade, and another of 1529 ending the right of alien printers to set up shop in England, it is apparent that England felt she had grown equal to the task of supplying her own literary wares. Despite this confidence, however, it was not until 1540 or 1550 that England's printers could keep abreast of local demands for liturgical books alone.28

For all its technical inferiority and few practitioners, the English book trade was clearly established in the first third of the sixteenth century. Living by the sale of its wares, it was certain to reflect the climate of England's intellectual life in the books it produced. In some of these we see the level of English interest in and knowledge of the outer world—distant lands that would one day be familiar parts of the British empire.

## NOTES TO CHAPTER I

1 James A. Williamson, *Maritime enterprise* (Oxford: Clarendon Press, 1913), pp. 15–17.
2 Ephraim Lipson, *The history of the woolen and worsted industries* (London: A. & C. Black, Ltd., 1921), pp. 9–13.
3 Charles L. Kingsford, 'The beginnings of English maritime enterprise,' *History*, XIII (October, 1928), 193–98.
4 Alice Bearwood, 'Alien merchants and the English crown in the later fourteenth century,' *Economic history review*, II (January, 1930), 229.
5 Kingsford, *History*, XIII, 200–3.
6 Goldwin Albert Smith, *A history of England* (New York: Charles Scribner's Sons, 1949), p. 155; Lipson, p. 16; 'The rise of the Merchant Adventurers,' *Statist*, CXL (October 16, 1934), 739–40.
7 E. M. Carus-Wilson, *The overseas trade of Bristol in the later Middle Ages* (n.p.: For the Bristol Record Society, 1937), pp. 30–130.
8 Ernest R. Cooper. 'The Dunwich Iceland ships,' *The mariner's mirror*, XV (April, 1939), 170–77; E. M. Carus-Wilson, 'The Iceland trade,' *Studies in English trade in the fifteenth century*, ed. Eileen Power and M. M. Postan (London: George

Routledge and Sons, Ltd., 1933), pp. 155–82.; G. J. Marcus, 'The first English voyages to Iceland,' *The mariner's mirror*, XLII (1956), 313–18.

9 Alwyn A. Ruddock, 'Alien merchants in Southampton in the later Middle Ages,' *The English historical review*, LXI (January, 1946), 1–17; 'The method of handling cargoes of medieval merchant galleys,' *Bulletin of the Institute of Historical Research*, XIX (1942), 140–48; *Italian merchants and shipping in Southampton, 1270–1600* (Southampton: University College, 1951), *passim*.

10 Charles L. Kingsford, *Prejudice and promise in XVth century England* (Oxford; Clarendon Press, 1925), p. 122; A. Weiner, 'Early commercial intercourse between England and Germany,' *Economica*, II (June, 1922), 127–48.

11 E. M. Carus-Wilson, 'The overseas trade of Bristol' *Studies in English trade in the fifteenth century*, ed. Power and Postan, p. 244.

12 F. R. Salter, 'The Hanse, Cologne and the crisis of 1468,' *Economic history review*, III (January, 1931), 93–96.

13 David B. Quinn, 'Edward IV and exploration,' *The mariner's mirror*, XXI (July, 1935), 275, 279.

14 George B. Parks, *The English traveler to Italy* (Stanford: University Press, [1934]), pp. 395–402.

15 J. J. Jusserand, *English wayfaring life in the Middle Ages* (London: T. Fisher Unwin, 1889), pp. 361–62, 380.

16 Quoted in A. R. Myers, *England in the late Middle Ages* (Harmondsworth, Middlesex: Penguin Books, Ltd., 1956), p. 154.

17 Parks, *The English traveler to Italy*, pp. 356–59; William Wey, *The itineraries of William Wey* (London: The Roxburgh Club, 1857), p. 154; H. Maynard Smith, *Pre-Reformation England* (London: Macmillan & Co., Ltd., 1938), p. 195.

18 J. J. Jusserand, *A literary history of the English people* (3 vols.; London: T. Fisher Unwin, 1895), I, 237, 242, 267–372.

19 H. S. Bennett, 'Science and information in English writings of the fifteenth century,' *Modern language review*, XXXIX (January, 1944), 1–8.

20 Charles L. Kingsford, *Prejudice and promise in XVth century England*, p. 25.

21 Charles L. Kingsford, *English history in contemporary poetry*, Vol. II: *Lancaster and York* (London: For the Historical Association by George Bell and Sons, Ltd., 1913), p. 13.

22 Sir George Warner (ed.), *The libelle of Englyshe polycye* (Oxford: Clarendon Press, 1926), passim. For a more extended treatment of this work see p. 31 below.

23 E. Gordon Duff, *A century of the English book trade* (London: The Bibliographical Society, 1905), pp. xi, xii, 1–176, *passim*.

24 Henry R. Plomer, 'The importation of books into England in the 15th and 16th centuries,' *The library*, 4th series, IV (September, 1923), 146–50; 'The importation of Low Country and French books into England, 1480 and 1502–3,' *The library*, 4th series, IX (September, 1928), 164; *Wynkyn de Worde and his contemporaries* (London: Grafton and Company, 1925), pp. 22–33; M. E. Kronenberg, 'Notes on English printing in the Low Countries,' *The library*, 4th series, IX (September, 1928), 141.

25 Kronenberg, p. 140.

26 J. M. Lenhart, 'Pre-Reformation printers and their services to the Church,' *Ecclesiastical review*, LXXXI (August, 1929), 156.

27 Quoted in Plomer, *Wynkyn de Worde*, p. 38.

28 Kronenberg, p. 141.

## Chapter II

## THE AGE OF CABOT AND CAXTON

When the art of printing came to England, the intellectual life of the English people was largely in the hands of ecclesiastics. They dominated the universities and the Civil Service and held important positions in the government. The awakening influence of Italian humanism, as it came to England in the fifteenth century, was channeled through their thinking, and as a result it came into English cultural life as a tool for the refinement of scholasticism rather than a new intellectual system, carrying with it new learning in many areas other than theology.[1] This utilitarian approach to humanism may have served the ecclesiastics well in the religious conflicts of the next century, but it did little to invite English interest in the age of exploration which vied with the Reformation for attention in some countries on the Continent. Nevertheless, the seed of interest in overseas exploration was planted in some English minds in the fifteenth century, and an interest in travel abroad actually manifested itself in English books published in the last two decades of that century.

Bristol was the starting point of the age of discovery in England. The voyages to Iceland already referred to gave Bristol sailors experience in navigating far from their native port, and in their seamanship they were undoubtedly indebted to the Portuguese, Spanish, and French with whom they were in frequent contact. By the late fifteenth century, compasses, charts, pilot books, means of determining latitude and some knowledge of finding longitude were known, and it is likely that in this knowledge English pilots were not far behind Continental navigators.[2]

English confidence in the ability of seamen to navigate unknown parts of the Atlantic is indicated by the expedition of John Jay of Bristol which, on July 15, 1480, set out into the Atlantic in search of the island of Brasil and was at sea nine weeks before storms drove it to port in Ireland. The following year Thomas Croft, also of Bristol, was exonerated by a jury of the charge of trading illegally in salt on the ground that the ships of which he owned one-eighth part were not trading in salt, but were 'seeking and discovering a certain island called the Isle of Brasile.'[3] The outcome of these voyages encouraged the Bristol men to continue their westward sailing. In 1498 Pedro de Ayala, the Spanish ambassador, wrote from London, 'for the last seven years the people of Bristol have equipped two, three and four caravels in search of the island of Brazil and the Seven Cities.'[4]

This suggests that at some time toward the beginning of that seven year period some land in the western Atlantic was found, and this appears to be corroborated by the recently discovered letter of John Day, an Englishman living in Andalusia, who wrote in the winter of 1497–98 that the land found by John Cabot in 1497 had been discovered *en otros tiempos* by Bristol men. Cabot was tempted by reports of the land the Bristol sailors had found. He considered the possibility that this might be a northeastern appendage of Asia, and with this in mind he secured a patent from Henry VII in 1496.[5] With this royal assistance and with a ship outfitted by Bristol merchants, Cabot reached the North American mainland the following year. He undoubtedly believed he had reached the coast of Asia, and in 1498 he was granted letters patent to make another voyage to the same region. The outcome of this second voyage remains in doubt, but if it failed it did not deter Henry from his interest in expanding England's commerce abroad. To this end he had concluded treaties with Denmark and Riga, made commercial agreements in the Mediterranean and built ships to form the beginning of an English merchant marine.

With such interests in overseas trade, it is not unnatural that he should have learned of the explorations of the Azorean Corte Real brothers and their countryman João Fernandes and of their findings in the Greenland-Labrador region in the period before 1501. Fernandes, in collaboration with Bristolmen, secured a patent from Henry and continued the English-sponsored exploration of the northeastern coast of North America in 1501 and 1502.[6] In December, 1502, Henry issued to Hugh Elyot and Thomas Asshehurst, Bristolmen, and Francisco Fernandes and João Gonsalvez, Azoreans, a patent which indicates that permanent settlements in the newly discovered lands were contemplated. These or other Bristol merchants continued to explore until 1505 under the title of 'The Company of Adventurers into the New Found Lands.'[7] Since monopolies were granted, an attempt at establishing a permanent overseas trade must have been intended, but it apparently was not sufficiently profitable to warrant its continuation after a few years' experience.

It is evident that in England's most natural area of interest, the

North Atlantic, her King and western sailors were abreast of the very latest information. It was the very accuracy of that information that discouraged England from further ventures into the northwest for some time. When Sebastian Cabot returned from his voyage in 1509, it was apparent that a land barrier stood between Europe and the Far East. He had found no northern passage; he had no teeming populations, no productive regions to report. Indeed, no report was made to the public, for these early Bristol-based voyages produced no accounts of travel or exploration in the North Atlantic, and it is likely that the general public, even the literate public, was either unaware of or apathetic toward these early ventures.

If these voyages had resulted in printed narratives, as did the early Spanish and Portuguese explorations, such books would have found a substantial literate public, for the fifteenth century in England was a period of expanding literacy and educational progress, marked by the founding of many new schools. The ability to read began to extend through the various ranks of society and to both sexes and was sufficiently widespread to call forth books of considerable variety from the English press, as well as from booksellers abroad with an eye to the English market.[8]

The Bristol voyages, however, interested no printer, and indeed such geographical literature as appeared before 1510 shows no interest in English or other explorations of the period. With the medieval spirit dominant, England's first generation of printers produced editions of earlier works of geographical interest which had an eastern orientation, while the first voyages of the age of discovery with their exciting tales of new found lands were entirely disregarded. Caxton started Englishmen off in their study of geography by publishing two books of some importance to that branch of learning, Gautier of Metz's *The mirrour of the world*, 1481 and Ranulf Higden's *Polichronicon*, 1482.

Gautier's work was a thirteenth century encyclopedia of knowledge which Caxton translated from the French himself. The description of the earth which it contained was in most ways inferior to that contained in the editions of Ptolemy and Strabo which were appearing on the Continent at this time. Nevertheless, Caxton and his merchant patron, Hugh Bryce, gave to England a geography which in its medieval character was not unlike many works being published in Europe. Africa was ill-defined, stretching 'from the south unto ye west',[9] and Asia began with the terrestrial paradise and extended somewhere beyond the vague region of India with its precious stones guarded by griffons and dragons, its horned pygmies, beasts with the bodies of men and the heads of dogs, and innumerable other wonders. Yet here it was explicitly stated that the world was a sphere, 'and yf it were so that by adventure two men departed that one from that other and that one went all the way toward the east, and that other toward the weste, so that both two went egally, it behoved that they shold mete agayn in the opposite place from where as they departed.'10 This sphere, however, was 'not enhabyted but in one quarter...'11 Whatever its defects, Caxton's translation was sufficiently in tune with popular taste to justify subsequent editions in 1490 and 1527.

The *Polichronicon* of Ranulf Higden, a Benedictine monk of the thirteenth century, was similar, but more abundant in geographical information of a specific nature. Numerous regions are described in some detail, with the information based on classical and medieval authorities. The division of the earth was based upon Saint Augustine, 'The grete see of Ocoean beclyppeth alle the erthe aboute. And the Erthe is departed in thre grete partyes... Asia one of the thre conteyneth half the erthe.'12 Pliny contributes to Higden's description of Africa, and Solinus is quoted on the Red Sea. A section on the Atlantic islands contains descriptions of the Canary and Fortunate Islands as well as Iceland, all of which presumably lay beyond Gades where 'hyrcules sette his pilers... in the uttermost ende of the world.'13 Here again Caxton gave to England a geography that could have been the beginning of a fund of geographical knowledge to which new information could have been added, yet it was republished quite without alteration in 1495 and 1527.

To these medieval encyclopedias of Caxton, Wynkyn de Worde added another which had considerable geographic information. This was the *Proprietatibus rerum* of Bartholomaeus Anglicus in an English edition of 1495. Written by an English Franciscan about the middle of the thirteenth century, this work was translated into English by the sometime Oxford scholar John de Trevisa in 1397 'as a thynge profitable to me & peraventure to many other whyche understonde not latyn, nor have not the knowledge of the propyrtees of thynges.'14

After chapters on the properties of angels, the elements, time, air, vapors, etc., Book 15 'declareth and sheweth the cytees of all provinces habitable with theyr names.' It begins with a division of the earth into three parts according to Isidore of Seville. Relying heavily on 'Ysider', Bartholomaeus catalogued 174 countries and regions, giving the typical medieval description of each, with classical and Biblical allusions, legends, the location, and distinctive characteristics. Again, here was a well constructed, systematic geography which could have incorporated new information, but the edition of 1535 was published without important alteration of the earlier printed text.

It was through these books published by Caxton and Wynkyn de Worde that England had access to classical geography in her own tongue, although the classical learning came through such interpreters as Isidore of Seville. Among the original medieval writings in geographical literature, no work was more popular on the Continent than the *Travels* of Sir John Mandeville. Mandeville called St. Albans his birthplace, and he must rank as the father of English travel literature; yet his book was not the result of a journey by the author, nor was it calculated to inspire interest in travel. It appears to have had no other cause than the author's desire to inform and entertain, but it unquestionably did stimulate a great curiosity about the lands of the East.[15] The popularity of this work, which produced at least thirty editions on the Continent before 1500, also reached to England. Richard Pynson issued the first English version in 1496, and de Worde followed with an illustrated edition of 1499 and another perhaps two years later.[16] A fragment of a 1503 printing by an unknown printer also exists. All of these early English editions are somewhat abridged, and the illustrations are generally of lower quality than those found in the illustrated incunabular editions published on the Continent, although they were copied from the woodcuts accompanying the Vesler edition.[17]

The fact that Mandeville's *Travels* were imaginative in the extreme, does not diminish the importance of the book, nor does his appropriation of the adventures of actual eastern travelers into his own narrative. Most people who read it believed it, even though the veracity of the work was called into question in the fifteenth century. The medieval mind appreciated the wonderful, and relished the thought of gold-digging ants, dog-headed men, and similar marvels. Moreover, these elements of fantasy were incorporated into narratives that also told of pepper, precious stones, and other legitimate products of the east so as to make it difficult for even the discerning mind to know where fantasy ended and reality began. Long after the questioning had started Mandeville still held his place near the forefront of travel writers. Samuel Purchas, in the seventeenth century, wrote of him as 'the greatest Asian traveller that ever the world had,' possibly excepting Marco Polo. Despite this appreciation of him, it cannot be said that the four editions which appeared in England prior to 1510 had the effect of stimulating Englishmen to travel to the East, or to write accounts of their travels elsewhere. Mandeville's work stayed in the English mind as a guide to eastern regions, and if not altogether factual, surely it was considered useful. The praise accorded by Purchas was justified by the library on the ship Martin Frobisher sailed as he sought the northwest passage, for he carried Mandeville's book with him.[18]

As a New World was being discovered in the west, English eyes were still fastened on the east. No English edition of the Columbus *Letter* stood on the shelves beside Mandeville's *Travels* in the 1490s. The eastward-trudging pilgrim was more interesting to most English minds than the voyages of John Cabot and his Bristol companions. Hence, we find Wynkyn de Worde publishing in 1498 the anonymous *Informacon for pylgrymes unto the Holy Londe*. Here the pilgrim could find a mileage chart of the various stages of the route to Palestine together with information on the exchange of money en route. Advice for the sea voyage included the suggestion that the pilgrim get a berth amidships 'to kepe your brayne and stomacke in tempre.'[19] The penitent was to insist upon hot meals and was to provide himself with two barrels of wine, as well as beds, pillows, drugs, and 'a cage for half a dosen hennes or chekys.'[20] The itinerary is a tedious listing of towns, distances, temples and chapels. The work concludes with a smattering of Greek, Turkish and Moorish vocabulary. While Cabot and Columbus were ignored by the printers, this pilgrim's guide was re-published in 1515 and 1524.

The pilgrim books and medieval encyclopedias that came to the printer were a logical continuation of several centuries of manuscript tradition, and their publication might be explained by the willingness of the publisher to offer his readers whatever came to hand. The composition of new works of geographic interest, however, show the mentality of the period even more clearly. The first post-incunabular English book to contain material of geographic interest reveals how far its author was from understanding the activities of explorers and merchants who were opening up a New World and establishing direct contact with the Orient. This book was Richard Arnold's *Chronicle*, published in 1503. It contained a section entitled 'The copye of a carete cumpasyng the circuet of the wolde and the compase of every yland comprehendid in the same.'[21] This treatise is nothing more than a crude sketching of the world's geography which would have been useful only as a listing of place names and distances. It made no mention of the New World. Yet this was the work of a merchant who was in frequent touch with Flanders and who would have had opportunity to absorb some of the

new geography during his visits there. Some aspect of this *Chronicle*—
not necessarily its geography—rendered it sufficiently popular to induce Peter Treveris of Southwark to publish a new edition in 1521.

It is noteworthy that the voyages of Columbus, Vespucci, Pinzón,
Vasco da Gama, Cabral and others whose exploits were described in
many publications on the Continent should not have found a reporter
in England until the end of the first Tudor reign, which was marked
by a very considerable royal interest in overseas commerce. Not until
1509, the year that reign ended, did a book appear in which the
discovery of America was mentioned, and this was in a strictly literary
and moralistic work, Sebastian Brant's *Ship of Fools*, printed by both
Pynson and de Worde from separate translations. The following passage of Brant's poem, originally published in Basle in 1494 gave English
readers the news of 1492 in their own language:

> *For nowe of late hath large londe and grounde*
> *Ben founde by maryners and crafty governours*
> *The whiche londes were neuer knowen nor founde*
> *Byfore our tyme by our predecessours*
> *And here after shall our successours*
> *Parchaunce mo be founde wherin men dwell*
> *Of whom we neuer before this same harde tell*
>
> *Ferdynandus that late was kynge of spayne*
> *Of londe and people hath founde plenty and store*
> *Of whome the bydynge to us was uncertayne*
> *No christen man of them harde tell before*
> *Thus it is foly to tende unto the lore*
> *And unsure science of vayne geometry*
> *Syns none can knowe all the worlde perfytely.*[22]

It surely was not these lines which made Brant's book popular in England, but rather the fact that it appealed to the national interest in the
church and in morality. In fact, the Barclay translation was really an
adaptation, 'an English ship, formed and fashioned after the Ship of
Fools of the World.'[23] Thus it was a nationalist and a moralist, not a
geographer, that first brought the discovery of America to the attention
of English readers.

## NOTES TO CHAPTER II

1 R. Weiss, *Humanism in England during the fifteenth century* (Oxford; Basil Blackwell, 1957), *passim.*

2 Dorothy Burwash, *English merchant shipping, 1460–1540* (Toronto: University of Toronto Press, 1947), *pp. 13–18.*

3 W. E. C. Harrison, 'An early voyage of discovery,' *The mariner's mirror,* XVI (April, 1930), 199.

4 David B. Quinn, 'The argument for the English discovery of America between 1480 and 1494,' *The geographical journal,* CXXVII, (September, 1961) 279. Professor Quinn offers two alternatives in assigning dates to the seven year period mentioned by Ayala; James A. Williamson, *The Cabot voyages and Bristol discovery under Henry VII* (Cambridge: For the Hakluyt Society, 1962), pp. 19–32.

5 Williamson, *Cabot voyages,* pp. 29–32.

6 John B. Brebner, *The explorers of North America, 1492–1806* (Garden City: Doubleday Anchor, 1955), p. 93.

7 James A. Williamson, *The voyages of John and Sebastian Cabot* (London: For the Historical Association, 1937), pp. 15–16.

8 Kingsford, *Prejudice and promise in XVth century England,* pp. 35–39; J. W. Adamson, 'The extent of literacy in England in the fifteenth and sixteenth centuries,' *The library,* 4th series, X (September, 1929), 163–93.

9 Gautier of Metz, *The mirrour of the world* [Westminster: William Caxton, 1481], fol. d8 recto.

10 *Ibid.* fol. d2 recto.

11 *Ibid.,* fol. d5 verso.

12 Ranulf Higden, *Polichronicon* [Westminster: William Caxton, 1482], fol. x verso.

13 *Ibid.,* fol. xxxix verso.

14 Bartholomaeus Anglicus, *Proprietatibus rerum* [Westminster: Wynkyn de Worde, 1495], fol. A2 recto.

15 Josephine W. Bennett, *The rediscovery of Sir John Mandeville* (New York: The Modern Language Association, 1954), *passim;* Malcolm Letts, *Sir John Mandeville, the man and his book* (London: Batchworth Press, 1949), pp. 13–22.

16 Sir John Mandeville, *The boke of John Maundvyle* (London: Richard Pynson, 1496). De Worde's edition of 1499 begins, *Here begynneth a lytell treatyse or booke named Johan Maundevyll knight…* The fragments remaining of the other two early editions do not include title pages.

17 Malcolm Letts, 'The source of the woodcuts in Wynkyn de Worde's edition of Mandeville's *Travels,* 1499,' *The library,* 5th series, VI (June, 1951), 154–61.

18 See p. 62 below.

19 E. Gordon Duff (ed.), *Information for pilgrims unto the Holy Land* (London: Lawrence and Bullen, 1893), fol. b4 verso.

20 *Ibid.,* fol. b6 verso.

21 Richard Arnold, *Chronicle of London* ([Antwerp: Adrien van Berghen, 1503]), fols. lii verso – liiii verso. Arnold's book was published without a title, and is also referred to as the *Customs of London.* Actually it is not a chronicle but a collection of antiquities.

22 Sebastian Brant, *This present boke named the shyp of folys of the worlde…* trans. Alexander Barclay (London: Richard Pynson, 1509), fols. cxxxix verso – cxl recto.

23 Sebastian Brant, *The ship of fools,* ed. T. H. Jamieson (2 vols.; Edinburgh: William Paterson, 1874), I, xviii-xix. In adapting the verses to the English language and in fitting them to English life, Barclay made the text four times as long as it had been in the Locher Latin edition from which he worked, according to Aurelius Pompen, *The English versions of the Ship of Fools* (London: Longmans, Green and Co., 1925), p. 310.

# Chapter III

## MERCHANTS AND INTELLECTUALS

The seamen of Bristol and the printers of London proved their competence in their respective arts during the first Tudor reign, yet no exploration literature appeared in England during the rule of Henry VII. This must be attributed to a lack of public interest, and as if taking his direction from his people, Henry VIII, too, showed but slight interest in the opening up of the New World and the establishment of direct trade with India. This is not to say that he was not concerned with navigation and trade. He saw to the building of the *Henry Grace a Dieu*, the largest ship yet to be constructed in England; he required regular recording of shipping statistics, a reporting of the sailing qualities of individual ships; and he reorganized Trinity House in 1515 to train pilots and consider other navigational matters.[1]

Henry's reign and the commerce of his nation, however, were Europe-oriented. It is possible that the concern of Henry VII with commercial affairs had left England in such a good position in conventional areas of commerce that there was no wish to exchange this security for the uncertainties of exploration. It is certain that interest in western exploration declined to such a low point that Sebastian Cabot was permitted to transfer his services to Spain. The cause of this decline was not necessarily personal apathy on the part of the ruler: the chief commercial facts of European history in the reign of Henry VIII were the rise of Spain and Portugal as commercial powers and the consequent decline of Venice. Antwerp was a part of the Iberian commercial network, and London came to absorb some of Antwerp's trade when civil strife impaired that city's commercial facilities to some degree. As England came to participate more directly and frequently in European trade, its ruler was forced to contend with powerful Continental monarchs. But these were gradual developments of which printers and the majority of the people took no note.

Their efforts and emotions were much more attracted to the nationalistic outburst expressed in the English Reformation, which captured the attention of Englishmen of all classes and dominated the monarch's activities as well. With the rising merchant class attracted more than

ever to Europe, with the King engaged with the Pope and other Continental powers, and with the populace in general concerned with the
religious controversy, there remained only a few individuals to be actively concerned with western exploration, and fewer still to be interested in publishing books about it. It was primarily the merchants
of Plymouth and the London intellectuals who maintained a spark of
interest in building an English empire while the King and people
attended to the nationalistic controversy at home.

The interest of the intellectual group owed much to its Continental
counterparts for its knowledge on geography. The circle in which Sir
Thomas More moved held the better minds of London; this group was
acquainted with the German mathematician Simon Grynaeus, the
Portuguese poet and historian Damião de Goes, the Swiss geographer
Glareanus, as well as Erasmus and others[2]—men who could give their
colleagues in London information on geographical discoveries. When
the first book in the English language containing an account of sixteenth-century voyages to the East and West Indies appeared, it too
came from the Continent. Printed by Jan van Doesborch during the
second decade of the sixteenth century, *Of the newe landes...* gave Englishmen an opportunity to read in their own language of matters that
were widely published on the Continent. By 1511, the earliest date
attributed to this book, Vespucci's voyages had been described in Italian, Latin and German, the Columbus *Letter* had been printed in six
countries, and German and Italian presses had printed numerous news
letters announcing Portuguese progress in India.[3] Yet England's printers had seen no opportunity for profit in such books, and, significantly,
Doesborch's tract knew only one edition.

This little book contained three unrelated sections, as if it were
designed to make the broadest possible appeal. The first of these was
titled *Of the newe landes and of ye people founde by the messengers of the Kynge
of Portyngale named Emanuel*. It was made up of portions of other of
Doesborch's publications, beginning with a brief description of America, called 'Armenica'. This is a slightly enlarged version of a Latin
broadside, made up very probably of extracts from narratives of the
Vespucci voyages and published by Doesborch about 1509 or 1510.[4]
The account dwells primarily on the habits of the natives of South
America, whose cannibalistic customs are especially prominent, both
in the text and in the accompanying woodcuts.

This section includes a translation of a portion of *Die Reyse van Lissebone*, containing observations from the eastern travels of Balthasar

Springer, an agent of the German financier Anton Welser.[5] Springer's narrative included descriptions of the Canary Islands, the west African mainland, the east African area of Delagoa Bay, called 'Allago', and the commercially important cities of Mombassa, Sofala, Kilwa, and Melindi on the east African coast. While he mentions animals and products, he is particularly concerned with the manner of dress and appearance of native peoples, with distances from place to place, and with the conquests of the Portuguese on the eastern coast of Africa. He describes Calicut and Cochin in India as great sources of spices and precious stones. Whereas the earlier Flemish version continues with a narrative of the events of the voyage, the English version stops at this point.

The second portion of Doesborch's book is titled *Of the .X. dyvers nacyons crystened,* and is a translation of a description of the ten nations of Christendom: Latin, Greek, Indian, Jacobite, Nestorian, Maronite, Armenian, Georgian, Syrian and Arabian.[6] It is little more than a religious gazetteer, noting the allegiance, or lack of it, that the various Christian sects bore to Rome. While its origin is quite obscure, its frequent publication testifies to the interest Europeans had in Eastern Christians.[7] As a description of distant peoples and places, however, it has little value.

The third section of this tract contains a version of the Prester John *Letter,* a fictitious account of an unidentified region which had originated in the twelfth century. It went through numerous translations in manuscript and was frequently printed in the late fifteenth and early sixteenth centuries before it came into print in English. While it was by no means contemporary travel literature, the finding of the Ethiopian Christians by the Portuguese at the end of the fifteenth century revived the interest in Prester John, the legendary Christian ruler, and gave to the *Letter* a contemporary interest far greater than most medieval works. It contains a description—much of it fantastic— of the flora and fauna of Prester John's kingdom. The power and wealth of the potentate are stressed also, though it was frequently modified to give it pertinence to one or more European monarchs; hence the request in this English version that 'the kynge of Fraunce... wyll us recommaunde to the myghty kyng of England.'[8]

This publication of Jan van Doesborch illustrates the ease with which recent and earlier travel literature could be gathered for publication in the English language. Pirating of texts was a continuing practice, and had there been any opportunity for profit in such publications,

England would have had a constant supply of such literature in her own language from the Continent. Here we find Doesborch attempting to attract interest with the contemporary, the factual-religious, and the legendary types of material, but apparently none of them was sufficiently interesting to English readers at that time to warrant another venture in travel literature in English, and we find none of his colleagues emulating his attempt.

The second decade of the sixteenth century found England's printers venturing more into pilgrimage literature than into accounts of voyages to India and America which were receiving wide attention on the Continent. In 1511 Richard Pynson published the first account of an English pilgrimage to the Holy Land, the narrative of Sir Richard Guylforde's pilgrimage. Guylforde was a person of prominence in England, having held several important positions during the reign of Henry VII, including that of Privy Councillor. He was accompanied on his journey by a number of other Englishmen, and they set out in 1505, but neither Guylforde nor his most prominent companion, John Whitby, Prior of Giseburn, lived to return to England. The journal of their voyage, and of the return following their deaths in the Holy Land, was kept by Guylforde's chaplain.[9]

While this book is primarily an account of places related to Biblical events and contains an abundance of statements on distances from one city to another and the relics to be found in each—features common to descriptions of pilgrimages—there are some observations on more mundane subjects. For example, in Venice the author noted various machines of war and a group of one hundred men and women 'that do no thynge but dayly make Ropes and Cables.'[10] He noted fortifications along the Dalmatian coast, and one of the islands of Greece, 'where as be tooles made of yrron that never lose their egge, by myracle of seynt Nycholas';[11] and of the Jordan River he observed that it 'rennyth into the deed see and passeth Clerely thoroughe the same, and gothe forthe out of the sayde deed see at the other ende, without takying any parte of the sayd deed see with it.'[12]

This English view of the pilgrimage route is known in only one edition, but that there was interest in pilgrimage literature in this period is indicated by the fact that the *Informacon for pylgrymes unto the Holy Londe* was published again in 1515 by Wynkyn de Worde under the title *The way to the Holy Lande.*

While the attention of readers was being called to the East by such books, a first attempt to publicize the New World was made in a play published in 1517 which satirized persons respondible for the failure of an intended voyage to America. John Rastell, brother-in-law of Sir Thomas More, and a lawyer, printer and author, planned a voyage to the New World about 1517, and when it failed he wrote and published *A new interlude... of the four elements*. A member of England's most enlightened circle, Rastell had access to the best Continental knowledge, as is evident by the direct relationship that has been found between his play and the major early sixteenth-century works on geography, cosmography and exploration. He undoubtedly added to his knowledge of the most recent discoveries in the northern part of the New World from oral reports of fishermen who frequented those latitudes.[13] Whatever the exact state of his knowledge, Rastell readied two ships, the *Barbara* and the *Mary Barking*, for a voyage to 'the new found land.' The expedition had gone no further than Waterford when Ravyn, the purser, and Richards, the master of the *Barbara*, suggested that piracy replace exploration as a motive of the journey. When Rastell refused, the officers left him and sold the provisions.[14]

This inconclusive attempt at New World exploration gave Rastell the opportunity to write and publish England's first native exploration literature and to present to the English people for the first time a plea for empire. *A new interlude... of the four elements* is a moral drama in which nature, humanity, experience, ignorance, sensuality and studiousness are portrayed. Experience tells of the New World, of successful voyages in the northern regions thereof. He cites the abundance of copper, wood, and other necessities, and alludes to the possibility of a northwest passage to the Pacific Ocean and to Asia. In so doing he carries out the author's two purposes in writing the play: to vent Rastell's bitterness at his associates and to propagandize for a further effort.

There is no reason to believe that Rastell's play was in response to popular demand, for it was written and published by him, and it knew only one edition. Whatever its public reception, it inspired no further publishing on the subject of England's interest in the exploration of North America. It is interesting, nevertheless, as a beginning of English imperialistic literature, for the first time publicly calling Englishmen to become active in overseas colonization:

> *O what a thynge had be than*
> *Yf that they that be englyshe men*
> *Myght have ben the furst of all*

*That there shulde have take possessyon*
*And made furst buylding & habytacion,*
*A memory perpetuall!*[15]

The nationalistic dream of carrying English people and institutions abroad was a part of English exploration literature from the beginning, and Rastell's nationalism extended to his defense of the English language as one worthy of the Latin texts, which, if translated, would give Englishmen the understanding needed for overseas exploits.[16] His little dream of empire, however, had insurmountable competition for the hearts of nationalists in the reign of Henry VIII. Rastell's grievances and hopes were of minor importance compared to the religious and national conflicts that crowded the second Tudor reign.

While the *Interlude* can hardly be called a book of major importance to English overseas interests, there is a possibility that it was linked to a proposed voyage to America in 1521. Sir Thomas More and others of his group came into the services of Henry VIII during the years 1517–19; and it was in 1520, while More was a member of the King's Council, that a plan was originated by the government for a voyage to North America for which Henry offered a ship of his navy and asked the London companies to show their interest by making five ships available.[17] Other ports were solicited also and Bristol promised two ships, but the expedition was never organized, for the London merchants feared the loss of their well-established Spanish and other Continental trade if they attempted to compete abroad. The decision to wage war against France in 1521 made a voyage of this type unthinkable, and again England's Continental orientation frustrated the few persons who might have been enthusiastic about the expedition. If this proposed enterprise was the brainchild of the intellectuals at court, it is apparent that their influence was not sufficient in 1521 to turn England toward the course that she would ultimately follow.

London might not venture to the brink of empire, but Bristol continued to see its future in the western ocean and the lands that lay beyond it. In 1527 Robert Thorne, a Bristol merchant resident in Spain, addressed to his sovereign and to Dr. Lee, the English ambassador to Spain, a serious plea for the discovery of a northwest passage to the East Indies. These two letters, later called *The book of Robert Thorne*, were full of hope and optimism, but they found no printer in 1527.[18]

Contemporary printers also overlooked the voyage of John Rut, who set out for America in June, 1527, arriving at Newfoundland on July 21.

Rut and his companions sailed as far north as 53 degrees, where ice blocked their path, and the two ships, the *Samson* and *Mary of Gilford*, which made up the expedition were separated. According to the Spanish historian, Oviedo, the *Mary of Gilford* actually sailed as far south as the West Indies, presumably searching for a waterway through the continent.[19] This voyage was a continuation of the Cabot and Rastell approach to the exploration of North America, and if Henry VIII lent support to the expedition, it was probably due to the converging upon him of pressure from Bristol merchants and opinions of his advisers in the King's Council.

Something of the English state of mind with regard to interest in overseas regions can be seen when it is noted that an expedition such as Rut's went unnoticed in the 1520s along with the numerous Spanish and Portuguese voyages which were a subject of popular interest on the Continent, while in that decade two books concerned with other distant regions did appear.

About 1520 Richard Pynson published, under the patronage of Edward, Duke of Buckingham, Earl of Gloucester, Stafford and Northampton, a history of Asia by the Armenian Christian Prince of Korghos, Hethum. It was first written in French and translated into Latin in 1307. The English translation was made by Pynson. This is a traditional history of Asia, dwelling largely on the wars of Mohammedan rulers, but the first twelve pages contain the best description of Asia to appear in English in the first half of the sixteenth century. This is not an attempt at narrative, but a description of the geography, ethnology, and social and religious customs of 'the xiiii pryncipall realmes that be in Asye.' Cathay is 'counted and holden for ye moost noble and rich realme of ye world'; in Tharsay 'the people... be... moche ingenious to lerne artes and sciences'; Turkestan has 'fewe good Cytes, but many grete playnes & large feldes'; India has 'marchauntes and all manner of marchaundises', etc.[20] The entire work is well written, informative, and includes a brief itinerary for travel to the Holy Land via Armenia.

In contrast is *The pylgrimage of M. Robert Langton*, published in 1522 by Robert Copland. This is a dreary catalog of cities visited by the author en route to Compostela in Spain. It was very probably a useful book, and one with some emotional appeal, since it lists the relics to be found in the various cities. Guidebooks of this kind had been used by pilgrims to the shrine of St. James of Compostela since the twelfth century, and Langton, who held a prebend in Lincoln Cathedral and was archdeacon of Dorset and treasurer of York Minster, borrowed from these earlier works. It is also likely that he had seen *Informacon for pylgrymes unto the Holy Londe*.[21]

These two items from the 1520s testify to England's continued orientation toward Europe and Asia, as does a new edition of *The mirrour: and dyscription of the world* published in 1527 by Laurence Andrew, with numerous Mandevillian woodcuts added. The absence of other types of travel literature shows an apparent disinterest in English voyages in the Atlantic and in the voyages of the Spanish and Portuguese as well. Indeed, the only book published in the next two decades to show English concern with European discoveries appeared in 1533, and again it was the intellectual circle which was responsible for it. *The legacye or embassate of Prester John unto Emanuell, Kynge of Portyngale*, printed by William Rastell, son of the author of the *Interlude of the four elements*, was the only translation from Portuguese travel literature to appear in the English language to the middle of the sixteenth century. The translator was John More, son of Sir Thomas More, and he may be suspected of having something other than interest in travel in mind when he made the translation and had it published. In 1513 the first embassy from Prester John had come to the Portuguese court. Sir Thomas More's *Utopia* appeared shortly thereafter. In 1531 the second Ethiopian embassy came to Lisbon, and in that year also appeared a book in the form of a letter from Damião de Goes to Johannes Magnus, Archbishop of Uppsala, with the account of the first embassy published in Dordrecht in 1518 as *Legatio magni imperatoris Indorum Presbyteri Joannes*. It is possible that this second embassy and the reappearance of the *Legatio* inspired the younger More to strike a blow for religious orthodoxy. In the preface to his translation he praised the steadfastness of the African Christian in contrast to England's current errors, and the picture of ideal Africa which follows may have been the son's attempt at a *Utopia* of his own.[22] Whatever its motivation, More's translation gave England its first near-contemporary news of Africa, and compared to the other two works of geographic interest printed in the 1530s, it is indeed an enlightening piece of literature.

In that decade Robert Wyer printed two books based upon outmoded geographic knowledge and alarming in their crudeness, considering that Wyer was a prominent printer who accounted for about one hundred titles during his career. The first of these geographies, *The compost of Ptholomeus*, actually an adaptation of the 1528 English edition of the *Shepherd's kalendar*, is a traditional description of the regions of the earth and the great circles. This is followed by a 'rutter' five pages in length, giving distances between various places from Ireland to Trebizond, with the greatest emphasis on the Mediterranean area.[23] The other publication, entitled *Mappa mundi otherwise called the compasse and cyrcuet of the world*, is nothing more than a reproduction of the crude original in *Arnold's chronicle* of 1503, but with additional information on the Earthly Paradise and Hell. Its claim to be 'Very necessary for all Marchauntes, and Maryners'[24] seems an extravagant boast even for those times.

The impression is unavoidable that between 1520 and 1540 most Englishmen were but little interested in the new discoveries and resulting opportunities for commerce and missionary work. Henry's earlier interest in America gave way before domestic problems, and the merchant community of London produced no overseas ventures. The intellectuals of London, more acutely aware of the European explorations, believed sufficiently in the advisability of overseas ventures to participate in one in 1536 when one hundred and twenty men, thirty being gentlemen, embarked for America in two ships. Among the sailors was John Rastell, another son of the dramatist. Under the leadership of Captain Richard Hore, this expedition coasted Newfoundland, gathering a cargo of fish, in the course of which the gentlemen suffered sufficient privations to prove to themselves the difficulty of establishing the colonies in America which they had been advocating.[25] We need not be surprised that the Rastell press printed no account of this venture.

Meanwhile, with no help from the monarch and no advice from the scholars, significant voyages were being made from England to Brazil by way of West Africa. William Hawkins of Plymouth, who had traded actively with La Rochelle and Rouen, apparently learned of the profitable opportunities in Brazil through French interlopers upon what was thought to be the preserve of Portugal. Hawkins is believed to have made voyages to Brazil in the 1520s, and he requested a loan of two thousand pounds from Henry VIII to expand his operations. The loan does not appear to have been made; apparently Henry was not interested in competing with Portugal in South America.[26] His attitude appears to have reflected public opinion, for there was no printer or bookseller willing to invest his money and time in publishing for English readers an account of this new trade.

Nor were the declining years of Henry's reign of any value to those few who had an interest in trade with the New World. The voyages to

Brazil were probably discontinued in the 1540s because of the war with France which required large vessels for the defense of the island and left piracy as the major outlet for England's adventurous seamen of the southwest coast. Would-be adventurers to the East also felt the royal disinterest, for a request made by the Privy Council to permit Englishmen to travel in Portuguese ships to Calicut, the center of the eastern spice trade, was turned down.[27]

In 1540–41 Henry was presented with another plan for an overseas venture, and again it was a Bristol Merchant, Roger Barlow, who sought royal assistance. Barlow had long been resident in Seville where he was associated with Robert Thorne. He had undertaken a voyage to the East Indies in a Spanish ship in 1526, but had got no farther than the Paraná River in South America. The plan which he and Thorne developed was to send English ships north-northeast from England, across the North Pole to the East Indies. Thorne's death in 1532 prevented the plan from being presented to the King until 1540, and at that time Barlow accompanied his proposal with a manuscript geography which described the coasts of the known world. Translated from Martin Fernández de Enciso's *Suma de geographia*, but with numerous interpolations based upon Barlow's own experiences, particularly his expedition to the Paraná, it has become known as *A brief summe of geographie*.[28]

In addressing his work to his sovereign, Barlow expressed the wish that 'your grace may comande it to be corrected and amended and to geve your auctoritie to be put fourthe in prynte,'[29] but Henry apparently had no interest in doing so. Barlow was to be disappointed in his plans for a northern expedition also, for there is no record of any such undertaking, although the Spanish ambassador wrote from England in May 1541 that a voyage was being planned to explore waters between Iceland and Greenland 'for the Northern Regions where it was thought that owing to the extreme cold, English woolen cloths would be very acceptable.'[30] The Walton Manuscript, a document relating to Barlow and drawn up in 1739, reports that at the time of Henry's death an expedition to the north was being planned under Barlow's leadership.[31]

Henry's unwillingness to launch England on an imperialistic course, and his aloofness from overseas mercantile adventures must be attributed in the main to his desire and that of his chief ministers, Wolsey and Cromwell, to enhance England's prestige in Europe and to keep her from foreign interference while liquidating the old church order, thus establishing English dominance in the British Isles.[32] All of these were prerequisites to empire, but it is unlikely that Henry saw beyond them. Such concerns inspired no travel literature, and from 1535 to the end of Henry's reign none appeared. The primary interest of Englishmen in that period was the religious settlement following the break with Rome. The emotional appeal of a Brazilian chief brought to Whitehall was insufficient to induce a printer to publish a description of him, but pamphlets growing out of the religious conflict flourished. England in the reign of Henry VIII was still in the first phase of nationalism—the struggle for independence from foreign control—and no literature could have more appeal than that which linked religion with this struggle.

Although the controversies set in motion by his father dominated the short reign of Edward VI, the Protectorate government of the Duke of Northumberland did interest itself in overseas ventures; but until the appearance of Richard Eden on the literary scene at the conclusion of that reign, this new interest was reflected but slightly, if at all, in travel literature. It seems probable that a broadside or leaflet, no longer extant, bearing the title *Of the newe founde landes* was printed in 1551 or 1552, for Richard Eden mentions it in the Dedication of his *Treatyse of the newe India* where he described it as 'a sheite of printed paper, (more-worthy to bee called then a boke).' It may have been the tract of Jan van Doesborch or a reprint of it. Whatever its form or date, it seems to have been a poor effort even by English standards, for Eden says of it, 'there seemed too me no lesse inequalitye between the tytle and the booke, then if a man woulde profess to wryte of Englande, and entreated onelye of Trumpington a vyllage wythin a myle of Cambrydge.'[33] Considering the apparent poverty of this effort at publicizing the new discoveries and the obvious failure of England's printers to register any real interest in Renaissance exploration and travel, it is not surprising that the voyages of Vespucci received only the slightest mention—Rastell's statement that America was named for Americus, its discoverer—until after mid-century, when in 1551 Ralph Robinson translated Sir Thomas More's *Utopia* into English. There Vespucci and the new discoveries became partners to political satire and fantasy before they were portrayed as reality by the publishing trade.[34]

Similarly, the second book by an Englishman to describe America, Anthony Ascham's *Astronomy*, brought the New World into its discussion as a means of pointing out the opposite seasons in the northern and southern hemispheres. Ascham's handling of this subject illustrates

the little progress that had been made toward absorbing the new knowledge of geography. He wrote, 'Knowe that the people dwellynge in
the countre of Brasilia, beynge in that parte of the worlde called America, with all the portes and havens called Canibales, where be founde
many precious stones, and also the region of the Giauntes, where
Magellanus that passed the strayght and narowe see, beyond America,
dyd measure them to be ten fote longe, & also the yle Madagascar
perteynynge to the great Cham where groweth Peper, sylke, and Precious stones, hathe wynter when we have sommer.'[35] This lack of information seems to have been a natural counterpart of the lack of
enthusiasm for overseas trade and possessions in the first half century
after the world was divided between Spain and Portugal. Only Rastell's
*New Interlude of the four elements* shows the projection of English nationalism beyond English shores in the desire to expand the realms of the
sovereign and improve the homeland by so doing.

This is not to say that overseas interests were non-existent in England during the fifteenth and early sixteenth centuries. Manuscripts
exist which show a concern for the improvement of England's position
with respect to other nations through a more aggressive foreign policy.
The earliest of these was *The libelle of Englyshe polycye*, a poem written
in 1436, which urged England to a more vigorous commercial and
maritime program. This anonymous poem contains the ingredients of
an expansionist outlook which presents to English statesmen an alternative to territorial aggrandizement at a time when England was engaged in wars on the Continent:

> *Cheryshe marchandyse, kepe thamaralte,*
> *That we bee maysteres of the narowe see.*[36]

This domination of the Channel is the pillar of the poet's policy, and
through that strength he would make England a great trade center:

> *For yef marchaundes were cherysshede to here spede,*
> *We were not lykelye to fayle in ony nede;*
> *Yff they bee riche, thane in prosperite*
> *Shalbe oure londe, lordes and comonte.*[37]

The author sees England not as a weak hanger-on to Europe's wool
industry, but as a potential controller of it. To Flanders he says:

> *The grete substaunce of youre clothe at the fulle*
> *Ye wot ye make hit of oure English wolle.*[38]

And from this fact he draws a significant conclusion:

> *Flaundres of nede must wyth us have pease*
> *Or ellis he is distroyde wythowghten less.*[39]

Nevertheless, the dependence upon the Continent as a market for wool is very much in the author's mind, as is shown in his concern for Calais:

> *And for the love of God and of his bliss*
> *Cherishe ye Caleise better than it is.*[40]

But he could see westward also, and the thoughts of controlling non-English peoples in imperial fashion appealed to him as he advised

> *To kepen Yrelond that it be not loste*
> *For it is a boterasse and a poste*
> *Undre England, and Wales is another.*[41]

The approval given to the spirit of this poem a century and a half later by Richard Hakluyt testifies to a feeling of kinship between Elizabethan imperialism and this earlier concern of England's overseas interests.

A more forceful statement of English expansionism, and one based upon contemporary commercial geopolitics, was *The book of Robert Thorne* in which the author sought to place England in a more favorable position to trade with the East Indies and Cathay. By vigorously prosecuting discoveries to the northwest, he thought, she would be enabled to compete effectively with Spain and Portugal who dominated the trade with the newly discovered areas. Thorne recognized the imperialist urge as a force present in all princes and commented on Henry VIII's 'great paine and labour' in his war with France, but he advised the King that greater glory was to be won with little cost, for 'with a small number of ships there may bee discovered divers New landes and kingdomes, in the which without doubt your Grace shall winne perpetuall glory and your subjects infinite profite.'[42]

A similar tone is maintained in the concluding paragraphs of Roger Barlow's *A brief summe of geographie* where he states 'ther resteth this waie of the northe onelie for to discover which resteth onto your graces charge, for that the situation of this realme toward that partie is more apt for it than eny other... And for such an enterprise no man shuld thinke upon the cost in comparison to the grete profyght that may therby succede, nor thinke the labour grete where so moche profyt honor and glory may folow unto this our naturall realm and king.'[43]

It is apparent that while the English monarch and most of his subjects were primarily concerned with the first phase of nationalism— the freedom of England from the influence of Rome and other Continental powers—there were a few voices, chiefly merchants and intellectuals acquainted with Continental knowledge of geography, speaking for the next phase—the expansion of England abroad. Yet these voices, with the exception of Rastell, spoke privately and did not get into print. The fact that examples of expansionist sentiment did not get published must be attributed to the recognition by the printers of no widespread enthusiasm for English expansion during the reigns of the Tudor kings, to the lack of concern among the classes capable of patronizing such literature, and to the absence of any one person who would take it upon himself to whip up such enthusiasm through the use of the press, which was constantly in use as a weapon against foreign influences in England.

## NOTES TO CHAPTER III

[1] Burwash, *English merchant shipping*, pp. 29–31.
[2] E. G. R. Taylor, *Tudor geography* (London: Methuen & Co., Ltd., 1930), p. 8.
[3] Edward Arber, *The first three English books on America* (Westminster: Archibald Constable and Co., 1895), p. xxvi dates this tract *ca.* 1511. The Library of Congress dates it 1522. Others have given various dates between these two. The books printed by Jan van Doesborch are described in Robert Proctor, *Jan van Doesborch* (London: For the Bibliographical Society, 1894).
[4] This broadside was titled *De novo mundo* and contained woodcuts of American and African natives, all of which were used again in *Of the newe landes*. It is similar in format and information concerning America to three German broadsides issued in 1505–6. See Joseph Sabin, *Bibliotheca Americana*, nos. 99360–67.
[5] Balthasar Springer, *Die Reyse van Lissebone* (Antwerp: Jan van Doesborch, 1508). Springer went to India with the Portuguese fleet of 1505, returning the next year. His account of his voyage circulated in manuscript until this edition was published. The following year it was printed in German, probably at Augsburg, with outstanding woodcuts by Hans Burgkmair, who had done his work from Springer's own descriptions of eastern peoples in 1508. Doesborch's woodcuts, which were used in both the Flemish and English editions, show that in some instances they were attempts at imitation of Burgkmair's art. They are much inferior, even

as the text as published in Flemish was an abridgement of Springer's narrative. See C. H. Coote, *The voyage from Lisbon to India*, 1505-6 (London: B. F. Stevens, 1894), pp. 1-49; Henry Harrisse, *Americus Vespuccius* (London: B. F. Stevens, 1895), pp. 37-67; and Franz Schulze (ed.), *Balthasar Springers Indienfahrt, 1505-06* (Strassburg: J. H. Ed. Heitz, 1902), which contains a facsimile of the German 1509 edition with the Burgkmair woodcuts.

6  *Of the newe landes*, fols. Di recto–E4 recto.

7  Friedrich Zarncke states that there is no known manuscript of this treatise. From the description given of the Greek Christians he dates it before 1453. See his 'Der Priester Johannes, Zwejte Abhandlung' *Abhandlungen der philologische-historischen Classe der Königlich Sächsischen Gesellschaft der Wissenachaften*, VIII, (1883), 187. Francis M. Rogers believes the treatise on the ten Christian nations originates with Jacques de Vitry, see his *The quest for Eastern Christians* (Minneapolis: University of Minnesota Press, 1962), p. 82.

8  *Of the new landes*, fol. E4 recto. This mention of the King of England is obviously an interpolation. Vsevolod Slessarev notes the appearance of the Prester John *Letter* in several languages in his *Prester John, the letter and the legend* (Minneapolis: University of Minnesota Press, 1959), pp. 3-8.

9  Sir Henry Ellis, *The pylgrymage of Sir Richard Guylforde to the Holy Land, A. D. 1506* ([London]: For the Camden Society, 1851), pp. v–vii.

10 *This is the begynnynge and contynuance of the pylgrymage of Sir Richarde Gylforde* (London: Richard Pynson, 1511), fol. v. recto.

11 *Ibid.*, fol. ix verso.

12 *Ibid.*, fol. xxxviii verso.

13 Arthur W. Reed, 'John Rastell's voyage in the year 1517,' *The mariner's mirror*, IX (May, 1923), 137-47; M. E. Borish, 'Source and intention of *The four elements*,' *Studies in philology*, XXXV (April, 1938), 149-63; E. M. Nugent, 'Sources of John Rastell's *The nature of the four elements*,' *PMLA*, LVII (March, 1942), 74-88; Johnstone Parr, 'More sources of Rastell's *Interlude of the four elements*,' *PMLA*, XL (March, 1945), 48-58; George B. Parks, 'The geography of *The interlude of the four elements*,' *Philological quarterly*, XVII (July, 1938), 261.

14 Arthur W. Reed, *Early Tudor drama* (London: Methuen & Co. Ltd., 1921), pp. 12-13.

15 John Rastell, *A new interlude... of the iiii elements* (n.p.n.d.), fol. Ci verso.

16 Borish, *Studies in philology*, XXXV, 150.

17 E. M. G. Routh, *Sir Thomas More and his friends* (London: Oxford University Press, 1934), pp. 89-110; James A. Williamson, *The voyages of the Cabots and the English discovery of North America under Henry VII and Henry VIII* (London: The Argonaut Press, 1929), p. 250.

18 Richard Hakluyt, *The principal navigations, voyages, traffiques and discoveries of the English nation* (8 vols.; London: J. M. Dent and Sons Ltd., 1910), I, 212-16. Thorne's letter to Henry VIII has never been dated precisely. The letter to Dr. Lee, which is similar in tone, is dated 1527 from internal evidence. Williamson, *Maritime enterprise*, p. 258. The content of these letters is described more completely on p. 32.

19 F. A. Kirkpatrick, 'The first recorded English voyage to the West Indies,' *The English historical review*, XX (January, 1905), 115-24; Williamson, *Voyages of the Cabots* (1929), pp. 255-62; H. P. Biggar, 'An English expedition to America in 1527,' *Mélanges d'histoire offerts a M. Charles Bémont* (Paris: Felix Alcan, 1913), pp. 457-72.

20 Hethum, Prince of Korghos, *Here begynneth a lytell cronycle...* ([London]: Richard Pynson, [ca., 1520]), fols. Bii recto; Aiii recto; Aiii verso; Aiv recto; Av recto.

21 Robert Langton, *The pylgrimage of M. Robert Langton* (London: Robert Copland,

1522); R. J. Mitchell, 'Robert Langton's *Pylgrymage*,' *The library*, 5th series, VIII (March, 1953), 43.

22 Taylor, *Tudor geography*, p. 10, Athur W. Reed, 'The editor of Sir Thomas More's English works: William Rastell, *The library*, 4th series, IV (June, 1923), 33–34.

23 Claudius Ptolemy, *Here begynneth the compost of Ptholomeus* (London: Robert Wyer, 1532? ). Two other undated editions are attributed to 1535 and 1540 by *STC*.

24 *Mappa mundi, otherwise called the compasse and cyrcuet of the worlde* (Londen, R. Wyer, [1535]), fol. Ciii verso.

25 E. G. R. Taylor, 'Master Hore's voyage of 1536,' *The geographical journal*, LXXVII (May, 1931), 469–70.

26 James A. Williamson, *Sir John Hawkins* (Oxford: Clarendon Press, 1927), pp. 8–9, 12, 13.

27 Williamson, *Maritime enterprise*, p. 269.

28 Roger Barlow, *A brief summe of geographie*, ed. E. G. R. Taylor (London: The Hakluyt Society, 1932), pp. xxi–xli; Fernandez de Enciso's book was first published in Seville by J. Cromberger in 1519.

29 *Ibid.*, p. 1.

30 *Ibid.*, p. li.

31 *Ibid.*, p. lii.

32 Conyers Read, *The Tudors* (New York: Henry Holt and Co., 1936), p. 91.

33 Sebastian Münster, *A treatyse of the new India*. trans. Richard Eden (London: Edward Sutton, 1553) fol. aaiii recto.

34 Sir Thomas More, *A fruteful and pleasaunt worke of the beste state of a publyque weale, and of the new yle called Utopia*, trans. Ralph Robinson (London: A. Vele, 1551). Prior to Robinson's translation the *Utopia* was published in the following editions: Louvain, 1516; Paris, 1517; Basle, March 1518 and December 1518; Venice, 1519; and Louvain, 1548. Subsequent English editions were published in 1556 1597.

35 Anthony Ascham, *A lytel treatyse of astronomy* (London: William Powell, 1552), fols. xvii verso – xviii recto.

36 Sir George Warner (ed.) *The libelle of Englyshe polycye* (Oxford: Clarendon Press, 1926), p. 1.

37 *Ibid.*, p. 25.

38 *Ibid.*, p. 5.

39 *Ibid.*, p. 6.

40 *Ibid.* p. 42

41 *Ibid.*, p. 36

42 Hakluyt, *Principal navigations*, I, 213–14.

43 Barlow, pp. 180–81.

## Chapter IV

## RICHARD EDEN: PROPAGANDIST FOR EMPIRE

Historians of Tudor England are not agreed as to the exact nature or intensity of the forces that worked for change in the nation's economy in the first half of the sixteenth century, yet certain changes of significance in England's attitude toward overseas trade and settlement are identifiable. The general rise in prices and the changing nature of agriculture were to be instrumental in England's earliest plans for expansion of trade and settlement abroad.

Throughout the first half of the sixteenth century a general price rise occurred in western Europe, due to the increase of money rather than a shortage of goods. To this inflation, England added a price spiral of its own as debasement of the currency was undertaken particularly between 1544 and 1551 to pay for state expenses—primarily war. As the value of English currency declined in relation to Continental money, prices rose sharply, and exports had to be increased to meet the pressure on the debased coin. The chief export was woolen cloth, and as more of this commodity was required at rising prices, country towns turned toward manufacturing of cloth. The country, too, turned more to grazing than heretofore, as the landowner could no longer maintain himself in accustomed fashion with prices rising while his rents were fixed. The increase in grazing meant a reduction in husbandry, and those who left the land left it with bitterness. The road from farm to factory was peopled with paupers and vagabonds, appearing to some to be an element superfluous to England's needs and a source of unrest. A contemporary observer sums up the relationship of exports, devaluation and popular unrest: 'The fall of the exchange within thus iiii dayse hathe cawsyd and wyll cause to be boughte for lvi *li.* the packe whyche before would not have ben bowghte for lii *li.* the packe; so that yow may perseve that the exchange doth ingendar dere clothe, and dere clothe doth ingender dere wolle, and dere wolle doth ingendar mych pastor and dere, and mych pastor ys the dekaye of tyllage, and owte of the dekay of tyllage spryngthe ii evylls, skarsyte of korne and pepull unrowghte, and consequently the darth of all thynges.'[1]

It is not surprising that unrest rose with prices and exports, yet the latter could not rise indefinitely, for by 1551 Antwerp was glutted with English woolens, and complaints of overproduction were heard in England. It was obvious that English ability to compete effectively in the cloth trade could be established only by a reliable currency, so a fifty per cent devaluation was put into effect between May and August of that year. But the solution was not to be found at once, and exports continued to decline—from 132,000 short cloths in 1550 to 122,000 in 1551 and 85,000 in 1552.[2] With production facilities expanded and the traditional market at Antwerp declining it was apparent that new outlets were needed for English production and possibly for English population. In this situation lay the beginnings of expansion, although it produced no theories of empire at once, for English imperialism was to be forced upon its monarchs and merchants, who changed slowly from their accustomed orientation to the Continent and who might indeed have avoided overseas expansion had it been possible to achieve reasonable prosperity and social calm without it.

It was indeed the merchants, with the backing of the Duke of Northumberland in the government, who first attempted a solution not based on the European market, with voyages undertaken to Africa and Russia in 1551 and 1553. These had government approval, it is true, but they were essentially mercantile ventures. The financial requirements of these undertakings called into existence a new type of business organization, the joint-stock company, which permitted the merging of funds from numerous investors who became share holders in a continuing organization. This development made it possible for the number of persons interested in voyages of exploration and distant commerce to be considerably increased, and it might be expected that such a broadening of opportunity for investment would provide a potentially larger market for published accounts of overseas voyages and trade. Indeed, as merchants of London planned new areas for England's trade, books did appear to give information and encouragement to the venturers.

After the return to England of Sebastian Cabot in 1548, a merchant group in London began to consider the northeast approach to China, long before advocated by Robert Thorne and Roger Barlow. The merchants' information on the Far East had come from no English publication, but they had at the head of their organization Sebastian Cabot who had returned from Spain and who was surely abreast of the latest European thinking on routes to the East. The knowledge of John Dee, England's leading geographer, was also made available to this group of merchants. The preference for the northeast over the northwest route is understandable considering the failures of earlier attempts to penetrate the American continent in its northern latitudes. Cabot's group sent out Sir Hugh Willoughby and Richard Chancellor in May, 1553, to probe the northern coast of Europe and Asia for a sea passage into the Pacific, to China and the East Indies. That this projected voyage had aroused some public enthusiasm is shown by the account supposedly originating with Richard Chancellor, of the departure of the three ships: 'And being come neere to Greenewich, (where the Court then lay) presently upon the newes therof, the Courtiers came running out, and common people flockt together, standing very thicke upon the shoare: the privie Counsel, they lookt out at the windowes of the Court, and the rest ranne up on the toppes of the towers: the shippes hereupon discharge their Ordinance, and shoot off their pieces after the maner of warre, and of the sea...'[3]

The same year Richard Eden, England's first literary imperialist, published his first book, a portion of Sebastian Münster's *Cosmographia* under the title *A treatyse of the newe India*. Eden was a minor civil servant, born in Herefordshire and educated at Cambridge where he studied under Sir Thomas Smith, a professor of civil law with a considerable reputation in astronomy. Eden held a position in the Treasury from 1544 to 1546 and, was destined for the office of the Distillery at the time of Henry VIII's death. During the reign of Edward VI he must have been employed by some state official, possibly Sir William Cecil, during which time he translated two Spanish works of significance to English interest in overseas navigation and trade.[4]

Eden commended his book to the English public as a means of learning by the mistakes and success of others so that Englishmen might 'direct theyr viage to their most commoditie.'[5] In dedicating the book to the Duke of Northumberland, he warned that not all overseas adventures would be profitable, and that venturers should not 'be dismayd as with shame and dishonor to leave wyth losse, but rather to the death persist in a godly, honeste, & lawful purpose, knowing... the same is more honourably spent in such attemptes as may be to the glorye of God & commoditie of our countrey, then in soft beddes at home, among the teares & weping of women.'[6] His praise for those Englishmen who 'have of late... attempted with new viages to serche ye seas and newe found landes,'[7] could only refer to the Willoughby-Chancellor expedition, for the support of which he commended the Duke of Northumberland. This dedication had in it sentiments which will be noted repeatedly in the dedications and epistles to the reader in travel literature of the sixteenth century: a concern for the national economy, the possibility of serving God in exploits abroad, and a contempt for the lack of courage attributed to Englishmen who were not interested in overseas explorations, commerce, or colonization. The emphasis here, however, was clearly on the 'commoditie of our countrie.'

In Eden's lengthy Epistle to the Reader, the economic motive was joined by another argument which was to be found frequently in the writings of enthusiasts for overseas adventure. Eden urged his countrymen to acquire the knowledge requisite to imperialism, and it was knowledge gained through experience rather than traditional learning which he recommended. He attacked the general acceptance of Ptolemy as the authority for the study of geography, affirming that 'albeit he was an excellent man, yet were there many thinges hyd from his knowledge, as not sufficientelye tryed or searched at those daies...'[8] While advancing the principle of the value of experience to learning, he used that principle to justify the northeast exploration then under way, noting that belief in such a passage was discouraged by the maps and globes then current which were based on the concepts of Ptolemy. He was perfectly aware that the voyage he espoused was an experiment and he was far from being as dogmatic about the existence of a passage as some writers two centuries later were to be. The search for knowledge justified it, for 'yf no good can be done this way, it were worthy the adventure to attempt.'[9] The general level of learning in geography among Englishmen of that time can be seen from the truths Eden sought to prove in his Epistle to the Reader. He dwelt on such facts as the roundness of the earth, and the habitability of the southern regions. He seems to have been trying, in a few pages, to bring England up to date on the fundamentals of geography which would have to be accepted to give credence to his major idea of trading with this newly found, inhabited, opposite side of the earth.

It is significant to Eden's purpose to note that the portions he selected from Münster's *Cosmographia* were those describing the East and West Indies. The East was made to appear a region of unimaginable wealth —the major source of various spices, silks, drugs and precious stones. Information on the interior of Asia was less precise, but no less encouraging. The city of Cambalu was described thus: 'there passeth not a daye in the yeare in which there are not about a thousand waynes laden with silke which are brought to this citie by straunge marchauntes.'[10]

While such statements are typical of Münster's picture of the East, the West Indies were described in less favorable terms. From the narratives of Columbus and Vespucci, the most frequently printed accounts of the New World, Eden gave his English readers the impression that America was a curious, cannibal-infested region of no particular promise for commerce. His own attitude toward English interest in America at that time is suggested in his portrayal of Spanish America '...where the Eagle (yet not in every place) hath so spled [sic] his wings, that other poor byrdes may not without offence seke theyre praye within the compasse of the same, I will speake nothing hereof, because I wold be loth to lay an egge, whereof other men might hatche a serpent.'[11] His book was published not more than a month before the end of the reign of Edward VI, and Eden, knowing the possibilities of a rise in Spanish influence upon the accession of Mary Tudor, had good reason not to compromise any future he might have in the civil service by advocating all-out competition with Spain in the New World. Here again, Eden was reflecting an attitude which was to be frequently met in the later sixteenth century. While lethargy and lack of courage were disparaged, the thought of a clash with Spain gave him pause.

In this book Richard Eden established in print the attitudes of the imperialist-minded nationalists for whom mere independence from Continental influence no longer sufficed. His purpose in writing the book may have been nothing more than the result of 'the good affeccion, whiche I have ever borne to the science of Cosmographie... much more by ye good will, whyche of duetie I beare to my native countrey & countreymen,'[12] and his continued activities in publishing more extensive works of a similar type give reason for accepting his stated motives in bringing this book to the press. Yet the fact that *A treatyse of the newe India* appeared just at the time Eden's friend Sebastian Cabot was promoting the first northern voyage of his company of merchants, and that Eden praised this venture, suggests strongly that this little book was no publisher's venture, but a subsidized publication, designed to praise and advertise this voyage which was only the first of many to the northeast.

Richard Chancellor's ship alone survived the challenge of the Arctic, but he made his way from the northern coast of Russia to Moscow, where he secured trading privileges from the government of Czar Ivan for his associates in London. With this commercial foothold in Muscovy, the London merchants accepted defeat in their attempt to get their ships to the Pacific Ocean by a northeast passage, and in 1555 they were incorporated into a new company, generally known as the Russia, or Muscovy Company, which was given a monopoly on trade with regions 'lying northwards, northeastwards or northwestwards.'[13] Fleets were sent out annually after 1555, and a continuing trade developed in which the company claimed to be sending fourteen or fifteen 'tall merchaunts shippes yerelie.'[14] The owners of these ships were not merchants alone. A joint stock organization, the Russia Company was heavily weighted with peers, knights and holders of high office. These would seem to have been, in part at least, men of some education, and their participation in the company's trade to a distant land could have inspired publications of books on Muscovy and other eastern regions —for surely there was in England a great dearth of information on the peoples and products of eastern Europe and Asia. One cannot help wondering why an English translation of Herberstein's account of his travels in Russia did not appear about 1555, for it had already been published in both Latin and Italian by that time. Perhaps the answer lies in the limiting factors that existed within the company. There appear to have been 201 charter members of the company, and all were Londoners except Edward Pryme of Bristol.[15] This group of investors was sufficiently small and localized to enable them to share what information they had with each other, making the publication of information on their newly found market unnecessary—and in fact undesirable—for it could only stimulate competition and possibly arouse the Hanse merchants who were accustomed to dominating England's trade in northern and eastern commodities. The company, therefore, had no interest in advertising its venture, and if a portion of England's population had an interest in this attempt at finding a market for England's woolens it did not impress the printers of London with numbers sufficient to provide a profitable market for books on Russia during the early years of the Company's activities.

The pressure to seek overseas markets drove Englishmen southward also. The coast of Africa had been the school of Portuguese imperialism, from which the Portuguese had moved on to India, leaving a weak network of trading stations along Africa's western shores. These were manned by the servants of a royal monopoly which could do little against foreign interlopers who chose to load slaves there for the plantations of Spanish America. There may have been some English voyages to Africa between those of William Hawkins and mid-century, but they had no continuity, and it was not until 1551 that an organized effort began. In that year a group of London merchants sent Thomas

Wyndham in charge of a voyage to Morocco. Results apparently were encouraging, for the following year three ships were sent out by the same group.

As Morocco had led the Portuguese southward, the English also responded to the lure of Guinea. In 1553 the London merchants of the Morocco trade promoted an expedition to Guinea; the Gold Coast and Benin were their objectives, where gold and pepper were presumably to be found. Despite the loss of all but forty of a crew of 140, the voyage was a financial success, and the syndicate of merchants began to take on the form of a company. Their voyages would undoubtedly have been continued on an annual basis had not the trade been ordered stopped by Queen Mary in response to Portuguese protests.[16]

It is unquestionably coincidental that in 1554, when the Guinea trade was getting under way, a small book appeared from the press of William Powell purporting to describe Africa. Based on the *Omnium gentium mores, leges et ritus* of Johann Boemus, this was the first of a projected series of geographies which were to include volumes on Africa, Asia and Europe.[17] Since Africa was the first continent to be discussed by Boemus, William Prat's translation, called *The discription of the countrey of Aphrique*, was to be the first volume of the series. Actually it was the only one that ever appeared in Prat's translation or over Powell's imprint. Prat's dedication of the book to Edward Courtenay, Earl of Devonshire, contains no hint of his purpose in publishing this translation, other than using it as a means to praise Courtenay, 'A worthy conceller, a preserver of the publicke weale, & a fortherer of her good & godli laws,'[18] and to flay the late government of the Duke of Northumberland. Nothing in the introductory matter bears any relevance to English interest in Africa, and there is no editorial comment in the text to indicate a knowledge of or concern for European or English commerce and conquest along the African coast.

Boemus had based his work for the most part on ancient writings, although he did claim to have used modern authors as well. He divided his description of Africa into three major parts: Ethiopia, Egypt, and various other regions. Most of his description of Ethiopia is taken from the writings of Sabellicus, whose *Enneads* had been frequently published in the late fifteenth and early sixteenth centuries.[19] This section contained a substantial account of the kingdom of Prester John, which would have been of considerable interest in Europe when Boemus first published it, but by 1554 it can hardly have been novel, even in England. No mention was made of the Portuguese contact with Ethiopia, and for the most part the customs, laws and habits of the Ethiopians predominated in the description of that area. The account of Egypt was based very largely on classical writings, owing much to Pliny, Plato, Diodorus, and perhaps other Greek authors. Again it was the manners and customs of the people that received most of the attention, and the same was true in the following section on various African peoples.

In concluding with 'a general description of Afrique', Boemus was very general, and the translator added nothing to make the book timely. While the ancient voyages of Hanno and Eudoxus around Africa were mentioned in the description of Ethiopia, the voyages of the Portuguese during the previous fifty years were nowhere referred to. Prat's translation, therefore, must be considered as an appeal to English classical learning rather than a part of the budding urge of imperialism.

William Prat did not complete his projected translation of all three parts of Boemus' work. His intention to do so is made clear from his statements in the dedication, in which he named the persons to whom the subsequent parts were to be dedicated.[20] However, in the following year William Waterman translated the Africa and Asia sections of Boemus' book, under the title of *The fardle of facions*. This also was translated from the French, and the English rendition of Boemus' Asia was similar to Prat's translation of the Africa in that the translator was content with the ancient authorities, and made no effort to include knowledge that had been acquired and published in Europe during the first half of the sixteenth century. Waterman translated the philosophy that governed the author's approach to scholarship, 'I rather fansie... to folowe the founteines of the first Authors, then brokes [*sic*] of abredgers, which often bring with them much puddle.'[21] Thus he presented Assyria from Herodotus and Sabellicus, Palestine from Josephus, and Tartary from Vincent of Beauvais. India was described as if the Portuguese had not yet found it.

In these two translations of Boemus and in Eden's *Newe India* we see the presentation of the earliest and the latest sources of travel literature which were to continue to develop side by side through the remainder of the sixteenth century. Yet neither the concern for new geographical information nor knowledge based upon the ancient geographers was of sufficient public interest in the 1550s to bring from the publishers many books of either type, and Richard Eden alone was to persist in urging England to empire in that decade. This is not to say that information was not being gathered and made available to interested persons in manuscript form, for when Richard Chancellor returned from his voyage to Muscovy he gave Clement Adams, a geographer and friend of Richard Eden, an excellent report on the voyage which Adams undoubtedly made available to his friends and members of the Muscovy Company in the Latin text which remained unpublished until 1589. But neither Adams nor the Company saw any advantage in making known to the public Chancellor's interesting observations on Russia.

The unhappiness which the reign of Mary Tudor brought to England reached its apogee in her marriage in 1554 to Philip, heir apparent to the crown of Spain. While it prompted revolts in England, it served as an inspiration to Richard Eden to give Englishmen a history of Spanish exploration. His *Decades of the Newe World* constituted his own translation of the first three *Decades* of Pietro Martire d'Anghiera, usually known as Peter Martyr, the noted Italian historian, and passages from numerous other authors.[22] This book was destined to be the foremost English work on the West Indies until the last quarter of the century.

Eden sounded the first note in the shift of English nationalism from a religion-centered emotion to an interest in overseas imperialism. In his long note to the reader he was loud in his praise of Spain for her work in discovering and exploring the New World and critical of Englishmen for their bickering and slandering against Spain. He advised his countrymen to accept the religion of Mary and Philip who 'holde theyr armes abrode to embrase thee yf thou wylt drawe nere unto them,' and he asked Englishmen to 'consider what benefits thau [sic] mayst receane [sic] at theyr handes.'[23] These were probably words of expediency, and when coupled with the fact that the book was dedicated to Philip and Mary, it appears that Eden was attempting to feather his own nest. He was indeed given a place in the English Treasury of Philip shortly thereafter. Yet his fondness for Spain and her religion must have been suspect, for despite his scolding of Englishmen for their recent errors—'thou oughteste to knowe the daungiour thou wast in,'[24] —he was subsequently relieved of his office on suspicion of heresy.[25]

There can be no doubt of Eden's strong nationalistic spirit. His previous book established it, and subsequent publications give no evidence of any weakening of his interest in establishing an English empire. It would appear, rather, that his imperialistic sentiments were so strong that he attempted to mask his natural English hatred for Spain, to pretend to admire and approve Spanish conquests in the New World, and to convince his countrymen that by accepting Spanish leadership they could learn what they must know if they were to be a force in the western Atlantic. In writing 'stoope England stoope, and learne to knowe thy lorde and master, as horses and other brute beasts are taught to doo,'[26] he was asking England to adopt humility as the means to greatness. Nowhere did he suggest that England become a challenger to Spain's dominance of the New World, nor did he criticize the treatment accorded the natives in New Spain as some Spaniards were doing at that time.[27] He hoped, rather, to make his country a student of the nation that had succeeded best in overseas ventures. While his approach may not have been very deceptive, Eden was offering Englishmen a chance to make the best of the unfortunate circumstance of having a Spaniard sharing the throne of England.

Eden's book was not well named, for while Peter Martyr's three *Decades* carry the history of the Spanish in the West Indies to 1516 and constitute 166 numbered leaves, they comprise only a portion of the whole volume. Immediately following the third *Decade* of Martyr is the papal bull of 1493 in which Spain was granted the right to possess lands of the New World. The similar grant to Portugal of the right to the East Indies was not published by Eden, suggesting where his major interest for England lay. Not content with the information presented by Peter Martyr, Eden added to his portrayal of the New World excerpts from the history of the West Indies by Gonzalo Fernández de Oviedo y Valdés.[28] His purpose was to present more recent information, 'forasmuche as of later dayes those countreys have byn better knowen and searched, and dyvers suche particular and notable thynges founde as are conteyned in the hystories of later wryters...'[29] From this source he presented very little history of Spanish conquest, but a wealth of information on the minerals, the climate, the flora and fauna, the navigation of the West Indies, and the customs of the natives.

Having demonstrated Spain's claim to the New World, told the history of her conquests there, and described the natural history of the West Indies, Eden proceeded to the voyage of Magellan, 'one of the greatest and moste marveylous thynges that hath bynne knowen to owre tyme.'[30] He published the introductory material only from the account of the voyage written by Maximilianus *Transylvanus*,[31] which is informative on the products of the East Indies, and then he gave in part the narrative of Antonio Pigafetta, who sailed with Magellan's fleet. In these accounts of Spanish navigation and conquest, Englishmen were presented for the first time in their own language with the possibilities inherent in westward navigation, and as if to lure them on, Eden followed the Pigafetta narrative with descriptions of precious stones and the places where they were to be found, as well as the prices for which they could be bought.

To further proclaim the greatness of the Spanish empire, Eden selected a brief section from the *Historia general de las Indias* of López de Gómara in which he told of the conflict between Spain and Portugal over the ownership of the Moluccas and the conference of navigators in 1524 that decided in favor of Spain.[32] This added to Spain's rich American empire the Spice Islands which were the major prize in the East. Eden concluded this section of his book with excerpts from the writings of Vespucci, Andrea Corsali and Alvise de Cadamosto. These dealt considerably with navigation and may have been included here to demonstrate the ease with which navigation could be undertaken in the southern hemisphere.

Having demonstrated what England might learn from a close association with Spain, Eden then turned his attention to the northeast passage and to northern Europe, where England might further her interests without any regard to Spain. He quoted at length from 'Galeatius Butrigarius' on the desirability of reaching Cathay, and the possibility of doing so by a northeast passage.[33] In the course of this treatise appeared a *roteiro* of the route from Muscovy to Cathay, making the voyage appear to be a clear possibility. A route involving the Caspian Sea and the rivers flowing into it from the north was also alluded to. Eden then left the northeast route to consider the possibility of a northwest passage and the opportunities for settlement in the New World. His enthusiasm burst all restraint as he wrote, 'Oh what doo the Christian Princes meane that in such landes discovered they do not assigne certaine colonies to inhabite the same...'[34]

Passing over the voyage of Richard Chancellor, which he said had been 'largely and faithfully written in the Laten tonge by that lerned young man Clement Adams,' Eden went on to a description of Muscovy from the writings of John Faber, Sebastion Münster and Giacomo Gastaldi, including many aspects of Russian life.[35] He then went on to similar descriptions of Scandinavia based on the descriptions of Jacob Ziegler.[36] Turning his attention then to eastern Asia, Eden presented a translation from the writings of Bishop Paolo Giovio of Nuceria, who had written an account of Muscovy and the lands east of it, based upon information provided by Demetrius, ambassador to Pope Clement VII from the Prince of Muscovy.[37] His account relates to the possibility of a route from the Indus River to the Oxus, thence into the Caspian Sea, and northward to Muscovy. In rendering the translation of Giovio's description of the peoples and products to be found along this route, Eden showed himself to be a critical editor as he elaborated on the author's description of Dvina River and at one point added a comment based upon information supplied to him by Richard Chancellor. Eden's final description of Muscovy was taken from the popular work of Sigmund von Herberstein, which includes an account of the Tatars, a description of the Don River and accounts of various regions from Muscovy to Cathay. Again Eden demonstrated an acquaintance with other sources of information as he quoted from Mandeville, Marco Polo and Maciej Miechowita in editorial and marginal notes.[38]

The closeness with which Eden followed England's commercial interests, and his intention to make his book pertinent to the current situation, are made clear by his inclusion of two very significant documents. These are the letter sent by Edward VI to 'the Kynges, Princes, & other potentates inhabytynge the Northeast partes of the worlde towarde the myghtye Empire of Cathay,' and the reply of Ivan IV of Muscovy. Edward's letter was sent with Willoughby and Chancellor in 1553, and it was a typical formalistic request for friendship, amity and commerce between England and whatever prince might receive the letter. Ivan's reply was encouraging, as he was 'willynge that yow sende unto us with your shyppes and vessels when and as often as they may have passage, with good assuraunce on owre partie to see them harmlesse.'[39] In addition to all of the encouragements Eden gave to Englishmen to develop trade with Muscovy, he added a map based upon the one which had appeared in the 1549 edition of Herberstein's narrative. It showed the inviting river system which led from northern Russia to the Caspian Sea, a reservoir for Asiatic goods. Altogether, Eden's account of Russia and adjacent lands gave to English merchants a more complete study of an area and its trade than was to appear in English until the publication of Federici's account of the Near and Middle East in 1588.

His work on the northeast regions completed, Eden again turned to America with accounts of Columbus from López de Gómara and Sebastian Cabot. He went on to report the voyages of Juan de Solis and Cabot to the Plate River in 1515 and Cabot to the same river in 1527. Then followed descriptions of Labrador, Baccalaos and the discovery of Florida. This section conluded with some theoretical geography and the note that some of the information was taken from a map made by

Sebastian Cabot.[40] Perhaps the least pertinent portion of Eden's book was his translation from the *Pyrotechnia* of Vannucio Biringoccio where he explained 'the generation' of metals.[41] He explained its inclusion by stating 'that it seemeth to me a thynge undecent to reade so much of golde and sylver, and to knowe lyttel or nothynge of the naturall generation thereof.'[42] He was apparently attempting to educate Englishmen in the nature and mining of precious metals.

As he came to the conclusion of his work, Eden reported that some of his friends had come to him and insisted that he include accounts of the recent voyages to Guinea in 1553 and 1554, in order that posterity might know of these enterprises. Eden agreed, and in his account of the 1553 voyage, he discussed the difficulties encountered, supporting the position of the Portuguese captain, Pinteado, against the English Captain Wyndham, as to the proper conduct of the voyage. Here again, Eden was urging England to accept foreign superiority in matters of navigation. The 1554 voyage was presented in very brief form, being little more than a journal of distances, rivers, soundings, and other matters of navigational interest. Eden implied that a want of navigational information made this approach necessary.[43]

Richard Eden's book as a whole is evidence of his world view of England's opportunities abroad. Realizing her handicap of ignorance in world geography, he urged upon her a close relationship with Spain which might help to remedy that condition. He made no plea for a special region or undertaking, but opened the New World, the Strait of Magellan, the East Indies, Cathay, Muscovy, and lesser regions to Englishmen's eyes. He wrote not as a merchant or as a government official, but as an intellectual, conversant with Continental languages and literatures. In his translations from several languages, he brought forth information that anticipated and served most of England's commercial undertakings abroad to the end of the sixteenth century. No collection of geographical literature published in English in the sixteenth century surpassed this one for pertinence to England's situation, and in form and content it anticipated the *Principall navigations* of Richard Hakluyt which is generally more highly regarded. In his nationalistic motive, and in his learning and realization of England's need for learning, Eden was in the tradition of John Rastell and the intellectual nationalists of the Thomas More group.

If it is true that with Eden's book 'England awoke to the new day,'[44] it is even more demonstrably true that most Englishmen did not clamor for the type of information it contained. Voyage literature was readily available to any publisher who wanted to collect and publish it, but apparently none saw in it an opportunity for profit. It is certain, however, that by the end of Mary's reign some Englishmen were absorbing knowledge of the new discoveries. Although Eden's books alone had described the Portuguese East Indies, Robert Record's *Castle of knowledge*, published in 1556, presents a dialogue between a 'master' and a 'scholar' in which the master says 'who is it hath not hearde of the isles of Molucca, and Samatra, where the Portingales gette the great plentye of rich drugges and fine spices?' [45]

Record wrote with familiarity of Calicut, Peru, and Cape of Good Hope and other newly found lands, to illustrate the various positions of the earth with respect to the sun in what was essentially a treatise on spheres. A reasonably good map of the eastern hemisphere was included which shows that some Englishmen had developed a picture of the East, despite the lack of any large amount of English literature on the subject. Robert Record, recognizing as he did the necessity of knowledge and experience in navigation as the key to successful ventures abroad, held promise as a real servant of overseas enterprise. In 1557 he published his *Whetstone of witte*, an arithmetic book which he dedicated to the Muscovy Company. Seeking patronage for this book, he promised that if it was accepted by the Company, he would shortly produce another one on navigation, with particular attention to the problems of the 'Northlie Navigations'. He promised also to show the way to the 'Northe Easte Indies', a region more accessible than the more southerly Cathay.[46] He referred disparagingly to those who complained against expeditions of this type, as many of his successors in the field of imperialistic literature were to do for the next two generations. Record died in 1558, before his promised book could be published.

William Cuningham, a physician, astrologer and engraver, attempted to give the impression of the same familiarity with the new discoveries that Record had shown, but *The cosmographical glasse*, the first geographical publication of importance in Elizabeth's reign, demonstrated no great erudition on the part of its author. Fearful that he might bore his readers with things that everyone know about India and America, he went on to write of 'the Navigation to Calicute (of which voiage Vesputius, & Columbus were the first authors, & nowe more frequented of the spanierdes, then sayling into countries nie adjacent to us)...' [47] This confusion is documented by an extremely crude map of the eastern hemisphere included in the book. Nevertheless, Cuningham showed some acquaintance with recent information, for he mentioned Chancellor's voyage of 1553 in connection with his description of Muscovy, and the reader is referred to 'Sigismunde' [Herberstein] for a further description of Russia. Cuningham took a critical view of the Mandevillian types of peoples currently attributed to Africa, Asia and America, but he offered nothing more than sketchy accounts of the peoples and places on those continents.

Cuningham's book, like Record's *Castle of knowledge,* called for no reprint, indicating that the public showed no marked preference for good geographies over mediocrities. The number of persons interested at all in lands beyond England's shores was probably very small; Richard Eden confirmed this in 1561 when he referred to them and praised them as he wrote '... in certeyne small and obscure members of the common wealth, consisteth no small increase to the perfection of the whole.'[48] These words from his introduction to *The arte of navigation,* a very useful book he translated from the Spanish of Martin Cortés, convey the impression that it was not the leaders of society or politics who were interested in the outer world, but—as had been true previously—lesser folk who were probably persons of scholarly attainments. In translating this valuable navigation handbook Eden showed a correct understanding of England's deficiencies in the science of navigation, and the book helped to convince Englishmen of their need for better sailing technology. They responded by calling for six editions of this practical work before the end of the sixteenth century. Eden's translation was also tied in with the overseas interests of the Muscovy Company, for he dedicated it to William Garrard and Thomas Lodge, aldermen of London and governors of the Muscovy Company, praising them and others who had 'maintained' him and who had taken personal losses in the attempt to find a northeast passage. There were others in England who shared Eden's knowledge and possibly his enthusiasm for harnessing it in overseas ventures, but no one else at that time put these two forces together in books that could influence the reading public.

## NOTES TO CHAPTER IV

[1] Quoted in F. J. Fisher, 'Commercial trends and policy in sixteenth century England,' *Economic history review*, X (November, 1940), 97.

[2] S. T. Bindoff, *Tudor England* (Harmondsworth, Middlesex: Penguin Books, Ltd., 1958), pp. 128–38; also G. R. Elton, *England under the Tudors* (London: Methuen & Co., Ltd., 1959), pp. 224–51.

[3] Hakluyt, *Principal navigations*. I, 271

[4] Edward Arber, *The first three English books on America*, pp. xxxvii–xlvi. Sebastian Münster's book was first published as *Cosmographei oder Beschreibung aller Lander* (Basel: Henric Petri, 1544).

[5] Sebastian Münster, *A treatise of the newe India*, trans. Richard Eden (London: Edward Sutton, 1553), fol. aaiii verso.

[6] *Ibid.*, fols. aaiii verso – aaiiii recto.

[7] *Ibid.*, fols. aaiii recto–verso.

[8] *Ibid.*, fol. aaviii verso.

[9] *Ibid.*, fol. Ai verso.

[10] *Ibid.*, fol. Fiiii rectol.

[11] *Ibid.*, fol. Aii recto.

[12] *Ibid.*, fol. aaiii recto.

[13] T. S. Willan, 'Trade between England and Russia in the second half of the sixteenth century,' *English historical review*, LXIII (July, 1948), 309.

[14] *Ibid.*, p. 315.

[15] T. S. Willan, *The Muscovy merchants of 1555* (Manchester: Manchester University Press, 1953), pp. 5–10.

[16] Williamson, *Sir John Hawkins*, pp. 44–46.

[17] The original edition was published in Augsburg by S. Grim and M. Wirsung in 1520. Three Latin editions appeared in 1536, and Latin editions were published in 1538, 1540 and 1541 also. Italian editions were printed in Venice in 1543 and 1549. French editions appeared in 1540 and 1542, two editions being published in the latter year. It was presumably from one of these French editions that Prat translated into English.

[18] Johann Boemus, *The discription of the countrey of Aphrique*, William Prat trans. (London: William Powell, 1554), fol. A3 verso.

[19] The *Enneads* of Marco Antonio Coccio, called *Sabellico*, constituted a chronological history of the world. It was first printed in Venice, 1498, and subsequently in Venice, 1504; Milan, 1507; and Basle, 1515.

[20] The description of Asia was to be dedicated to 'my lorde of Darbie,' and that of Europe to 'my good mistres Clarentius.' See fol. Avii recto.

[21] Johann Boemus, *The fardle of facions*, trans. William Waterman (London: John Kingstone and Henry Sutton, 1555), fol. Iiii recto.

[22] Richard Eden, *The decades of the Newe Worlde or West India* (London. William Powell, 1555). Four different printers issued this work for Powell; they were Richard Jugge, Robert Toy, Edward Sutton, and William Seres. Peter Martyr's first *Decade* was published in Venice, 1504; another edition was published in Seville, 1511; and the first three *Decades* were printed in Alcalá, 1516, and again in Basle, 1533. Eden worked from the 1516 edition.

[23] Eden, *Decades*, fol. bii recto – verso.

[24] *Ibid.*, fol. bii verso.

[25] Arber, p. xl.

[26] Eden, *Decades*, fol. bi verso.

[27] The classic Spanish criticism of that nation's policies with respect to the American

natives is Bartolomé de las Casas, *Brevissima relación de la destruycion de las Indias* (Seville: Sebastian Trugillo, 1552).

28 Gonzalo Fernández de Oviedo y Valdés, *De la natural hystoria de las Indias* (Toledo: Remō de petras, 1526). George B. Parks suggests that the appearance of many names in Italian in the text probably means that Eden did not translate from the original Spanish, but from Giovanni Battista Ramusio, *Delle navigationi et viaggi* (Venice: L. A. Giunta, 1550 or 1554); see his *The contents and sources of Ramusio's 'Navigationi'* (New York: The New York Public Library, 1955), p. 32.

29 Eden, *Decades*, fol. 173 verso.

30 *Ibid.*, fol. 214 verso.

31 Maximilianus *Transylvanus, De Moluccis insulis* (Cologne E. Cervincorni, 1523).

32 Francisco López de Gómara, *Primera y segunda parte de la historia general de los Indias* (Saragossa, Agustin Millan, 1552); The treaty of Tordesillas had provided for the division of the undiscovered regions between Spain and Portugal in 1494. Upon the discovery of the Moluccas with their valuable spices, it became necessary to determine their location with respect to the dividing line, which lay opposite the parallel lying 370 leagues west of the Cape Verde Islands.

33 According to Eden, Galleazzo Botrigari presented this information in a conversation in the home of Francastro, the poet. Ramusio reproduces the conversation, but he does not attribute it to Botrigari, but to 'un gentil huome, grandissimo philosopho et mathematico,' and R. H. Major demonstrates that this could not have been Botrigari, who was Bishop of Gaeta. See his *Notes upon Russia* (2 vols.; London: The Hakluyt Society, 1850–52), II, 183.

34 Eden, *Decades*, fol. 254 recto.

35 Faber's work was first published as *Epistola de Moscovitarum juxta mare glaciale regione, seu dogmatibus Moscou* (Tübingen, 1525); Gastaldi was the editor of the first edition of Ptolemy's *Geographia* in Italian. It was published in Venice by G. B. Pedrezzano, 1548.

36 Jacob Ziegler, *Quae intus continentur: Syria... Palestina... Arabia Petrea...* [etc.] (Strassburg, Peter Opilio, 1532).

37 First published as *Libellus de legatione Basilii Magni Principis Moschoviae ad Clementum VII* (Rome, 1525). An Italian edition was published in Venice, 1545.

38 Miechovita was a Polish physician whose *Tractatus de duabus Sarmatii* ([Cracow]: J. Haller, 1517), was based on observations he made during travels in Russia. Latin and German editions were published in 1518 also.

39 Eden, *Decades*, fol. 308; Ivan's reply is found on an unnumbered leaf inserted between folios 309 and 310.

40 This must refer to Cabot's planisphere variously dated 1544, 1547 and 1549. Clement Adams who was appointed schoolmaster to the King's henchmen at Greenwhich in 1552 and was an exploration enthusiast, engraved this map, but no copy has survived. The inscriptions from it are preserved in Nathan Chytraeus, *Variorum in Europa itinerum deliciae* (Herborn: 1594), pp. 779–81.

41 Vannucio Biringocci, *Pyrotechnia* (Venice: V. Roffinello, 1540). A second edition was published in Venice, 1550.

42 Eden, *Decades*, fol. 325 verso.

43 *Ibid.*, fols. 343 recto–360 verso.

44 George B. Parks, *Richard Hakluyt and the English voyages* (New York: American Geographical Society, 1928), p. 23.

45 Robert Record, *The castle of knowledge* (London: Reginald Wolfe, 1556), p. 65.

46 Robert Record, *The whetstone of witte* (London: John Kyngstone, 1557), fol. aiii recto–verso.

47 William Cuningham, *The cosmographical glasse* (London: John Day, 1559), p. 67. Cuningham was a physician, astrologer, and engraver who published several

works on astrology. The woodcuts in *The cosmographical glasse* are from his own hand.

48 Martin Cortés, *The arte of navigation*, trans. Richard Eden (London: Richard Jugge, 1561), fol. ii recto. The original edition was *Breve compendio de la sphera y de arte de navegar* (Seville: Anton Alvarez, 1551). The importance of Eden's translation to the development of the science of navigation in England is discussed at some length in David W. Waters, *The art of navigation in England in Elizabethan and early Stuart times* (London: Hollis and Carter, 1958), pp. 104–105.

## Chapter V

## BEGINNINGS IN AMERICA

The death of Mary Tudor and the accession of Elizabeth in 1558 brought forth no literary show of imperialism such as Mary's marriage to Philip had done. Mary's demise relieved England of its uncomfortably close relationship with Spain, and her successor began at once to go her way of independence for England, giving as little offense to Spain as possible as she did so. There were genuine reasons why Protestant England and Catholic Spain should not offend each other, and these had implications for any overseas interests that might appear in England. One reason was France, which lay between Spain and her most valuable European province, the Low Countries. The commerce that flowed between them was constantly menaced by France, and Spain needed the help of an English fleet to balance the power of French raiders in the Channel. Another area where French sea power molested the Spaniards was the American waters, where the French menace forced the Spaniards to use an expensive and cumbersome convoy system.[1] Spain had no wish to have England join France in this piracy if it could be prevented.

On the other hand, Elizabeth had a very good reason for not wishing to break the Spanish alliance formed by the marriage of Mary and Philip. She had a rival in Mary Stuart, Queen of Scots, who was allied with France. The Spanish alliance, therefore, while obnoxious to English Protestants and to those few who saw a future for England in America, was expedient on other grounds. Unwillingness to offend Spain, Europe's most powerful nation, and the general lethargy toward imperialistic undertakings would account for the absence of any expansionist literature concerning America during the first five years of Elizabeth's reign—a period of marked activity from the standpoint of commercial ventures in Eastern Europe and Asia where Spain had no claims.

The Muscovy Company had been frustrated in its search for a northeast seaway to the East Indies and Cathay and the trade which developed with Russia after Chancellor's voyage did not satisfy the company's ambitions; thus the hope for direct trade with the East forced consideration of overland routes into Asia. To this end Anthony Jenkinson was sent, in 1557, to search for a route through Russia. Jenkinson's remarkable adventure took him from the White Sea to the Caspian, but in seeking to tap the eastern trade by a land route he was actually attempting to establish a variant upon the earlier east-west trade connection which had already been outflanked by Portuguese navigation. The knowledge he added of political turmoil in the areas through which he passed did not recommend this northern approach as an orderly way for England to get her eastern goods.[2] This discouragement may account for the failure of Eden or anyone else connected with the company to publish a description of Jenkinson's journey when he returned to England in 1560, for it must surely be assumed that Eden had access to and would have been keenly interested in Jenkinson's description of his travels in Russia and Persia.

Jenkinson apparently held out some hope for developing a profitable trade with the Caspian and Persian Gulf areas, and in 1561 he went out to Russia again, in the service of the Queen and the company. Had he succeeded, the Muscovy Company would have had access to the trade of India at the Persian Gulf and would have deprived the Turks of their profit in handling the goods that flowed westward from India. But Jenkinson encountered international rivalries in the Near East. The Turks and Persians were at peace at the time of his visit, and although he did succeed in establishing trade with the Persian province of Shirvan, the Shah of Persia was in no position to offend his Turkish rival for the benefit of the English. Jenkinson returned to England in 1563 an advocate of a water route to the East Indies, although he went back to Russia again in 1572 and the company continued to prosecute the Persian trade until 1581.[3]

Throughout this series of commercial adventures into Russia and Persia, and in spite of the availability of literature on Russia to supplement the first-hand information on the area from the White Sea to the Persian Gulf which Jenkinson brought back, no printer ventured to produce a book describing these regions of admitted interest to England's economy. The lack of interest on the part of the publishers must be attributed to a lack of enthusiasm among the public for the Muscovy Company's ventures. The company had a monopoly on the trade, and even investigating it involved sufficient expense so that few independent merchants would be interested in Russia and Persia from a practical business standpoint. Jenkinson's employers, on the other hand had no reason for wanting to share with others the information they received from him. The Queen's interest was indicated by the fact that during his 1561 mission he was in her service as well as that of the company; yet she and her advisers needed no printed accounts of his travels to inform them of the lands Jenkinson visited. All of these factors combined to keep this series of colorful and adventurous travels from being described in print at the time when there ought to have been the greatest interest in them. There may have been a map in circulation that showed the lands Jenkinson visited, for he or someone close to him must have drawn a map after his return from Russia. In 1570 a map depicting Jenkinson's travels appeared in the *Theatrum orbis terrarum*, an atlas published in Antwerp by Abraham Ortelius; however no comparable map bearing an English imprint exists.[4]

The other newly established overseas trade which Elizabeth inherited was that of western Africa, where English merchants had gained a foothold through the voyages of Thomas Wyndham in 1551 and 1553. Despite the prohibition Mary placed upon English trade to Guinea, it continued; Elizabeth gave it official sanction by refusing to recognize Portuguese occupation as effective occupation, and Sir William Cecil added that England did not recognize the papal grant under which the Portuguese claims were made.[5] In sanctioning the Guinea trade Elizabeth had in mind a permanent commercial relationship there, for in 1561 when John Lok, a London merchant, was placed in command of a fleet bound for that coast, his orders included instructions to select a site for English occupation.[6] The next year Sir John Hawkins, in company with a group of London merchants, brought England into the African slave trade by capturing 300 Negroes in Sierra Leone and shipping them to the West Indies for sale to the Spanish plantations. In 1564 he repeated the voyage, accompanied by several gentlemen— and among the subscribers to the expedition was Queen Elizabeth herself. Hawkins sailed not only as a merchant, but as the Queen's officer.

In participating in the slave trade from Africa to the Spanish West Indies, Hawkins and his Queen were violating Spain's restriction upon trade with her American possessions. It is doubtful that Elizabeth would thus seek to annoy the Spanish with whom she was officially in alliance, and whose help she might need. It is more likely that she and Hawkins were trying to demonstrate the value the English could be to Spain by supplying slaves and goods to the plantations, while in return for this right to trade, England would hunt down the French corsairs in the Caribbean.[7]

This projected partnership with Spain could not be exposed to public view, and consequently it gave rise to no published literature on either Africa or America. On the other hand, Hawkins had the possibility of cooperating with France in despoiling the Spanish empire, and this opportunity did inspire the publication of Jean Ribaut's *The whole and true discoverye of Terra Florida*. Ribaut was a Huguenot captain who advanced the most daring scheme for the plunder of Spanish shipping yet. In 1562 he planted a settlement at Charlesfort on the coast of what is now South Carolina with the undoubted intention of using it as a base for raiding the Spanish treasure fleet which must sail along the coast with the Gulf Stream. He returned to France, leaving some colonists behind, and upon discovering in his own country that the Huguenots were losing in their civil war, he crossed over to England where he secured approval for his idea from the English government, and where a plan was made for an Anglo-Huguenot enterprise in Florida with the adventurer Thomas Stukeley named to assist Ribaut in planning the venture. A part of the promotion program was the publication of Ribaut's description of Florida which had previously circulated in manuscript.[8]

The book took the form of a statement from Ribaut to some person in authority in France, probably the Huguenot leader Coligny, and this edition for English readers was dedicated to Sir Martin Bowes, alderman of London. In this instance the publisher appears as an enthusiastic participant in plans for overseas exploits, for Thomas Hacket commended 'the forwardnes in these late yeares of Englysche men'[9] with respect to navigation. Despite the effort required, voyages abroad were well worth while, in Hacket's view, and he noted the success of Spain and Portugal as a result of their initiative. Actually, Hacket was printing what the promoters of the Ribaut-Stukeley enterprise wanted him to print, for he was shortly to publish exactly opposite sentiments.

Ribaut's account of Florida was an entirely favorable picture of a region that abounded in all manner of natural products, including a 'great aboundance of golde & silver, precious stones, & other great riches.'[10] The vegetable products were pictured as sufficient to make settlement easily undertaken, and the possibility of producing silk easily was to give the settlement a stable industry. 'To be short,' said Ribaut, 'it is a thing unspeakeable to consider the thinges that be seene there, & shalbe founde more & more, in this incomparable lande, whiche never yet broken with Ploughe yrons, bringeth forthe all things according to his first nature, where-with the eternall God endewed [sic] it.'[11] To the appeal of precious metals and life-sustaining products, he added a third motive for settlement in mentioning the conversion of the natives to Protestant Christianity. In this first English propaganda to support an overseas settlement, therefore, are to be found the three appeals most frequently appearing in English exploration and colonization literature in the sixteenth century. The products to support settlers were given the greatest prominence, either as a mask of the true intent of the colony or out of realization that the Huguenot-English raiders would need a firm base of operations if they were to get precious metals either inland or in the Gulf Stream. The missionary motive received the weakest expression of the three.

Thomas Stukeley was not the type of person to be intrusted with building an empire at the expense of Spain. He revealed the plans of Ribaut to the Spanish ambassador and was forthwith removed from his responsibilities. This must have caused the public no great annoyance, for in a broadside ballad issued before Stukeley's fall, Robert Seall had felt it necessary to defend Stukeley and the Florida venture against critics. In twenty-eight crude verses he compared the taunts of these doubters to those hurled at Columbus, and he advised

> *Now Stuetley hoice thy sail,*
> *Thy wisshed land to finde:*
> *And never doo regard vain talke,*
> *For wurds they are but winde.*[12]

Seall's abounding faith in Florida far surpassed his knowledge of that region, and his optimism was based on its favorable evaluation by the French, Spanish and Portuguese. He firmly believed that Stukeley would have the last word with his critics, for

> *... if it fall his lot*
> *With fortunes helping hand:*
> *He may wel make a law[p]hing stock,*
> *Of them which him withstand.*[13]

Apparently the vocal opposition to the Florida project did not deter the Queen, for her officer, Sir John Hawkins, in making his Africa-West Indies voyage of 1564, was aware that Ribaut and René de Laudonnière were en route to Florida to reinforce the French settlement there, and he took with him a Dieppe pilot who knew the Florida coast.[14] Clearly Elizabeth was trying both a pro-Spanish and an anti-Spanish entrance into the Caribbean, and Hawkins was to discover which was likely to be most advantageous to England.

Hawkins loaded Negroes in Sierra Leone, sailed for the Caribbean in January, 1565, and succeeded in trading profitably in the Spanish West Indies despite the Spanish King's decrees prohibiting such trade. He then sailed to Florida, where he found most of the French colonists anxious to depart. He offered them passage home, for he was now convinced that trade with the West Indies would be more beneficial than raids upon Spanish shipping. Laudonnière refused the offer of transportation back to France, and Hawkins returned to England with a profit and with plans that could not be served by Hacket's book advertising the riches of Florida. By 1582 Richard Hakluyt was saying that this book was 'not nowe to be had, unless I had caused it to be printed againe.'[15] If it had convinced Englishmen of the value of a settlement in Florida, that conviction was soon challenged by events in the French base there and by a second book published by Hacket which reported these events and presented a frankly anti-imperialistic point of view. This was a translation from the French of the account of what befell the French garrison in Florida under Laudonnière and the reinforcements which Ribaut sought to bring him. Both groups were caught unprepared in 1565 by the Spanish commander Pedro Mendénez de Avilés, and most of them were killed. One who escaped was the carpenter Le Challeux, and his narrative of the destruction of the French settlement went through three editions in French before Hacket published an English translation of it titled *A true and perfect description of the last voyage... attempted by Capitaine John Rybaut*.[16] The text reported the massacre of the French in Florida, but the dedicatory epistle instead of being an expression of outraged anger at the brutality of the Spanish was a firmly expressed anti-colonial statement. It took the form of a letter from Le Challeux to a friend, and it admonished the craftsman to keep to his tools and the householder to his wife, lest the home decay in his absence. 'Let them go to Florida who list, for my part I would not wishe, that that man, that is a householder should leave his occupation, for to seeke his adventure in a straunge countrey, and for greater profit of gaine.'[17]

The publication of these sentiments constitute an abrupt about-face on the part of Hacket after his earlier expression of admiration for Englishmen who were engaging in distant navigations. He was expressing a pessimism that may have been widespread in England, although there are no other contemporary evidences of it in print, and knowingly or not, he was reflecting the decision of the Queen and her advisers to cast their lot with the Spanish West Indian trade and to discourage interest in the partnership with the Huguenots.

Two years later Hacket published his third book on America, and once again he was the champion of overseas enterprise with an English edition of André Thevet's *Les singularitez de la France antarctique*, dedicated to Sir Henry Sidney, Lord President of Wales and Lord Deputy of Ireland.[18] Sir Henry was in high favor with the Queen and these positions made him one of the key figures in the first phase of England's imperialism—the subjugation of non-English peoples in the British Isles. In using Henry Bynneman as his printer, Hacket was drawing upon the services of one who called himself the servant of Sir Christopher Hatton, another favorite at court.[19] Hacket was now unrestrained in his praise of those who would leave the easy, comfortable life of England to face 'a thousande imminent evils, onely to encrease the fame and good renowme [sic] of their countrey,'[20] but he lamented as Eden had done, that most men are given to idleness. It seems likely that in this publication Hacket was again encouraged, if not subsidized, by interests close to the court, even though the book was not propaganda for English cooperation in any specific French colony in the New World which Thevet had described.

Whatever his motivation, Hacket presented to English readers their first comprehensive view of America in his translation of Thevet's book. It was based on the experiences and observations of the author who had left France with Villegagnon to establish a Huguenot colony near Rio de Janeiro in 1555. In connection with this Atlantic voyage Thevet gave descriptions of the African coast and the Atlantic islands, and even brought Madagascar and the East Indies into the picture. He followed this with a description of Rio de Janeiro, then carried his narrative northward along the coast of Brazil, thence to Florida, and finally along the coast of Canada and Newfoundland en route to the Azores and back to Europe. The account of America probably covered substantially more than did the travels of its author, but its veracity was not a matter for debate in the sixteenth century. Thevet gave his readers a substantial account of the natives, minerals, climate, etc., and in Hacket's translation England had a book of geographic, economic, and ethnological interest relating to the New World as a whole. The fact that this book was to be in the ship of Martin Frobisher when he sailed for America eight years later, yet was published in only one edition in English, bears out Hacket's opinion as to the lack of interest in overseas ventures, for Thevet's book was sufficiently broad in its portrayal of the New World to have interested readers who were curious about any aspect of the American continents.

Meanwhile, the overseas interests of the Queen and her chief adventurer abroad, Sir John Hawkins, continued to center on the Spanish West Indies. In 1566–67 another slaving voyage was made by John Lovell in command of three ships, but with no great success, for the Spaniards deprived him of many of his slaves without making payment.[21] In 1567 Hawkins undertook another voyage. He called at Sierra Leone where he acquired a cargo of nearly 500 Negroes and departed for the Spanish Main. He traded at Margarita Island, at Borburata in Venezuela, at Rio de la Hacha, and at Cartagena, although he met with increasing resistance from Spanish colonial officials who put up a show of wanting to comply with their King's order not to trade with foreigners. In sailing for home, Hawkins found it necessary to put into the harbor of San Juan de Ulúa to repair the Queen's ship, the *Jesus of Lubeck*. Here he was caught by the Spanish treasure fleet and badly mauled. The *Jesus* had to be abandoned, while Hawkins and what was left of his party escaped in two small vessels.[22]

Now it was clear that the Spanish were not agreeable to accepting English trade and English assistance in the Caribbean. With this episode closed, Hawkins gave to English readers an account of his ill-fated third voyage into the Spanish West Indies. His *True declaration of the troublesome voyadge* described in detail the English defeat at the hands of the Spanish fleet, and he lamented, 'If all the miseries and troublesome affayres of this sorowefull voyadge shoulde be perfectlye and throughlye written, there shoulde nede a paynfull man with his penne, and as greate a tyme as he had that wrote the lives and deathes of the martyrs.'[23] Hawkins' book has no preface, dedication, or introductory material to suggest the reason for its publication. Its publisher, Lucas Harrison, does not appear again as a publisher of this type of literature. The impression his book left must have been one of pessimism as strong as that of the Le Challeux account of the massacre of the French in Florida, but England's pessimists were not numerous enough to require a second edition.

Elizabeth's earliest programs for extending English trade into American waters, therefore, did not send large numbers of readers to the bookstalls of London seeking accounts of the new lands that English sailors were visiting. Booksellers found a more active market in the field of classical and medieval geography than in accounts of current explorations, for the intellectual development of England in this period was toward the classical and away from the medieval learning which was, however, still quite firmly entrenched.[24] In 1566 Thomas Hacket offered an abstracted version of Pliny's *Natural history*, translated from the French, and the information he chose to publish pertains chiefly to the conditions and traits of men and animals in little-known lands such as Asia, India and Ethiopia. Recognizing the incredibility of some of the information, the translator, who signed himself merely 'I. A.', defended questionable passages by affirming 'nothing is impossible unto God.'[25]

Such works as this were published to meet the growing interest in the ancient writers as sources of a new type of learning, even as new discoveries were making the classical geographers increasingly obsolete. Sir John Mandeville, on the other hand, represented medieval geography, with its flair for the fantastic, and a new edition of his travels, published in 1568,[26] was carried with Martin Frobisher on his voyage of 1576, along with Hacket's translation of Thevet and the *Arte de navegar* written by Pedro de Medina.[27] This indicates that England's foremost navigators, like other Englishmen, were as yet unable to discern with certainty the comparative value of the modern writers and medieval legends. If Frobisher valued Mandeville's book sufficiently to take it with him, it is unlikely that its publisher, Thomas East, published it merely because 'the English have always loved a good liar.'[28]

While England's two major commercial schemes prior to 1570— direct trade with Asia and a working agreement with Spain for West Indian trade—had failed to produce much significant popular literature, they also failed in providing England with new markets for her goods. Asiatic tribes, Near Eastern politics, and Spanish sea power made it plain to the expansionists near the Queen that expansion must be undertaken in another direction, and the early 1570s found a small but influential group of men considering seriously what England's next move should be, for the economic pressures had been increasingly severe in the decade just past. This problem seems to have made no impression on the general reading public or the booksellers, for the book trade carried nothing of worth to students of geography in the years 1570–75.

The science of navigation, however, was served by a second edition of *The arte of navigation* published in 1572 and the first English book of navigation, William Bourne's *Regiment for the sea*, 1574. While the former was essentially a reprint of the earlier translation of Richard Eden, the *Regiment* of Bourne was the first original English work on navigation. Bourne wrote nothing of empire as an objective or motive in writing this book, but cited England's insular situation to indicate that he expected it to be useful to his countrymen. In protesting his own inadequacy, he stated that 'the learned sorte of Seafaring men have no neede of this booke, yet I am assured that it is a necessarie booke for the simplest sort of Seafaring men.'[29] Despite his modesty, he did claim to cover some points not included in the work of Martin Cortes, and indeed, he supplemented Cortes admirably with information on the use of instruments of navigation which the Spanish author had merely described. That Bourne was not a mere theoretician and that he was aware of the range of English seafaring is evident, for he planned his book to be useful to navigators to all parts of Europe, to Africa and 'neare unto the coast of America.'[30] This awareness of modern discoveries together with his use of astrology illustrates the emergence of modern scientific thought which was not yet free of medieval traits.

While sailors were thus well instructed in navigation, those who were interested in the ends of navigation—the discovery and exploration of distant lands—had no such good fortune. They found Henry Bynneman, in 1572, publishing a translation of the classical geography of Dionysius *Periegetes*, an Alexandrian geographer of the second century. Thomas Twine, in introducing this book to the English reader, leaves the impression that he had translated it because it was a classic rather than because of any intrinsic merit the text might contain. Hopefully, he concluded, 'if thou receive any plesure of commoditie therby, then have I for my part, atteyned to my desire.'[31] The text which follows is an Alexandrian view of the world without commentary by the translator. It was altered from the rhymed version which had made it popular on the Continent two generations earlier to a dull prose which was typical of its translator.

The same year Sebastian Münster's *Cosmographia* was published in an abridged edition, and the result was an unusual hodgepodge of encyclopedic information. The random selection of material gave England's searchers for geographic information accounts of Persia, India, Cathay and Prester John, but also they found here comments on a variety of European subjects including alpine mice, an abnormal birth in Germany, Mount Vesuvius, the properties of the eagle, and other miscellaneous knowledge. Such a book can have had no other motive than an appeal to a great diversity of readers, and the appearance of a second edition in 1574 indicates it was more successful than the books of Eden and Hacket with their concern for overseas matters.[32]

While the book trade shed no light on England's export problems, the expansionists in the court circle developed two alternatives of overseas enterprise toward that end. These were the finding of a northwest passage to the East Indies—an idea as old in England as the voyages of John Cabot—and the discovery of a great southern continent, generally believed to lie to the south and west of the Strait of Magellan. This latter was accepted by all learned geographers of the time but was championed most vigorously in England by Sir Richard Grenville, who in 1573–74 planned a project to take an English fleet through the Strait of Magellan into the South Pacific. He presented his petition to the Queen on March 22, 1574, asking for the right to discover for England and to establish English trade in 'all or any lands, islands and countries southward beyond the equinoctial... which lands... be not already possessed or subdued by or to the use of any Christian Prince in Europe...'[33] The partners to this proposed venture were to be largely within the Grenville relationship, but the Queen was also to be included.

Elizabeth did not permit the voyage to be undertaken, however, and as nothing was printed to advocate or criticize the venture, it attracted little notice. There were several factors inherent in the plan which worked to prevent any publicity of it. The small group involved made any sort of public appeal unnecessary and possibly disadvantageous, for the Queen knew that Spain and Portugal would strenuously oppose such an expedition if it were announced. Furthermore, the geography involved in Grenville's plan was not controversial. There was no need to prove the existence of the Strait of Magellan or the great continent that lay somewhere to the south of it, for all of the major cartographers indicated these features of the earth's surface on their maps.

The northwest passage idea presented an opposite set of circumstances. The area was controversial as to its true geography, but it was unclaimed. And a large number of people became involved in it. The first Elizabethan actively to interest himself in the northwest passage was Sir Humphrey Gilbert, whose study of geography convinced him that the passage could be found, and in 1566 in association with Anthony Jenkinson he petitioned the Queen for the right to discover it.

At that time Gilbert had shown no interest in advertising his plan of discovery publicly, and it appears that his and Jenkinson's interests were more private than national, for they requested a monopoly on trade passing through the passage they hoped to discover.[34] There is no record of the Queen's reply, but if they were refused Gilbert and Jenkinson still had a more favorable climate of opinion in which to continue their plans than Grenville did. A part of this climate was due to the continuing belief among European scholars that a passage existed to the north of America, and it was frequently shown on maps from the mid-sixteenth century onward. England's leading geographer of the Elizabethan period, John Dee, believed in it. Futhermore, there was a feeling among Englishmen—and it had existed as early as John Rastell's time—that if England had a natural right to and talent for exploration in any part of the world, that part was the ocean to the north and west of the British Isles.

The most enthusiastic support for the northwestern exploration came from among a group of adventurers in the Queen's service in Ireland, among whom was Gilbert. It may be too much to say that 'the inevitable result of service in Ireland seems to have been a passionate desire on the part of the English to go somewhere else,'[35] but this group in the Queen's service in Ireland, including Gilbert, Martin Frobisher, Sir Henry Sidney, and others, subsequently became the enthusiasts for the colonization of America. Ireland was their first experience in empire-building, and it is not strange that one of them should have been the author of the first of a series of books on the northwest passage. Gilbert's *Discourse of a discoverie for a new passage to Cataia*, was composed in 1566 at the time Gilbert petitioned the Queen for a monopoly on the passage he hoped to discover.[36] His apparent failure to secure permission to sail did not discourage him at once, for he tried again the following year, but failure in this attempt brought no further plans for him, and his *Discourse* remained unpublished and little known. Five years later, however, Gilbert was to meet with Martin Frobisher, and in the mind of this practical sailor the theory of the northwest passage found ready acceptance.

Frobisher was a Yorkshireman of an aggressive family and a nephew of Sir John Yorke, a rising merchant of London. Young Martin was sent to his uncle when he was eleven or twelve years old, and he soon found his calling as a sailor. In 1554, when John Lok and a syndicate of merchants sent ships to West Africa, young Martin Frobisher was aboard. In the 1560s he was occasionally brought to the attention of the Queen's Council for acts of piracy, and it was probably these demonstrations of skill and daring that recommended him to her Majesty's service. It appears that he was sent to Ireland in 1572 to assist in subduing rebellion there, and two years later he came into association with Michael Lok who was deeply interested in the northwest passage idea, and who had discussed it with Gilbert. Undoubtedly influenced by the learning of Gilbert and Lok, Frobisher went to the Earl of Warwick with plans for finding a passage through North America to Asia, and Warwick carried the plan to the Queen's chief advisers.[37]

Despite the opposition of the Muscovy Company to the northwest passage exploration, Frobisher's plan received the blessing of the Privy Council, and Lok, a member of the Muscovy Company, came strongly to Frobisher's assistance. First he undertook to sell subscriptions to the voyage to other merchants, but he had little success. He then underwrote most of the expenses of the voyage himself. There is no evidence that he went to the book trade to arouse interest in the project, and when Gilbert's *Discourse* appeared in print a month or two before the voyage began, it was the poet George Gascoigne who claimed to be responsible for seeing it into print, although Gilbert's considerable revision of it after his return from Ireland in 1570 suggests that he had a wider audience in mind.

It was in April or May of 1576 that the *Discourse* came into print,[38] and in the Epistle to the Reader Gascoigne described how he saw it in Gilbert's study and took it home to read because he had become interested in the idea of a northwest passage due to his relationship with Martin Frobisher.[39] Upon reading it he decided that it should be printed, although he noted it was not written for publication. He recognized its theoretical nature in declaring, 'whereas other cosmographical workes doe but shew us things already knowen and treated of, this Discoverie doeth tend to a very profitable and commendable practice of a thing to bee discovered.'[40] Gascoigne presented a defensive tone, noting the arguments that he expected to be used against Gilbert's theories, and he admitted that arguments of the book 'doe not fully proove so much as may be expected.'[41] It appears that Gascoigne was not merely anticipating criticisms but replying to those who had already criticised the venture, presumably the Muscovy merchants. In his hands, Gilbert's book, which was originally intended as a scientific argument, became a promotion piece to attract adventurers to this first Frobisher-Lok enterprise. Gascoigne was not among the eighteen subscribers to the voyage, but he was vigorous in trying to promote it and to overcome opposition to it. In the tradition of Rastell and Eden, this poet exhorted his countrymen to greater support for expeditions of this kind, saying, 'we are by as great reason bounde to encourage and commend the industrie of the diligent, as to dispraise and punish the slouth or abuse of the negligent... We see the good huswife is no lesse curious to decke her bees hive, to rub and perfume it with sweet herbes, to cover and defend it from raine... then Shee is readie to wreck her malice on the drones...'[42]

Gilbert's *Discourse* in its published form retains many features of a private treatise. It opens with a covering letter, dated the last of June, 1566, to his brother, Sir John Gilbert. Here Sir Humphrey recognized incredulity within his own family, for he wrote: 'Knowing you to be one that may easily be induced to hearken, and yeelde to reason, I will briefly open unto you, some fewe of the grounds of mine opinion, to the end you may better understand, that my hope of this discoverie and passage, was not so rashe, or foolishe as you heretofore have deemed.'[43] In printing this letter, Gascoigne was admitting that doubt of the existence of the passage prevailed as well as opposition to a voyage to prove that it did exist. Thus defensiveness with respect to the existence of a northwest passage, a feature to be noted in subsequent northwest passage literature, was established in the earliest English espousal of belief in this northwest route to the Orient.

In his opening chapter Gilbert drew upon the ancient writers such as Plato, Crantor, Proclus and Philo to prove that America was an island, namely the remnant of Atlantis, which had been flooded and covered after an earthquake. He supported this view with evidence from medieval authors, Lucio Marineo and Marcilio Ficino,[44] and then brought to bear the authority of the leading contemporary authors and cartographers, concluding with Ortelius 'who doth coast out in his generall Mappe (set out Anno 1569) al ye countries and capes, on the Northwestside [sic] of America... making both Gronland & America Ilands disjoyned by a great sea, from any part of Asia.'[45] This was clearly a post-1570 revision. From the evidence of ancient and modern thought Gilbert concluded that between Greenland, America, and Asia was a sea route 'by the which any man of our country, that will give the attempt, may with small danger passe to Cataia, the Moluccae, India, and all other places in ye East in much shorter time, than either the Spaniard or the Portingale doth...'[46]

The remaining nine chapters of the *Discourse* contain arguments of varying quality to prove the existence of this route to the East. In

Chapter Two, Gilbert presented a series of arguments of a scientific nature to prove the existence of the passage. He showed that there was no evidence of either commerce or migration of peoples and animals between Asia and America, and no indication of exploration of either continent by inhabitants of the other. This would prove the separation of them by a substantial body of water. Then, using Jacques Cartier as his major source, he showed how ocean currents flowed westward from the Cape of Good Hope, and then, being unable to pass through the Strait of Magellan, they flowed northward along the North American coast. Since they did not appear to flow toward Scandinavia, it must follow that they found an outlet into the Pacific.

Gilbert used the reports of early travelers to Asia in Chapter Three to prove the separation of Asia and America. He stated that Marco Polo 'sailed, 1500 myles, upon the coastes of Mangia, and Anian, towards the Northeast: always finding the Seas open before him, not onley as farre as he went: but as far as he could discerne.'[47] João de Barros was cited as an authority, following the testimony of Chinese geographers, to prove that the Chinese coast extended northward without touching America.[48] Coronado, Gómara, Nuñez de Balboa, Fracastoro, Verazano, and Sebastian Cabot were marshalled among the believers in the insularity of America. The next three chapters are less impressive, since they attempt to prove the existence of the passage by repeating old stories of Indians who landed on the European coast as early as 57 B.C. Gilbert took these to be Asiatic peoples rather than American natives. Nevertheless, his arguments show a considerable knowledge of early source materials.

Returning to contemporary evidence again, and with another post-1570 addition, Gilbert reported that a Spaniard named Salvaterra had said in the presence of Sir Henry Sidney, 'in my hearing,' that the people in America believed in the passage, and that Andrew Urdenata had come from the South Sea to Germany through the passage. Salvaterra supported his own talk by offering to accompany Gilbert in the search for the passage.[49] Then turning to contemporary objections by proponents of the northeastern approach to Asia, Gilbert advanced counter arguments of unfavorable weather to the northeast, the greater distance to the Moluccas that way, the likely opposition of Russia, and the proximity of England to the northwestern route as reasons for an expedition to the northwest. Finally he noted the probable benefits to be gained for England by discovering this passage, revealing the motives which he considered most likely to move the Queen and her

Council to favorable action. The foremost of these were underselling the Portuguese in eastern wares, finding gold, planting colonies of needy and discontented people, selling English cloth, and increasing home manufactures by creating industries 'to make trifles and such like, which the Indians and those people doe much esteem.'[50]

Gilbert's learning and Gascoigne's initiative mark the beginning of what was to become an extensive literature on the northwest passage. The author's argument was a serious and logical treatment of the problem of enlarging England's overseas trade by reaching the East Indies, yet in his Epistle to the Reader Gascoigne gave the publication an air of defensiveness, as if he did not expect Gilbert's ideas to be accepted. He stated that 'of thinges uncertaine, the greatest Clerke that ever was could write but probably.'[51] It is paradoxical that a treatise so weighted with authority should have been so uncertain. It suggests that a large number of Englishmen interested in the idea of a northwest passage did not really believe in its existence, and it bears out the fact that any belief in the passage in high places was discouraged by the Muscovy Company. Despite the impending voyage of Frobisher, and the apparent controversy over the passage, the *Discourse* did not arouse anyone to publish a commentary on it, and its publication should not be viewed as a publisher's venture into geographical literature, for Gascoigne wrote that he 'thought it very meete... to give it out in publike. Wherupon I have (as you see) caused my friends great travaile, and mine owne greater presumption to be registered in print.'[52]

This necessity for a vested interest to provide the public with information, while the book trade ignored events at the beginning of the northwest passage enterprise, is further evidenced by the manner in which printers ignored Frobisher's return, which was a spectacular event. He arrived in England in October, 1576, believing that he had found the entrance to the desired passage. He brought with him an Eskimo taken from his homeland and also some rock which was believed to contain gold. The greatest excitement concerning the voyage centered around this ore, in which one assayer claimed to find particles of gold. Now it became clear which of the motives mentioned by Gilbert had the greatest impact in England. Whereas the Lok-Frobisher enterprise for exploring a trade route had interested only eighteen subscribers who invested 875 pounds, of which Michael Lok paid 738 pounds in addition to another 100 pounds, to get the expedition under way, Frobisher's second voyage attracted many willing hands. Early in 1577 the Company of Cathay was formed to undertake the second voyage, and 4,400 pounds was quickly subscribed, including a 1,000 pound subscription from the Queen who loaned a ship for the voyage as well. The needs of England's merchants and woolgrowers were now clearly secondary to the hopes of the investors for an arctic Peru. The entire expedition was fitted out with shiploads of ore in mind, rather than a voyage to Cathay. It was understood that if the ore did not appear promising, Frobisher was to go on to Cathay, but without the Queen's ship—indicating her primary interest.[53]

This second expedition sailed on May 26, 1577, and its members set about digging ore on Baffin Island between Greenland and Labrador. Those in the expedition who wanted to continue westward in search of the passage were restrained by Frobisher who held to his orders to load the ships with ore. The three ships returned in September, laden with 200 tons of worthless rocks, and Henry Middleton appears to have been induced to publish an account of the voyage written by one of the participants, Dionyse Settle, whose *True reporte of the laste voyage into the west and northwest regions* is the first book to contain English eyewitness impressions of America.

Settle's book was a commendable effort at reporting the land and people of the part of America he had visited, and he gave a brief indication of the reasons he felt that Englishmen ought to become interested in northern North America. His Epistle to the Christian Reader revealed some religious enthusiasm for 'Gods good will and pleasure, that they [natives] should be instructed in his divine service and religion,'[54] and he recommended that Englishmen interest themselves in the northwest passage rather than other areas already dominated by Spain, Portugal or France, since it was an area 'more agreeing to our temperature.'[55] For the most part, however, his book was a straightforward description of the voyage and things seen in America. His enthusiasm fell far short of that of Abraham Fleming who introduced the book with a four-verse 'rythme decasyllabicall, upon this last luckie voyage of worthie Capteine Forbisher,' in this tone:

> *A right Heroicall heart of Britanne blood,*
> *Ulysses match in skill and Martiall might:*
> *For Princes fame, and countries speciall good,*
> *Through brakish waters seas (where Neptune reignes by right)*
> *Hath safely saild, in perils great despight:*
> *The Golden fleece (like Jason) hath he got,*
> *And rich returned, saunce losse or lucklesse lot.*[56]

Settle dedicated his book to the Earl of Cumberland and identified himself on the title page as Cumberland's servant. That he had the interest of Cumberland at heart when he sailed is confirmed by the words 'in this last voyage of [Frobisher]... under whome (as your Honours unworthie servant) I was one in the said voyage.'[57] It is possible that Cumberland might have intervened with Lok and Frobisher in order to have Settle included among the crew members, for the grateful author wrote, 'I am not oblivious, neither careless, when, and how, your Honour (above my noble expectation) nobly satisfied the request of me your humble servant.'[58] Apart from this voyage and book, Settle is unknown to history, but his brief attachment to Cumberland linked him to other writers on geography who were to find patronage in the household of Cumberland's wife who was Margaret, third daughter of Francis Russell, Earl of Bedford.

Although Cumberland had subscribed twenty-five pounds to the second Frobisher voyage, his man Settle gave out no strong encouragement for belief in the future of gold-mining in the northern islands of the New World, nor did he find the area very attractive in any respect. Of the weather he said, 'we tasted cold stormes, insomuch that it seemed, we had chaunged Summer with winter, if the length of dayes had not removed us from that opinion.'[59] The commodities of the natives he held in low esteem. 'Their riches are neyther Gold, Silver or precious Draperie... [but] trifles, more to be wondered at for their strangeness, than for any other commoditie needful to our use.'[60] He despaired of any temperature that could dissolve the huge icebergs of the northern waters, and he found the natives unattractive, eaters of decayed flesh and possibly cannibalistic. He saw deer, hares, wolves, bears and sea fowl in abundance, but of vegetation he wrote 'there is nothing fitte, or profitable for ye use of man, which that Countrie with roote yeeldeth, or bringeth forth.'[61] As for the main purposes of the voyage, Settle admitted that gold was the chief objective, and while he warned that 'all is not golde that glistereth,'[62] he added cautiously, 'There is much to be said of the commodities of these Countries, which are couched within the bowels of the earth, and which I let passe till more perfect triall be made thereof.'[63] He was equally cautious about the secondary purpose of the voyage, the discovery of the northwest passage. In referring to Frobisher Bay he wrote, 'This said streight, is supposed to have passage into the Sea of Sur, [South Sea] which I leave unknowne as yet...'[64]

Such was the first English eyewitness account of America. While it is predominantly negative in its impression, there is nothing to suggest that it was inspired by opponents of the Cathay Company. It is, in fact, an accurate account of the region of Frobisher Bay. That it went through two editions proves the existence of an active interest in the northwest passage, although it seems probable that the hope for gold was much more a stimulant to interest than the idea of finding a water route to Asia. The voyage and the book aroused interest on the Continent also, as a French edition appeared in 1578, Latin and German editions were published in Nuremberg in 1580, and an Italian edition was published in Naples in 1582.

## NOTES TO CHAPTER V

1 James A. Williamson, *Hawkins of Plymouth* (London: Adam and Charles Black, 1949), p. 47.

2 Earnest V. Vaughn, 'English trading expeditions into Asia under the authority of the Muscovy Company (1557–1581),' *Studies in the history of English commerce in the Tudor period* (New York: D. Appleton and Co., 1912), pp. 39–41.

3 Sir William Foster, *England's quest of eastern trade* (London: A. & C. Black, Ltd., 1933), pp. 26–30, 35–41.

4 John Webb, 'The Van Deutecum map of Russia and Tartary,' *Merchants and scholars*, John Parker ed., (Minneapolis: University of Minnesota Press, 1965).

5 Williamson, *Hawkins of Plymouth*, p. 45.

6 Williamson, *Sir John Hawkins*, p. 55.

7 Williamson, *Hawkins of Plymouth*, p. 66.

8 Jean Ribaut, *The whole and true discoverye of Terra Florida* (London: R. Hall for Thomas Hacket, 1563). It seems certain that this English edition was the first, and perhaps the only one, despite the fact that Paul Gaffarel in his *Histoire de la Florida française* (Paris, 1875) gave a French title to Ribaut's work: *Histoire de l'expedition française en Florida*. No other bibliographer has described a French edition. See H. P. Biggar, 'Jean Ribaut's discoverye of Terra Florida,' *The English historical review*, XXXII (April, 1917), 253–54.

9 Ribaut, first page of dedication.

10 *Ibid.*, fol. Biiii verso.

11 *Ibid.*, fol. Biii verso.

12 Robert Seall, *A commendation of the adventerus viage of the wurthy captain M. Thomas Stutely... towards the land called Terra Florida* (London: John Alde [1563]).

13 *Ibid.*

14 Williamson, *Hawkins of Plymouth*, p. 65.

15 Richard Hakluyt, *Divers voyages touching the discoverie of America* (London: For Thomas Woodcocke by Thomas Dawson, 1582), fols. 3 verso – 4 recto.

16 The first French edition was published as *Discours de l'histoire de la Floride* (Dieppe, 1566). A second edition, enlarged, was also probably published at Dieppe, and a third edition, with variations, at Lyons, both in 1566. The English edition is based on the Lyons printing. See John Gilmary Shea, 'Ancient Florida,' *Narrative and critical history of America*, ed. Justin Winsor (8 vols.; Boston: Houghton, Mifflin and Co., 1889), II, 296.

[17] Nicolas Le Challeux, *A true and perfect description of the last voyage... attempted by Captain John Rybaut* (London: Henry Denham for Thomas Hacket, [1566]), fol. Aiiii verso.

[18] Hacket's translation was titled *The new found worlde, or Antarctike* (London: Henry Bynneman for Thomas Hacket, 1568). The original French edition was published in Paris, 1557; another printing with a new title page appeared the following year.

[19] Eric St. John Brooks, *Sir Christopher Hatton* (London: Jonathan Cape, Ltd., 1947), pp. 18–19.

[20] Thevet, fol. *iii recto.

[21] Williamson, *Hawkins of Plymouth*, pp. 93–99.

[22] *Ibid.*, pp. 132–46.

[23] Sir John Hawkins, *A true declaration of the troublesome voyadge... to the parties of Guynea and the West Indies* (London: Thomas Purfoote for Lucas Harrison, 1569), fol. b7 verso.

[24] C. H. Conley, *The first English translations of the classics* (New Haven: Yale University Press, 1927), *passim*.

[25] Plinius Secundus, *A summarie of the antiquities, and wonders of the worlde*, trans. I. A. (London: Henry Denham for Thomas Hacket, [1566]). This is a translation of *Sommaire des singularitez de Pline*, trans. Pierre de Changy (Paris: R. Breton, 1559). Two other French editions were published in Lyons in 1562 and 1566.

[26] Sir John Mandeville, *The voiage and travayle...* (London: Thomas East, 1568).

[27] Vilhjalmur Stefansson, (ed.). *The three voyages of Martin Frobisher* (2 vols.; London: The Argonaut Press, 1938), I, ci, cii.

[28] Malcolm Letts, *Sir John Mandeville, the man and his book* (London: Batchworth Press, 1949), p. 40.

[29] William Bourne, *A regiment for the sea* (London: Thomas Hacket [1574]), fol. aiii verso.

[30] *Ibid.*, aiiii recto.

[31] Dionysius *Periegetes, The surveye of the world*, trans. Thomas Twine (London: Henry Bynneman, 1572). fol. *iiii verso. The translator was a physician, fellow of Corpus Christi College, Oxford, and a student of medicine at Cambridge. He was a friend of John Dee, England's foremost geographer of the time. This is one of several translations he made, in varous areas of interest. His biographer says of him, 'He inclines to dulness both in prose and verse.' *DNB*, LVII, 404.

[32] Sebastian Münster, *A brief collection and compendious extract of straunge and memorable thinges gathered out of the Cosmographye of Sebastian Munster* (London: Thomas Marshe, 1572). The 1574 edition was also published by Marshe.

[33] Quoted in A. L. Rowse, *Sir Richard Grenville* (London: Jonathan Cape, 1937), p. 90.

[34] Carlos Slafter, *Sir Humphrey Gylberte and his enterprise of colonization in America* (Boston: The Prince Society, 1903), pp. 1–13.

[35] William McFee, *Sir Martin Frobisher* (London: John Lane, the Bodley Head, Ltd., 1928), p. 27.

[36] A. L. Rowse, *The expansion of Elizabethan England* (London: Macmillan, 1955), pp. 137, 191.

[37] McFee, pp. 5–28.

[38] David B. Quinn, *The voyages and colonising enterprises of Sir Humphrey Gilbert* (2 vols.; London: The Hakluyt Society, 1940), I, 30.

[39] While Gascoigne refers to Frobisher as his 'kinsman,' the relationship is somewhat remote. Frobisher's great grandfather had married a sister of Sir William Scargill. Sir William was Gascoigne's great-grandfather, the grandfather of his mother, Margaten Scargill.

[40] Sir Humphrey Gilbert, *A discourse of a discoverie for a new passage to Cataia* (London: Henry Middleton for Richard Jhones, 1576), fol. ¶¶ iiii recto-verso.

[41] *Ibid.*, fol. ¶¶ iii verso.

[42] *Ibid.*, fol. ¶ ii recto-verso.

[43] *Ibid.*, fols. ¶¶¶ iii recto-¶¶¶¶ i verso.

[44] Lucio Marineo was the author of two histories of Spain, *De Hispaniae laudibus* (Burgos, ca. 1497) and *De primis Aragonie regibus* (Saragossa, 1509); Marsilio Ficino was a fifteenth-century Florentine who wrote numerous works on medicine, astronomy and religion.

[45] Gilbert, fol. Biii verso. Abraham Ortelius of Antwerp was the foremost map publisher of this period. The map referred to by Gilbert is the world map in Ortelius' *Theatrum orbis terrarum*, actually published in 1570, which clearly shows a northwest passage. It may have been issued separately prior to the publication of the collection in 1570.

[46] Gilbert, fols. Biii verso Biiii recto.

[47] *Ibid.*, fol. Dii recto.

[48] João de Barros, *Asia* (3 vols; Lisbon: G. Galharde, 1552-53; J. de Barreira, 1563).

[49] Gilbert, fol. Fiii verso.

[50] *Ibid.*, fol. Hii recto.

[51] *Ibid.*, fols. iii verso – iiii recto.

[52] *Ibid.*, fol. ii verso.

[53] Stefansson, I, ci, cxii-cxiii.

[54] Dionyse Settle, *A true reporte of the laste voyage into the west and northwest regions* (London: Henrie Middleton, 1577), fol. Aiii verso. Louis B. Wright, *Religion and empire* (Chapel Hill: University of North Carolina Press, 1943), p. 5, says 'Religion was a motive of greater consequence in early British expansion than we have hitherto realized.' I shall attempt in the later chapters to balance the religious motive as a popular appeal against others as indicated in the popular colonization and travel literature of the later Tudor and early Stuart periods.

[55] Settle, fol. Aiiii recto.

[56] *Ibid.*, fol. Ai verso.

[57] *Ibid.*, fol. Aii recto.

[58] *Ibid.*

[59] *Ibid.*, fol. Bv recto.

[60] *Ibid.*, fols. Ci verso-Cii recto.

[61] *Ibid.*, fol. Di verso.

[62] *Ibid.*, fol. Bviii recto.

[63] *Ibid.*, fol. Diii recto.

[64] *Ibid.*, fol. Biiii verso.

## Chapter VI

## THE FLOURISHING AGE

The first two Frobisher voyages gave England its earliest imperialistic urge, for together they held promise of both gold and Eastern trade, the sources of the wealth and power that had come to Spain and Portugal. The Muscovy expeditions had given no promise of empire, and the Hawkins penetrations in the West Indies had been feelers for trade in a hostile region. The northwest was open to England, and for all of its natural hostility it looked inviting in 1577. So much so that on May 27, 1578, before any final opinions on the northern ore had been given, Frobisher left with another fleet for America. This time his plans called for a group of thirty Cornish miners, thirty soldiers, and forty seamen to be left in America with three ships, while the remaining twelve ships were to return laden with ore.[1]

As this first plan for an English settlement in the New World was taking form, several books appeared showing the concern of a small group of imperialists who saw in these voyages an opportunity for England to take its place with Spain and Portugal as an overseas power. From this group, and from this period, came the beginnings of a stream of imperialist literature that was to be relatively constant throughout the remainder of the Elizabethan period.

The interest in China which was reflected in naming Frobisher's group the 'Cathay Company' is further shown in the publication of a newsletter translated from the Spanish by Thomas Nicholas about 1577. This *Strange and marveilous newes lately come from the great kingdome of Chyna* reported Spanish military, missionary, and commercial activity in islands along the coast of China. The Spaniards were represented to have discovered more than forty leagues of the China coast, and in the course of doing so, to have come into conflict 'with those Indians,'[2] while some Spaniards were taken as prisoners to the mainland. The Spaniards provided information on a place called Ander which is described as to fortifications, government, religion and products. The islands off the coast from which they approached the mainland are not named and may have been the Philippines, but accounts of attacks upon the coast by 'Turks' and continued reference to 'Indians' where

Chinese apparently were meant added confusion to this limited view of the Far East. However, references to such products as silk, purple, wheat, rice, horses, fruits, cloth, pepper, cloves, wool, and great quantities of gold carried the common impression that China was a goal worthy of great effort on the part of European merchants.

The confused picture of China which Nicholas brought into English may not have been his own fault, for he had translated from a letter written by a merchant in Mexico to a friend in Andalusia. This Spanish source was based on a letter which was apparently being readied for the Spanish King before the sailing of the next fleet. Noting that it 'dooth conteyne more then .xx. sheetes of Paper,' the Spanish merchant condensed its contents and may have garbled them in the process.[3]

In 1577 also appeared the first of six translations by John Frampton, an English merchant who had lived in Spain and had fallen into the hands of the Spanish Inquisition. His unhappy fate not only embittered him against Spain, but it also gave him the opportunity to become familiar with Spanish exploration literature which he determined to use against his captors upon his liberation in 1562.[4] His first work is generally known as *Joyfull newes out of the new founde worlde*, although it was published with a less attractive title.[5] This translation brought into the English language the American herbal written by Dr. Nicolás Monardes, destined to be the most frequently issued book of overseas interest in the Elizabethan period. This popularity must be ascribed to the value the book had for physicians rather than any imperial urge it inspired, for while Monardes' descriptions of tobacco, sassafras, and other medicinal plants were also in a manner a description of the New World, Frampton did not advance any proposals for invading the Spanish preserve in America. It is, in fact, the only one of Frampton's translations in which the political motive is not evident, his only expressed motive being the desire 'to passe the tyme to some benefite of my countrie and to avoyde idelnesse.'[6]

The *Joyfull newes*, however, was destined to be of real interest to expansionists of the next decade, for Hakluyt, Raleigh, and Hariot were keenly interested in medicinal plants, and Frampton's translation must have been their major source of information. Two issues in 1577, another in 1580, and still another in 1596 were not in keeping with the tendency of most English travel books of this period to appear in only one edition, even when they were vigorously imperialistic. Only its utilitarian value to medical practitioners can account for this popularity.

The enthusiasm of England's expansionists for the discovery of a northwest passage did not escape Richard Eden, who had been inspired by the voyages to the northeast to publish his *Decades of the newe worlde* in 1555. During the subsequent twenty-two years, this apostle of empire continued to assemble more accounts of voyages, and in 1577 a new edition of his *Decades* was published as *A history of travayle in the West and East Indies*. He died just prior to its publication, however, and the components of the new edition were assembled, edited, and augmented by Richard Willes, a poet who had studied at Winchester, Oxford, Mainz and Perugia. It was he who dedicated the book to Lady Brigit, Countess of Bedford, who had been Willes's patroness shortly before he engaged in this work.[7]

Willes's long Epistle Dedicatory contained the first plea for an increased study of geography to be published in England and presented a strong case for the utility of travel literature. Where Eden had extolled the virtues of travel, Willes saw great value in the study of it. Like Eden, he was very much aware of the opportunities of the age in which he lived. He believed that succeeding periods of history had different interests and therefore increased or decreased emphasis on various aspects of learning. 'Learnyng may bee ryght well compared unto the floures & fruites of the earth... In May, floures: in June, Cheries: at Harvest, corne: in September, Grapes: so fareth it in the study of good letters.'[8] He cited the past emphasis on grammar, the earlier interest in poetry, the rise and fall of the study of Greek, the growing interest in logic and astrology which had only 'weeried the heades of young schollers.' He then noted the long dormancy of geography as a subject for popular interest, but added that 'of late who taketh not uppon him to discourse of the whole worlde, and eche province thereof particulerly, even by hearesay, although in the first principles of that arte, he bee altogeather ignorant and unskylfull?'[9]

Willes reviewed for his readers the history of Portuguese exploration of Africa and India and showed how all peoples were dependent upon a knowledge of geography. 'I dare be bold to say, that generally all Christians, Jewes, Turkes, Moores, Infidels, & Barbares be this day in love with Geographie... Set Geographie asyde, you shal neyther be able to get intelligences of... any citie, nor the limites and boundes of any countrey... nor be able wel to travayle out of your owne doores.'[10] He called attention to the riches gained for Portugal and Spain through travel abroad; he noted the riches brought to England by the trade with Barbary, Guinea, and Muscovy; and he predicted that 'The Northwesterne voyage, be it never so full of difficulties, will become as plausible as any other journey, if our passengers may returne with plentie of silver, silkes, and perle.'[11]

But the passengers received no more praise than the authors, for Willes praised Barros for his histories of Portuguese explorations, Peter Martyr for his writings on the New World, and Richard Eden as well for bringing into English the writings of Martyr and Oviedo in his earlier edition. Now he praised Eden further for providing a translation of Varthema's account of the East Indies and the narratives of English merchants who had traveled to Muscovy and Persia. In taking over this work from Eden, Willes was clearly placing himself in the tradition of these men he had praised, yet he made no show of ardent nationalism equal to that of Eden. He claimed no other motive for his work than 'Christian charitie... unto the party departed,'[12] yet it is apparent from his references to the wealth acquired by other nations from overseas ventures that he had the economy of his country in mind in recommending to his contemporaries closer attention to travels and travel literature. It was also England he was addressing when he lamented, 'I knowe this day no place, no preferment, no publike chayre, no ordinarie lecture, no commune stipende, no special rewarde due unto the studentes in Geography: no not at this time, when this faculty was never more set by: no not in this realme, where yt never more flourished.'[13] These words not only show a concern for England's acquiring the necessary knowledge of geography but demonstrate again that it was neither the crown nor the merchants who felt strongly enough about this failure to publish a work of geography or to establish geography as an important study in the universities. The poet Willes was following in the tradition of Rastell and Eden, a scholar-nationalist with an awareness that travel literature was necessary to greatness in the sixteenth century.

Willes was also keenly aware of what was pertinent, and in editing this second edition he omitted the several sections dealing with astronomy and metals. He added three important chapters on the northwest passage and the Far East, and an abridgement of the fifth, sixth, seventh, and eighth *Decades* of Peter Martyr. Also, to the writings of Martyr and Oviedo which had appeared in the 1555 edition, Eden and Willes added 'certaine speciall reports of new Spaine or Mexico, of Peru, of Rio de la Plata, & the countrey lying therunto, of the lands of Laborador & Baccalaos, with the discoveryng of Florida.'[14] Another improvement of the second edition over the first was the inclusion of significant material on Persia and the East Indies.

These additions show an increased interest on the part of Willes and Eden in the opportunities for trade in both Asia and America and are quite devoid of the interest in mining gold that was a common appeal made for exploration in Elizabethan England. While Peru was described as the richest land known, its gold was not held out as a possible English acquisition. New Spain, the Plate River region, and Baccalaos were described mainly in terms of peoples and products, and the discovery of Florida was presented primarily from the narratives of Ponce de Leon and De Soto.

To Willes the existence of a northwest passage was a distinct probability[15], for though he said, 'the way is dangerous, the passage doubtful, the voyage not throughly [sic] knowen, and therefore gaynesayde by many,'[16] he went about demolishing the arguments of the doubters in much the same manner used by Gilbert, and in doing so he showed a real familiarity with maps and geographies published on the Continent. He concluded on this subject, 'M. Furbishers prosperous voyage and happie returne wyl absolutely decide these controversies, ... and what commodities the paynfull travayler can reape therby, what gaine the venterous merchant may looke for, what wealth, what honor, what fame wyll our Englyshe nation therof ensue.'[17] Significantly, he followed his treatise on the passage with descriptions of China, Japan, and other eastern islands.

His description of China was dedicated to Elizabeth Morison in gratitude for 'the singular care you ever have had of my well dooyng, and speciall favour I have founde among your Honorable frendes for your sake...'[18] It was a translation from the Italian of Galeotto Pereira,[19] and was far more reliable than '*The strange and marveilous newes* of Thomas Nicholas. Pereira's work, a very general report on China, included everything from the price of various kinds of meat to the treatment of criminals, but it dwelt particularly on political organization and administration of the thirteen 'shires' of China and of the central government.

The first account of Japan in the English language which follows the description of China, was translated by Willes from the Latin of Giovanni Pietro Maffei, 'my olde acquainted friend.'[20] Maffei's descriptions of eastern countries were based on a number of sources, but the portion Willes chose as being most important was a letter from the missionary Aloysius Froes who had been in the Far East from 1563 to

1597.[21] It contained details of the government and customs of the Japanese, who were presented as an honorable, law-abiding people with great curiosity.

The arrangement of this material by Willes in such a way that the descriptions of the Far East followed the northwest passage material indicates that he thought of the northwest passage and eastern Asia as being closely related. Richard Eden, on the other hand, was still looking eastward to Asia. In the *History of travayle* he gave brief accounts of the voyages to Persia in 1561, 1567, and 1568, showing the Persian trade of the Muscovy Company as well as he dared, 'Forasmuch as many thinges myght bee written touchyng this voyage, and the merchauntes trafique in these regions, whiche for many great considerations ought not to be published or put in prynt... it shall suffice to the reader to understande the description of the regions, with the maners and customes of the people.'[22] The restrictiveness of the Muscovy merchants was further confirmed, 'for that I coulde not orderly have any information of them that came from Persia.'[23] Nevertheless, Eden pieced together from several sources a picture of the commercial opportunities in Persia. He gave a brief description of the route from St. Nicholas in the far north to the Caspian Sea, chiefly on the rivers, and then overland to Persia from the Caspian. This was followed by extracts from an account of Jenkinson's voyage of 1561, information obtained from Geoffrey Ducket, who went to Persia in 1568, and material relating to the travels of Arthur Edwards who was in Persia in 1565.[24] Eden supplemented this with information based on the travels of Marco Polo, the description of Asia by Hethum, and a discourse on Persia's trade with other countries. Altogether, he produced a good picture of the Persian people, their customs, religion, government and economy.

Arber states that the final literary work of Eden's productive life was his translation of the *Itinerario* of Lodovico de Varthema,[25] a very popular description of the countries from Egypt to the East Indian archipelago by an adventurer who traveled between 1503 and 1508 merely to see distant lands. It brought into English reports of many places hitherto unknown to most Englishmen. Varthema's narrative tells of his visits to the leading cities of the East, including Aden, Ormuz, Cambay, Goa, Calicut, Tenasserim, and Malacca. While much of it is devoted to personal adventures, it contains interesting accounts of native customs, cities, buildings, products, business methods, and other aspects of eastern life which had already aroused great interest

on the Continent.[26] Through it, English readers gained their first acquaintance with the vast area dominated by the Portuguese merchants
who were one day to give way to English and Dutch traders.

Considered as a whole, the *History of travayle* is one of the outstanding
compilations of travel literature to be published in England. Despite
the inclusion of portions of Peter Martyr's *Decades*, it is clear that the
main emphasis of Willes was on Asia, with the northwest passage as
the probable means of reaching the markets of the Far East, while Eden
kept alive the hope of a satisfactory overland route to Persia. Both
Willes and Eden were out of step with the court group in not emphasizing the dream of large quantities of gold coming into England without the export of English goods. Nor did either of them make any
concession to the religious element, for they gave no indication of
interest in missionary enterprises. The *History of travayle* was motivated
primarily by an interest in commerce.

Meanwhile, the winter of 1577–78 found England awaiting the ver-
dict of the goldsmiths and assayers who were examining the ore brought
from America with Frobisher's second voyage. Before a conclusive
opinion could be given, a new voyage was planned, despite criticism
of it. New subscribers came forward willingly; the Crown assumed
direct supervision as fifteen ships were assembled; and plans were made
for the establishment of the first English fort in America which was to
be maintained by one hundred men. This optimistic plan brought
forth a subscription of 1,350 pounds from the Queen in an enterprise
that required 2,452 pounds.[27] The planners of the third Frobisher expedition had a vociferous spokesman in Thomas Churchyard, a writer
of innumerable miscellaneous pamphlets. His *A prayse and reporte of
Maister Martyne Forboishers voyage to Meta Incognita* is a belligerent defense
of the idea of overseas ventures in general and the present one in particular. While Churchyard may be suspected of using this piece as a lever
to secure favor at court where he had been rebuffed, it contains sentiments frequently heard in later times.[28] In his dedication to Dr. Thomas Wilson, a member of the Privy Council, he confirmed the popularity of Frobisher's voyage as a topic for discussion when he wrote, 'I
have chosen familiar thinges too write upon... presenting to the people
that whiche they are beste acquainted withal...'[29] He confirmed also
that much of the discussion was negative in tone, for 'many maie mis-
like this travail, and shew many perswasions for the maintenance of
their dislikyng...,' but he added, 'the mislikers should either hold their
peace, or put in practice a matter of more importance, or at the least

beholde the successe of the nexte journey with more silence and lesse murmuryng.'[30]

Churchyard's plea was not for one voyage. It was for a movement—a general and official awareness of the need for a colonial policy. He wrote 'for the encouragement of any forward minde (servyng for the maintenance of a commonwealth) to shewe a little at large the goodnes that riseth by traveiling abroad, and commoditie that cometh by seekyng out such soiles and Countries, as maie make our countrimen here happie at home.'[31] As he awaited the outcome of the third Frobisher voyage, Churchyard, like the rest of England, was waiting for gold, but he was able to see the possibility of other gains to be made in North America. 'Albeit great wealth and commoditie maie rise to us... yet the purpose of manifestyng Gods mightie woorde... among those... [natives] doeth argue not onely a blessed successe, but perswadeth a prosperous and beneficiall retourne.'[32] The appeal to England to save the souls of Eskimos was coupled with the suggestion made here in a specific manner for the first time that the New World might take from England some of her more troublesome people. Churchyard saw England a kingdom in danger from shortage of food and abundance of thieves who stood as a constant menace to property. 'I feare in a whyle,' he warned, 'we shall have neither meate for our mouthes nor houses for our heades. I wonder why there is more men hanged in Englande in the space of one yere, then in five regions our neighbors in the space of ten yeres put to execution.'[33] This concern for the abundance of thieves will recur in colonization literature; it reflects here the beginning of the realization that England's ills might not be solved simply by exporting more cloth and reflects also the beginning of public discussion of the idea of exporting people for the benefit of the homeland. This suggestion is the chief value of Churchyard's book, for his account of the second Frobisher voyage is undistinguished, rambling and sketchy. The book as a whole is entirely in the literary-nationalist tradition—but is more nationalist than literary. It is also less precise and complete in its view of the establishment of a colony abroad than the instructions penned by Richard Hakluyt the Elder as a part of the preparation for the voyage in 1578, but these instructions were not published until four years later.

Frobisher's third voyage carried with it England's hopes for the discovery of a great gold mine in the Arctic regions of North America, and it could hardly have been more disappointing. A part of the prefabricated fort, which was to house the thirty soldiers who were to

remain in America, was lost with the *Dennis;* the ice in Frobisher
Bay was unusually troublesome; provisions were not ample for leaving
the shore party; fog was heavy and tides severe. When the ships returned to England it was discovered that faith in the value of the ore had
suddenly declined during the summer and that the Company of Cathay
was bankrupt and torn with dissention. Frobisher was charged with
abuses against the Company, and Michael Lok was thrown into prison
for debt, despite the destitution of his wife and fifteen children.[34]

The ships of this defeated fleet straggled home to various ports about
October 1, 1578, and public interest in the voyage was met by an
account of it written by Thomas Ellis, a member of the expedition.
His *True report of the third and last voyage into Meta Incognita* told of the
difficulties encountered in battling the mountains of ice in the northern
waters, the difficulties in navigation and finding suitable places to land,
and the inability to maintain continued relations with the Eskimos.
The only point at which Ellis ventured judgment was his unreserved
praise for those who planned to remain in America 'among a barbarous and uncivill people, Infidels and miscreantes.'[35] For all of his
unhappiness with America, Ellis was not one to blame Frobisher for
the expedition's failures. His book opened with another of Abraham
Fleming's poems, another 'rythme decasyllabicall' which sang with
hope:

> *Long last thy lucke, thy fortune never faile,*
> *Not as Ulysses aged and unknowne,*
> *But Gallant like arrive among thine owne.*[36]

When the grim story of the voyage had been told, the narrative was
followed by three poems in praise of Frobisher by Ellis, John Stanley
and John Kirkham, all of whom probably were rude sailors, and poets
only upon this occasion.

In protesting humbly his inability to write adequately of his voyage
to America, Thomas Ellis had predicted that others would report on
it more ably when they arrived back in England. In this anticipation
he was correct, for George Best, one of Frobisher's officers, shortly
thereafter published an account of all three voyages, and it is far superior to anything else published at that time in connection with the
northwestern undertaking. Best's *True discourse of the late voyages of discoverie* was dedicated to Sir Christopher Hatton, a favorite at court,
and was published by Hatton's 'servant', Henry Bynneman. Hatton

had been an investor in the voyage, and the naming of an island 'Hatton's Headland' and a promontory on it Cape Best testifies to some close relationship between the two men.[37] It seems likely, therefore, that Best's book was an effort by some of those connected with the Frobisher expeditions to defend Frobisher and to lecture England on some of the fundamentals of exploration.

In these respects it answered a demand for literature on the northwest passage, for it is apparent that the defenders of Frobisher had adversaries in some number. Best wrote of their 'many trifling Pamphlets... secretly thrust out,'[38] although no such pamphlets have survived. In Best's view, defense of the enterprise was called for when 'by sundrie mens fantasies, sundry untruths are spred abroad, to the gret slaunder of this so honest and honorable an action.'[39] A defeat such as Frobisher had suffered called not for carping and blind criticism but stood as a lesson of great value for the future. Best listed the achievements of these voyages: 'many unknowen lands and Ilands... made knowen unto us: Christ's name spred: the Gospell preached, Infidels like to be converted to Christianitie...: Shipping and Seafaring men have bin employed: navigation and the Navie (which is the chief strength of our Realm) maintayned: and Gentlemen in the Sea service, for the better service of the Country, wel experienced.'[40]

The failure of the Company of Cathay did not discourage Best from hoping for better fortune in the future. He called attention to the great vigor of the age in which he lived: 'behold the greate industrie of our present age, and the invincible mindes of our Englishe nation, who have never lefte anye worthy thing unattempted, nor anye part almoste of the whole world unsearched,... So that, if now the passage to Cataya ... be made open unto us... we may truely infer, that the Englishman in these our dayes, in his notable discoveries, to the Spaniard and Portingale is nothing inferior: and for his hard adventures, and valiant resolutions, greatly superior.'[41] In answer to the multitude that criticized Frobisher and his venture, he gave the highest praise to the men who served at sea with him and condemned England, rather, for being so late upon the scene in the 'flourishing age,' attributing this tardiness to the 'lacke of liberalitie in the Nobility' and the 'want of skill in the Cosmographie, and the Art of Navigation.'[42] He noted with satisfaction that these wants were now repaired, as the Queen and nobility had come to give moral and financial encouragement to exploration. The publisher, Bynneman, added his recognition of the need for the publication of accounts of voyages as a further encouragement. This is the earliest recognition by a member of the publishing trade of such an obligation, and it may well have been born of Bynneman's association with Hatton; but, whether out of interest or patronage, Bynneman continued to publish books of a similar type, allying himself with the literary-nationalist group which was eager to put geographical literature before the public.

Best introduced his accounts of the three voyages with an essay on the new age that had come about by the application of newly discovered scientific knowledge. Man is no longer content with the goods and ideas of his ancestors, he wrote, and, with respect to ideas and their propagation, he mentioned the printing press specifically. [43] The sailor here was of one mind with the printer and the patron. It was not enough for Best that Englishmen know of the new scientific developments. These must be applied to England's interests. His essay drifted into navigation and then into a general geographic treatise of good quality. It showed real familiarity with Europe's major geographers, and it leaned toward a concern for the northern regions, for 'this parte of the world hath beene most or onely made by English industrie.' [44] He also described the trade to Guinea and Persia developed by England and showed pride in this accomplishment as well as an interest in continuing the expansion of England's markets. The seaman's narrative was thus prefaced by ardent propaganda for empire.

The account of the first voyage contained an interesting revelation of the lack of enthusiasm which the merchant community had shown toward Frobisher before the rumors of gold in North America became current. Best reported that Frobisher had long known of the passage and that for fifteen years he dealt with various merchants to get support for the voyage, but to no avail because merchants 'never regarde Vertue, without sure, certayne and present gaynes.' [45] The three voyages are described in terms of the difficulties encountered, the islands and waterways explored, the relations with the Eskimos, and above all, the search for gold. Best made no attempt to glorify the part of America he saw but noted the cold, the disease, the ice, and the hostility of the people as disadvantages. He had little good news to report from the three voyages, but held hope for the future as he wrote, 'although the passage to Cataya were not found out, neither yet the golde ore proved good, wher of both, the hope is good & gret.' [46] He also defended the whole experience as one good for the training of seamen in England's service.

So the promise of Gilbert's *Discourse* had come to nothing more than a hope that the passage might yet be found. In spite of the two crude maps included in Best's book, one showing the passage clearly, the other identifying the many islands between Greenland and Labrador discovered by Frobisher, it was obvious to any English reader that the passage would not easily be found and that an Asiatic market for English woolens was remote indeed. The hope Best offered for England's further participation in the 'flourishing age' was general and vague.

In spite of their failure, the Company of Cathay and Martin Frobisher had a lasting influence upon England. Their effort to carry English maritime activity into new regions—whether to seek a passage to China or to dig ore in America—aroused in Englishmen a greater interest in the outer world than they had previously known, and this interest was reflected in an immediate increase in the publication of exploration literature which in turn gave further stimulus to interests in overseas navigation, trade and empire. The idea of a northwest passage was not given up, and England's confidence that her sailors could discover the secrets of the northern waters grew in spite of the failure of Frobisher's voyages, as did English interest in the Far East. Indeed, in 1578, Sir Humphrey Gilbert planned an expedition to America and received permission to sail. He got no farther than Ireland, and the real destination and purpose of his voyage are still unknown.[47] It is likely that he intended to examine the North American coast near Spanish America for a place to plant an English colony. A destination in this area becomes quite plausible upon consideration of two books that appeared in 1578, both translations by former prisoners of the Inquisition.

John Frampton translated the geography of the West Indies written in 1519 by Martin Fernández de Enciso, calling it *A briefe description of the portes, bayes and havens of the Weast India,* and dedicated it to Gilbert, praising him for being the first to enlighten England on the northwest passage. Frampton expressed the hope, perhaps facetiously, that his book might be of use to English sailors driven by storms to the West Indies, and he hoped also that it might help his countrymen 'to be awaked out of their heavy sleepe wherein they have long lein... and with other nations rather late than never to make themselves shine with brightnesse of knowledge.'[48] Frampton's text is a composite of navigation information and socio-economic geography with some products, native customs, animals and vegetation described. Except for a description of the Canary Islands, and a final paragraph on Labrador, the entire work dealt with Spanish America. Richard Eden could not have asked for better education at the feet of the Spanish masters, and Frampton did his former captors no service by bringing this information to the attention of such persons as Gilbert who were both eager for learning and energetic for overseas ventures.

Thomas Nicholas, another English merchant who had been held prisoner by the Spanish for his religion, also had some revenge in 1578 with the publication of his translation of López de Gómara's history of Spanish exploration and conquest in America as *The pleasant historie of the conquest of the Weast India*. This translation was clearly inspired by the Frobisher voyages, and the dedication to Sir Francis Walsingham pointed out the error of the belief that gold was to be found only in the southern part of the New World. He asserted that Frobisher had proved that there was gold in the lands of the north which were previously thought valueless. He could not doubt that God had made it England's destiny to rule over these peoples of America, and 'also be a meane that the name of Christ may be knowen unto this Heathenish and Savage generation.'[49] The book was clearly in print before Frobisher's return from his third voyage, but its message went beyond the mere hope for gold. It was a guide to the management of imperialistic ventures, just as George Best's work had been an invitation to England to participate more vigorously in overseas exploration, and like Best's book, it was published by Henry Bynneman. It called itself 'a Mirrour and an excellent president [*sic*] for all such as shall take in hande to governe newe Discoveries: for here they shall behold how Glorie Renowne and perfite Felicitie, is not gotten but with greate paines, travaile, perill and daunger of life.'[50]

More than a lesson in discipline, Nicholas' translation carried the strongest propaganda for colonization yet seen in England. Although he wrote in parable fashion and did not elaborate, Nicholas told of meeting Augustín de Zárate, a seventy year old Spaniard who was on his way to get permission to set forth with four ships on a voyage of discovery. Nicholas had asked him if it were not more suitable for him to be preparing for the next life, and the old man replied that we came into the world to do some good for our country and our fellows. He said that he longed only to know that persons whom he took along to the New World would say 'oh happie day, when old Zárate... brought us from penurie, yea from a number of perils that were like to fall into.'[51] And he added, 'I hope also, that the royall estate of my Prince shall be my paynes... enlarged: beleeve you me, this is the onley sumtuous Tumbe that I pretende to build for my poor carkas.'[52] Zárate then added a word of scorn for those who were content with their country's situation, for such persons considered neither their God, their prince, nor their neighbors. Having said all of this for English benefit by translating the words of a Spanish colonial administrator, Nicholas went on to praise the forwardness with which Walsingham had supported the Frobisher voyages.

The text does not particularly fit the introduction, for it is a history of the Spanish conquest of Mexico, a story full of blood and gold, with little in the New World appearing as an improvement upon the woes of the old. Nevertheless, until England had successful explorations and colonies of her own to publicize, she had only the histories of the successful to introduce her to the problems and values of colonization. The approach Nicholas used to colonization does not suggest that his book was designed to arouse mass interest in leaving England for the New World. It appears, rather, like Best's *True discourse* to have come into print through the interest of an influential expansionist in the Court as a means of keeping the New World on the edge, at least, of the thinking of those who guided England's policies.

More popular in its appeal was Thomas Churchyard's lengthy poem in praise of Gilbert's abortive venture of 1578 which the ambitious poet appended to his account of the Queen's journeys to Suffolk and Norfolk. Once more it was Henry Bynneman, 'servant to the right Honourable Sir Christopher Hatton,' who published this *Commendation of Sir Humphrey Gilberts ventrous journey* which praised overseas undertakings in general and Gilbert's voyage in particular. Through more than five hundred lines of crude poetry, Churchyard rambled on in praise of Gilbert, Raleigh, Knolles, and other participants in the voyage, and he promised:

> *Well noble Pilgrims, as in verse*
> *I write this for your sake,*
> *In prose at your returne*
> *looke for a greater prayse,*
> *A Booke that to the loftie Skyes,*
> *your rare renowne shall rayse.*[53]

Yet for all his lack of ability as a poet, Churchyard saw clearly who were the enthusiasts for empire, just as he saw the need for colonization in his *Prayse and reporte*. If the message of his poem can be summarized, it is most cogently stated in these lines:

*What charges you are at,*
  *what venter you have made,*
*And how you seeke to traffike there,*
  *where never yet was trade.*
*And most of you such men,*
  *as livings have at home,*
*So great and good, that sure abrode*
  *yee need not for to rome.*[54]

Churchyard's contrasting of the sloth, thievery, wantonness, and other
sins of England with the noble virtues to be found in traveling abroad
are naive in the extreme, but the poet was a propagandist for empire
and was not bothered by realities, except for the unpleasant ones he
found in England. Nor was he downcast with the return of Frobisher
from his third voyage. While Bynneman was preparing Churchyard's
book for publication, Frobisher returned, and the prolific poet rushed
in with 'A welcome home to Master Martin Frobusher,' for inclusion
in the volume. In verse he again praised explorers and showed his
appreciation of the improvement their knowledge would bring to England, and he was, as ever, impatient with those who were less enthusiastic about empire than he.

*O mizers mindes, and wretches hartes,*
  *if all men sought their ease,*
*And none should search out golden mines,*
  *nor seeke their gaine by seas,*
*The worlde would sone be at an end,*
  *or meate and clothe would fayle,*
*And those that now doe laugh and smyle,*
  *at length would weepe and wayle.*[55]

Churchyard, like Henry Bynneman, was in the patronage of Sir Christopher Hatton at the time these lines were written, and in view of his
constant poverty, we may assume that he was writing to express sentiments close to the interests of his patron when he concluded in prose,
'Thus have I playnely expressed with pen, what portion of good will
I beare to all those that valiantly and worthily are workers to the
enriching & honour of our common wealth.'[56] Representing the arts
among the Queen's favorites, Hatton with the help of his humble pro-
tegé spoke more loudly for empire than anyone in the land, thereby

continuing the tradition which Rastell, More, Eden and Willes had established of a close alliance between letters and expansionism.

The sudden enthusiasm over American gold and Churchyard's thoughts about exporting troublesome people to the New World were by-products of the earlier idea of finding a new outlet for England's woolens in China by a northern route. This motive was never entirely lost in the gold rush of 1577–78, and it continued to bring descriptions of Asia into print after the failure of the Company of Cathay. With that failure there was a renewed interest in a northeast sea route to China, and literature appeared which was intended to be helpful in exploring the northern side of Eurasia.

Again it was John Frampton who provided information on those parts of Asia which had been described in Spanish and Portuguese, and his patron in these literary undertakings was Edward Dyer, a poet of importance who had been a subscriber to Frobisher's first two voyages and had been instrumental in interesting others at court to support Frobisher.[57] In 1579 two of Frampton's translations were published. His edition of Marco Polo's *Travels* gave Englishmen their first opportunity to read this classic in their own language, although it had been in print in other vernacular languages for more than a century. In his introduction Frampton stated that he was urged to publish it because of the numerous 'Merchauntes, Pilots, and Marriners, and others of dyvers degrees, much bent to Discoveries'[58] who came to him to read his manuscript translation, and he considered it of potential utility, believing 'that it mighte give greate lighte to our Seamen, if ever this nation chaunced to find a passage out of the frozen Zone to the South Seas.'[59] It is also probable that a major part of the impetus to publish Marco Polo's *Travels* came from Edward Dyer to whom Frampton admitted being 'more bound... than to anye man in England.'[60] The merchants and mariners were not sufficient to call for a second edition of Frampton's book but Dyer was consistent in his support of the translations Frampton produced, and without his patronage it is doubtful that they would have been published at all. Elizabeth's England called for only one edition of this greatest of travel books, whereas Spain had published editions in 1503, 1507, 1518, and 1520, and 1527.

The inclusion of Nicolo de Conti's travels to the east in the fifteenth century might have given the book greater interest, but there was not sufficient concern for eastern travel to call for another printing of this narrative either. This modest level of public interest in the East is again indicated in the case of Frampton's publication of Bernardino

de Escalante's *Discourse of the navigation which the Portugales doe make to...
the east partes of the world*, for it too satisfied the public with one edition,
although it was more modern in content, being devoted to the current
Portuguese supremacy in the East Indies. Frampton's statement that
the book was born of the need for information 'by personnes of sundry
callynges, and especially by diverse moste excellent Pilottes, Maisters,
and towardly young Marriners' [61] is rather vague, and his dedication to
Dyer even more so as it expressed the hope that the book 'maye geve
lyght to our Nation and woorke in many respectes benefite to all suche,
as shall by Northeast, or by Northwest attempt discoveries of Dominions and Territories, wtihin [*sic*] the circle Artike, or with out the same
to the Tropicke of Cancer.' [62] Rather than a response to enthusiasm
for discovery, this translation, like others of Frampton's books, appears
to be much more an attempt by Frampton and Dyer to generate
enthusiasm among the reading public. While Frampton seems to have
considered this book a supplement to his Marco Polo translation, it
was in fact far more pertinent to England's interest in the Far East.
The first five chapters relate the history of Portuguese conquest in the
East Indies, and the remaining eleven chapters describe China and the
Philippines, the very regions English navigators hoped to reach by the
northern passages.

The failure of the Company of Cathay, and the continued opposition to it by the Muscovy Company, placed upon the latter group the
obligation to 'put into practice a matter of more importance,' to use
Churchyard's words. Moreover, their Persian trade, which had shown
some promise in the early years of the decade, was now suffering from
political turmoil in Western Asia, and the long route via Muscovy, the
Volga and the Caspian no longer seemed the best possible means to
tap the wealth of the East. Once again, therefore, the Muscovy Company mounted an expedition to attempt a northeast water route to the
Far East. The occasion provided more work for John Frampton, for
as Arthur Pet and Charles Jackman prepared to make the voyage,
Frampton translated and sent with them, in manuscript, selections on
the people of the northern regions from Johann Boemus' *Omnium gentium mores et leges*. Actually his translation was twice removed from the
original, since he used Támara's Spanish edition as the basis for his
translation which appeared as *A discoverie of the countries of Tartaria,
Scithia, & Cataya* in 1580, the year Pet and Jackman sailed. [63]

In this instance Frampton did not dedicate his book to Dyer but to
Rowland Hayward and George Barne, both governors of the Muscovy

Company who had a closer interest in the voyage than did Edward Dyer.[64] The book is divided into four parts: 'Of the region of Tartaria'; 'Of the countrie of Scithia'; 'Of the countrie that is called the other side of the Ganges, and of Cataya, and the region of Sinas'; and 'Of many notable things that are found in the land of Tartaria and in East India.' Clearly, Frampton was trying to give the Pet-Jackman expedition information on whatever lands they might find in the east if the voyage were successful.

Through Frampton's efforts and the interest of his patron Edward Dyer, Englishmen looking toward Asia for new markets had better information than had been available to the pioneers of the Muscovy Company. They also had some recently published books on navigation. In 1580 a new edition of Bourne's *Regiment for the sea* appeared.[65] Added to Bourne's book was a timely note—a discussion, included for the first time, of five possible ways to Cathay, among which were the northwest and northeast passages and a route over the north pole, in addition to the two southern routes. No such significant addition was made in the new printing of Eden's translation of *The arte of navigation* in 1579, for it was substantially the same work as the 1572 edition.[66] Although John Dee held the position of primacy among England's theoreticians in the field of navigation, his book, *General and rare memorials pertayning to the perfect arte of navigation*, published in 1577,[67] showed his involvement in the Frobisher enterprise. It was, however, little more than a long-winded plea for recognition of his invention of 'the paradoxicall cumpas' twenty-four years earlier and was no more significant than Edward Hellowes' translation of Antonio de Guevara's book on navigation which was published in 1578 as *A booke of the invention of the art of navigation*. Hellowes, in his note to the reader, may have recorded contemporary attitudes toward navigation when he wrote of 'the opinion of certeine, which affirme, that so unremoveable bounds [the sea] declareth Gods omnipotent ordinance, that every country so divided ought to content themselves to live, by the gifts of the same God and countrie,'[68] but his translation was far less current in its interest, being merely a series of references to classical navigation, followed by an entertaining collection of 'privileges of the Gallie' and other sea lore of no scientific value.

A knowledge of navigation and geography were obvious prerequisites to empire in the minds of England's imperialists of the 1570s, yet to William Bourne these were not enough, and he equipped the explorer and traveler with a textbook on the science of travel when in 1578 he published his comprehensive and detailed *Treasure for traveilers*. Here for the first time in English letters, travel was viewed as a science. Bourne was scornful of people who did not take proper advantage of their travel abroad, 'and when they have come home, they have no judgement of their travayle, but have been utterly ignoraunt of suche thinges as were most meetest to a Travailer to be noted...' [69] He advised persons going into strange countries to observe the state of civilization of the region, the nature of the fortifications, access to the sea, the government, laws, buildings, natural enemies and friends among neighboring states, the major items in trade, commodities produced, customs and tolls, manner of waging war, etc. With such observations Bourne believed the traveler could render a greater service to his country. Correct method of travel was to him as important as travel itself was to other expansionists of the time. Bourne's writings, along with those of Dee and Hellowes, illustrate a mounting interest in techniques potentially applicable to overseas ventures as the Frobisher voyages opened the era of active English exploration in America and the Muscovy Company renewed its attempt at a northeast passage.

Despite the help and hope of Frampton, Bourne and the Muscovy Company, and its own heroic efforts, the expedition of Pet and Jackman failed to get beyond Vaigats, and it returned to Norway from whence Pet came back to England to report the failure. Jackman tried again from Norway, but his ship with its company was lost in the attempt. This failure marked the end of England's reliance upon the northern waters to lead her sailors and merchants to a profitable eastern market for her woolens. By 1580 English merchants were negotiating for eastern trade with the Sultan of Turkey, and Sir Francis Drake's voyage had convinced Englishmen of their ability to use the southern routes to the East Indies.

The failures of Frobisher as well as the success of Drake exhibited a high degree of competence on the part of England's seamen, but the readiness of these seamen to carry English interest abroad was far in advance of the interest of most Englishmen in overseas trade or exploration. The history of publishing in England during these years of the beginnings of overseas enterprise proves the apathy of the general reading public, in spite of the fact that Richard Eden's 'certeyne small and obscure members of the commonwealth' were vigorous imperialists. Almost no area of potential reader interest was less regulated by the Company of Stationers than travel literature, for it could not conceivably fall under any of the monopolies that were granted to various printers in London.[70] The lack of travel and geographical literature, therefore, must be attributed to a lack of demand for such books. While the northeast and northwest passage attempts stimulated some popular interest, the number of persons responsible for most of the books that appeared were few: Eden, Dyer, Frampton, Hatton, Nicholas, and Bourne.

Controversial voyages produced books, but many other expeditions received less attention by English publishers and readers. The continuing trade to West Africa brought no accounts of that region or of the voyages there. The Russian trade produced only Clement Adams' descriptions of English enterprise there, but no translations of continental works on Russia appeared until Frampton's translation of Támara's version of Boemus in 1580, and this was intended as a guide book on peoples to be met on the way to the Pacific Ocean. In the first three years of the 1570s, Francis Drake successfully raided Spanish holdings in America, yet no book survives describing these triumphs. Gilbert Horseley returned to England in 1575, rich with plunder from the coast of South America, but no evidence exists that printers took any note of it. If successes went unpublished, it is not to be expected that failures would be broadcast. The voyages of Stephen Borough in search of a northeast passage in 1556 and 1557, of John Noble to South America in 1574, of Andrew Barker to the Caribbean in 1576, and of John Oxenham to Darien in 1576 all ended in failure–and in silence.

Nevertheless, by 1580 English readers had access to sixteenth century information on the New World, China, India, the Philippines, inner Russia, Persia, Egypt, the Levant, and the East Indies. Most of this information came through translations rather than works on English exploration, and in general it was accompanied by imperialistic expressions from England's literary group. We find no policy-maker in the Queen's circle equal in his patronage of imperialism to Sir Christopher Hatton, whose greatest influence with Elizabeth was in the areas of entertainment; no London merchant to compete with the poets, Edward Dyer, Richard Willes, George Gascoigne, and Thomas Churchyard. While such men of the sea as George Best, Dionyse Settle and Thomas Ellis described the voyages in which the Queen had been a subscriber, she received no book in dedication in this period, and there is no indication that she was interested in expansionist literature.

There were reasons why England showed so little interest in literature of overseas interest in the first half of Elizabeth's reign. In the first place, Elizabeth was in no position to espouse imperialistic projects openly, for as royal marriages tended to bring Spain and Portugal together, any aggressive move in almost any part of the world could be interpreted as a threat to Spain, the most powerful nation on the Continent. Offending Spain meant not only the likelihood of armed conflict abroad but also of rebellion at home, for in the view of those loyal to the Roman Church, Elizabeth was the bastard child of a heretic and not a legitimate Queen. Spain would surely have exploited those sentiments. Elizabeth would not, therefore, encourage the imperialist spirit until she could stand against this mighty adversary at home and abroad.

The apathy of the merchant community can be attributed to London's continued orientation toward the Continent in its commerce and to the fact that joint-stock companies that ventured abroad were still small groups which did not need the printing press to advise shareholders of the progress of their enterprise. It was chiefly the cloth trade that called for the expansion of markets, and from mid-century until 1580 there was a fairly steady improvement in cloth exports, even though they remained below the figures for the first half of the century. England's dominant port, therefore, felt no compelling urgency to arouse the country to the need for overseas markets.

The general public's lack of concern for literature describing the outer world can be understood when the position of modern languages, of geography, and of history in the schools of Elizabethan England is recalled. Education at that time had little to do with information. Throughout the sixteenth and seventeenth centuries, grammar and rhetoric constituted the bulwark of the grammar school curriculum, and though mathematics, natural sciences and vernacular languages became increasingly popular as they increased in usefulness, they were seldom taught in the schools.[71] Learning by rote rather than by inquiry tended to keep subject matter and methods the same from one generation to another. In 1582 Richard Hakluyt was pleading for one adequate chair of geography in England. History was viewed as a subject suitable to nobles and gentlemen, and such histories as were read were usually chronicles of England or classical history. Current history had less prestige, for it was from the past that lessons of virtue and steadfastness were to be learned, and those readers who sought escape from the dominant moral tone of the time found it more in literature of entertainment than of learning.[72] Those who had the leisure to be educated, therefore, could not easily become acquainted with the knowledge requisite for an interest in exploration and the literature which grew out of it.

As the merchant which he was, the bookseller had to examine public interests and cater to public taste within the limits prescribed by law and the regulations of the Company of Stationers. There was no security in his profession unless he had one of the more lucrative monopolies on certain types of books. In this struggle for existence the unprivileged printer leaned toward the cheap and the sensational in preference to what he may have recognized as better and more lasting literature.[73] Literature of a quality above the most popular taste in reading still frequently required patronage, and most of the travel literature published prior to 1580 was patronized by persons with enthusiasm for empire far in advance of the general literate public. Indeed a recurrent theme in the dedicatory epistles is the lethargy of Englishmen towards overseas ventures. Yet this was an age when patronage in general was giving way to the newer economics of publishing for the public—an age when pages addressed 'to the reader' came to assume prominence equal to the dedication to the patron.[74] But travel and exploration literature had not yet arrived to the point where the readers could support it.

What this type of book lacked was an emotional appeal to large numbers of readers or a truly utilitarian appeal, for it dealt with places and events far away from the experience and primary concerns of most Englishmen. At the level of public affairs, English emotions in the first half of Elizabeth's reign were still dominated by religion and nationalism. However, there were inhibitions upon both of them, and they were dependent upon one another so that neither could run its full course without the other. Whereas the earlier Tudors had united the country, reduced local authority, and shattered the authority of the Papacy in England, Elizabeth's problems were different. Her first task was to keep herself at the head of her nation by a policy of religious moderation that did not too vigorously arouse her Catholic subjects, who made up half of the population of the realm. In doing so she had to turn a deaf ear to the arguments of the Calvinists, a militant element that wanted the Reformation to continue so that churches in England might be stripped of Roman trappings. It was this reforming element which had the zeal to send England abroad in a missionary effort and which would ultimately do so. But in 1580 it was clear that opposition to such an expansionist program would come not from Rome but from Madrid. The real power of the Catholic Church was the well-financed

Philip II, who had at his back the wealth of the Indies and the devotion of the Society of Jesus. With an official religion less aggressive than either Calvinism or Catholicism, England was deprived of an emotional drive that could have had wide popular appeal. Nationalism was strong, but without its religious counterpart it could have no broad popular appeal, and until it was shown that overseas ventures held potential profit for English investors, the utilitarian motive could not be brought into play. The sheer belief in England's greatness was enough for a Dyer or a Hatton, as it had been for Rastell and Eden, but it gave the average reader no compelling reason to want to go abroad. Nationalism had not yet grown to imperialism in the common mind.

## NOTES TO CHAPTER VI

1 Stefansson, I, 81–2.
2 *The strange and marveilous newes lately come from the great kingdome of Chyna*, trans. T[homas] N[icholas] (London: Thomas Gardyner and Thomas Dawson, [1577]), fol. Aiii verso. Nicholas had lived in the Canary Islands as a merchant. He was arrested for heresy in 1560, and was released upon the intercession of the English ambassador, Sir William Chamberlain, but he was arrested again shortly. In 1564 Queen Elizabeth interceded for him, and he was released the following year. He had been confined in Seville, and it was probably here that he acquired the letter from which he translated.
3 *Ibid.*, Aiii recto.
4 Lawrence C. Wroth, 'An Elizabethan merchant and man of letters,' *The Huntington Library quarterly*, XVII (August, 1954), 304–6.
5 First published in English as *The three bookes written in the Spanish tonge*, trans. John Frampton (London: Willyam Norton, 1577). A later issue of the same year was entitled *Joyfull newes out of the new founde worlde*. The first Spanish edition appeared in 1569, and a second edition was published in 1571. The two editions were combined into a larger work, *Primera y segunda y tercera partes de la historia medicinal... de nuestras Indias occidentales*. It was from this edition, published in 1574, that Frampton translated. See F. Guerra, *Nicolas Bautista Monardes, su vida y su obra* (Mexico City: Compañia Fundidora de Fierro y Acero de Monterrey, 1961).
6 *Ibid.*, fol. *ii recto.
7 Lady Brigit was the second wife of Francis Russell, second Earl of Bedford, a prominent official in Elizabeth's government. In 1576 he was Lord President of Wales, after having served as governor of Berwick. She had been widowed by Sir Richard Morison and by Henry Manners, Earl of Rutland. On folio ❧ii Willes acknowledges that 'The first yeerely pension I ever was assured of in England, to have ben by your Ladiship bestowed on me.'
8 Richard Eden, *A history of travayle in the West and East Indies* (London: Richard Jugge, 1577), fol. (.) ii recto–verso.
9 *Ibid.*, fol. (.) ii verso.

[10] *Ibid.*, fols. (.) iii verso–iiii recto.
[11] *Ibid.*, fol. (.) iiii recto.
[12] *Ibid.*, fol. ᷒i verso.
[13] *Ibid.*
[14] *Ibid.*, fol. ᷒iiii recto.
[15] *Ibid.*, fol. 230 verso. This section was dedicated to Lady Anne, third wife of Ambrose Dudley, Earl of Warwick. It was he to whom Frobisher first presented his plan for exploration to the northwest, and he was a major promoter of the first voyage. These dedications to prominent ladies suggests that in the mind of Willes, at least, geography was becoming a suitable interest for ladies.
[16] *Ibid.*, fol. 231 recto.
[17] *Ibid.*, fol. 236 recto.
[18] *Ibid.*, fol. 236 verso. Elizabeth Morison was the daughter of Sir Charles Morison and granddaughter of Sir Richard Morison and Lady Brigit, who was Willes's patroness.
[19] Galeotto Pereira, *Alcune cose del paese della China* (Venice, ca. 1561).
[20] Eden, *History*, fol. 253 verso. The translation is from *Rerum a Societate Jesu in oriente gestarum tractatus* (Naples, 1573). Also printed in Cologne in 1574, this work consists of Jesuit letters from the Far East and a Dedicatory Epistle by Giovanni Pietro Maffei.
[21] Early activity of Froes and other Portuguese priests in Japan is described in C.R. Boxer, *The Christian century in Japan* (Berkeley: University of California Press, 1951).
[22] Eden, *History*, fol. 321 recto.
[23] *Ibid.*
[24] Geoffrey Ducket and Thomas Banister were sent to Persia in 1568 in the company of Thomas Randolph, who was to attempt negotitations for improved trading conditions on behalf of Queen Elizabeth. Ducket's travels took him down the Volga, into the Caspian Sea, and to a number of cities in Persia. Banister died in Persia and Ducket and his party lost most of their good to pirates. Ducket returned to England in 1574. Edwards went to Persia in 1565 along with Richard Johnson and Alexander Kitchin. He visited Schmekha and Astrakhan in Persia, and other members of the party travelled to other parts of Persia. Edwards headed another expedition into Persia in 1579. See Foster, *England's quest of eastern trade*, pp. 32–41.
[25] Arber, *The first three English books on America*, p. xlviii; Varthema's work was first published as *Itinerario de Ludovico de Varthema Bolognese...* (Rome: Stephano Guillireti de Loreno and Hercule de Nani, 1510).
[26] In addition to five Italian editions by 1523, Varthema's account of the East was translated into Latin, Spanish, German, French and Dutch before Eden translated it into English.
[27] Stefansson, II, 116.
[28] Churchyard was the first of Sir Christopher Hatton's literary dependents according to Brooks, p. 124. A soldier, adventurer and poet who was always impoverished and constantly seeking assistance at court, he intended the *Prayse and reporte* for Walsingham's attention, but lamented, 'my work neither found free passage nor acces to his noble judgement,' Thomas Churchyard, *A prayse and reporte of Maister Martyne Forboishers voyage to Meta Incognita* (London: Andrew Maunsell, 1578 ), fol. Aiii recto.
[29] *Ibid.*, fols. Aiii verso–Aiiii recto.
[30] *Ibid.*, fol. Biii verso.
[31] *Ibid.*, fol. Av recto–verso.
[32] *Ibid.*, fols. Avi verso–Avii recto.

[33] *Ibid.*, fol. Ciiii verso.

[34] McFee, *Martin Frobisher*, p. 115.

[35] Thomas Ellis, *A true report of the third and last voyage into Meta Incognita* (London: Thomas Dawson, [1578]), fol. Bvi recto. Ellis documented his accounts of icebergs with four crude woodcut illustrations.

[36] *Ibid.*, fol. Ai verso.

[37] The association between Hatton and Best is not clear. Best refers to Hatton as 'my singular good Mayster,' George Best, *A true discourse of the late voyages of discoverie, for the finding of a passage to Cathaya by the northweast* (London: Henry Bynneman, 1578), fol. aiii recto. Best is called 'a man of Hatton's,' at whose murder Hatton was distressed with the Queen for failing to prosecute the assailant. See Brooks, *Sir Christopher Hatton*, p. 93.

[38] Best, fol. biii recto. No printed works are extant which are hostile to Frobisher's voyages, nor are any recorded in the *Stationers register* which appear to have been hostile. It is unlikely that such pamphlets could have been licensed in view of the Queen's support of the voyages. Four books which were licensed by the Company of Stationers, but of which no copies are known or recorded at any previous time are: *Fullers farewell to master Froubousier and other gentlemen adventurers whoe labour to discover the right passage to Catay*, licensed to John Jugge, 20 May 1577; *A thing touching Fourboyser*, A. Maunsell, 1 July 1577; *A discription of... those strange kind of people which the worthie master Martin Fourbosier brought into England*, John Aldee, 30 January 1578; *A pamphlet in the praise of master Captaine Frobisher in forme of a farewell at his third voiage*, R. Jones, 13 May 1578. See Edward Arber (ed.), *A transcript of the registers of the Company of Stationers of London* (5 vols.; London, Birmingham: Privately printed, 1874–94), II, 312, 323, 327. (Hereafter cited as Arber (ed.) *Stationers register*.)

[39] Best, fol. Aiii recto.

[40] *Ibid.*, fols. Aiiii verso – bi recto.

[41] *Ibid.*, fol. aiiii recto–verso.

[42] *Ibid.*, fols. bi verso, bii recto.

[43] *Ibid.*, p. 3. Bynneman's Epistle to the Reader states that Best's narrative was published without the author's knowledge or consent, but the dedication to Hatton, and Best's eloquent description of the 'flourishing age' indicate that it was meant for a public audience.

[44] *Ibid.*, p. 9.

[45] *Ibid.*, p. 46.

[46] *Ibid.*, fol. bi recto.

[47] Quinn, *The voyages and colonising enterprises of Sir Humphrey Gilbert*, I, 37–44.

[48] Martin Fernández de Enciso, *A briefe description of the portes, creekes, bayes and havens of the Weast India*, trans. John Frampton (London: Henry Bynneman, 1578), fol. Aii verso; Frampton translated only a portion of the *Suma de geographia* (Seville: Jacob Cromberger, 1519). The merchant Roger Barlow had translated it in revised form in 1541, but his work remained in manuscript until it was edited by E. G. R. Taylor in 1932.

[49] Francisco López de Gómara, *The pleasant historie of the conquest of the Weast India, now called New Spayne*, trans. Thomas Nicholas (London: Henry Bynneman, 1578), fol. Aii verso. This was first published as *Primera y segunda parte de la historia general de las Indias* (Saragossa, 1553).

[50] *Ibid.*, fol. Aii verso.

[51] *Ibid.*, fol. aiii verso.

[52] *Ibid.*

[53] Thomas Churchyard, *A discourse of the Queenes Majesties entertainment in Suffolk and Norfolk... whereunto is adjoyned a commendation of Sir Humphrey Gilberts ventrous journey*

(London: Henry Bynneman, [1578]), fols. Kii verso–Kiii recto. Churchyard entitled his poem 'A matter touching the journey of Sir Humphrey Gilbarte knight.'

54  *Ibid.*, fols. Hiiii verso–Ii recto.

55  *Ibid.*, fol. Lii recto.

56  *Ibid.*, fol. Liiii recto.

57  Ralph M. Sargent, *At the court of Queen Elizabeth; the life and lyrics of Sir Edward Dyer* (London: Oxford University Press, 1935), pp. 41–43.

58  Marco Polo, *The most noble and famous travels of Marcus Paulus*, trans. John Frampton (London: Ralph Newberry, 1579), fol. *ii recto. Marco Polo's *Travels* were first published by F. Creusner in Nuremberg in 1477. Frampton translated from the Castilian edition of Rodrigo Fernández de Santaella y Córdoba, published in Seville, 1503.

59  *Ibid.*, fol. *ii recto.

60  *Ibid.*, fol. *ii verso.

61  Bernardino de Escalante, *A discourse of the navigation which the Portugales doe make to... the east partes of the worlde*, trans. John Frampton (London: Thomas Dawson, 1579), fol. 2 verso. This was first published as *Discurso de la navegacion que los Portugueses hazen... del Oriente* (Seville: Alonso Escrivano, 1577).

62  *Ibid.*, fol. 3 recto.

63  Francisco Támara, *A discoverie of the countries of Tartaria, Scithia, & Cataya, by the northeast*, trans. John Frampton (London: Thomas Dawson, 1580). Támara's translation was first published as *El libro de las costumbres de todas las gentes del mundo, y de las Indias* (Antwerp: Martin Nucio, 1556). The work of Johann Boemus from which Támara translated was first published as *Repertorium librorum trium* (Augsburg: S. Grim and M. Wirsung, 1520), and it went through many editions in various languages in the sixteenth century, a frequently used Latin title being *Omnium gentium mores et leges.*

64  The only copy of this book located was the British Museum copy. The dedication apparently wants one leaf, leaving very little text other than the identification of Hayward and Barne as aldermen of the city of London and governors of the Muscovy Company.

65  William Bourne, *A regiment for the sea* (London: Thomas East, 1580). See E. G. R. Taylor (ed.), *A regiment for the sea and other writings on navigation by William Bourne* (Cambridge, For the Hakluyt Society, 1963).

66  Martin Cortés, *The arte of navigation*, trans. Richard Eden (London: Widow of Richard Jugge, 1579).

67  John Dee, *General and rare memorials pertayning to the perfect arte of navigation.* (London: John Day, 1577).

68  Antonio de Guevara, *A booke of the invention of art of navigation*, trans. Edward Hellowes (London: Ralph Newberrie, 1578), fol. Bbv recto.

69  William Bourne, *A booke called the treasure for traveilers* (London: For Thomas Woodcocke, 1578), fol. **iii verso.

70  Arber (ed.), *Stationers' register*, I, 111, records the following monopolies whichs were probably granted by Queen Elizabeth at her accession: John Jugge, Bibles and testaments, in addition to being the Queen's printer; Richart Tothill, 'all kinds of lawe bookes'; John Daye, The A. B. C. and catechisms; James Robertes and Richard Watkyns, almanacks and prognostications; Thomas Marshe, 'latten bookes used in the gramer scoles of England'; Thomas Vautrollier, 'other latten bookes, as the newe Testament and others'; William Byrde, music and ruled paper; William Seres, psalters, primers, and prayer books; Francis Flower, 'the Gramer.'

71  Foster Watson, *The beginnings of the teaching of modern subjects in England* (London: Sir Isaac Pitman & Sons, Ltd., 1909), p. xxii.

[72] *Ibid.*, p. 63; Louis B. Wright, 'The Elizabethan middle class taste for history,' *The journal of modern history*, III (June, 1931), 175–97; Edwin H. Miller, *The professional writer in Elizabethan England* (Cambridge, Mass.: Harvard University Press, 1959) pp. 63–93.

[73] Phoebe Sheavyn, 'Writers and the publishing trade, circa 1600,' *The library*, 2nd series, VII (October, 1906), 364–65.

[74] P. Thomson, 'The patronage of letters under Elizabeth and James I,' *English*, VII (1949), 278–82; Franklin B. Williams, Jr. *Index of dedications and commendatory verses in English books before 1941* (London: The Bibliographical Society, 1962), pp. ix–xi note trends toward and away from patronage in various areas of English publishing.

## Chapter VII

## PROPOSALS FOR WESTERN PLANTING

In the history of Elizabethan overseas interests and in the literature that made these interests known to the public, the year 1580 stands as a dividing line. In that year Sir Francis Drake returned from his circumnavigation of the earth, proving that England had access to the East Indies without recourse to a northern passage and proving also the competence of English seamanship. The same year Elizabeth and Sultan Murad III of Turkey exchanged letters which confirmed the privilege of Englishmen to trade directly with Turkey. This gave England an approach to eastern goods that did not require the long and troublesome journey through Russia and Persia. In 1580, also, Richard Hakluyt who was to become the foremost literary imperialist of the sixteenth century emerged as the ardent advocate of colonization of North America. The events which proceeded from these beginnings ultimately committed England to direct trade with the East Indies and the Levant and brought her by the end of Elizabeth's reign to the verge of colonization in the New World. Like the imperialistic ventures encountered thus far, these developments were the result of England's continuing concern for new markets for her primary export product—woolen cloth.

To the economic crisis which confronted English merchants in Antwerp in the early 1550s was added a political-religious difficulty in the 1560s; for the Netherlands, with an expanding economy and strong Protestant tendencies, were smarting under the control of Philip II of Spain, who saw English heresy coming into Antwerp along with English wool.[1] As the Inquisition came down upon this busy mercantile center of the Low Countries, 'the foreign merchants, manufacturers, and artisans fled from her gates as if the plague were raging within them.'[2] English merchants tried other cities in the Netherlands, and in Germany as well, but without much success, and by the 1580s the hope of restoring their trade to its traditional Continental port was gone, and London was being shaken out of its complacency.

As the Antwerp market declined, a change gradually took place in English woolen manufactures. Whereas unfinished cloth had displaced wool in the fifteenth century, there now developed, with the assistance of recent exiles from the Low Countries, the 'new draperies.' These more highly finished cloths could not depend upon a market in western Europe, where they would meet strong local competition, but found their most ready acceptance in the Mediterranean area. Other commercial developments also focused English attention on the Mediterranean. Rising populations in the southern European countries brought greater demands for food than those countries could supply, a development which opened a market for both grain and fish from the north. The rebellion of the Netherlands against Spain caused the Hapsburg monarchy to move its financial center from Antwerp to Genoa, and repercussions of this were bound to be felt in England. The decline of Venice as a trading center with strong connections in northern Europe invited England to fill a growing need in that area, and English merchants in supplying northern goods to the Mediterranean found a ready market for tin and lead to supply military needs in the south of Europe.[3]

England's need of imports as well as her desire to export brought the Mediterranean more closely to the attention of her merchants. Most eastern goods had heretofore come to London by way of Antwerp, but with the weakening of this connection the alternatives were to import from Spain, thereby enriching the chief enemy of Protestantism, or to import from the eastern Mediterranean ports directly. The French had chosen the latter course with good success, and their example stimulated the hope in Englishmen that they could do as well.[4]

In 1553 Anthony Jenkinson had made preparations for the opening of English trade with Turkey, but Queen Mary had espoused a policy of not trading with infidels, and Jenkinson's plans came to nothing.[5] There is no recorded trade between the two countries from that time to the late 1570s. In 1575 Edward Osborne, a London cloth merchant, and his partner, Richard Staper, secured from Sultan Murad III a safe conduct for their agent, William Harborne, who, in 1578 secured trading privileges from the Sultan with the support of Queen Elizabeth.[6] She convinced the Sultan of the wisdom of opening the trade with Turkey to all English subjects, a move which actually gave her control over it. Then, in 1581, she granted a patent to Osborne, Staper, Thomas Smith, and William Garret, all of London, 'and such other person and persons, Englishmen borne, not exceeding the number of twelve, as they... shall appoint.'[7] This group was required to do business to the value of five hundred pounds annually, and it was to be organized on a joint-stock plan.[8] With the details of operation clarified, Harborne returned to Turkey in 1582 and began setting up English trading stations in various parts of the Sultan's dominions.

It was not Osborne and Staper, however, who excited the multitude in England in 1580. The return that year of Francis Drake from his voyage around the world established him as England's most brilliant seaman to that time, and the Spanish gold in his ship warmed the hearts of nationalists. To the less ardent Spain-haters, however, Drake was a menace whom they would have sacrificed in order to keep peace with Spain.[9] The emotions which were aroused by his return probably obscured for all but a few the real purposes of his voyage. Historians and biographers of Drake have not agreed on these purposes, but it seems likely that establishing commercial relations with the undiscovered Terra Australis Incognita was considered at some point in his plans and that reaching the Moluccas was his foremost objective.[10] The raiding of Spanish shipping would be a natural consequence of an English voyage into Spanish waters, and in view of the hope widely held for a northwest passage when Drake departed in 1577, his probing of the west coast of North America was a natural phase of the voyage.[11] Nevertheless, it was the gold returned to England and the voyage as a feat of navigation that captured the popular fancy.

Actually, Drake had not only performed outstanding feats of navigation and piracy, but he had also arranged a treaty of commerce with the King of Ternate. This aspect of the voyage interested the Muscovy Company, which willingly accepted an invitation to participate in a voyage to exploit this newly-established trade in the Moluccas. Edward Fenton set out under the auspices of the Earl of Leicester with the support of the Muscovy Company in 1582.[12] Although he failed to get even as far as the Plate estuary, England was to continue to think of the Strait of Magellan as a possible route to the East Indies.

While London's merchants were looking to the Levant and the East Indies, Sir Humphrey Gilbert was continuing his plans for an expedition of an unspecified nature to North America. In 1580 he sent out a reconnaissance ship to explore the American mainland. It returned three months later, apparently with encouraging news, for Gilbert proceeded to organize a colonizing project. About the same time the earliest literary undertaking of Richard Hakluyt appeared in print.

Born about 1551, the son of a member of the Skinners' Company of London, Richard Hakluyt attended Westminster School and went to Oxford in 1570 where he was to prepare for the ministry. He came very much under the influence of his cousin, also named Richard Hakluyt, a lawyer with a keen interest in geography, navigation and England's commerce abroad. After seven years of study at Oxford, the young Richard Hakluyt appears to have given lectures in geography.[13] His interests were by no means purely academic, however, for he quickly applied his knowledge to England's commercial and population problems, became the first outspoken advocate of colonization and eagerly put his opinions into print.

John Rastell had mourned England's lost opportunity to settle people in the New World; Eden's 'Butrigarius' had advocated it. Gilbert, Nicholas, and Churchyard had seen colonization as a means of relieving the more distressed elements of England's population. But none of these had made a strong case for the removal of Englishmen to the New World. Now, while Gilbert's plans for a settlement took form, Hakluyt appeared as the champion of colonization in his encouragement of and participation in the publication of John Florio's translation of the narratives of Cartier's first and second voyages which Henry Bynneman published as *A shorte and briefe narration of the two navigations and discoveries to... New Fraunce.* 'Translating at the request and erneste solicitations of divers my very good frends heere in Oxforde,'[14] Florio appears to have been writing at the suggestion or orders of Hakluyt, for his ideas exactly correspond with those expressed by Hakluyt in subsequent publications.

Speaking through Florio, the son of an Italian Protestant refugee and a teacher of languages in Oxford, Hakluyt was unrestrained in his enthusiasm for colonization, and countering the popular belief that Spain's wealth was easily gained, he stated 'the Spanyards never prospered or prevailed, but where they planted.'[15] While Gilbert hid the true motives of his earlier abortive voyages of 1578–79,[16] Hakluyt launched out boldly, seeing no reason why a colony in America should not be founded, both to facilitate further searching westward for the water route to Cathay and to serve as a base for trading with the natives of the New World and exploring the land for minerals. He defended England's right to North America, basing his claim on the Cabot voyages and the continuing westward sailing of English ships. 'So there is no nation,' he wrote, 'more fit for this purpose, than they are, who travayling yearely into those partes with 50 or 60 sail of shippes, might very commodiouslye transporte a sufficient number of men to plant a Colonie.'[17] Hakluyt saw ships as one need and information as another, and he called for additional translations from European sources, 'whiche Bookes, if they were translated into English by the liberalitie of some noble Personage, our Seamen of England... shoulde know many worthy secrets, which hitherto have beene concealed.'[18] Hakluyt, like Richard Eden before him, showed a sense of urgency, and when he arranged for the translation of the Cartier narratives in 1580, it was for no academic reason but 'for the benefite and behoofe of those that shall attempt any newe discoverie in the Northwest partes of America.'[19] In 1580 he must have had Sir Humphrey Gilbert's American venture in mind.

The text is well suited to such a motive, giving descriptions of Cartier's voyages up the St. Lawrence River in 1534 and 1535. The narrative of the first voyage is primarily navigational in interest, describing the sailing in and out of one bay and another but noting along the way trees, birds, fish, and other commodities. The opening of trade between the French and the natives and the enthusiasm of the Indians for French goods are also described. This narrative concludes with about sixty words of the vocabulary of these Indians. The account of the second voyage deals more closely with French and Indian relations, with the voyage up the St. Lawrence to Hochelaga and Stadcona making up most of the narrative. Another hundred words are added to the vocabulary, and the book concludes with an expression of hope for a passage to the Pacific: 'They of Canada saye, that it is a monthes sayling to go to a land where Cinamonds and cloves are gathered.'[20]

While Gilbert's enterprise competed for public attention with the beginnings of the Levant Company and the return of Drake and was in fact less promising of long range results than either of these, it was the only one of the three ventures to result in the publication of a book in 1580. The translation of the Cartier narratives and the publication of Frampton's translation of Tamara's book on the northeastern regions in 1580 show the persistence of England's interest in the northern approach to the East Indies, among patrons at least, even as other routes were being tried. It must be noted, however, that these books did not reflect a strong public interest, for Frampton was surely subsidized in his work by the Muscovy Company, and it was again Henry Bynneman, Sir Christopher Hatton's printer, who published Florio's translation. The impetus for its publication assuredly came from Hakluyt and not from the publisher's belief that it would be of great public interest and a profitable venture. Similarly, the continued patronage of Edward Dyer caused a second and enlarged edition of Frampton's *Joyful newes out of the new founde worlde* to appear in 1580, prompted, according to Frampton, by the urgings of Dr. Hector Nunes, a Portuguese physician living in London.

Compared to the thought of establishing a colony in America, the formation of an organization to trade in Turkey was unspectacular and of immediate interest to only a handful of chosen merchants. It was actually only a proposed extension of the already existing Mediterranean trade and called for no popular notice, so it is not surprising that the book trade and the literary patrons took no notice of it. Drake's voyage, on the other hand, was a spectacular event, and it is remarkable that no contemporary book describing or commenting on this most brilliant accomplishment of English seamanship is extant. The most acceptable explanation of this apparent silence by the entire literary profession is that the Queen, in order to prevent undue annoyance of Spain, forbade the publication of any account of the voyage. It is certain that she had plans to follow up Drake's success with other voyages to the East Indies, and that she could gain nothing by permitting the advertising of her intentions.

It is hard to believe, however, that there was any ban on commendatory volumes, for one—and only one—appeared in 1581. This was Thomas Nicholas' translation of Zárate's *Discovery and conquest of Peru*, in which Nicholas in his dedication to Thomas Wilson, a secretary of state to the Queen, praised Drake for his voyage. We find here no indication of an awareness of restrictions upon publishing accounts of Drake's circumnavigation, for Nicholas stated that others would 'justly sett foorth his paynes and travell.'[21] The purpose of his translation appears to have been to show Drake as the example of what was required of Englishmen if their country was to rival Spain in power, for it 'set forth the dutie, and royall service, of the Subject to his Prince... and the highe waye to Honour is great paine, and daunger of lyfe.'[22] Nicholas had similarly called attention to the hard road to empire in his translation from Gómara in 1578.

The example of royal service which Nicholas brought to English readers was that of Pizarro in his conquest of Peru. While the narrative was primarily concerned with military matters, it did bring into the English language some information on the geography, natural history, cities, peoples and customs of Peru. A description of Chile was also included in Book Three, which carried the account of Diego de Almagro's expedition into that region, and this was followed by a report of the explorations of Gonzalo Pizarro in the vicinity of Quito, then considered a part of Peru. Finally, a three-page description of the mines of

Potosí in Peru was added, showing the most tangible type of reward that awaited the servant of his country who endured the hardships of exploration and conquest.

If Nicholas' purpose was to celebrate heroic actions in the national interest, he could have done it equally well with a translation of some book describing a gallant voyage, such as the Columbus *Letter* or one of the accounts of Magellan's circumnavigation. These were more akin to Drake's achievement and showed equally well the mettle required of men in building an empire. But it was the appeal of gold primarily that held English eyes on America, and Nicholas suited his selection of an account of overseas enterprise to the prevailing taste.

While investors in American enterprises were to think chiefly in terms of enriching themselves through the discovery of gold mines, the appeal of settlements to relieve England of her paupers and establish an English nation in the New World persisted in the thinking of a few imperialists. Foremost among these was Sir Humphrey Gilbert, who in 1582 launched a new colonial venture which showed an appreciation of England's social and economic problems for which the New World could be expected to provide some answers. He offered England's capitalists vast expanses of land in which to invest. He intended to make his colony a refuge for those who could not accept Elizabeth's religious settlement; he would transport paupers and provide them with land; he would establish North American bases as an English balance against Spain in the New World; he would guarantee the protection of a northwest passage if one should be found. To manage this undertaking a joint-stock company was formed under the title 'The Merchant Adventurers with Sir Humphrey Gilbert.' It was controlled from Southampton, and it excluded from participation all members of the Muscovy Company.[23] In this latter provision we may see Gilbert's recognition of the fact that the Muscovy Company was casting about for new enterprises and it appeared to have an agent in Christopher Carleill who looked to the merchants of Bristol and London, likely sources of sufficient capital, to support an American colony. It was still the seaports of the south and west of England that looked toward America, however, and as colonization became a part of that westward orientation they were the group most interested in it, while the London merchants in general showed no great interest.[24] In leadership, management and interest, the Gilbert colonization scheme was a west-country undertaking.

As Gilbert made ready for his departure, Richard Hakluyt issued from the press of Thomas Dawson an eloquent plea for colonization. Hakluyt was by this time about thirty years old, and he had made it a point to be acquainted with England's foremost seamen and merchants. The knowledge he acquired was apparently too great for him to organize into a coherent colonial propaganda message, but there can be no question about the sincerity with which he attempted to use it to promote imperialism. His biographer states that Hakluyt's *Divers voyages*, published in 1582, declared his maturity.[25] This mature view saw the futility of hanging petty criminals in England when a continent across the ocean awaited their coming. Hakluyt knew where England stood in the 'flourishing age,' but he did not often relate his knowledge of the outer world to England's problems of pauperism and discontent in a style that made stimulating reading.

The *Divers voyages* is a great source of information on America, most of it without commentary, revealing the compiler to be a master collector, wanting in both system and popular appeal as an editor. Preceding his dedication to Sir Philip Sidney, he inserted three pages of miscellany including a list of 'certaine late writers of Geographie,' 'certaine late travaylers, both by sea and by land,' and 'a verie late and great probabilitie of a passage, by the Northwest part of America.'[26] The lists of writers and travelers appear somewhat arbitrary, and the northwest passage argument is clearly an insertion of the last moment which 'may bee well annexed unto the other eight reasons mentioned in my epistle dedicatorie.'[27]

The Epistle Dedicatory to Sidney had several purposes. At the outset it declared the folly of hanging able men for petty crimes instead of using them for colonists. Hakluyt's view of colonization was based upon the principle of using the New World to rid England of her 'superfluous people.' He then went to the defense of the idea of searching for a northwest passage, advancing proofs for its existence, much in the manner of Gilbert's *Discourse*, only with brevity. Finally, he revealed what appears to be the main object of his dedication. He felt that the great lack in England was knowledge of navigation and geography, and he favored the establishment of a lectureship in these subjects. This would have to be paid for by some generous person, and he stated that Sir Francis Drake had agreed to give twenty pounds annually for that purpose. The candidate for the position, however, had asked forty pounds for his services, and Hakluyt concluded, 'Nowe if God shoulde put it into the head of any noble man to contribute other twentie pounde, to make this lecture a competent living for a learned man, the whole realme no doubt might reape no small benefite thereby.'[28] In this concern he was reiterating the plea Richard Willes had made five years earlier; he was in effect urging the nobility to become a partner in the improvement of England, just as he had done in Florio's translation of Cartier's narratives, when he urged the nobility to promote the translation of useful books. A response to his plea was made in 1588 by Sir Thomas Smith and Lord Lumley who sponsored Thomas Hood as Mathematical Lecturer to the City of London.[29]

The text of the *Divers voyages* contains a great variety of material relating to North America including letters patent from Henry VII to John Cabot, a note on Sebastian Cabot's voyage of 1498, and remarks from Ramusio on Cabot. Here for the first time was published Robert Thorne's *Declaration of the Indes* and Thorne's 'Book' of 1527, which noted the progress of Portugal and Spain as well as England's hope for an improved trade if a northern passage could be found. Other items included were Verazano's description of North America which was a favorable view of the coast and its products based upon his voyage of 1524; an account of the Zeno Brothers' voyage to Greenland in 1380;[30] a reprint of the Ribaut narrative of 1563; and instructions for settlement in the form of 'Notes framed by a Gentleman heretofore to bee given to one that prepared for a discoverie, and went not.'[3] He included the map of North America made by Robert Thorne in 1527 and another by Michael Lok in 1582. The former he acknowledged to be out of date, but he did not apologize for the latter which is hardly more accurate and is completely at variance with the major maps of North America of that time in its portrayal of the 'Sea of Verazano' reaching eastward from the Pacific to within a few miles of the Atlantic seaboard.[32]

It was either Hakluyt's rather indiscriminate gathering of material or great breadth of purpose that led him to include in this book a set of instructions given to Pet and Jackman for their northeastern venture for the Muscovy Company in 1580. He considered these 'not altogether unfit for some other enterprises of discoverie.'[33] This information on Nova Zemlya and Cambalu was hardly pertinent to the Gilbert expedition then pending, and the fact that members of the Muscovy Company were excluded from participation in Gilbert's colony would not have made the inclusion of this material popular with Gilbert and his associates. Its inclusion may have served the Muscovy Company's interest, however, and any English agency of expansion could expect the good will of Richard Hakluyt.

There is ample evidence in the text and in the dedication to Sidney, a supporter of Gilbert, that the *Divers voyages* was intended as propaganda for Gilbert's proposed voyage. If it is considered as propaganda rather than as historical material, it has obvious failings, for while it provided England with much useful information, it lacked the continuity and emotional appeal which could have been given to it in an elementary commentary. Despite his own deep convictions about expansion, Hakluyt did not see his function to be that of actively arousing his generation to the cause, for aside from his deep concern for petty criminals bound for the gallows he appealed to no group.

Hakluyt's zeal for translations could have been used to improve his book had he been able to add to his *Divers voyages* a translation of the work of a contemporary, Stephan Parmenius, a Hungarian at Oxford, whose passion for bringing Christianity to the American natives was not shared by Gilbert, and probably not by Hakluyt. Permenius looked to the New World with hope: 'Am I deceived, or is this the golden age about to dawn again... But if we may not yet admit that this golden age has come again in our world, what is there to prevent its existence in lands unknown.'[34] Of the New World he believed, 'There a man's value will not be measured by birth, nor the people's liberty crushed by riches.' He called for help on behalf of the American natives at the hands of the Spaniards and their religion. 'Why,' he asked, 'do we see men reduced by fire, starvation or the sword in the name of religion.'[35] Here were appeals that might have aided Hakluyt's cause, and they would be made again during his lifetime with some success. These were words of conviction with the zealous Hungarian, for he sailed with Gilbert and lost his life in the voyage.

On June 11, 1583, Gilbert set forth with five ships, carrying with him a token from the Queen, 'an ancor guyded by a lady.' One of the ships put back into Plymouth two days later, apparently for want of adequate provisions. The remaining ships arrived in St. John's harbor, Newfoundland, in August, and Gilbert set himself to establishing control over the international colony of fishermen which frequented those shores. He spent a brief period prospecting and mapping on the island and then took three ships on an exploratory voyage to the west and northwest. This terminated with the wreck of one of the ships and a loss of eighty men. With provisions low, and the crew discouraged and homesick, Gilbert decided to return to England, although planning to be back in Newfoundland the next year. On the night of September 9, however, Gilbert's little ship, the *Squirrel*, went down, and he with it.

Gilbert's death brought no serious interruption in the efforts of his group to establish a colony in America, for he had gathered around him men of enthusiasm for the undertaking, notably Sir George Peckham, Christopher Carleill, and Sir Thomas Gerrard, as well as Sir Philip Sidney. Also, the proposed colony had become more than a private undertaking, for it came to appeal somewhat to a group of Catholics and Catholic sympathizers who were feeling the pressure of Elizabeth's stiffening religious policy which levied fines of twenty pounds per month for noncomformity. As Peckham and Gerrard were both Catholics, they tied into Gilbert's plan for removal of members of their faith to America, and had Elizabeth been willing to let them go without requiring the payment of fines by the wealthier Catholics, the Gilbert expedition might well have been largely Catholic in makeup.[36] Thus America had almost come to assume the position Churchyard, Gilbert and Hakluyt had envisioned for it, a refuge for people not wanted in England, although their concern had been primarily for the economically distressed. It was such a function that could give the New World a genuine popular appeal.

After Gilbert's death it was Sir George Peckham who most actively promoted this colonization scheme, although it is impossible to say to what degree his efforts were based upon his Catholic sentiments. He received a grant of land from Sidney, who had been accused of Catholic sympathies, and late in 1583 he published a work of considerable interest as propaganda, his *True reporte of the late discoveries... of the new-found landes*. Until that time no book had been so clearly related to a particular colonial undertaking. Peckham dedicated his pamphlet to Sir Francis Walsingham, who had played a prominent part in bringing Gilbert and the Catholic group together, commending him for his interest in furthering western discoveries. He then attempted to show the popularity of his plan by publishing commendatory poems under names of persons of distinction. Sir William Pelham appeared as the author of four verses in this vein:

> *Our forren neighbours bordering hard at hand,*
> *Have found it true, to many thousands gaine:*
> *And are inricht by this abounding land,*
> *While pent at home, like sluggards we remaine.*
> *But though they have, to satisfie their will*
> *Inough is left, our cofers yet to fill.*[37]

Then followed fourteen lines attributed to Sir Francis Drake, who foretold benefits in America for all types of Englishmen, concluding,

> *So that, for each degree, this Treatise dooth unfolde:*
> *The path to Fame, the proofe of Zeale, the way to purchase gold.*[38]

John Hawkins, treasurer of the navy, spoke 'his opinion on this intended voyage,'

> *So England that is pestered nowe, and choakt through want of ground*
> *Shall find a soile where roome inough, and perfect doth abound.*[39]

Peckham's intended enterprise was similarly praised in verse by Captains Richard Bingham and John Chester, the poet Matthew Roydon, merchants Anthony Parkhurst, Arthur Hawkins and John Ashley and by Martin Frobisher, who saw in this venture 'a certaine gaine, a never dying praise.'[40]

Peckham's text was to the point and convincing. He described Gilbert's taking possession of the new land for England in the presence of foreign fishermen, and he assured the reader that this was a good title, permitting him to propose settlements for English colonists between thirty and sixty degrees north latitude. In stating the purpose of his book, he expressed a desire to convince those who had opposed western planting 'by reason perhappes that they have not deliberately and advisedly entered into the judgement of the matter,'[41] and he called on those who had wealth to leave off spending it in luxurious living and use it instead to support his venture. He showed how trade and colonization would benefit all England: there would be an English harbor for fishermen, cloth from England would clothe natives in America, the navy would be enlarged, and idle men and women would be given employment. He showed that noblemen and gentlemen might find in America a good climate, good hunting, good wine. Merchants could choose from more than seventy products listed, and in associating themselves with Peckham's enterprise they would be bound to only one adventure, and that with a promise of monopoly for the future to the original investors. He saw no great effort required to establish a colony, as he wrote, 'Planting in these parts is a thing that may be doone without the aide of Princes power and purse.'[42] Food was there, armor was not needed, the voyage was easy.

Here was an argument more potent than Hakluyt's. It offered profit to England and to every class of Englishmen. It promised to bring national and private gain without help from the Crown and without heavy military investment. While Peckham's *True reporte* acknowledged that the savages of America would benefit from the arrival of English men there, his chief appeal was the benefits Englishmen would receive, particularly the merchant group. In this he was ably seconded by Christopher Carleill whose *Discourse upon the entended voyage to... America* was even more directly intended for England's merchants. Carleill wrote this tract in April, 1583, and he went straight to the point on the title page to describe the difficulties the promoters of this colonizing venture had experienced in trying to raise money for it. The tract was written, he said. 'for the better inducement to satisfie suche Marchauntes, as in disbursing their money towardes the furniture of the present charge: doe demaunde forthwith a present returne of gaine: albeit their saied perticuler disburcementes are in such slender sommes, as are not worth the speakyng of.'[43]

Carleill invited comparison of the commercial potential of America with the benefits deriving from other areas where English merchants were engaged in commerce. He called attention to the heavy investment required of the Muscovy merchants before the trade there began to yield a profit, and he went on to warn of the instability of the Russian government which made the Muscovy Company's trade undependable. He observed that the voyage to Russia could be made only once a year, and that merchants using the Baltic route were subject to the good will of the Danish king. The rising competition from Dutch merchants trading to Russia was also pointed out. Turning to the 'Easterling' trade, through which England derived much-needed goods from the Baltic region, Carleill pointed out its unreliability, mentioning the recent denial of English commercial rights in that area. The Levant trade, he noted, was extremely competitive and was based on commercial intercourse with non-Christian peoples, while the Mediterranean commerce placed English seamen in constant danger from pirates and forced English merchants in Spain and Portugal to live under continual pressure to renounce their Protestant faith.

America, on the other hand, offered a voyage that could be completed in four months. The winds were favorable, there was no danger from foreign governments, and good harbors in England and Ireland faced westward toward the New World. Carleill did not promise immediate profits on a large scale, but he did make the prediction that in thirty years there would be two ships returning with goods from

America for every one coming from Muscovy. He described the products immediately available, chiefly fish and naval stores, and saw in the future a good production of grapes, wax, honey, and salt. In so large a country, he believed, there must ultimately be a great demand for English woolens, and he held out the hope that somewhere in that vast continent might lie the passage to the Pacific Ocean which Englishmen had sought so long. He cautioned, however, against great hopes for gold, noting that people had been disappointed by such promises before.

Like Hakluyt, Carleill recognized the necessity of planting an English population in America, and he referred to the hundred colonists that were ready to go with his proposed voyage. The poor people of England who were a menace to the well-to-do would, he believed, do well in this new environment. He made it clear, however, that his appeal was not to them, but to the merchants; when the project was under way it would be time to explain to the common sort those things about America which were beyond their present understanding. Citing the recent success of the French in the St. Lawrence region, he concluded with a plea to the merchants to support his undertaking, in which he was investing far more than he asked from them.

Carleill's *Discourse* makes it abundantly clear that the merchants of England were not willing to invest in this enterprise, and were, therefore, the major stumbling block in the way of the establishment of an English colony in America; for until investment was assured no appeal for settlers could be made. Considering the Catholicism of the major promoters of the colony, it was impossible to use religion as an appeal to gain the merchants' support, for London's merchants were, in the main, conformists to the Queen's church. Without an emotional approach, and unable to promise 'a present returne of gaine', the North American venture of Peckham and Carleill never materialized. The reason was a simple lack of interest on the part of those with the means to invest. Despite the eloquent pleas of Peckham and Carleill, whose publications represent the first campaign for support of a particular colonial undertaking, only Exeter is known to have promised funds, and then only seven men were sufficiently interested to invest twelve pounds, ten shillings each.[44] The royal purse was not called upon and was not offered in support of the colony. Indeed, the Crown may have been actively opposed, for in 1584 Peckham's solicitations were stopped when he was imprisoned for his Catholic activities.

These were hard years on dissenters from the official faith: while the Society of Jesus was sending priests into England in disguise, English policy was taking note of malcontents and possible defectors in preparation for the inevitable showdown with the champion of the Roman church. A Protestant merchant observing the struggle of the neighboring United Provinces of the Netherlands to establish their independence from Spain might well turn a deaf ear to the pleas of proponents of a Catholic-sponsored colony in America. Catholicism in the Netherlands represented—in the eyes of Englishmen of 1584—a threat to the English nation and to its Protestant religion.

It was precisely this atmosphere of anti-Catholicism that brought into the English language the critical account of Spanish doings in America by Bartolomé de las Casas, Bishop of Chiapa, whose criticism of his own countrymen abroad was used as evidence of the cruelty of the Spaniards to those who did not bend to their will and their religion. The bishop's indictment of Spanish administrators in America was translated from Spanish into French in 1579 'to serve as a warning to the XII provinces of the lowe Countries' of the true nature of their adversary. The unknown English translator, who titled his book *The Spanish colonie... in the West Indies*, took the French translation whole, including the translators declaration of purpose, suggesting that its purpose in England was the same as it had been in the Netherlands.[45] He gave to his readers a book about America which told little of the New World except of the cruelty with which the Spaniards used the natives in their colonies. In spite of the religious and nationalistic appeal inherent in this book, it knew only one English edition; even accounts of Spanish atrocities could not assure a publisher of a large audience for a book that related to America.

England was by no means aroused to an interest in the outer world. The apathy that apparently greeted the translation of Las Casas extended to works on the East Indies also. Just two years after Drake's circumnavigation proclaimed the accessibility of the East Indies to English shipping, Nicholas Lichfield published his translation of the first book of Lopes de Castanheda's monumental history of Portuguese expansion into Asia. This *Historie of the discoverie and conquest of the East Indies* was dedicated to Sir Francis Drake, and the translator promised that if this first book were well received by English readers, the second and third books of Castanheda would be forthcoming shortly. They never appeared. In translating this history of Portuguese eastern imperialism to 1525, Nicholas Lichfield gave to English readers the accounts of Diaz, Covilhan, Da Gama, Cabral, the cousins Albuquerque, Pacheco and other Portuguese pioneers of eastern exploration, trade and conquest. In these narratives he set forth the navigations, battles, difficulties, and triumphs of the first East Indian empire; he also revealed the 'commodities and riches that every of these places doth yield.' [46]

While Thomas East, the publisher of this important and informative work, apparently was not encouraged by its sale to publish the second and third books of Castanheda, he did see fit to publish a new edition of Sir John Mandeville's *Travels* in 1583. Using the same illustrations as had appeared in the 1568 edition, East made no attempt to edit or correct, but merely reproduced a very unsophisticated book for his Elizabethan clientele. [47]

Not all Elizabethans, however, were satisfied with such crude literature on the outer world. While nobody published a criticism of Mandeville, André Thevet, the French royal cosmographer, was taken sharply to task by Thomas Nicholas, the merchant, who had been in the Canary Islands for seven years. When he read the account of those islands by Thevet in the English edition of 1568, he forthwith wrote his *Pleasant description of the Fortunate Ilands* to correct the information given out by Thevet, 'who wrote of the Fortunate Ilandes by hearesay.' [48] Nicholas' work is a handbook, with no apparent motive other than to provide correct information concerning islands which he knew well. He conjectured briefly on the origin of the islands and their earliest inhabitants, and then related their discovery in modern times, providing a good account of the natural products of the islands, their government, size, topography and towns. This handbook must be regarded as a useful guide to the Canary Islands, although it was very badly printed by Thomas East.

In publishing three books of overseas interest in 1582 and 1583, Thomas East was apparently trying the book market in an area where he had ventured only once before with his 1568 edition of Mandeville. He was able to test the general interest in travel literature with these three books of entirely different types and it is significant that none of these books was issued by him again—in fact, he did not undertake the publication of any more travel accounts even though he continued to publish until 1609.

Despite this apparent apathy toward overseas subjects on the part of the general public and despite the concern of the Crown for the forthcoming showdown with Spain, the current of interest in North

America set in motion by Gilbert's voyage, and swelled by the efforts of Sidney and Peckham, continued to grow. Upon Gilbert's death the major proponent of North American planting came to be his half-brother, Sir Walter Raleigh, who had been interested enough in Gilbert's plans to captain one of the ships of the abortive voyage of 1578–79. In subsequent years Raleigh advanced in position at court and received command of a company of troops in Ireland. Returning at the end of 1581, he came to the attention of the Queen, and his rise in her service enabled him to invest perhaps 2,000 pounds in Gilbert's voyage of 1583.[49] On March 25, 1584, the patent formerly held by Gilbert was transferred to Raleigh, and a month later Captains Amadas and Barlowe set out to reconnoiter the American coast at a point farther south than Gilbert had attempted to explore. Raleigh's decision to concentrate on more southerly latitudes shows a willingness to approach the dominions of Spain; in place of the earlier inclination of Englishmen to accept banishment to the northerly regions, it revealed an attitude of confidence in England's ability to maintain a colony on the edge of the enemy's sphere of influence.

The belief that a colony could be planted and successfully maintained on the American coast just north of Spanish Florida was bolstered by optimistic reports brought back by Amadas and Barlowe in September, 1584. Further hope for its success was provided by Richard Hakluyt, who drafted a report on the types of settlers that would be required, the products to be produced, the damage that such a settlement could do to Spanish shipping, and the general long range benefits that England might reap from developing a new economy across the Atlantic. This *Discourse of western planting* was not published, and it therefore made no appeal to dissidents and others whom Hakluyt would have included in the proposed colony. Instead of making a public appeal as Peckham and Carleill had done, the planners chose to communicate only with those at the policy-making level of government. This decision has been attributed to the necessity of secrecy in order that the Spaniards might not know of the location of the intended colony.[50] There was undoubtedly virtue in an official silence, but the expression of English interest in America, both in print and in action, could have left no doubt in Spanish minds that the interest was genuine, at least on the part of a few vigorous imperialists. If keeping the exact location of the colony a secret was the intention, and if publication of a prospectus on the new colony had been considered worth while, it would have put no strain upon Elizabethan morality to have published intentions of inhabiting an area some distance to the north of the intended site of the settlement.

Surely there was nothing to be gained, except public interest, in the publication of the plans for this American colony. But Spanish knowledge of the settlement was a certainty, regardless of publicity, and the colony must have been planned with the confidence that Spain either would not interfere, or that her opposition could be fended off by English sea power. The lack of publicity, therefore, was likely less due to Spanish attitudes than to the fact that the idea of making overseas ventures a public concern had not yet occurred to the planners. They spoke of *sending* unwanted elements of the population to America, but they had not yet reached the point of *offering* these people the opportunity of going there. They apparently had sufficient financial backing and did not need to make the appeal that Peckham and Carleill had made. If the public was indifferent, that was of little concern to those who planned the venture, for they had no need of public support.

The evidence of public indifference had been noted by those who were confident of England's abilities and ambitions for empire from the time of Richard Eden; now, as competence in navigation was becoming increasingly apparent, the lack of public interest continued as the great frustration of ardent imperialists. In 1585 England's greatest hero, Sir Francis Drake, sailed for the West Indies with Spanish plunder in mind, and at his departure a *Friendly farewell* was written by Henry Roberts, a hanger-on at court whose crude poetry is reminiscent of Thomas Churchyard's verses of 1578. Roberts' purpose was as much to rouse England out of her lethargy toward her heroes of the sea as it was to commend Drake. He cited the English custom 'to represent unto our betters whom we honour some simple gift as a farewell in writing whereby their names might be remembered in their absence,'[51] and continued that, 'seeing none of the learned sort have undertaken to write according to custom,'[52] it fell to him to make some gesture of appreciation to a national hero. He was offended by scholars who wrote of less heroic people, noting that Drake had not yet been adequately presented to the English people and that, when one such as Gilbert was gone, he was quickly forgotten. Roberts was keenly aware that imperialism had not caught on in England.

Roberts' *Friendly farewell* is actually a laudatory poem to Drake, a simple doggerel verse, the sense and spirit of which are contained in these lines:

*For dastardes use at home to stay, and there will sit and talk.*
*When you in many a forren soil in danger daily walk.*[53]

*Thy parting nowe is blased abroad, as every tongue can tell,*
*Thy ships are lancht, thy sailes are hoist, Syr Francis Drake farewell.*[54]

For all its crudeness, this is an attempt to make English imperialism a popular interest; yet the poor quality of the printing suggests that these vigorous sentiments were a marginal type of literature, handled by marginal craftsmen.

Drake's return was also celebrated with poetry, as Thomas Greepe, an obscure rustic, composed a ballad of seventy-one verses which he called *The True and perfecte newes of the woorthy and valiaunt exploytes, performed and doone by... Syr Frauncis Drake.* Although slightly better poetry than that of Roberts, these verses were intended for the same purpose: to praise Drake and to give the English readers an appreciation of the significance and facts of his hero's raid into Spanish America. Greepe acknowledged that this news of Drake would not be unfamiliar to the Earl of Cumberland, to whom he dedicated his book, 'yet the vulgar sort of people in the Realme having hearde, and yet wanting the veritie of the same, may by this pamphlet be the better advertised.'[55] He recognized his particular qualifications for telling the story to them, saying, 'howe much the playner it is written by mee, the better it is to be understoode of the simplest, who in this case I seeke most to please, beeing my self a rude Countriman.'[56]

A confidence in an aroused England is apparent in Greepe's Epistle to the Reader where he wrote: 'But nowe may the enemie see what woulde come to passe, if our gracious Queene would bende her whole force against them...'[57] The stature of England's greatest seaman was unsurpassed in Greepe's view:

*Ulisses with his Navie great*
*In ten yeeres space great valour wonne:*
*Yet all this time did no such feate,*
*As Drake within one yeere hath doone,*
    *Both Turke and Pope and all our foes:*
    *Doo dread this Drake where ere he goes.*[58]

For the most part, however, the ballad is a narrative of Drake's voyage, showing that the author had access to more information than was available to the general public. In fact, this ballad was the first account of the voyage to be published, but Greepe chose to omit the significant information that the voyage was a financial failure, as investors realized only fifteen shillings on the pound.[59]

Another fact that Greepe did not mention was that among those who returned to England in Drake's ship was a group of English colonists who had attempted to get Raleigh's American colony under way. On April 9, 1585, Sir Richard Grenville sailed for the New World from Plymouth with seven ships and some 300 to 400 men in addition to the ships' crews. During July and August the colony established itself on Roanoke Island, and in September Grenville returned to England, leaving 107 settlers under the command of Ralph Lane as governor. On his return, Grenville brought to England Spanish ships and cargoes to the value of at least 15,000 pounds,[60] which kept in the forefront of English imperialist thinking the possibility of great wealth without settlement and cultivation in the New World.

As Grenville left Roanoke for England, Drake was leaving England for the West Indies on a raiding mission that took him to Cuba, Santo Domingo, the Spanish Main and Florida. A part of the plan for this voyage was for Drake to call at Grenville's colony on his way home, and when he arrived there on June 9, 1586, he found the colony in need of provisions and anxiously awaiting reinforcements. The provisions Drake offered to leave were destroyed in a storm and it was decided that the colony should be abandoned and that the settlers should return to England with Drake. Later in 1586 a supply ship sent by Raleigh arrived to provision the colony, but it arrived after the colonists had left and turned back to England with the supplies. Grenville also returned to Roanoke, not knowing that his colonists had departed, and when he found no trace of them, he left another company of fifteen men to retain posession of the land for England. These disappeared, leaving no evidence of their fate. In spite of the gloom being spread by most of the settlers who returned from Roanoke with Drake, Raleigh continued to plan for more American settlements: in 1587, before the fate of Grenville's fifteen colonists was known, another group was sent out to settle at Chesapeake Bay with John White as the leader. One hundred ten settlers were left in the new settlement when White returned to England in August, 1587.[61]

Those who knew America from a brief colonial experience said little in its favor, but the optimism and hope of those who had not been there are reflected in two publications of 1587 relating to the New World. A description of the travels of Antonio de Espejo in North America, which had been an addition to Gonzales de Mendoza's description of China and had been separately published in both Spanish and French by Richard Hakluyt in Paris, was translated into English in 1587 as *New Mexico, Otherwise, the voiage of Anthony of Espejo*.[62] Dedicated to Henry Anderson, merchant, this pamphlet of sixteen pages conveniently tied together English hopes for a large population in North America and the still active hope for a northwest passage to Asia, as it recounted Espejo's journeys in the southwest part of North America in 1582. It reported fruitful lands and large populations, with towns of 40,000 souls mentioned in an area that was vaguely linked by rivers to the northern part of the continent. The dedication claimed the pamphlet 'revealeth more rivers and people, toward our northern parts then others heretofore have done.'[63] This becomes more noteworthy when read in connection with the following from the title page, '... and some suppose that the same way men may by places inhabited go to the land tearmed De Labrador.' The idea of a water passage from Labrador to a well-populated region in western North America was entirely in harmony with the hope for an easy access to a large market for England's surplus woolens.

Optimism over England's future in America continued also to be expressed in the writings of Richard Hakluyt, who, although living in Paris much of the time between 1587 and 1588, still showed an active interest in the Roanoke colony. In 1587 he translated Laudonnière's account of the French attempts to settle Florida in the 1560s. His *Notable historie containing foure voyages... unto Florida* was directly related to the Roanoke venture, for he dedicated it to Raleigh and stated that the errors of the French recorded in this book ought to stand as a warning to England. He encouraged Raleigh to continue his Virginia planting, reaffirming his previously expressed view that it would yield a rich harvest for England when planted and filled with European products. He believed that Virginia could be easily managed because it would be proved shortly by the voyages of John Davis that this land mass did not extend very far to the west. Also he contended that a force of ten thousand men could hold it against Spain, and he felt that this many men could be spared. The Indians would not be difficult, he believed, because they were more agreeable than those to be found in New Spain. The translation of Laudonnière's preface gave Hakluyt a chance to say in English that two reasons existed for colonizing: the desire to discover new commodities and the need to find an outlet for surplus population. And when people were sent out to colonize, they should be 'of so juste and sufficient number, that [they] may not bee defeited by strangers.' [64]

The text contained a description of the fruitfulness of Florida, followed by the details of the loss of the French establishment there. Dissension and lack of military strength were clearly the reasons for the French failure, according to the narrative, for they invited Spanish attack. The lesson was plain for Englishmen to read, and the book was more a lecture to England's promoters of colonies than propaganda directed toward prospective settlers. Hakluyt's message was badly timed. England could not spare ten thousand men for the defense of Virginia in 1587. She could not spare Grenville and enough shipping to keep alive the little colony on Roanoke the following year, for the inevitability of a showdown with Spain was becoming more apparent. Furthermore, Hakluyt's plea for unity of command and strength of leadership was daily challenged by those who had returned from Roanoke with no kind words for that colony.

It is obvious that residence in the Roanoke settlement did not develop an enthusiasm for imperialism among the colonists, for it was in defense of the colony and its management that the only book to describe it was published. Thomas Hariot had been sent to Virginia by Raleigh to observe the natural products of the region, and his *Brief and true report* was published primarily to correct the false impressions being spread abroad in England to the prejudice of any continued effort in Virginia. The title page declared that the book was 'Directed to the Adventurers, Favourers, and Welwillers of the action, for the inhabiting and planting there,' and to the reader it was quickly apparent that it was directed against the 'many which had little understanding, lesse discretion, and more tongue then was needful or requisite.' [65]

Following the introduction, the text was divided into two major subjects, the commodities of Virginia and the native inhabitants. The former was given the greater emphasis, and the discussion of products was divided among commodities which could be sold profitably, goods available to sustain the colonists, and other products such as building materials. Among the merchantable commodities Hariot listed and described silks, dyes, gums and fruits. Among the native commodities for the sustenance of life he enumerated a great variety of fruits, fowl, fish and animals, while building material was described as abundant in the form of stone and timber of great variety.

The Indians of Virginia were portrayed as poor by English standards, but not wanting in intelligence, 'for although they have no such tooles, nor any such craftes, sciences and artes as wee; yet in those things they doe, they shewe excellencie of wit.'[66] Hariot indicated no great passion to carry England's religion to these people. 'Some religion they have alreadie,' he wrote, 'which although it be farre from the truth, yet beyng as it is, there is hope that it may bee easier and sooner reformed,' and he added that 'through conversing with us they were brought into great doubts of their owne, and no small admiration of ours, with earnest desire in many, to learne more than we had meanes for want of perfect utterance in their language to express.'[67] He was more concerned that the natives become obedient and agreeable than that they should be assured of salvation.

In his conclusion, Hariot summed up his reasons for optimism: 'Seeing therefore the ayre is so temperate and holsome, the soyle so fertile and yeelding such commodities as I have before mentioned, the voyage also thither to and from being sufficiently experimented, to bee performed thrise a yeere with ease and at any season thereof: And the dealing of Sir Walter Raleigh so liberall in large giving and granting land there, as is alreadie knowen, with many helpes and furtherances els:... I hope there remaine no cause wherby the action should be misliked.'[68] Hariot's optimism served two causes: it was both a defense of Raleigh and his colony that had failed, and an attempt to hold the adventurers to the cause and keep alive in England the prospect of a settlement in America. Yet his concern was that interest be maintained at the level of investment rather than settlement, for his book is clearly not an appeal to settlers, and the statement of Ralph Lane, governor of the colony, that it was published at the request of certain of his friends shows it to be an attempt to maintain some investor interest, rather than a response to a positive public interest.

For all of its defensiveness, Hariot's *Briefe and true report* was the most convincing plea for North American colonization made thus far in Elizabeth's reign; though it lacked the emotion of Peckham's book, it was far more informative. It was not, however, sufficiently convincing to save the Roanoke colony. Events were against the colonizers. Grenville had four ships ready to sail with supplies for Virginia in 1588, but that was the year of the Armada, and he was restrained from sending more than two small boats which gave themselves to piracy and were in turn preyed upon and returned to England without reaching North America. When relief ships were finally sent in 1590 the colony had disappeared.

The great Armada victory, therefore, was not without cost to the dream of empire that had been nourished in the minds of Raleigh and his associates. There was no book published to mourn the loss, nor was there one to celebrate the victory. Literature designed to enlist English interest in North America was not to appear again until 1602, proving that Raleigh's colony and the books of Peckham, Carleill and Hariot had not aroused the type of public reponse that would induce a publisher in the intervening to years invest in books on this subject.

## NOTES TO CHAPTER VII

1 G. D. Ramsay, *English overseas trade during the centuries of emergence* (London: Macmillan & Co. Ltd., 1957), p. 31.
2 John Lothrop Motley, *The rise of the Dutch Republic* (3 vols.; New York, Harper & Brothers, 1874), I, 482.
3 Ramsey, pp. 33, 38–40.
4 Alfred C. Wood, *A history of the Levant Company* (London: Oxford University Press, 1935), p. 6.
5 Albert Lindsay Rowland, 'England and Turkey: The rise diplomatic and commercial relations,' *Studies in English commerce and exploration in the reign of Elizabeth* (Philadelphia: University of Pennsylvania Press, 1924), pp. xvi–xvii.
6 Wood, p. 10.
7 Rowland, p. 18.
8 William R. Scott, *The constitution and finance of English, Scottish and Irish joint stock companies to 1720* (3 vols.; Cambridge, Cambridge University Press, 1912), II, 84.
9 Rowse, *Sir Richard Grenville*, p. 154.
10 W. J. Harte, 'Some recent views on Drake's voyage around the world,' *History*, new series, XX (March, 1936), 348–53.
11 Henry R. Wagner, *Sir Francis Drake's voyage around the world* (San Francisco: John Howell, 1926), pp. 15–27, discusses possible motives and the historiography of Drake's voyage, noting the varying emphasis upon piracy, exploration, and statesmanship to fit different periods of English history.
12 E. G. R. Taylor (ed.) *The troublesome voyage of Captain Edward Fenton* (Cambridge: The Hakluyt Society, 1959), pp. xxx, xxxiv.
13 Parks, *Hakluyt*, pp. 57–60.
14 Jacques Cartier, *A shorte and briefe narration of the two navigations and discoveries to the northwest partes called New Fraunce*, trans. John Florio (London: Henry Bynneman, 1580), fol. Aii recto. Florio translated from the Italian version in Ramusio, *Delle navigationi et viaggi*, III, published in Venice, 1556. The narrative of the second voyage was first published as *Brief recit, & succincte narration de la navigation faicte es ysles de Canada* (Paris: Ponce Roffet & Anthoine le Clerc, 1545). Florio is best known for his Italian-English dictionary, but he was very much a part of the literary society in England. See Frances A. Gates, *John Florio* (Cambridge: Cambridge University Press, 1934).
15 Cartier, fol. Bii recto.
16 Quinn, *Gilbert*, I, 40, notes that in September, 1578, Gilbert had 500 men ready to sail. This strongly suggests a colony was planned. The armanent of 122 guns indicates that opposition from Spain was anticipated; therefore a far northern voyage cannot have been in Gilbert's mind.

17 Cartier, fol. Bii recto.
18 *Ibid.*, fol. Bii verso.
19 *Ibid.*, fol. Bi recto.
20 *Ibid.*, p. 80.
21 Augustín de Zárate, *The discoverie and conquest of the provinces of Peru*, trans. Thomas Nicholas (London: Richard Jhones, 1581), fol. ¶ i verso. The first edition was published as *Historia del descubrimiento y conquista del Peru* (Antwerp: Martin Nucio, 1555).
22 Zárate, *fol.* ¶ 4 verso.
23 Quinn, *Gilbert*, I, 55–61; William G. Gosling, *The life of Sir Humphrey Gilbert* (London: Constable and Co., 1911), pp. 206–13.
24 Quinn, *Gilbert*, I, 56.
25 Parks, *Hakluyt*, p. 68.
26 Richard Hakluyt, *Divers voyages touching the discoverie of America* (London: Thomas Dawson for Thomas Woodcocke, 1582), Title page, verso, and unnumbered second leaf, recto and verso.
27 *Ibid.*, unnumbered second leaf, verso.
28 *Ibid.*, fol. ¶ 3 verso.
29 E. G. R. Taylor, *The mathematical practitioners of Tudor and Stuart England.* (Cambridge: Cambridge University Press, 1954), p. 179.
30 The voyage of Antonio and Niccolo Zeno to Greenland is not accepted as authentic by many students of Arctic exploration. It first came to light in 1558 with the publication in Venice of an account of the voyage, together with a remarkably correct map of Greenland, supposedly based on an original manuscript source in the possession of a later member of the Zeno family who was responsible for the publication, which bore the title *De i commentarii del viaggio in Persia... et dello scoprimento dell' Isole Frislianda, Eslanda, Engrovenlanda...*
31 Hakluyt, *Divers voyages*, fol. K1 recto.
32 The 'Sea of Verazzanao' concept was based upon that explorer's belief that the Pacific Ocean lay just beyond a narrow neck of land comprising the eastern seaboard at about 40 degrees north latitude. It was shown repeatedly on portolan charts of the 1530's, but by 1580 the maps of Ortelius, Gastaldi and Mercator had given North America a very great westward extension at that latitude. Lok's belief in it can only be accounted for by his anxiety for finding a northwest passage.
33 Hakluyt, *Divers voyages*, fol. H1 recto.
34 Staphanus Parmenius, *De navigatione H. Gilberti, ad deducencam in novum orbem suscepta carmen* (London: T. Purfutium, 1582). The translation is from Gosling, *The life of Sir Humphrey Gilbert*, pp. 217–21.
35 *Ibid.*, pp. 219, 221.
36 Quinn, *Gilbert*, I, 71–75.
37 Sir George Peckham, *A true reporte of the late discoveries, and possession of the new-found landes* (London: J. Charlewood for John Hinde, 1583), fourth preliminary leaf, recto. See note 40 below regarding authorship.
38 *Ibid.*, verso.
39 *Ibid.*, fol. Si recto.
40 *Ibid.*, fol. Sii recto. The names used by Peckham as authors of these verses were for the most part names associated with overseas ventures. Drake and Frobisher were among the nation's foremost seamen. Captain Richard Bingham had early been an associate of Peckham's, as had Anthony Parkhurst. John Ashley was a London merchant and an acquaintance of the elder Richard Hakluyt. Matthew Roydon is the only member of this group who might have written verses commending the voyage, for he was a friend of Sir Philip Sidney's, took his A.M. at Oxford in 1580, and must therefore, have been known to Richard Hakluyt.

George B. Parks advances the theory that George Peele may have written the text and the poems. See his 'George Peele and his friends as 'ghost poets',' *The journal of English and German philology*, XLI (October, 1942), 527–36.

41 *Ibid.*, fol. Ci recto.

42 *Ibid.*, fol. Fiii verso.

43 Christopher Carleill, *A discourse upon the entended voyage to the hethermoste partes of America* (n. p. n. ca. 1583), fol. Ai recto. Another edition has the title *A breef and sommarie discourse uppon the entended voyage...*

44 Quinn, *Gilbert*, I, 93.

45 Bartholomé de las Casas, *The Spanish colonie, or briefe chronicle of the acts and gestes of the Spaniardes in the West Indies*, trans. M.M.S. (London: Thomas Dawson for William Brome, 1583); the French edition was published as *Tyrranies et cruautez des Espagnols, perpetrees e's Indes occidentales* (Antwerp: Franc. de Rafelenghien, 1579). The indictment of the Spanish administrators in America by Las Casas appeared in a series of nine tracts published in Seville in 1552 and 1553. See George Edward Ellis, 'Las Casas, and the relations of the Spaniards to the Indians,' in Justin Winsor ed., *Narrative and critical history of America*, II, 348. The tracts are listed on pp. 333–335. For a study of the development of Spanish attitudes toward the American Indian see Lewis Hanke, *Aristotle and the American Indians* (London: Hollis & Carter, 1959).

46 Fernão Lopes de Castanheda, *The first booke of the historie of the discoverie and conquest of the East Indies*, trans. N. L [ichfield] (London: Thomas East, 1582). fol. A2 recto. An edition of Castanheda's *Historia do descobrimento e conquista da India* was begun by J. de Barreyra and J. Alvarez in Coimbra, 1551. Only one volume was printed at that time. A new edition was undertaken in 1552 and completed in eight volumes in 1561.

47 Sir John Mandeville, *The voyages and travailes of Sir John Maundeville, knight* (London: Thomas East, [1583]).

48 [Thomas Nicholas], *A pleasant description of the Fortunate Ilands, called the Ilands of Canaria* (London: Thomas East, 1583), fol. A2 verso. See John G. Underhill, *Spanish literature in the England of the Tudors* (New York: Columbia University Press, 1899), p. 167.

49 David B. Quinn, *Raleigh and the British Empire* (New York: Collier Books, 1962), pp. 31–41.

50 Hakluyt viewed America as a possible replacement for many of England's other overseas trading outlets. See Parks, *Hakluyt*, pp. 87–98; also David B. Quinn, *The Roanoke voyages* (2 vols.; London: The Hakluyt Society, 1955), I, 6–7.

51 Henry Roberts, *A most friendly farewell... to... Sir Frauncis Drake.* (London: Walter Mantell and Thomas Lawe, [1585]), fol. A2 verso.

52 *Ibid.*

53 *Ibid.*, fol. B2 verso.

54 *Ibid.*, fol. B3 verso.

55 Thomas Greepe, *The true and perfecte newes of the woorthy and valiaunt exploytes performed and doone by ... Sir Frauncis Drake* (London: I. Charlewood for Thomas Hacket, [1587]), fol. Aii recto.

56 *Ibid.*, fol. Aii recto-verso.

57 *Ibid.*, fol. Aiii verso.

58 *Ibid.*, fol. C2 recto.

59 *Ibid.*, ed. David W. Waters (Hartford, Conn: For Henry C. Taylor, 1955), pp. 41–42.

60 Quinn, *Roanoke voyages*, I, 171.

61 Quinn, *Roanoke voyages*, II, 497–98, 539–42. Among those settling in America were eleven women and nine children, indicating the intended permanence of

the settlement. Two children were born to settlers during the summer of 1587.

62 The English edition was published in London by Thomas Cadman. For the first Spanish version see Juan González de Mendoza, *Historia de las cosas mas notables, ritos y costumbres, del gran reyno de la China* (Madrid: Pedro Madrigal, 1586). Hakluyt's Spanish edition was entitled *El viaje que hizo Antonio de Espejo* (Paris, 1586); The French edition is *Histoire des terres nouvellement descouvertes... par Antoine de Espejo* (Paris; Nicolas Roffet, 1586). Espejo's journey is mentioned in the Rome, 1585 edition of Gonzalez de Mendoza, p. 351.

63 Antonio de Espejo, *New Mexico*, ed. F. W. Hodge (Lancaster: Pa. Lancaster Press, Inc., 1928), p. 6.

64 René Goulaine de Laudonnière, *A notable historie containing foure voyages made by certayne French captaynes unto Florida*, trans. Richard Hakluyt (London: Thomas Dawson, 1587), fol. A1 verso. First published as *L'histoire notable de la Floride* (Paris: Guillaume Auvray, 1586). Laudonnière was in command of the French Florida colony at the time Hawkins called there in June 1563. He was subsequently succeeded by Ribaut as commander just before the colony was overcome by the Spaniards.

65 Thomas Hariot, *A brief and true report of the new found land of Virginia* (London: Robert Robinson , 1588) fol. A4 verso.

66 *Ibid.*, fol. E2 verso.

67 *Ibid.*, fols. E3 verso–E4 recto.

68 *Ibid.*, fol. F3 verso.

## Chapter VIII

## FAR EAST, NEAR EAST AND WEST

Among those Englishmen who looked abroad as they thought of their own and England's future, few saw in America opportunities that compared with the fabled wealth of the East. England accepted the view that the American continents were primarily a barrier preventing easy access to Asia, and while Raleigh and his compatriots sought to establish a small colony on this massive barrier, others busied themselves in assaulting the northern and southern flanks of the New World.

In 1586 Thomas Cavendish set out to duplicate Drake's circumnavigation of the earth, arriving home just after the Armada victory. He had navigated the Strait of Magellan and touched at the Philippines and at Java, staying close to Drake's route most of the time. His voyage produced no books in England, presumably for the same reason Drake's great achievement had been kept from publication.[1] Meanwhile, in 1585, 1586, and 1587, John Davis had returned to the northwest passage in an attempt to succeed where Frobisher had failed. In this effort he worked his way well into the strait between Baffin Island and Greenland that now bears his name. He had the backing of Raleigh and Walsingham, and of William Sanderson, who was also an associate of Raleigh in his Virginia colony.[2] In spite of Davis' repeated and courageous efforts, and the important people who supported him, no printer undertook to publish an account of any of his three voyages. That London was less concerned than it had been with Frobisher is attributable to the absence of any hope for immediate wealth through the discovery of gold during Davis' voyages and also to the absence of a vocal opposition such as the Muscovy Company had presented during Frobisher's voyages.

No one in England followed these voyages toward the markets of the Far East more closely than Richard Hakluyt who, although deeply interested in the colonization of America, also looked beyond the barrier to the Spice Islands and the Asiatic mainland. He took notice of the voyages of Davis and Cavendish in the introduction to Robert Parke's translation of González de Mendoza's *Historie of the great and mightie kingdome of China*, in which Cavendish was urged to lead England to China by a northern route.³ While the book was dedicated to Cavendish by Parke, the sentiments expressed in the dedication appear to be those of Hakluyt, who encouraged Parke to make the translation. Whoever the author, they reveal that the fundamental reason for expansion—the sale of English woolens—had not been lost sight of, nor had it been satisfied with markets. Here the Willoughby-Chancellor voyage was recalled as an attempt to spread Christianity and to find 'ample vent of the cloth of England... foreseeing withal how beneficiall ample vent would rise to all degrees... and especially to the infinite number of the poore sort distressed by the lacke of worke.' The author then recalled to Cavendish his recent voyage to the Philippines and the vicinity of Japan and China, declaring the great likelihood of reaching these areas by a northwest passage. He went on to assure Cavendish of the interest of 'many worshipfull and wealthie merchants of this citie and other places [who] would most willingly joyne their purses with yours.'⁴

In urging Cavendish to take up the northwest passage exploration, Hakluyt and Parke took an optimistic view that was not entirely supported by the facts. Although Cavendish was urged to take over the explorations of Davis, one of the really great navigators of his time, it was stated that Davis' efforts had produced 'reasonable contentment for the time, of the adventurers.'⁵ Why then was Cavendish being invited to undertake the northwest exploration? The answer appears to lie in the unwillingness of the backers of Davis to support a fourth voyage after three attempts had not given any reason to believe that China could be reached by this northern route.⁶ Hakluyt's hope was to interest a new group in supporting a new explorer, and he implied as much by having Parke write that the purpose in publishing this book was for the better understanding of China by 'the subjects of Englande ... and specially for the illuminating of the mindes of those, that are to take the voyage next in hande to Japan, China, and the Phillippinas.'⁷

Hakluyt's enthusiasm carried him somewhat beyond accuracy also when Parke assured Cavendish of strong support from London's merchants. Actually, of 1,175 pounds raised for the 1586 voyage, the merchants of London subscribed only 162 pounds ten shillings and were far below the cities of Exeter and Totnes in the amount subscribed. Of the 'other places' from which Cavendish was to draw support, only nine had indicated an interest in 1586, and in four instances these were not groups of merchants but individual merchants who subscribed. The withdrawal of the Exeter merchants before the beginning of Davis' third voyage proved that there was no unshakable enthusiasm among the adventurers.[8]

Parke's translation was, therefore, a vehicle to revive interest where it had waned, and while it launched no expeditions, it was nevertheless an excellent work to acquaint Englishmen with the Far East. Part One of Gonzáles de Mendoza's book describes the borders and natural products, the religion and religious ceremonies, the political organization, learning, shipbuilding, and fishing of China as well as the early Spanish contact with that country. Part Two treats the approach to China from the Philippines and gives an account of missionary activities in the islands and on the mainland. Parke took the precaution of advising the English reader that the favorable accounts of activities of Spanish priests were to be 'rather imputed unto the first writer... than to any fault of mine.'[9] The last 105 pages describe the voyage from Spain to China, via the Canary Islands, Santo Domingo, Mexico, New Mexico, Acapulco, the Ladrones, and the Philippines. Mention is made of commodities to be had in the various places, the condition of the peoples met with, and a wide variety of other useful information. Japan, Cochin China, Malaya, and India are then described in similar fashion. In short, the *Historie of China* was an advertisement of nearly all of the Spanish and Portuguese overseas connections. It gave English readers an account of many parts of the world in which they would ultimately become interested and was a fitting book to be dedicated to the circumnavigator Cavendish.

At the time it was published, however, Parke's translation probably was not of compelling interest to a large number of English readers. Indeed, the many areas described in it were not among the chief concerns of English merchants venturing abroad. The newly-formed Levant Company was a more promising enterprise than any other that had appeared to this time, and when Englishmen ultimately went to the East Indies, it was to be through the commercial arteries of the Near East. Reflecting this interest in the Levant was the publication in 1585 of a translation of Nicholas de Nicolay's very popular description of his *Navigations, peregrinations and voyages, made into Turkey.*[10] While the book is concerned primarily with the customs, religion, and dress of the peoples living under Turkish rule, it was nevertheless of imperialistic purpose, for the dedication by the translator, Thomas Washington, to Sir Henry Sidney scolded scholars who stayed at home rather than going abroad to observe other peoples and nations. In urging Englishmen to go abroad, Washington was clearly working in the interests of an expanded trade to the east, and he attempted to find in the book and the region it described marvels equal to those found in the writings of Peter Martyr and Oviedo who had described the West Indies. He might well have claimed for it considerable artistic merit, for it contains numerous engravings made in smaller format after those in the original French edition of 1567 depicting the peoples of the Near East in their native costumes. While this book might have met with greater interest in England than did the *Historie of China*, the public was again content with one edition of what must have been, due to its many illustrations, an expensive book. It was printed at the expense of John Stell who apparently was one of the Londoners becoming interested in the Levant trade.

While this trade was, in the 1580s both profitable and popular, it was not without its dangerous aspects, for the menace of pirates was a constant one, and of the many tales of capture and escape which must have been told, only the *True discription and breefe discourse of a most lamentable voiage* by Thomas Saunders, published in 1587, found its way into print.[11] The voyage of Thomas Saunders to Tripoli in Barbary in the service of the Levant Company was an unsuccessful one, for following a dispute with the ruler of Tripoli, the English party were made slaves and as captives endured a series of depressing adventures before being released. The narrative is tedious and appears to have had no particular motivation other than the telling of a story. While it could not have encouraged an interest in traveling or trading in the Mediterranean, it surely was not intended to diminish the interest that existed.

Englishmen were interested in the eastern Mediterranean for more reasons than were offered by the opportunities for trade in that area. The Levant was not only an emporium for eastern goods but was also the gateway to Persia, India, China, and the islands of the East Indies. The purposes to which English Levant merchants were to put their newly-won rights to trade in the sultan's region were soon apparent. While a brisk trade with the Levant was developing in January, 1581, the merchant traveler John Newbery was on his way from Aleppo to Ormuz, the great commercial rendezvous of the Middle East in the Persian Gulf. Two years later the Levant Company sent him and Ralph Fitch off to India and beyond. Newberry appears to have died in India, but Fitch continued on as far as Malacca, returning to England only in 1591.

The Levant Company did not publish Newbery's report on his first journey, but in 1588 a translation of the narrative of an Italian, Cesare Federici, was published which gave evidence of this English interest in the Middle East. Federici was a Venetian merchant who had spent eighteen years in the East Indies. His book, published in Venice in 1587, was read by Thomas Hickock, presumably a London merchant, who was returning to London from the Levant in the *Hercules of London*. Hickock was sufficiently impressed with Federici's observations to undertake a translation immediately, although he admitted that he was not equal to the literary task. He published this *Voyage and travaile... into the East India* in order 'that Merchants and other my Cuntrimen may reape by it.'[12]

It is not difficult to understand why Federici's book impressed Hickock, for it is a thorough description of cities and islands of the East Indies from a merchant's point of view. In giving it to English readers, Hickock did not discuss the benefit that might come to England as a nation from eastern ventures, as was commonly done in literature describing North America. He pointed out that Federici had profited greatly from a small investment, and the reader was told 'so mayest thou if thou wilt travell those Countries.'[13] No sixteenth century book, with the exception of Linschoten's *Itinerario*[14] brought into the English language so much current information on the East, and while it did not lack material on the social and religious customs of the various peoples, it was essentially a merchant's guidebook.

Federici's narrative was based on his travels that started from Venice in 1563. He went to Cyprus, Tripoli, and Aleppo before embarking on the Euphrates at Bir on a boat that carried him to Feluchia, a day and a half by land from Babylon, a city 'of great trade of Strangers.'[15] From there he went to Basra, noting en route 'a hole in the earth, which continually throweth pitch into the ayre...'[16] At Ormuz, at the head of the Persian Gulf, he again noted an abundance of commercial activity, which in this instance was under the dominance of the Portuguese who held what Federici called the most barren and dry island in all the world. Taking ship at Ormuz, the Venetian sailed to Goa and then to the nearby city of Cambaietta, and 'if I had not seene it I could not have beleeved, that there should be such a trade.'[17] He noted the goods: spices, silks, sandalwood, ivory, velvets, gold, etc. Such riches inevitably attracted thieves, and he explained the necessity of remaining in Bezenger for seven months because of the danger of highwaymen. Federici traveled as far east as Malacca, where he again remarked on the extensive trade of the city; he then turned westward, visiting Siam, Pegu and the Ganges River area. On the Ganges the Venetian merchant was amazed to find merchants attending fairs every day of the week.

With this account of Federici's eighteen years of travel in the East now in their own language, Englishmen did not lack opportunity to know of the eastern trade that lay beyond the preserve of the Levant Company. Yet the enthusiasm for such information was not sufficient to call for another edition of Federici's book in English, although Hakluyt included it in the second edition of his *Principall navigations*.

During these years of travel and trade in the Near and Middle East by Englishmen, books describing the regions continued to be published which were based on classical scholarship and contained nothing in the way of modern commentary of the ancient authorities. The criticism of scholars by such rough but enthusiastic literary artisans as Henry Roberts can be understood; for in 1585, the year of his *Farewell* to Drake, and the year of Grenville's departure for Virginia, Arthur Golding translated and published an inadequate version of Pomponius Mela's *De situ orbis*.[18] He stated in his dedication to Sir William Cecil that he wished to use the classic source for the three continents known to antiquity and to add something of later writers for the new discoveries. It apparently was never finished, and after it had lain unpublished for many years, he decided that it was better than nothing, and took it to press. It was without commentary and makes no mention of America, yet to the printer, Thomas Hacket, it must have been a profitable venture, for it was issued again in 1590.[19]

Equally out of keeping with the development of modern knowledge but in step with the strength of the classics in English learning was the publication by Hacket in 1585 of a new edition of Pliny's *Natural history* under the title, *The secrets and wonders of the worlde*, which was sufficiently popular to support another printing two years later.[20] In 1587 he also issued the *Polyhistor* of Solinus, a collection of geographical and historical tales from a third century Roman geographer which had little value for persons seriously interested in geography in the late sixteenth century.[21] It is possible that such translations were made and published because of the demand for them in English schools where they were learned by rote, but this explanation would not account for the rash of classical geographies at this time, when they had been less abundant previously. It seems more likely that the voyages of Drake and the colonial plans of Raleigh and Gilbert stimulated an increased interest in geography, and enterprising translators and publishers capitalized on England's still medieval mentality which instinctively turned back to the Biblical, the classical, and the legendary for its explanations of the world.[22]

While classical authors maintained their popularity, the interest in overseas efforts, which had produced diverse but incessant attempts at trading, exploring, gold-hunting, and colonizing since the voyages of Frobisher, had by 1589 enabled the geographer Thomas Blundeville to draw some conclusions about England's favorite project, the northwest passage, in his handbook on the use of maps and charts, *A briefe description of universal mappes and cardes*. Here he had some hard things to say about the optimism with which Englishmen portrayed the passage in the north, 'all which they make islands, and yet never sayled about them.'[23] Blundeville did not think the routes to the north held any possibility for persons coming from a moderate climate, yet he commended 'those valiaunt mindes that doe attempt such desparate voyages.'[24] With Blundeville's book, the literature of the northwest passage had passed from the enthusiasm of Rastell through the defensive optimism of Gilbert and the hopeful accounts of Frobisher's voyages to actual disbelief. He challenged Bourne's opinion that the Arctic waters would be navigable in the summer months because of the long hours of sunshine by asking what heat the sun could give in the high latitudes when it rose no higher than twenty-three and a half degrees. Yet these arguments were laid aside by seekers for the northern passage who followed the Arctic summer hopefully until late in the eighteenth century. And as Blundeville foreclosed the hopes for a northern route to the Asiatic markets in the minds of those who could be convinced, the traditional ports of the Low Countries were closed by the Spaniards, making the export problem temporarily worse, for adequate outlets for English woolens in Germany were sought in vain.[25]

Nevertheless, the last years of the 1580's were not without cheer to the English. The failures in the northwest were countered by success in the Levant trade. The Armada victory was a great promise of English dominance in the Atlantic, and even as the Roanoke settlement perished and Drake returned from the West Indies with loss to report to his backers, Englishmen found satisfaction in the destruction he had wrought in the Spanish settlements in America. His raids into West Indian ports were reported in a spectacular publication by Walter Bigges, entitled *A summarie and true discourse of Sir Frances Drakes West Indian voyage*. Bigges had begun to compose the narrative while on board one of Drake's ships, but he had died before its completion.

Thomas Cates, who brought the book to press, stated that he believed it was finished by Lieutenant Crofts, another member of the expedition.[26] A spectacular book, it contained four exquisitely engraved maps of West Indian ports and was written with a swagger England's seamen had earned, for Cates said in his dedication to the Earl of Essex that the book was 'a very fit thing to be published, that they [Englishmen] may see what great victories a fewe English men have made upon great numbers of the Spaniardes.'[27] This volume may have contained a map titled *The famouse West Indian voyadge made by the English fleete*, although it is sometimes found separately. It shows the route of Drake's ships and gives an up-to-date portrayal of the Atlantic coast of North and part of South America and the Caribbean islands.[28]

To Richard Hakluyt, both the recent victories and the recent failures paled beside the persistent achievements of Englishmen abroad throughout the nation's history, and in 1589 he celebrated the greatness of English seamen with a mighty volume, *The principall navigations, voiages, and discoveries of the English nation*. With an admirable passion for completeness, and with an equal insistence upon authentic sources, Hakluyt produced a bibliographical landmark in the history of English overseas expansion. The conception of his book was not entirely original for it followed the pattern of Ramusio's *Delle navigationi et viaggi* in its division of materials according to geography, and then by chronology within each geographic section. On the other hand, Hakluyt's motive was quite different, for while Ramusio collected the voyages of all European peoples, Hakluyt confined himself to English travelers and explorers, as he sought to establish the long-standing importance of England as a nation interested in travel and exploration. To his credit it must be said that Hakluyt was more concerned with exactness, especially with regard to documents.

This collection of materials relating to the history of English interests abroad which Hakluyt published is the work of an historian, a geographer and a collector, and in that context it is a work of the highest order. It is also a testimony to Hakluyt's patriotism, for he made it apparent in his dedication to Walsingham that the book was a defense of his homeland. 'Thus both hearing and reading the obloquie of our nation, and finding few or none of our owne men to replie heerin: and further, not seeing any man to have care to recommend to the world, the industrious labors, and painefull travels of our countrey men: for stopping the mouthes of the reprochers, my self... determined... to undertake the burden of that worke.' The insults he had felt undoubtedly came as a part of his periodic residence in France from 1583 to 1588, and his massive compilation of evidence of England's interests abroad and abilities at sea attempted to prove that 'in compassing the vaste globe of the earth more than once, [Englishmen] have excelled all nations and people of the earth.'[29]

Hakluyt's patriotism did not diminish his value as an historian, although his emotions show clearly in his attacks upon other writers of travel literature from abroad who had probably taunted him for England's deficiencies. He returned the taunts, mentioning 'those wearie volumes bearing the titles of universall Cosmographie which some men that I could name have published as their own...'[30] This appears to refer to André Thevet, the French royal cosmographer whose Cosmographie universelle had appeared in 1575, and to a similar work by François Belleforest, which was published in three editions in the 1570s.[31]

When including Hakluyt among his Worthies of England, Thomas Fuller described his assembling of this vast accumulation of English travel literature in naval terms: 'In a word many of such useful tracts of sea adventurers, which were before scattered as several ships, Master Hackluit hath embodied into a fleet, divided into three squadrons...'[34] The three squadrons were the three divisions of the book: the Near East and Africa, the northeast toward Asia, and the New World. The fleet is impressive in its totality, containing some three quarters of a million words,[35] and the component ships carry the history of English overseas interests from the earliest times. Hakluyt filled about fifty-five pages with the narrative of Mandeville's travels and a brief life of Mandeville, all of it in Latin, and without an English commentary. Twenty-three additional pages describe travels to the Levant between 337 and 1270, and these are of little interest to Hakluyt's period, except to prove his point that Englishmen had long been avid seagoers.

After eighty pages of such material, Hakluyt came to the travels of Anthony Jenkinson to Aleppo, and then followed accounts of voyages to Guinea from 1552 to 1566. He introduced a series of documents on the Turkey and Morocco trade, and on Malta before going on to the travels of Fitch and Newbery into the Middle East. Business and sailing directions were set forth for the Near East as were two voyages there by Laurence Aldersey, a London merchant who traveled to the Near East in 1581 and 1586. The section on Africa and the Near East concluded with patents for trade in Barbary, Senegal, and Gambia dated 1585 and 1588. Here Hakluyt was at his best as a collector of source materials, and he continued at a high level in his Part II, which is a collection of narratives of travels to the northeast. He apparently could not resist including six pages of pre-1400 navigations in that direction before presenting the writings of Robert Thorne on the northern passage, Sebastian Cabot's instructions for northern navigation, and the Willoughby-Chancellor expedition in Latin and English from the pen of Clement Adams. He then recorded the various travels into Russia by agents of the Muscovy Company down to narratives of the Pet-Jackman voyage of 1580, setting forth the most complete selection of sources existing on the early Russian and Persian commerce of England.

Hakluyt's treatment of the New World was also very comprehensive. Here again he exhibited the priority of Englishmen in seafaring by beginning his New World section with the supposed voyage of Madoc, the Welshman, to America in 1170. This is followed by some notes on Columbus' attempt to interest Henry VII in his proposed voyage and the letters patent granted to John Cabot by Henry VII. Actual accounts of voyages begin with the North American explorations of Sebastian Cabot and Master Hore, followed by the Brazilian voyage of William Hawkins in 1530 and the 1564 voyage of Sir John Hawkins. Hakluyt included in this portion of Part III interesting accounts of New Spain by a number of Englishmen who had lived there for several years, giving information on Spanish commerce and native commodities and also telling the strange story of David Ingram who with two companions, Richard Browne and Richard Twide, claimed to have gone ashore in Mexico from the San Juan de Ulúa fleet of Sir John Hawkins and to have walked northeastwardly across the continent to Canada where they were picked up by a French ship in 1569.[36]

In turning to the northwest passage Hakluyt reprinted Gilbert's *Discourse*, the observations of Richard Willes, the accounts of the second Frobisher voyage from Dionyse Settle and the third from Thomas Ellis, and added an account of the first voyage by Christopher Hall. He then directed his attention to Brazil, presenting letters describing voyages there, following these by an account of the attempted voyage of Edward Fenton to the East Indies via the Strait of Magellan in 1582. He again took up the northern voyages, with a printing of Gilbert's patent and an account of Gilbert's voyage of 1583, Peckham's *True report*, Raleigh's patent and his voyages of 1584, 1585 and 1586, Hariot's *Briefe and true report*, and the voyages to Roanoke in 1587 and 1588.

Moving still farther north in his interest, Hakluyt then presented the first publication of the accounts of the three voyages into the northwest passage by John Davis. This was followed by an account of the Earl of Cumberland's voyage of 1586, which was primarily concerned with piracy. The great volume concluded with a miscellaneous gathering of travel items, including four pages of distances in Brazil, a narrative of Cavendish's circumnavigation, published here for the first time, an account of a voyage to Benin in 1588, and finally, Ambassador Jerome Horsey's description of the coronation of the Russian emperor in 1584. At the last moment, Hakluyt decided to include an account of Drake's circumnavigation in his volume, for twelve pages containing a description of the voyage were inserted, unnumbered, between pages 643 and 644.

As an archive of English overseas interests, Hakluyt's great compilation is worthy of all the praise it has received. This praise continues to come from historians of our age who value it as a mine of dependable information. While it demonstrated England's long-standing interest and skill in overseas travel, it could not obscure the words published by Eden, Willes, Churchyard, Best and Roberts, chastising the English in the Elizabethan period for their lack of enthusiasm for overseas ventures and their lack of curiosity about the new areas of the world being opened up by others. There is no doubt that Hakluyt was an ardent believer in colonization, but his *Principall navigations* appears not to have been an effort at overt propaganda to that end, for it lacked the fervent commentary necessary to convince readers of a point of view. It makes no plea for colonies, or for a continued interest in the East and West Indies. Hakluyt showed no anti-Spanish tendencies which could have given his book greater appeal the year after the Armada. Yet in its inclusiveness, and in the evidence of painstaking accuracy that went into it, Hakluyt's book is an impressive anthology. What it lacked in emotion it made up abundantly in information which must have gone far toward giving Englishmen both pride and confidence in the achievements of their countrymen abroad. It is not easy, however, to judge the book's influence in its own time. One can believe it was entirely satisfactory to Edward Dyer and William Sanderson who are identified in the preface as financial supporters of its publication, but it probably aroused no sudden large-scale interest in travel and exploration literature. At least we find no attempts by English publishers to produce similar collections of travels, and for the first five years of the 1590s, the offerings of English publishers in this field constituted a rather drab assortment.

It is true, these were not active years from the standpoint of new undertakings by English merchants and explorers, and the west-country enthusiasts for empire were falling on evil times. In 1589 John Chidley and Andrew Meyrick took three ships to the Strait of Magellan, apparently in hopes of duplicating the voyage of Thomas Cavendish. After six weeks of trying to navigate the passage, and after two ships with their crews had been lost, they gave up, and only four men from the entire expedition of over three hundred lived to return to England.[37] In 1591 Sir Richard Grenville was carried dying off the *Revenge* after being defeated in an attempt to intercept the Spanish silver fleet. That same year John Davis and Thomas Cavendish undertook a voyage through the Strait of Magellan, Cavendish to plunder Spanish shipping and Davis to probe the western coast of North America for the elusive northern passage. Their expedition failed utterly, no ship being able to navigate the Strait of Magellan. Finally, in these years, Raleigh fell from his high favor with the Queen, owing to his love for another woman, and in 1592 he was imprisoned. Hakluyt was named as one of nineteen directors charged by Raleigh with keeping alive the interest in the settling of a colony in Virginia. The other members appear to have been London merchants who took little active interest in the project, so Hakluyt's enthusiasm was for the time being isolated.

Into this situation of arrested progress and declining prospects came a number of books that can have done little to improve it. Even the failures of Fenton and Grenville appear as great achievements compared to some of the books that were published within a few years of Hakluyt's great volume. In Robert Tanner's *A mirror for mathematiques* we see a genuine concern for a knowledge of astronomy and the instruments of astronomers, but no corresponding concern for geography, for his chapters on Asia and Africa are based heavily on Pliny and Strabo while his smattering of vague information on America could have been gleaned from Vespucci's letters or other very early sources. A table of locations for cities and countries in all parts of the world may have been more useful, although he used 21,600 miles as the circumference of the earth.[38] In 1590 an instruction book for travelers, reminiscent of Bourne's *Treasure for traveilers*, was published. Hakluyt apparently was instrumental in encouraging Philip Jones to translate the *Methodus* of Albertus Meierus into English, at least the dedication of the book to Sir Francis Drake was suggested by Hakluyt. It was the many 'expeditions, plantings, discoveries and voyages of the largest compasse'[39] that led the translator to bring into English the view that cosmography, astronomy, geography, chorography, topography, husbandry, navigation, political affairs, ecclesiastical literature, histories and chronicles of the countries visited were deserving of scrutiny by travelers. The author concluded with a quotation from Ortelius to the effect that those who visit foreign countries should record all possible information for future reference. While showing an admirable concern that Englishmen harness their travels abroad to some productive use, this work was not particularly adapted to England's overseas interests, being more concerned with travel into Europe. It was far more pertinent, however, than the new issues of the geographical works of Pomponius Mela and Solinus which also appeared in 1590, for they were merely re-issues of their 1585 and 1587 printings respectively—evidence of their continued appeal to English readers seeking geographical information based on ancient authority.

As if to remind England of her misfortunes, one Job Hortop returned to his homeland in 1590 after an absence of twenty-three years, and the following year published an account of what had befallen him since he had been put ashore in Mexico by John Hawkins during his ill-fated voyage to San Juan de Ulúa. *The rare travailes of Job Hortop* were dedicated to the Queen, the first book of overseas interest to be addressed to her. Hortop had been a gunner in the San Juan de Ulúa expedition, and upon its disastrous conclusion had decided, like David Ingram, to take his chances on land rather than on a crowded and ill-provisioned ship. He was taken by the Spaniards, served in the galleys, and was also imprisoned. In spite of all that he must have seen and heard concerning Spain's New World possessions, he reported very little, being more concerned with methods of hunting sea horses, with strange fish that came on land at night, and with similar wonders. The two editions which appeared in 1591 do not necessarily mean that the book had an unusually good sale. The first edition apparently was withdrawn shortly after it was issued in order to revise it to include Drake's participation in the battle of San Juan de Ulúa, thus bringing it into line with Hakluyt's account of the event.[40] The second edition, somewhat expanded, was titled *The travailes of an English man.*

Job Hortop's woes were matched by the misfortunes experienced by Edward Webbe in Russia and in the Mediterranean. He too described his adventures abroad as 'troublesome travailes' in his book published in 1590 as *The rare and most wonderful thinges which Edward Webbe… hath seene and passed.* Webbe served abroad first in Russia under Anthony Jenkinson, and in 1571 when the Crimean Tatars burned Moscow he was made a slave and carried off to the Crimea. After being ransomed he returned to England and then departed for Leghorn and the Levant on another ill-fated expedition during which he was taken by the Turks. Enslaved again, he served in the galleys and as a gunner, and ultimately found himself in service with the Turkish army in Persia, Damascus, and the land of Prester John. In the latter adventure he claimed to have seen the many marvels recorded in the Prester John *Letter*, such as sixty kings serving at Prester John's table, beasts with four heads, unicorns, and similar wonders. This flight of fancy terminates with Webbe's return to Constantinople where William Harborne of the Levant Company secured his release. His troubles were not ended, however, for in Italy he was held briefly as a spy and a heretic before he finally returned to England in May, 1589.

Webbe's story apparently aroused considerable interest, for three different publishers issued it.[41] This popularity can best be attributed to its brevity and to the fact that Webbe's adventures brought him into close contact with the Turkish army, whose strength was a subject of great interest in all of the western European countries, where it loomed as a threat to all Christendom. His conflict with the authorities in Italy added interest also, for the persecution of an Englishman for his religion at the hands of the Inquisition was a subject of established interest in England. The entire book spoke of the insecurity of Englishmen who ventured beyond the Baltic or Gibraltar.

In these troubled years not even the Russian trade could escape difficulties, although it had been established for a generation. In the latter 1580s Sir Jerome Horsey, the English envoy to Russia, labored with great effort to keep harmony between the English and Russian courts and to keep in force the monopoly the Muscovy Company held upon the northern shores of Russia. As Horsey succeeded with the Protector, Boris Godunov, the Anglophilic attitude of Godunov offended the nobility of Russia, and Horsey left in some haste in 1587 before the alliance between the two sovereigns could be drawn up.[42] To conclude the negotiations, Queen Elizabeth sent out Dr. Giles Fletcher in 1588. Fletcher was by this time well known as a poet and had held diplomatic posts in Scotland and Germany. He had undoubtedly learned much about Russia while in Scotland, for his superior there was Thomas Randolph who had once been ambassador to Russia. Fletcher's embassy in Moscow was not a happy one. He encountered both hostility and neglect at the hands of the Russians, and while he secured confirmation of the trading privileges asked by the Muscovy Company and

was back in England in 1589, he was not forgetful of the rude treatment
he had received from his Russian hosts. In this mood he wrote *Of the
Russe common wealth*, the first English book based upon an Englishman's
observations to describe Russia at length. Some of his remarks were
sufficiently hostile to worry the Muscovy Company into attempting
to have it suppressed, but for the most part Fletcher gave his information in a dispassionate manner, describing all aspects of Russian life.

Fletcher dedicated his book to the Queen, comparing her government briefly to that of Russia, thankful 'that you are a Prince of subjec-
tes, not of slaves...' [43] which must have jolted the Muscovy Company
into wondering what good the ambassador could have done them.
His first four chapters are given to the provinces and boundaries, the
soil and climate, the products, and the major cities of Russia. Then
follow ten chapters concerning government, and five more devoted to
information on the Russian military system. The book concluded with
chapters on certain of the northern peoples, a discussion of the Russian
church, the habits of the emperor and his household, and some notes
on the customs of the Russian people. It was, on the whole, a well
balanced picture of Russia; though more concerned with administration than with trade, it offered considerable information to Englishmen
interested in nearly any aspect of Russian civilization. Like most English travel books of this period, it was published in only one edition.

The inability of most English books describing foreign lands to attract sufficient interest to call for second and third editions was in
sharp contrast to the greater demand for books on navigation which
found much more intensive use and thus wore out quickly. In 1592
Bourne's *Regiment for the sea* was published in its sixth edition,[44] and in
spite of the failures of Davis and murmuring such as Blundeville's
against the belief in the northwest passage, the *Regiment* continued to
expound on the five ways to Cathay, which included three northern
routes. Such books were accepted by navigators as the tools of their
profession, as were sailing charts, the first of which to bear an English
imprint was issued by Thomas Hood in 1592. It showed the North
Atlantic Ocean from Cape Verde to northern Scotland, but did not
extend beyond the Azores to the west.[45] Books of travel had no such
obviously utilitarian purpose, and they encountered not only lethargy
but a very conservative attitude toward the kind of venturing abroad
advocated by Hakluyt and undertaken by Anthony Jenkinson or Thomas Hariot. The years following the Armada did not obliterate the
timidity that Eden, Churchyard and others had found in their society.

The illiberality toward overseas ventures on the part of the nobility mentioned by George Best was not overcome as Elizabeth's reign moved toward its last decade. In 1592 Sir John Stradling, a scholar and poet of considerable standing, translated an excerpt from the *Epistola de peregrinatione Italica* of Justus Lipsius for the benefit of the young Earl of Bedford who was about to undertake a trip abroad, most likely to well-known parts of Europe.[46] The advice of Lipsius, a distinguished Latinist at the University of Leyden, added up to a warning against association with foreigners, and showed the most extreme distaste for adventure. It is remarkable that the Earl of Bedford should have had such a book dedicated to him, for his sister, Anne, was married to the Earl of Warwick who had sponsored Martin Frobisher at Court, and another sister, Margaret, was married to George Clifford, Earl of Cumberland. Richard Eden and Richard Willes had both been patronized in their writing of travel literature by members of the Bedford family.

While one Elizabethan poet was a partner to the encouragement of timidity, Henry Roberts, the balladeer, was celebrating the return of Captain William Grafton, a pirate, with bad poetry and worse printing in *Our Ladys retorne to England*, which told of the capture of two Spanish ships laden with sugar and slaves.[47] Two years later he praised another English pirate, Edward Glenham, in *Newes from the Levante seas*, and he introduced his account of English piracy with a criticism of those who remained at home 'whereof England harboureth to many.'[48] Roberts' writings are crude expressions of imperialism, but they were the only expression of interest in overseas ventures published in the half decade after Hakluyt's *Principall navigations*. When Sir Francis Drake and Sir John Hawkins planned a new voyage to Spanish America in 1595, it was Roberts who sent them off with a nine-page poem, *The trumpet of fame*, praising them for their effort

> *That Phillips Regions may not more be stord*
> *With Pearle, Jewels and the purest gold.*[49]

Likewise, in the same year he sang loudly the praises of James Lancaster in his *Lancaster his allarums* which reported that captain's voyage to Pernambuco, his conflict with the Portuguese and his trade with the French there. Here he levelled a broadside against Londoners for not appreciating men of valor, for valuing money above men, and for refusing to 'imitate in good actions such noble Straungers as have lived in elder time.'[50]. In his customary doggerel he advised his readers:

*Learne by this man of woorth to guyde,*
*your selves in every place :*
*By land or sea to gaine renoune,*
*and enemies desgrace.*[51]

Henry Roberts' little tracts remain as more than attempts to stir Englishmen to overseas action. They were also the only printed material from the 1590–95 period which were primarily concerned with what Englishmen were doing outside the European theatre in these years. The publisher of all but one of Roberts' patriotic pieces, William Barley, apparently was sufficiently impressed with the demand for adventure stories to publish one in 1595 without any assistance from Roberts. His *Strange and wonderful things happened to Richard Hasleton* was not a good choice.[52] In dedicating his book to Richard Staper, one of the founders of the Levant trade, Barley gave it an important connection, but the narrative of Hasleton's adventures is a monotonous tale of ten years of captivity at the hands of Turks and Spaniards and far from appropriate to the encouragement of eastern Mediterranean commerce.

The enthusiastic balladry of Henry Roberts is notable for its spirit, but unlike Richard Eden, George Best, Richard Hakluyt, and others who were impatient for empire, Roberts did not have geographical knowledge to give him a philosophy of empire. He was at best a journalist whose emotions far surpassed his knowledge, and piracy appears to have had more appeal to him than exploration. This was not an unusual attitude for an Elizabethan, yet it was quite in contrast to the quiet persistence of Elizabethan England's last great exponent of the navigability of the northwest passage. To John Davis, the Dartmouth captain, spectacular piracies were no substitute for important feats of navigation, and in 1595 he again advanced the theory that the passage could be found, and the route laid open to China. In that year he published *The worldes hydrographical description,* which he dedicated to the Privy Council, urging them to support his belief in the passage.

Davis began his treatise much as Gilbert had done, by noting the usual objections to the passage: the failures of the past; the possibility that Asia and America were joined; ice, cold, and ignorance of navigation of the northern waters of America. He discounted these, claiming that he and Drake had proved the insularity of America—Drake by discovering the great distance between America and any part of Asia at forty-eight degrees north latitude, and himself in his three northern voyages. He attributed the discontinuance of his northern explorations, not to failure, but to the death of Sir Francis Walsingham, for 'when his honour died the voyage was frindles, and mens mindes alienated from adventuring therein.'[53] In addition to the lethargy noted among most Englishmen, he also mentioned the opposition 'of the malitious multitude that onely desire to hinder when themselves can doe no good.'[54] The persistence of the idea of the northwest passage was obviously due to the tenacity of a few seamen, not to any appeal it made to the public.

There was no doubt about the existence of the passage, however, as far as Davis was concerned, and he stated: 'The cause why I use this particular relation of all my proceedings for this discovery, is to stay this objection,—why hath noth Davis discovered this passage, being thrise that way imploied?'[55] The ensuing accounts of his three voyages in search of the passage show him returning from the first two because the season for northern navigation was ended, and from the third because he was convinced that the passage had been laid open toward the north. Then despite such good hopes, Walsingham's death ended the undertaking. In his plea to the Privy Council to take up the search once more, Davis asserted that the sea did not freeze in the latitudes he sailed, the air was not intolerably cold, and during the summer season the long daylight periods made the northern region especially apt for navigation. Finally, he outlined the benefits England would receive from discovering the passage. He was at some pains and eloquence to prove the spiritual values of bringing religion to the natives of the north 'it is onely we therefore that must be these shining messengers of the Lord, and none but we.'[56] As for material benefits, Davis saw England improving herself in comparison to her neighbors by selling goods directly to the East, rather than through European middlemen. He also showed how England would become the storehouse of eastern commodities for Europe. Considering these benefits, Davis regarded it 'impossible that any true English hart should be staied from willing contribution to the performance of this so excellent a discovery.'[57]

English hearts, however, showed no inclination to embark on another series of northern adventures at this time. Davis' enthusiasm and his unquestioned ability as a navigator left the would-be promoters of voyages unmoved. His book, more learned than Gilbert's, and incorporating greater experience, was forced into the same coaxing approach that was common to most northwest passage literature in Elizabeth's reign, revealing either lethargy or outright opposition to the undertaking on the part of most Englishmen. *The worldes hydrographical de-*

*scription* fell between Frobisher and Hudson, far enough from each to have little influence. It also was published at a time when overseas enthusiasts had another project to interest them, for in February, 1595, Sir Walter Raleigh sailed from Plymouth with five ships on a voyage to Guiana.

In seeking to restore himself to the royal favor, Raleigh was forced to adapt his colonial ambitions to the dominant spirit surrounding the Queen and the dominant spirit among Englishmen interested in overseas ventures. His Roanoke venture had been planned with a view to establishing English colonies where Englishmen might create permanent settlements and exploit the products of the New World just as Englishmen used the soil and forests of England. He used the term 'an English nation', and its objectives were to be merchandise and new territory added to the Queen's jurisdiction. But it was not merchants who were the royal favorites. Pirates were preferred; and similarly, the lust for gold made a greater appeal to most Englishmen than did the mere expansion of England's trade. While the Roanoke colony conformed to the requirement of overseas possession which the new and more aggressive nationalism demanded, it did not satisfy the gold-seekers. But Elizabeth was not going to attempt to take gold and territory by force in America, for she was trying hard to make peace with Spain. To suit the needs of the hour, Raleigh proposed to get both land and gold without war in the fabulous land of Guiana in South America.

Despite the distrust of many persons who feared Raleigh might be merely going to embroil England anew with Spain through piratical actions in America, others who thought he might be deserting to Spain, the forebodings of his wife, and a general mistrust by the people at large, Raleigh secured permission to sail. His voyage was not supported by the Queen but by friends and relatives. Its purposes were to establish friendly relations with the Indians of Guiana and to penetrate inland on the Orinoco River so as to learn of the interior. Both of these missions were accomplished, and Raleigh arrived back in England in September. He then set about to convince the Queen and her advisers of the potentialities of Guiana, and one of his devices was the publication of *The discoverie of the large, rich, and bewtiful empire of Guiana*.

Raleigh's book was more than an advertisement for Guiana. It was also a personal defense of the author, for in his dedication to Charles Howard and Sir Robert Cecil, Lord High Admiral and Lord Treasurer respectively, he stated, 'I am assured that whatsoever shall be done, or written by me, shall neede a double protection and defence.'[58]

Here he attempted to stand off his critics who were saying that he had never left Cornwall and that he was 'too easeful & sensuall to undertake a jorney of so great travel.'⁵⁹ Throughout his book Raleigh gave the impression of being a great servant of England, and in this he did himself some harm. He noted his impoverished condition after returning from a land of great wealth, and he explained it by saying that he declined to take native chiefs for ransom because it would have been wrong to have 'defaced an enterprise of so great assurance, untill I knew whether it pleased God to put a disposition in her princely and royall heart either to follow or forestow the same.'⁶⁰ Leaving gold in Guiana in the national interest was beyond the understanding of most of Raleigh's contemporaries who knew that he had not been averse to enriching himself in England. The fact that he brought no gold home was seized upon by his critics as proof that no gold was to be found in Guiana. Furthermore, the memories of Frobisher's ore must have returned when some of Raleigh's crew exhibited a type of rock picked up near Trinidad. In his Epistle to the Reader Raleigh was quick to identify this as 'marcasite' in an attempt to dispel any notion that this was the best wealth Guiana had to offer. Gold was to be had, he assured his readers, and it would do for England what Peru's gold had done for Spain, and 'if her Majesty will undertake it, I wilbe contented to lose her highnes favor and good opinion for ever, and my life withal, if the same be not found rather to exceede, then to equal whatsoever is in this discourse promised or declared.'⁶¹

Despite this most vigorous defense of Guiana as a source of gold in the introductory pages, Raleigh's description of the country was not unlike that of Hariot's *Virginia* in that it revealed more interest in the land, its products, and the natives, than in gold. He mentioned the abundance of stone pitch which would be useful for ships trading to that area; he considered the soil excellent for the production of sugar, ginger and other commodities; he listed flora and fauna to be found on Trinidad, and mentioned trade in cotton and brazil wood. His descriptions of the trade in gold and of the nation of the Amazons obviously came from hearsay. After describing the agreeable nature of the natives who, he said, would be willing to die to the last man against the Spaniards, Raleigh summed up his impressions of Guiana by saying 'that both for health, good ayre, pleasure and riches... I am resolved it caunot [sic] bee equalled by anie region eyther in the east or west.'⁶² He estimated that an army of three or four thousand would be sufficient to hold this great empire for England.

Raleigh's book was unquestionably published at his own expense or subsidized by one of his associates. Yet it was a popular book, for it went through two distinct and separate impressions, and three editions are known, all from 1596. The numerous typographical differences with the same content prove that the book was revised in its typographical aspects after the first printing, indicating a sizeable public demand. This is not to say conclusively that England was becoming enthusiastic about Guiana, or about the idea of an empire abroad. Raleigh was a controversial person, and his other books were also widely read, and this small volume undoubtedly found a literary as well as a practical audience. Nevertheless, as a propagandist for empire, Raleigh was outstanding, and his *Discoverie of Guiana* is an eloquent plea for both Guiana and the idea of empire. It showed Spain as cruel and powerful; it advertised well the gold and other products; it pointed out the navigability of the rivers, the defensibility of the land, the friendliness of the natives, and the agreeableness of the countryside. But it called for an army, and this would have been sufficient to defeat his plan even if there had not been personal enemies at work to undo it on other grounds. There was no precedent in English history for sending an army so far from home, and Elizabeth had measured out her military assistance to the Netherlands in their war of liberation against Spain with shrewd parsimony. Raleigh's lack of realism in this respect was matched by his attempt to gloss over his failure to bring back gold, and for all his eloquence these were weaknesses that touched at the heart of established English attitudes.

Raleigh was by no means discouraged by criticism, and in January, 1596, he sent out one of his captains, Lawrence Kemys, to follow up his own voyage by making further explorations along the Orinoco River. Kemys returned in June and published *A relation of the second voyage to Guiana*, which contained additional description of the potentialities of Guiana. But he too came home with no gold in hand, and even more than Raleigh, he emphasized the commercial opportunities of the region rather than the abundance of precious metal. The 'Orenoque' region, he wrote, 'yieldeth choise of fourtie severall great rivers... for our merchants and others, that doe now finds little profit in setting foorth for reprisall, to exercise trade in. To such as shall be willing to adventure in search of them I could promise some hope of gold mines,'[63] but with greater assurance he promised that the lands washed by these rivers yielded brazil wood, honey, cotton and drugs. If less outspoken in his optimism than Raleigh, Kemys was no less ardent in his wish to establish a colony in Guiana and to do so as soon as possible. He made an impassioned plea to the reader to throw off the contentment that infested England before Spain had taken everything, for then it would be too late. He warned 'To sleep then, because it costeth nothing... is the plaine high-way to fearfull downefall.'[64]

Kemys was fighting more than mere lethargy, however, for in his dedication to Raleigh he made it apparent that other projects were getting more attention in England, projects 'which requiring greater charge, yeeld not so large benefit and are subject to more doubtful events.'[65] In the eyes of the Queen and her advisers, however, no project could be more plagued by 'doubtful events' than sending an army to America to hold a tropical wilderness against Spain's certain opposition. English nationalism had by no means progressed to the point where the Queen's subjects would sing her praises for raising an army for distant imperial service.

Although Raleigh's proposals failed to excite either the Queen or the merchants of London, they apparently stimulated some interest in the subject of America, for in 1596 London's printers published new editions of Bigges's *Summarie and true discourse of Sir Francis Drakes West Indian Voyage*, Monardes' *Joyfull newes*, and Gomara's *Conquest of the Weast India*.[66] This flurry of books relating to America was the last attention English publishers paid to the New World in the sixteenth century, and it was the re-emergence of Raleigh as a colonizer that kept Englishmen concerned with the opportunities for settlement in America, even if they rejected his colonial schemes. Although he found no royal support, he did stimulate some merchants and adventurers, Dutch and French as well as English, to take an interest in the commerce of the north coast of South America, and for a generation settlement on that coast was repeatedly undertaken by Englishmen. The personality and reputation of Raleigh were unquestionably the most compelling factor in a revived English interest in the New World.

If the 1590's did not produce many good descriptions of America or other distant lands, they did see the publication of several significant works of navigational interest which showed concern for geographical knowledge and English expansion abroad. Foremost among these were the *Exercises* of Thomas Blundeville, a Cambridge educated mathematician. In 1594 he wrote 'I greatlie rejoyce to see so manie of our English Gentlemen, both of the Court and Countrie in these dayes so earnestlie given to travell as well by sea as land... and speciallie into the East and West Indies.'[67] He saw a close connection between this interest and the need for knowledge of navigation, and most of the material in the six treatises promised in the title of his book is given to mathematics, astronomy, discussions of spheres, etc. When describing Mercator's globes, however, he adds a brief description of the globe made by Emery Molyneux which traced the voyages of Drake and Cavendish around the world, and also the northwest passage voyages of Frobisher. Blundeville then described Drake's voyage briefly, concluding with the hope that Drake would publish a descriptive narrative of his circumnavigation 'shewing howe much he sayled in a day, and what watring places he found... and what good Ports and Havens he found... what beastes, fowles, or fishes, fruits, hearbes, plants, or other commodities he found...', thus doing the saide Sir Frances I say should greatly profite his countrie men.'[68] A more brief account of Cavendish's circumnavigation follows, with a comparison in several points between it and Drake's voyage.

Blundeville's concern for geography continues with his 'Plaine and full description of Petrus Plancius his universall map.' Plancius, one of the leading geographers of the Netherlands, had published a world map in 1592, and Blundeville gives descriptions of all parts of the world from the twelve sheets that made up the map.[69] Some of the map's inscriptions which he translated tell of the discovery and exploration of recently discovered areas. When a second edition of Blundeville's book appeared in 1597, two new treatises were added, including the previously published 'A briefe description of Universall maps and cards,' and 'The true order of making of Ptolemie his tables.'[70]

Another mathematician who used a discussion of globes as the means of imparting some knowledge of geography was Robert Hues who had sailed with Cavendish in his voyage around the world. His *Tractatus de globis et eorum usu*, published in 1594, was primarily a discourse on a pair of globes made by Emery Molyneux, but one chapter in Part III does discuss the known regions of the earth, setting late sixteenth century knowledge against the geographical writings of the ancients. Following the text, Hues presented a gazetteer of more than three thousand place names, giving locations by latitude and longitude. In his dedication to Raleigh he reviewed English maritime achievement and commended also the travels of Mandeville whom he cited for his 'strict view of all India, China, Tartary and Persia, with Regions adjoyning.'[71]

Neither Blundeville nor Hues made as close a connection between navigation and national overseas interests as did John Davis, who in 1594 dedicated *The seaman's secrets* to Lord Howard.[72] Published the following year, this aid to navigation deserves mention here for the author's insistence to Lord Howard that the northwest passage did exist and for his brief account of the luckless voyage he and Cavendish had made to the Strait of Magellan in 1591–93.

The publication of maps of unfamiliar lands had not progressed nearly as far as had navigational and travel literature, but these late years of the sixteenth century did produce several maps of varying degrees of quality. Foremost among them was the world map included in Hakluyt's *Principall navigations*. Based upon the 1585 world map of Ortelius, it was abreast of the most recent geographical information, and it must have been a help to the English reader finding his way among unfamiliar places mentioned in the text. It was surely the desire of the publisher, Thomas Wight, to give greater clarity to the Biblical history related in *A briefe description of Hierusalem* by the Dutch cleric Christiaan van Adrichem that prompted him to include a map of Jerusalem and its environs when he issued that work in 1595.[73] In the same year it was the fear of the Turks that led Abraham Hartwell to translate Giovanni Tommaso Minadoi's *History of the warres betweene the Turkes and the Persians* which contained a map of considerable interest, showing the area bounded by the Black and Caspian Seas, the western coast of India and the Persian Gulf. Apart from the map the book has little geographic interest, for the author states that 'to tell of the Mountaines, the Rivers, the Champaines, the Distances... and such other particularities, it would not be an enterprise fit for our handling.'[74]

The following year John Blagrave issued a map intended for the enlightenment of students of navigation in his book, *Astrolabium uranicum generale*.[75] The map is titled 'Nova orbis terrarum descriptio' and is made on a north polar projection, extending southward to the southern extremities of South America and Africa. It portrays a circumnavigation, presumably Drake's, and must be considered a work of quality comparable to polar projections issued in the Netherlands in the 1590's.[76]

Influence from the Low Countries is also apparent in two maps of Gabriel Tatton who spent a part of his life in the Netherlands. Both maps were engraved by Benjamin Wright and apparently were issued in 1600. They relate to the New World and the Pacific Ocean, the *Nova et rece terrarum et regnorum Californiae, Nova Hispaniae,...* portraying North and Central America from Lower California eastward beyond Florida, and from forty-five degrees north latitude to Nicaragua,[77] and the *Maris Pacifici* map includes that area but extends southward to the Strait of Magellan and westward to Japan and the East Indian archipelago. In the northwest portion of the latter map a vague coastline of 'Nova Albion' extends toward China. The most outstanding map produced in these late years of the sixteenth century was that based on the 1592 globe of Emery Molyneux, reflecting the most advanced cartografic knowledge and techniques to be found in England or anywhere else at that time. Hakluyt was to include it in the second edition of his *Principall navigations*, although most extant copies do not contain it.

These few maps do not suggest that England had arrived as a competitor to Italy or the Netherlands as a center of map production, but they do indicate the growth of a skill which would ultimately make English travel literature more attractive to its audience.

## NOTES TO CHAPTER VIII

[1] Emanuel van Meteren, the Dutch historian, translated an account of the Cavendish circumnavigation which was published as *Beschryvinge van de overtreffelijcke end wijdtvermaerde zee-vaert van den... Thomas Candish*. (Amsterdam: Cornelis Claesz, 1598). The manuscript from which Van Meteren worked was probably supplied to him by his friend Richard Hakluyt.

[2] Clements R. Markham, *A life of John Davis* (London: George Philip and Son, 1889), pp. 31–32. Sanderson was married to Raleigh's niece; Davis' partner in the enterprise, although he did not sail, was Adrian Gilbert, brother of Sir Humphrey and half-brother of Raleigh.

[3] Juan González de Mendoza, *The historie of the great and mightie kingdome of China*, trans. Robert Parke (London: J. Wolfe for Edward White, 1588). This was first published as *Historia de las cosas mas notables, ritos y costumbres, del gran reyno de la China* (Rome: V. Accolti, 1585). Apart from this translation, Parke is quite unknown to English history and literature.

[4] *Ibid.*, fols. 2 recto; 3 recto.

[5] *Ibid*, fol. 3 recto.

[6] Albert Hastings Markham (ed.), *The voyages and works of John Davis the navigator* (London: The Hakluyt Society, 1880), p. xxi.

[7] González de Mendoza, fol. 3 verso.

[8] Albert Hastings Markham, pp. xx–xxvi.

[9] González de Mendoza, fol. 4 verso.

[10] Nicholas de Nicolay, *The navigations, peregrinations and voyages, made into Turkey*, trans. Thomas Washington, the younger (London: Thomas Dawson, 1585), fol. 5 2. recto. This was first published as *Les quatre premiers livres des navigations et peregrinations orientales* (Lyons: Guillaume Rouille, 1567).

[11] Thomas Saunders, *A true discription and breefe discourse of a most lamentable voiage, made latelie to Tripolie in Barbarie* (London: Richard Jones for Edward White, 1587).

[12] Cesare Federici, *The voyage and travaile... into the East India, the Indies, and beyond the Indies*, trans. T[homas] H[ickock] (London: Richard Jones and Edward White,

1588), fol. Aii recto. First published as *Viaggio... nell' India orientale et oltra l'India* (Venice: Andre Muschio, 1587).

13 *Ibid.*, fol. Aiii verso.

14 See p. 160 below.

15 Federici, fol. 2 recto.

16 *Ibid.*, fol. 3 recto.

17 *Ibid.*, fol. 5 recto.

18 Pomponius Mela, *The worke of Pomponius Mela the cosmographer, concerning the situation of the world*, trans. Arthur Golding (London: For Thomas Hacket, 1585). The original work was written in the first century and was first published in 1471. Arthur Golding was a prominent translator of the Elizabethan period, and was patronized by some of England's leading figures, including Sir Christopher Hatton.

19 The 1590 edition was published with an edition of Solinus' *Polyhistor* of that year, which was made up of unsold sheets of an edition of 1587.

20 C. Plinius Secundus, *The secrets and wonders of the worlde* (London: Thomas Hacket, 1585). The 1587 edition had the same title.

21 C. Julius Solinus, *The excellent and pleasant work of Julius Solinus Polyhistor*, trans. Arthur Golding (London: I. Charlewood for Thomas Hacket, 1587).

22 Watson, *The beginnings of the teaching of modern subjects in England*, p. 89.

23 Thomas Blundeville, *A briefe description of universal mappes and cardes, and of their use* (London: Roger Ward for Thomas Cadman, 1589), fol. C1 verso.

24 *Ibid.*, fol. C2 verso.

25 J. D. Gould, 'The crisis in the export trade, 1586–87,' *The English historical review*, LXXI (April, 1956), 212–22.

26 Walter Bigges, *A summarie and true discourse of Sir Frances Drakes West Indian voyage* (London: Richard Field, 1589), fol. Aii recto. Two issues by Field and another by Roger Ward appeared in 1589. A Latin edition, *Expeditio Francisci Draki equitis Angli in Indias occidentales* (Leydon: F. Raphelengium, 1588), and a French translation, *Le voyage de Messire François Drake Chevalier, aux Inlex occidentales*, 1588, by the same publisher, preceded the English edition due to some dely incurred by Roger Ward in the year of the Armada. Quinn, *Roanoke voyages* I, 294.

27 Bigges, fol. Aii verso.

28 Baptisto Boazio, *The famouse West Indian voyadge made by the English fleete of 23 shippes and Barkes... from Plimmouth in the moneth of September 1585 and ended at Portesmouth in Julie 1586.* (n.p., ca. 1589).

29 Richard Hakluyt, *The principall navigations, voiages and discoveries of the English nation* (London: George Bishop and Ralph Newberie, 1589), fol. *2 verso. A facsimile edition was issued by the Hakluyt Society under the editorship of David B. Quinn, 1964.

30 *Ibid.*, fol. *3 verso.

31 André Thevet, *La cosmographie universelle* (2 vols.; Paris: P. L'Huilier, 1575); François de Belleforest, *La cosmographie universelle de tout le monde* (Paris, G. Mallot, 1570, 1572, 1577).

34 Thomas Fuller, *Worthies of England*, quoted in Parks, *Hakluyt*, p. 187.

35 Parks, *Hakluyt*, p. 175.

36 The authenticity of Ingram's journey has been questioned by some writers on the exploration of North America and defended by others.

37 A. L. Rowse, *The expansion of Elizabethan England* (London: Macmillan, 1955), p. 189.

38 Robert Tanner, *A mirror for mathematiques* (London: J. C. to be sold by Richard Watkins, 1587), fol. 36 verso.

39 Albertus Meierus, *Certaine briefe, and speciall instructions for gentlemen, merchants, students, souldiers, marriners, etc. employed in services abroade*, trans. Philip Jones (Lon-

don: John Wolfe, 1589 [i. e., 1590]), fol. A3 verso. First printed as *Methodus describendi regiones, urbes, et arces...* (Helmstadt, 1587).

40 Job Hortop, *The rare travailes of Job Hortop, an Englishman, who was not heard of in three and twentie yeeres space* (London: William Wright, 1591).

41 Edward Webbe, *The rare and most wonderful thinges which Edward Webbe an Englishman borne, hath seene and passed in his troublesome travailes* (London: Ralph Blower for Thomas Pavier, [1590]). A reprint of the original text, but with six woodcuts added, was published by William Barley, and another edition containing slight additions and corrections was published by William Wright. As the latter edition is dated 1590, it appears that all three editions must have been issued that year.

42 Edward A. Bond, *Russia at the close of the sixteenth century* (London: The Hakluyt Society, 1856), pp. lxix–lxxii.

43 Giles Fletcher, *Of the Russe common wealth* (London: T. D. for Thomas Charde, 1591), fol. A4 recto.

44 William Bourne, *A regiment for the sea* (London: Thomas East for Thomas Wright, 1592).

45 This chart is reproduced in Waters, *The art of navigation in England in Elizabethan and early Stuart times*, Plate XLIX, p. 193.

46 Justus Lipsius, *A direction for travailers... enlarged for the behoofe of the Earle of Bedford*, trans. Sir John Stradling (London: R. B[lower] for Cuthbert Burbie, 1592).

47 Henry Roberts, *Our Ladys retorne to England* (London: A. I. for William Barley, 1592). The contributions Roberts made to English pamphlet and ballad literature were first discussed by Louis B. Wright in his *Middle class culture in Elizabethan England* (Chapel Hill; University of North Carolina Press, 1935).

48 Henry Roberts, *Newes from the Levan t[e]seas* (London: For William Wright, 1594), fol. Aii recto.

49 Henry Roberts, *The trumpet of fame: or Sir Frauncis Drakes and Sir John Hawkins farewell* (London: Thomas Creede for William Barley, 1595), p. 9.

50 Henry Roberts, *Lancaster his allarums, honorable assaults... in Brasill* (London: A. I. for William Barley, 1595 ), fol. Bl recto.

51 *Ibid.*, fol. A4 verso.

52 Richard Hasleton, *Strange and wonderfull things happened... in his ten yeares travailes in many forraine countries* (London: A. I. for William Barley, 1595). Apart from this work, Hasleton is quite unknown both as an author and traveler.

53 John Davis, *The worldes hydrographical description* (London: Thomas Dawson, 1595), fol. B2 recto.

54 *Ibid.*, fol. B1 verso.

55 *Ibid.*, fol. B5 verso.

56 *Ibid.*, fol. E6 verso.

57 *Ibid.*, fol. E8 recto.

58 Sir Walter Raleigh, *The discoverie of the large, rich and bewtiful empire of Guiana* (London: Robert Robinson, 1596), fol. A2 recto–verso.

59 *Ibid.*, fol. A3 recto.

60 *Ibid.*, fol. ¶1 verso.

61 *Ibid.*, fol. ¶4 verso.

62 *Ibid.*, fol. N3 verso.

63 Lawrence Kemys, *A relation of the second voyage to Guiana* (London: Thomas Dawson, 1596), fol. E3 recto.

64 *Ibid.*, fol. A1 recto (Second A signature).

65 *Ibid.*, fol. A2 verso–A3 recto (First A signature).

66 Walter Bigges, *A summarie and true discourse of Sir Frances Drakes West Indian voyage* (London: For William Ponsonby, 1596). This is a close reprint of Field's second issue, but with the errata corrected. Nicolàs Monardes, *Joyfull newes out of the*

*new-found worlde*, trans. John Frampton (London: E. Allde by the assigne of Bonham Norton, 1596). Except for the addition of several pages inadvertently omitted from the 1580 edition, this is a near reprint of that edition. Francisco López de Gómara, *The pleasant historie of the conquest of the Weast India*, trans. Thomas Nicholas (London: Thomas Creede, 1596). The content is the same as the 1578 edition, with only minor variations in composition.

67 Thomas Blundeville, *M. Blundeville his exercises, containing six treatises* (London: John Windet, 1594), fol. A4 verso.

68 *Ibid.*, fol. 244 recto.

69 The world map of Plancius is reproduced in Frederik C. Wieder, *Monumenta cartographica* (5 vols.; The Hague: Martinus Nijhoff, 1925–33), plate 39.

70 Thomas Blundeville, *M. Blundeville his exercises, containing eight treatises* (London: John Windet, 1597).

71 Robert Hues, *Tractatus de globis et eorum usu* (London, Thomas Dawson, 1594). Translation from Clements R. Markham (ed.) *Tractatus de globis* (London: The Hakluyt Society, 1889), p. 3.

72 John Davis, *The seaman's secrets* (London: Thomas Dawson, 1595).

73 Christiaan van Adrichem, *A briefe description of Hierusalem and of the suburbs thereof* (London: Peter Short for Thomas Wight, 1595). This was first published as *Jerusalem sicut Christi tempore floruit* (Cologne: Godefridus Kempensis, 1584). It was included in van Adrichem's *Theatrum terrae sancti*, published in Cologne, 1590.

74 Giovanni Tommaso Minadoi, *The history of the warres betweene the Turkes and the Persians* (London: John Wolfe, 1595), p. 52. First published as *Historia della guerra fra Turchi et Persiani*. (Venice, A. Muschio, 1588).

75 John Blagrave, *Astrolabium uranicum generale* (London: T. Purfoot for W. Watts, 1596).

76 See Gerard de Jode's *Hemispherium ab aequinoctiali linea, ad circulum Poli Arctici...* [Antwerp, 1593] and Gerard Mercator's *Septentrionalium terrarum descriptio* [Duisburg, 1595].

77 Gabriel Tatton, *Nova et rece terrarum et regnorum Californiae, Nova Hispaniae, Mexicanae, et Peruviae...* Engraved by Benjamin Wright ([London, 1600]).

78 Gabriel Tatton, *Maris Pacifici quod vulgo Mar del Zur.* Engraved by Benjamin Wright ([London, 1600]).

## Chapter IX

## TO THE BRINK OF EMPIRE

The American adventures of Sir Walter Raleigh turned some English eyes to the New World, but the merchant community of London was more interested in the possibilities of the East. The return of Ralph Fitch in April, 1591, from his eastern travels coincided with the petition of the Levant Company for an extension of its letters patent. When Lord Burghley granted the new patent on January 7, 1592, it licensed Edward Osborne and fifty-two other persons, including Fitch, to trade for twelve years in the lands recently visited by Newbery, Fitch and their companions.[1] This potential extension of England's trade to Malaya was made without the publication of any account of the regions now opened to the Levant Company. Thomas Hickock's translation of Federici's narrative of eastern travels in 1588 had covered much of this area, but it was in no way related to the journey of Newberry and Fitch. In view of the monopoly system and the dominant position of London in this monopoly, the lack of public information is not surprising, for London also controlled the book trade of England.

There were other plans afoot also for English participation in the eastern trade. While the Levant Company was beginning to make a direct approach to the East Indies by way of the Mediterranean, a group of London merchants looked to the Cape of Good Hope route as the means of developing an eastern commerce. These merchants were probably members of the Levant company, for while their names are not recorded, the ships which departed in 1591 under the leadership of George Raymond were all previously engaged in the Levant trade.[2] This voyage was undertaken after a group of London merchants petitioned the Queen for permission to attempt to reach the East Indies by the old Portuguese route. Reconnaissance and piracy appear to have been the main purposes of the voyage, which turned out disastrously, as disease depleted one of the ships, another went down with all hands in a storm off the Cape of Good Hope, and, giving up the attempt to reach the East Indies, Sir James Lancaster turned the remaining ship toward the West Indies. Ultimately, he and eighteen others were marooned on the island of Mona by five men and a boy who made off with the ship, forcing Lancaster and his companions to return in a French ship in 1594.[3] It is not surprising that they did not publish an account of this adventure.

It is possible to understand Lawrence Kemys' concern for royal support of such enterprises 'subject to more doubtful events' than Raleigh's Guiana project. As Kemys wrote, another doubtful adventure was being readied, and late in 1596 Benjamin Wood sailed for the East Indies by the Cape of Good Hope. Only one man, a French crew member, lived to return from that voyage. Yet the promise of the East Indies was great, and the wealth to be gained from steady participation in trade there was proved by nearly a century of Portuguese enterprise. The Dutch were proving that the Indies could be reached by navigators other than the Portuguese, for within four years after the return of Cornelis Houtman, the first Dutch captain to make the voyage, perhaps sixty ships left the Netherlands to trade in the East Indies.[4] This was more than an example; it was a threat. England's approach to the East through the Levant was being outflanked by her near neighbor, and if England was to compete in the markets of western Europe, she must not fall behind the Dutch in wresting control of the eastern trade from the Spanish and Portuguese.

In this atmosphere it is not surprising to find two works useful to navigators, Bourne's *Regiment for the sea* and Record's *Castle of knowledge* being re-issued in 1596.[5] Nor is it surprising to see Richard Hakluyt relaxing his intense concern for colonies in America in favor of publishing translations of African and East Indian interest. In 1597 he apparently induced Abraham Hartwell to translate Duarte Lopes' account of Africa which was published as *A report of the kingdome of Congo.* Hartwell was not a good choice from the mercantile point of view, however, for he looked upon Africa as a field for missionary work primarily, hoping that Englishmen interested in Africa would 'not attempt these actions for commodity of Gold and Silver... but that they woulde first seeke the Kingdome of God & the salvation of many thousand soules...'[6] A contemporary of Hakluyt at Oxford, and subsequently secretary to John Whitgift, Archbishop of Canterbury, Hartwell had no love for the work he undertook in translating from the Italian, but he gave Hakluyt more than a translation. He edited his book with great care, commenting on the value of retaining the original style, referring the reader to other sources on controversial points, and taking issue with the Portuguese use of the term 'pirates' when referring to Drake and Cavendish. He considered seriously the effect of the sun on men's skin, the possibility of a nation of Amazons, and the value of Catholicism among the African natives as opposed to paganism.

This critical analysis accompanies a description of the western side of Africa particularly, with some attention to south and east Africa. In the text proper the religious aspect of Portuguese interest is less prominent than the commercial, as the rivers, climate, cities, and prodducts are described in some detail. The activity of the Portuguese priests, however, is also included. Its critical features, the inclusiveness of the information, and a very good map of Africa included in this volume make it one of the more distinguished geographical publications to be issued in England in the sixteenth century.

Africa was undoubtedly of interest to the navigators and merchants who sought to reach the East Indies by the Cape of Good Hope route, but the East Indies themselves were the real goal, and for this area the Dutch were the major source of information. The need which both the Dutch and English felt for an ally against Spain, as well as long-standing and mutually beneficial commercial connections, had brought them into a close relationship by the last years of the sixteenth century. The strength which the Dutch showed in liberating the northern provinces of the Netherlands from Spain also expressed itself in an aggressive mercantile policy. Dutch publishers were also aggressive, and voyages to the East Indies were quickly reported in volumes which the English picked up and translated. In the earliest of these translations from the Dutch, the hand of Richard Hakluyt is again to be seen, but with less force than he showed in the earlier works on America. More in evidence than Hakluyt were the translator, William Phillip, and the publisher, John Wolfe.

In the year following Houtman's return from his first East Indian voyage, and the publication of an account of it, Phillip translated his journal into English for Wolfe, who published it as *The description of a voyage made by certaine ships of Holland into the East Indies*. Phillip, who, apart from his translations of Dutch travel literature, was an obscure person, appears to have been an enthusiast for Dutch enterprise, and in his dedication to Sir James Scudmore he stated that he believed this voyage of Houtman's was 'deserving no lesse commendation then those of our Countrey men... as at large appeareth in a book by M. Richard Haclute...'[7] He told Scudmore that if he received this book favorably the forthcoming translation of Linschoten's *Itinerario* would be dedicated to him also; then, without effort at propagandizing for East Indian voyages, he merely translated the narrative of Houtman's voyage. Houtman's landing on the African mainland and on Madagascar were described, as were products and harbors in Java, prices of commodities in East Indian markets, dealings with Eastern rulers, difficulties with the Portuguese, and other events of the voyage. His book includes pictures of coins used in Java, maps of Java, Sumatra, and other islands. It is a superior piece of travel literature, full of both the quaint and the practical. It apparently did not appeal to Sir James Scudmore, however, for a sequel to it, *An addition to the sea journal... of the Hollanders unto Java*, was dedicated to an obscure Mathias Rutten.[8] The term 'addition' is very suitable for this pamphlet, for it has no continuity, but contains nine plates, a map, and several silhouette maps with text describing them. Some vocabularies of East Indian islands are included, and a more complete description of Bali than was to be found in the earlier publication was added.

These translations by William Phillip are not without significance, but they were dwarfed both in size and importance by his translation of Linschoten's *Itinerario*, also published in 1598. Sir James Scudmore was again passed over, as the book was dedicated to Julius Caesar, who had been appointed Judge of the High Court of Admiralty in 1580 and subsequently held a variety of other positions in the government during the reigns of Elizabeth and James I. Linschoten's book came into the English language at the suggestion of Hakluyt who recommended it to Wolfe, 'which book being commended by Maister Richard Hakluyt... the printer thought good to cause the same to be translated into the English tongue.'[9] In the hands of Phillip, however, it did not take on the character of vigorous empire propaganda, for the translator seems to have had no imperialistic spirit; he admired navigators more for what they could endure than for the benefit they might bring to England. In his dedication he merely expressed the hope that the judge would find this book 'beneficial to our countrey men.'[10] To the reader he addressed a fear-laden statement of the great dangers of travel, remarking that sailors 'doo continually dye living and live dying.'[11] He made no mention of the situation which was responsible for the publication of the book: that the Portuguese empire was now open to the Dutch and English. With the greatest wealth of information on the East Indies published to that date in his translation, Phillip's strongest hope for it was that it would aid Englishmen in the 'exportation of such thinges wherein we doe abound, and importation of those Necessities whereof we stand in Neede.'[12] In suggesting that it be translated, Hakluyt was recognizing the merits of a book that was much better than his own from the standpoint of utility, maps and readability. Its usefulness to those contemplating eastern voyages was attested to by the fact that a group of London merchants, the forerunners of the East India Company, made a gift of ten pounds to Hakluyt for seeing this book into print and an additional thirty shillings for maps to be used in the book.[13]

Linschoten's work is divided into four books. The first concerns the East Indies, including eastern Africa. Islands, cities, methods of navigation, harbors, products, units of measurement, and other useful information is given for regions as far east as Japan. Book Two describes the navigation of the coast of West Africa, around the Cape of Good Hope to Arabia, and in addition contains a description of the New World based on a great variety of sources. Book Three is a massive *roteiro* made from the writings of the Portuguese Royal Pilot, Diego Affonso. It contains a route guide from Portugal to India and instructions for sailing from island to island in the East Indies; similar descriptions and instructions are given for the New World, particularly Brazil and Spanish America. Finally, Book Four is a translation from a Spanish source of 'a most true and certaine extract and summarie of all the rents, tributes, tenthes... and incomings of the King of Spain.'[14] Since the Portuguese empire was at that time under Spanish rule, this indicated the value of the various colonial regions to Spain.

In this one book, therefore, Englishmen had a vivid picture of the commerce of the newly discovered areas which had a vigorous trade. Well and authoritatively written by a Dutchman of a merchant family who had spent eleven years in the East Indies, and illustrated with up-to-date maps, it was a history and geography of the first order, and in recommending it to John Wolfe, Hakluyt was performing one of his greatest services to English imperialism.

As the work he recommended went to press, Hakluyt was finishing a new edition of his own great collection of travel accounts. The second edition of his *Principal navigations* was in fact an entirely new work, rather than a re-editing of the old one. Both the bulk and the scope of the book were greatly expanded; only the method remained the same. This was the method of the compiler, for to the end he was still 'essentially the bystander who recorded.'[15] His dedication to Charles Howard is more a personal note than a call to empire; it contains a hint of the author's relief that his book is finished: 'the ardent love of my countrey devoured all difficulties... and thrust me forward into this most troublesome and painfull action.'[16] Yet he noted with apparent pride the ancient accounts, many of them not related to England's situation, which he had discovered and included, proving that the 'troublesome and painfull action' was a labor of love after all.

In this second edition, it is the collector rather than the imperialist that shows most prominently. He increased the amount of medieval travel literature from the 70,000 words in the 1589 edition to nearly 250,000 in 1598. Now he was including non-English travels, so the material for the modern period could have been expanded almost without limit, yet while the medieval material increased three and one half times, the modern section increased from 629,000 words to 1,452,000 words, or less than two and one half times.[17] He simply could not resist including information he had gathered. Of the northeast passage he wrote, 'But now it is high time for us to weigh our ancre, to hoist up our sailes, to get clear of these boistrous, frosty and misty seas, and with all speed direct our course for the milde, lightsome, temperate, and warme Atlantic Ocean...'[18] But then he gave 590 pages to voyages and travels to the north and east.

Hakluyt's imperialism does show through in the dedication to Robert Cecil in Volume Two. It was a wishful imperialism, still directed to the crown rather than to potential colonists. He wished 'the Almighty to stirre up her Majesties heart... with transporting of one or two thousand of her people'[19] whom he knew would be willing to go as adventurers as well as for the purpose of bringing Christianity to natives of the New World. He wished also that the gentry would give this idea some consideration, rather than following their 'soft unprofitable pleasures.'[20] It seems that in Hakluyt's estimation it was the Queen and the gentry who stood in the way of empire. Yet it is obvious that by the end of the century Hakluyt's interests were more evenly divided between eastern trade and western planting than they had been ten years earlier. His second volume is concerned with the Levant trade and the Cape of Good Hope voyages, including much material on the reopening of the Levant to the English by Osborne and his associates and the travels of Fitch and Newbery to the East via the Levant.

Still his interest in the New World remained strong. In his coverage of voyages to the west and southwest he increased his text from 279,000 words to 812,000.[21] It is, however, chiefly an archive of documents and narratives. He brought his readers up to date on such recent events as Raleigh's voyage to Guiana. He also added much to the bulk of this section with the inclusion of accounts of non-English voyages, such as the expeditions of Verrazano, Ribaut, Laudonnière, and the Zeno brothers, as well as a large number of documents describing the West Indies from Spanish sources.

It is doubtful that Hakluyt's second edition was due to a strong public demand. He would probably have noted such an increase in interest had it existed instead of bemoaning the lack of interest on the part of the Queen and the gentry. He was confident that colonists could be found, but he gives no evidence of a public clamour for empire. The second edition may have grown from his recognition of a still unfilled need for geographical information in English which could not be supplied by accounts of English voyages alone—hence the inclusion of non-English narratives. His dedications to Howard and Cecil suggest agreement in high places with his motives. He did not use this additional mass of information to bolster any strong plea to either the people or the crown on behalf of an imperial ambition. He was aware of the momentum building up for an East Indian enterprise of large proportions, yet he did not use this book to encourage it openly or to solicit the public interest in it. Like his first edition, this one was an anthology of narratives and documents, gathered with great care, but loosely strung together and lacking in commentary. It is nevertheless the greatest historical source for England's interests abroad in the sixteenth century.

In the works of Hakluyt and Linschoten, Englishmen had access to the most important historical and geographical information relating to the discoveries of the sixteenth century; yet neither of these books was reprinted, possibly because of their cost. Popular interest in geography however was evident at quite another level and apparently quite divorced from current events, for George Abbot's comparatively primitive *Briefe description of the whole worlde*, which appeared in editions of both 1599 and 1600,[22] was destined to go through seven more editions by 1636.

Abbot's work was a general geography in which discoveries of the sixteenth century were but lightly mentioned. Except for Greece, European countries were in some cases described in less than one page. Eastern Mediterranean countries were described largely in terms of Greek and Roman history, and the account of China made no mention of European contact there. Although the Portuguese were mentioned in connection with India, the entire description of that country occupied less than two pages. Mention of 'recent' Portuguese explorations was made with reference to Africa, but most of these by this time were nearly a century old, and the East Indies were merely mentioned as sources of spices for the Spaniards. Abbot's description of the New World included brief accounts of Columbus and Cortés as well as English attempts at the northwest passage 'about the yeare 1570,'[23] and he was aware that Virginia had been abandoned 'to the olde inhabitants.'[24] He also referred to 'some of our English men'[25] sailing through the Strait of Magellan to the west coast of North America which they named New Albion. On the whole, Abbot, a bishop who was ultimately to become Archbishop of Canterbury, relied more on classical and Biblical sources than on sixteenth century works, and as a result his book is decidedly old-fashioned. Yet, like the translations from Münster and the classical geographers, it appears to have had far more appeal to the general public than well-founded accounts of recent geographical discoveries.

There was another public, however, a growing group of persons interested in the latest voyages of the Dutch to the East Indies, and English accounts of these voyages continued to come into print shortly after the return of Dutch ships from the East. In 1598 eight ships were sent to the East Indies by the Dutch under the command of Jacob van Neck and Wybrand van Warwick, four of them returning the following year with profitable cargo. In 1599 *A true report* of this voyage was published in the form of a news letter without preface or dedication but with an abundance of information on the East Indian voyage, some of which was useful, some merely interesting. The narrator observed the decline in the quality of the beer on the outward voyage after the Cape of Good Hope had been passed. He took pleasure in watching the natives hunt whales, and he observed without comment that on the island of Santa Maria, near Madagascar, 'We tooke the king prisoner, who paide for his Ransome a Cow and a fat calfe.'[26] Upon the arrival at Bantam there was a brief exchange of letters and gifts, and the author noted with satisfaction 'we were freely licensed to trade and trafficke...'[27] Four days after arrival they began to load their ships, and the author described the types of goods that were exchanged. He also noted that the price of pepper began to rise as the rumor spread that more Dutch ships would arrive shortly. When the Dutch departed, 'the people [at Bantam] were glad of their departure, having some mistrust of us...'[28] The joy with which the cargo of pepper, cloves, mace, nutmeg, and cinnamon was received in Holland is described, and the author, offering thanks to a benevolent Providence, viewed with the greatest satisfaction the fact that the voyage required only one year, two months and nineteen days. This anonymous narrative contains no suggestion of who wrote it. References to Van Neck make it clear he was not the author, and it could not have been Warwick, for he did not return with this part of the fleet. The lack of any known previous Dutch edition suggests that this may have been written by an Englishman with Van Neck's fleet.

It was now clear in London that the trade of the East Indies was being tapped at its easternmost source, and with substantial profits resulting to the Dutch merchants. Rumors spread that the Dutch were buying ships in England to increase their East India cargo fleet.[29] England responded with a group of 101 merchants subscribing 30,133 pounds on September 22, 1599, to send a fleet of merchant ships to the East Indies; many among the leaders of this group were members of the Levant Company whose eastern trade was now sorely threatened. The initial Dutch advantage created an air of urgency among the merchants, but trade had to wait on the royal will, for the Queen was negotiating peace with Spain. English ships sailing to the East Indies, nominally controlled by Spain, could only upset her long-cherished hopes for peace.

The merchants waited as negotiations with Spain dragged through the early months of 1600, and in September they were told to proceed with their plans for an East India voyage. James Lancaster and John Davis were selected to lead the voyage. Davis had sailed to the East Indies with the Dutch fleet of Cornelis Houtman. Four ships, together with stores and provisions, were purchased, and men at the refitting docks were hastened in their work with a barrel of beer a day. As preparations for the voyage advanced, the Privy Council pressured subscribers who were behind in their payments to pay up so that the ships might get under way at the earliest possible date. The charter of the new company was granted on December 31, 1600, and finally on the following February 13 the East India fleet departed from Woolwich.[30]

In the exciting days during which the fleet was being readied for the voyage, Richard Hakluyt was again active in supplying literary preparation for those interested in the East Indian venture. He induced William Walker, an otherwise unknown person, to translate *The journall or dayly register* of Jacob van Neck, which was licensed by the Company of Stationers less than a month before the fleet sailed. In dedicating the book to Sir Thomas Smith, governor of the East India Company, Walker—or possibly Hakluyt—recaptured the spirit of the 1570s as he wrote: 'That the searching of new trades, & above all other, this to the East Indies, is more than necessary, both the restraint of traffique in the King of Spaines dominions, and also the underrate of the Hollanders spices in regarde of those brought out of the Indies by way of Turkie, doe plainelie demonstrate.'[31] The purpose of the book is clearly stated: 'Heere therefore your Captaines, Masters and Factors... may in some sorte be directed how to shape their course to avoide many perils, and to enjoy severall kindes of Marchandize for which you send them.'[32]

The account of the voyage is similar in many points to the anonymous narrative of the same voyage published in 1599. It described Mauritius in greater detail as a provisioning place and included the voyage beyond Bantam to Amboina, Banda, and the Moluccas made by four ships of the fleet, while the other four returned. Some useful mercantile vocabulary was also included. No better brief collection of information could have been presented to the East India venturers than was to be found here, and in addition to being utilitarian, it carried the conviction that England could benefit from it.

Hakluyt was aware that the East Indian voyages would require some knowledge of Africa, for the Portuguese had used African bases for provisioning and refitting. Linschoten had viewed Africa as a part of the eastern voyage, and indeed, the lands and seas beyond the Cape of Good Hope were to become the preserve of the various European East India Companies. It was within this context that Hakluyt's influence in having the geography of Africa by Leo Africanus translated and published was related to the early preparations of the East India merchants, for England's African trade was not of major importance in the last decade of the sixteenth century. In publishing *A geographical historie of Africa*, John Pory, the translator, recognized the fact that Leo's work was badly out of date, having been written in 1526, and he buttressed it before and after with excerpts from Linschoten, Lopes, Alvares, and Goes, as well as with information from classical writers, 'both for the Reader's satisfaction, and that John Leo might not appeare too solitarie upon the stage.'[33] For this he earned the praise of Hakluyt who commended him on 'how... faithfully he hath done his part, and how he hath enlarged and graced this Geographicall history out of... the best ancient and moderne writers.'[34]

Early in his text, Pory wrote of the regions omitted by Leo, including eastern and central Africa particularly, with the various kingdoms supposedly ruled over by Prester John, and such important commercial cities as Sofala, Mozambique, and Kilwa, indicating his appreciation of the development of East Africa. He also added descriptions of the Portuguese lands of West Africa and various islands off the coasts and in the Red Sea. Leo's own description of Africa, though out of date, was detailed on the subject of the manners and customs of various African peoples, so that as a whole the work was a compendium of information, which, with the works of Linschoten and Lopes, gave to English readers an abundance of information on Africa, its peoples and its commercial opportunities.

Pory's book was dedicated to Sir Robert Cecil, who, in succeeding to the position of his father, Lord Burghley, became the most influential man in the English government. It was he who had given aid and comfort to Raleigh during his disgrace, and now he appears as Hakluyt's patron. It was, perhaps, at Cecil's charge that Pory's book was published, and in 1601 the dedication by Hakluyt of another book to Cecil was further revealing of their relationship. This book was *The discoveries of the world from their first original unto the yeere of our Lord 1555*, translated by Hakluyt from the Portuguese of Antonio Galvão. In making this translation Hakluyt was responding to the suggestion of a friend that he condense his *Principal navigations* 'to draw them into a short sum' for the benefit of 'men of great action and employment.'[35] Hakluyt's selection of Galvão's book for this purpose of brief information was not entirely suitable, for the Portuguese chronicle of eastern exploration terminated with the year *1555*, although it certainly reflected the flourishing East India interest. Galvão had used the *Asia* of Barros for his account of fifteenth-century Portuguese explorations on the African coast, and for the subsequent period he had relied on Gómara and Peter Martyr, so the information presented was far from recent, and Hakluyt made but slight effort to make it timely with editorial comment, inserting only a few marginal notes based on more recent information.

While these translations of 1599–1601 were closely related to a commercial enterprise based upon an acute concern for their eastern trade by the London merchants, none of them had a wide enough audience to call for a second edition. By comparison, the geography of Giovanni Botero, first published in English in 1601 as *The travellers breviat*, was general and historical in tone, but its extensive descriptions of India, China, Persia, Tartary and eastern Africa may indicate the new East Indian interest as a motive which induced John Jaggard to bring it into print.[36] Botero's book described the Spanish and Portuguese eastern commerce in some detail, and if this translation was less immediately practical than the accounts of Dutch East Indian voyages, it was far more acceptable to the English public, for it was published again in 1603, and in five more editions before 1640.

The sudden burst of interest in the East Indies by merchants of the Levant Company did not mean that the Levant area was to be abandoned. In 1597 Sir Anthony Sherley was asked by the Earl of Essex to go out to Persia for the double purposes of securing help against the Turks and attempting to improve commercial relations between England and Persia. This was not a spectacular mission, but it resulted in the publication of two accounts of his travels into Persia and his negotiations there. The first of these was an anonymous *True report*, apparently an unauthorized publication consisting primarily of documents relating to Sherley's mission.[37] After a brief listing of places visited en route to the Great Sophi, Sherley's oration to that ruler is given, along with his letters of credence from the Great Sophi granting permission to trade in Persia. This collection of documents confirmed England's active interest in continuing the Persian trade via the long-used Russian route despite the growing interest in the new southeast passage.

William Parry's account of the same mission contains more detail and observation, for he accompanied Sherley but it does not so clearly indicate the purpose of the embassy.[38] He did quote Sherley's remark to an eastern ruler that 'wee were Merchants, desirous to trade to the utmost confines of his countries,' [39] but the narrative took on the character of a series of private adventures and observations, noting, among other things, the use of carrier pigeons to fly news of coming East India cargoes to Mecca and Aleppo. From Persia Sherley's group went into Russia via the Caspian Sea and Volga River, departing from Russia at St. Nicholas on the White Sea. While informative, Parry's narrative lacked conviction concerning the Persian and Russian commerce and was more a work for entertainment than for developing an interest in the areas he visited.

While both merchant and royal attention was primarily directed toward the East Indian trade in the last years of the sixteenth century, America still had the interest of lesser folk. English fishermen continued to compete with the Bretons and Basques in the Newfoundland area, and though fishing was their main concern, they landed to trade with the natives also. Meanwhile, the idea of using the New World as a place to send undesirable and nonconformist people, advocated by Churchyard, Gilbert, and Peckham, continued to linger in English thought. In 1597 the island of Ramea in the St. Lawrence was sought as a refuge for a group of religious noncomformists who intended to sustain a settlement on walrus-hunting and cod fishing. They petitioned the Privy Council for the right to establish a colony there, and they appear to have been granted permission to settle. The colony was not established, however, possibly because of the opposition of Bretons and Basques, whose hostility to an English base in those international waters would be understandable.[40]

Through such small and unofficial groups information continued to flow to England from the New World, although the East India Company showed a brief interest in North America in 1602 when it sent out Captain George Weymouth to explore for a northwest passage to Asia. Weymouth sailed into the strait later named for Henry Hudson, but contrary winds and mutinous sailors forced him to return home. London's publishers took no note of this failure. The same year Raleigh sent two ships to North America to acquire products of commercial value, indicating that his interests were again centering on the North Atlantic seaboard of America where his patent of 1584 still gave him claim to a large territory. Furthermore, hope was still held out that some remnants of the Virginia colony might be found.

Meanwhile, another group led by Bartholomew Gosnold and Bartholomew Gilbert directed an attempt in 1602 to plant a settlement in America. They sent out one ship with thirty-two men who briefly established themselves on Cuttyhunk Island, south of Massachusetts. After staying less than a month they returned to England. Among the members of the expedition was one John Brereton, who upon his return wrote an account of the venture, *A brief and true relation of… the north part of Virginia*, 'being earnestly requested by a deere friend, to put down in print, some true relation of our late performed voyage.'[41] The friend could have been Richard Hakluyt, the most persistent encourager of recording such voyages in England. It is noteworthy that George Bishop, who had published the translations from Galvão and Leo Africanus as well as both editions of Hakluyt's *Principal navigations*, also published this book. In dedicating it to Raleigh, Brereton may have been seeking Raleigh's good will for himself and his associates, for their voyage was undertaken without his knowledge, and upon their return Raleigh was upset at the thought that the sassafras in their cargo would compete with that brought back recently by his two ships.[42]

Brereton's book appeared in two issues in 1602, the second issue being considerably augmented. The first portion of the book contains accounts of the goods discovered which Brereton considered economically useful, including fruits, trees, herbs, animals, stones, metals, etc. Then follows an account of a voyage of 1602 in search of Raleigh's lost colony, noting the products that expedition acquired in America. Brereton then

turned his attention to the north, presenting a statement by Edward
Hoyes in favor of making an effort to colonize in the Newfoundland
region, in which valuable commercial products are enumerated, including wood for England's navy. Four subsequent pages are taken up
with Hoyes' belief that a great river flowing to the Pacific lay just
beyond the mountains that hemmed the coastal area. An overland
route to the headwaters of this river would, he believed, give England
access to the East Indies. At this point the first issue ends, having
stressed the economic and strategic aspects of northern Virginia.

The second issue adds 'Inducements to the liking of the voyage
towards Virginia.' [43] This had been written in 1585 by the elder Richard Hakluyt as a support for Raleigh's colonial undertaking, but
was not published at that time, probably because of the certainty of
Spanish opposition to such forward colonial plans by the English.
Hakluyt presented thirty-one inducements, among them the increase
in the sale of English woolens, the possibility of finding a westward
passage to the Pacific, the abundance of furs and hides to be found in
America, and the possibility of growing sugar there. He summed up
his view of the purposes of such a colony: to spread Christianity, to
develop trade, or to conquer—or all three. He listed thirty-one types
of artisans to be included in such a colony, including farmers, drug-
gists, smiths, and brick-makers. Following the 'Inducements' are passages from De Soto and Hariot on the richness of Virginia.

Brereton's book, particularly the second issue, stands out as one of
the foremost arguments for American colonization in the Elizabethan
period, for it was not encumbered with personal pleading and defending
as was Hariot's *Virginia*. It did not hold out hopes of gold to lure the
investor as did Raleigh's and Kemys' works on Guiana. It stands between the Raleigh Virginia colony and the Jamestown settlement of
1607, involving the motives of both. It reflects the earlier views of
Raleigh and Hakluyt in that its northwest passage appeal was secondary to its trade appeal. America, like the East Indies, was being presented to Englishmen as a place where a profitable trade could be
driven. Hakluyt convinced a group of Bristol merchants of this opportunity, and, with Raleigh's permission, an expedition was planned for
1603.

In March, 1603, Queen Elizabeth died. At that time England held
no territory abroad, the first commercial voyage to the East Indies had
not yet returned, and America was just being noticed as having potential commercial value. If the greatest of the Tudor reigns had not

established an empire, it had seen England sufficiently equipped with publications on the newly discovered regions of the earth to enable overseas enterprises to get under way with excellent information widely disseminated. Yet in this effort the Queen took no direct part. She and her ministers undoubtedly had far more information than was published, but they showed no interest in making it known to the citizenry. The books that gave information on the outer world for the public to read during the last half of her reign resulted from the enthusiasm of no more than a dozen men, among whom Richard Hakluyt was clearly dominant. Among the others who wrote literature of geography and travel after 1580, only Raleigh, Kemys, Peckham, Davis, Brereton and Carleill seem to have had any interest in establishing English colonies abroad. The pleading and defensive tone often evident in their writing indicates that the idea of empire was but slowly gaining acceptance.

## NOTES TO CHAPTER IX

1 Rowland, *England and Turkey*, pp. 87–88.
2 Foster, *England's quest*, p. 128.
3 Clements R. Markham (ed.), *The voyages of Sir James Lancaster, Kt. to the East Indies* (London: The Hakluyt Society, 1877), pp. 24–34.
4 Foster, *England's quest*, p. 143.
5 William Bourne, *A regiment for the sea* (London: Thomas East for T. Wight, 1596); Robert Record, *The castle of knowledge* (London: V. Simms assigned by B. Norton, 1596).
6 Duarte Lopes, *A report of the kingdome of Congo*, trans. Abraham Hartwell (London: John Wolfe, 1597), fol. ❧ 3 recto. This was first published as *Relatione del reame di Congo et delle circonvicine contrade* (Rome: Bartolomeo Grassi, [1591]).
7 Bernardt Langenes, *The description of a voyage made by certaine ships of Holland into the East Indies*, trans. William Phillip (London: John Wolfe, 1598), fol. A2 recto. The *STC* attributes this work to Langenes, but there is no question but that it is Houtman's narrative. It was first published in Middelburg by Langenes, a bookseller, as *Verhael vande reyse by de Hollandtsche schepen gedaen naer Oost Indien in 1597.*
8 Cornelius Geraldson, *An addition to the sea journal or navigation of the Hollanders unto Java*, probably trans. William Phillip (London: John Wolfe, 1598). This is a translation of *Appendix oft by-voechsel achter t'journal vande reyse de Hollantsche schepen op Java* (Middelburg: B. Langenes, 1598). The printer was Cornelis Gerritszoon, to whom the *STC* attributes authorship, which probably belongs to Houtman.
9 Jan Huygen van Linschoten, *John Huighen van Linschoten, his discours of voyages into ye East and West Indies*, trans. William Phillip (London: John Wolfe, [1598]), fol. A3 verso. The original edition was *Itinerario, voyage ofte schipvaert... naer Oost ofte Portugaels Indien* (Amsterdam: Cornelis Claesz, 1596).
10 Linschoten, fols. A1 verso–A2 recto.
11 *Ibid.*, fol. A3 recto.
12 *Ibid.*, fol. A4 recto.
13 Foster, *England's quest*, p. 145.

14 Linschoten, p. [449].

15 Parks, *Hakluyt*, p. 180.

16 Richard Hakluyt, *The principal navigations, voyages traffiques and discoveries of the English nation* (3 vols.; London: George Bishop, Ralph Newberie and Robert Barker, 1598–1600), I, *2 recto.

17 Parks, *Hakluyt*, p. 175.

18 Hakluyt, *Principal navigations* (1598–1600), I, fols *4 verso–*5 recto.

19 *Ibid.*, II, *3 recto.

20 *Ibid.*

21 Parks, *Hakluyt* p. 175.

22 George Abbot, *A briefe description of the whole worlde* (London: T. Judson for John Browne, 1599). The 1600 edition was printed by R. B. for John Browne.

23 *Ibid.*, fol. D8 verso (1599 ed.).

24 *Ibid.*

25 *Ibid.*

26 *A true report of the gainefull, prosperous and speedy voiage to Java in the East Indies* (London: P. S[short] for W. Aspley, 1599), p. 3.

27 *Ibid.*, p. 6.

28 *Ibid.*, p. 8.

29 Foster, *England's quest*, p. 144.

30 *Ibid.*, pp. 147–55.

31 Jacob Corneliszoon van Neck, *The journall or dayly register contayning a true manifestation... of the voyage... under the conduct of Jacob Corneiliszen Neck*, trans. William Walker (London: For Cuthbert Burby and J. Flasket, 1601), fol. Ʂ2 recto.

32 *Ibid.*, verso.

33 Johannes Leo Africanus, *A geographical historie of Africa*, trans. John Pory (London: George Bishop, 1600), fourth preliminary leaf, recto. Leo was an 'African' geographer and traveler who was born in Spain and educated in Italy. His description of Africa was first published by Ramusio in 1550. Pory's translation was, for the most part, from a Latin version printed in Antwerp in 1556.

34 Leo Africanus, p. 57. Pory included a half page of 'approbation of the historie ensuing' by Hakluyt.

35 Antonio Galvão, *The discoveries of the world from their first originall unto the yeere of our Lord 1555*, trans. Richard Hakluyt (London: George Bishop, 1601), fol. A2 recto. The original Portuguese edition was *Tratado que compos o nobre e notavel capitão Antonio Galvão, dos diversos e desvayrados caminhos... veyo da India* ([Lisbon]: Joham da Barreira, 1563).

36 Giovanni Botero, *The travellers breviat, or an historical description of the most famous kingdomes in the world*, trans. Robert Johnson (London: E. Bollifant for John Jaggard, 1601). The first edition, *Le relationi universali* was published in Rome in 1591.

37 *A true report of Sir Anthony Shierlie's journey overland to Venice, from thence by sea to Antioch, Aleppo and Babilon* (London: R. B. [lore] for J. J[aggard], 1600). See Sir E. Denison Ross, *Sir Anthony Sherley and his Persian adventure* (London: George Routledge & Sons, Ltd., 1933).

38 William Parry, *A new and large discourse of the travels of Sir Anthony Sherley... to the Persian Empire* (London: Valentine Simmes for Felix Norton, 1601).

39 *Ibid.*, p. 9.

40 David B. Quinn, 'England and the St. Lawrence, 1577–1602,' *Merchants and scholars*, ed. John Parker.

41 John Brereton, *A briefe and true relation of the discoverie of the north part of Virginia* (London: George Bishop 1602), fol. A2 recto.

42 Quinn, *Raleigh*, p. 169.

43 Brereton, p. 25.

## Chapter X

## TRADE AND EMPIRE IN THE EAST

The England which James VI of Scotland inherited in 1603, and over which he ruled as James I until his death in 1625, was a nation just about to become aware of the role she was to play in modern history. The East India Company had its ships on the sea. The North American and Guiana Coasts were drawing increasing attention. Yet new ideas had to contend with a traditional cast of mind that looked to old ways instinctively. The forces of the future had allies, however, for there were developing certain attitudes which had implications for empire, especially when coupled with the policies of James. The long-standing hatred of the Papacy and Spain had given English nationalism an outlet in war, and it had provided English investors with a legitimate enterprise in fitting out privateering vessels to prey upon enemy ships. James was opposed to this popular war, and he concluded peace in 1605. Nationalist aspirations had to seek new outlets, and investors in overseas undertakings had to find new projects for profit. England was also possessed of a restive Protestant element which Elizabeth had held in check, and when James, a fellow-Calvinist, said of these Puritans 'I will make them conform, or else harry them out of the land,' he added another group to the list of undesirables that imperialists might consider as likely colonists. But this group was different. They had a missionary spirit which could indeed be harnessed to build an empire. James's attitude toward the Puritans resulted from his suspicion of their theocracy which ran contrary to his attitude toward good order in the state. Good order in his view proceeded from a chain of relationships between God and man, and between man and man, in which the king reigned by divine right and men obeyed their rulers without question. The questioning of royal prerogative had never been given up by Englishmen even under the strong Tudor monarchs, and an alien king viewing this practice with disfavor made the homeland less attractive to zealots for English law and added to the number of discontented citizens who might hope to find less oppression in the New World. Finally, James came from a country that was not nearly as commercially oriented as England, and his fluctuating policies with respect to England's overseas trading enterprises indicated no settled philosophy toward that element of the nation which was becoming stronger with each passing year and which was to be of major importance in the establishment of an empire. In being out of step with much that was English, James was the harbinger of England's time of troubles; yet in the first two decades of his reign we see the establishment of the beginnings of empire in the eastern and western hemispheres to the accompaniment of a steady flow of significant literature based upon these overseas interests and a growing output of general geographical works.

As James proceeded southward to his coronation in 1603, the four ships of the East India Company under Sir James Lancaster crept northward, returning from the first East Indian voyage, and while the company was entirely independent of government, it was of concern to the nation, for it was establishing what many voyages by other routes had attempted in the interests of English trade—a feasible water route to the East Indies. The fact that Lancaster was accorded an interview with the new monarch upon his return and had knighthood conferred upon him shows clearly that the Crown was interested in this private effort. And well it might be! It had cost 17,000 pounds to bury Elizabeth, and another 10,000 to bring James from Edinburgh.[1] The Exchequer had a deficit of 400,000 pounds to greet the new king. As the King and the company awaited Lancaster's return, some news of the East Indies appeared in an anonymous letter written in Amsterdam, apparently to a friend of the author in London, under the title *A true and perfect relation of the newes sent from Amsterdam, the 21. of February, 1603.* This was an account of the latest Dutch doings in the East Indies, 'forasmuch as the Maister of the Pinnace himselfe (called Cornelis Schoutein) arrived here yesternight.'[2] The Dutch correspondent related chiefly the story of the five ships that sailed to the East Indies from the Netherlands on April 23, 1601, and upon arriving at Bantam found a Portuguese fleet of twenty-two ships waiting for them. The Dutch went to the attack, drove the Portuguese out, and then sailed on to Banda and Ternate to lade spices. Brief mention is made of other Dutch ships in the East Indies, including two that went to China. To anxious watchers for the return of Lancaster the letter stated: 'Of the English and French shippes we have no newes at all.'[3]

This 'no newes' was the best news the company was to have in this period of waiting, for the affairs of the company were far from satisfactory. An investment of 68,000 pounds was tied up in Lancaster's voyage. The northwest attempt of Weymouth the previous year had been a complete loss and was not to be undertaken again. Trade was nearly stopped in London because of the plague, while the Dutch were sending out fleet after fleet to secure an advantage over the English in the East Indies. Governor Smith, meanwhile, was forced to give up his position as head of the new company on suspicion of having been involved in the Essex plot.[4] When Lancaster's ships did arrive, the cargo they brought back was primarily pepper acquired at Bantam, and now it was discovered that the Dutch voyages had satisfied the current demand for that commodity. The dividend that was declared was a dividend of pepper, while cash had to be borrowed to pay the seamen.[5]

While the immediate results of the voyage were not satisfactory, they were apparently of sufficient interest to warrant the printing of two accounts of the voyage. Both of these accounts reflect the true nature of the early voyages to the East Indies, for they show no nationalistic spirit, no missionnary idealism, but are straightforward journals of a voyage which was a purely business undertaking in an area where the Spanish, Portuguese, Dutch, Indians, Javanese, Chinese and others were already established.

*A true and large discourse of the voyage* was written by one of the men aboard the *Ascension* and, without preface, introduction or dedication, begins 'The 20 of April 1601, we wayed Anchor and set saile out of Torbay by Dartmouth.'[6] There is not an entry for each day, and many of the entries are as brief and cold as the first, such as 'The 2. of May one of our Admiralles men fell overboord from the maine yard and was drowned.'[7] Other entries, however, were very informative about the events of the voyage and convey the impression the eastern islands made on the English writer. He noted with calm casualness: 'The 21 of June we took a Portingall whose lading was Wine, Oyle, and Meale...'[8] He was more impressed with the arrival of the fleet at Saldanha Bay near the Cape of Good Hope, noting the 900 to 1,000 cattle and sheep bought there to reprovision the ships. He described the appearance of the people, their dress and speech, as well as the birds, animals and rivers of that region. He also found the reception given Lancaster by the King of Achin impressive, as he wrote 'The Dishes and Cuppes wherein they served, were most of goulde, and of a mettal much like Bell mettall, which is dearer then goulde, and every dishe covered, some with Purslain of China.'[9] The impact of eastern civilization upon English mentality shows through occasionally, but the main concern is with navigation and trade, and the author's tone is one of practicality, without any pretense at being popular or literary. This account was probably intended for the use of the company in manuscript form, for it contains such features as an East Indian vocabulary and a list of the 180 men who lost their lives during the voyage.

On June 6, 1603, at a meeting of the East India Company, two letters written by Roger Style and Edmund Highlord aboard the *Ascension* were delivered by a Frenchman whose ship had left the *Ascension* at St. Helena. It is not possible to know which of these letters came into the hands of William Aspley and his printer, Thomas Thorpe, who published it without registering it with the Company of Stationers. This *Letter written to the worshipfull the governours and assistants of the East Indian marchants in London* is much briefer than *A true and large discourse*, noting very few of the events at sea, omitting descriptions of the peoples encountered, and even reduces the necrology to the 'chiefe men of note which are dead in the voyage.'[10]

These three publications of 1603 provided for the possible extension of interest in the East India Company and its undertakings to the general public. It is also possible that the members of the company themselves needed some reinforcement of their interest, for they were called upon for funds to finance a second voyage immediately upon the return of Lancaster, who had left factors in Bantam with the full expectation that more voyages would follow. The company was not yet actually a joint-stock company in the sense that it had a continuing operation, for each voyage was separately planned and financed until 1613. The call for capital realized 60,452 pounds, and the next expedition was placed under the command of Henry Middleton, who had been with Lancaster in the 1601 voyage. The same four ships were to be used, and a group of merchants was included in the personnel of the voyage, as was a chaplain, who was to double as physician to the fleet.[11]

Departing the first week in April, 1604, Middleton made for the Cape Verde Islands, then for Table Bay, where his fleet put in with the crew scurvy-ridden and weak. Rested and restored by fresh meat and vegetables, they were at sea again August 20 and arrived at Bantam on December 23. Here the sick and bedraggled crew heard tales of woe told by the factors Lancaster had left there. The miseries of the climate and the treachery of the natives had not prevented them, however, from gathering a cargo of pepper sufficient to lade two ships. These were dispatched to England, and Middleton with the other two ships went on to Amboina, Banda, Tidore, and Ternate in search of spices other than pepper. Here he encountered an already rampant Dutch-Portuguese rivalry, and his presence further complicated the situation, for neither of the rivals was anxious to have the English establish themselves in these rich islands. Nevertheless, the *Dragon* loaded cloves in Tidore, and the *Ascension* came back from Banda with mace and nutmegs. Together they sailed for England on October 6, 1605.

Of the first two ships of the fleet to sail for England, the *Susan* disappeared without a trace, and the *Hector* was overtaken by the *Dragon* at Table Bay. The voyage was considered a success by the company, Middleton was knighted, plans were made for the next voyage, and two books appeared to inform the public of the peoples and products of the Spice Islands and the markets of the East Indies.

The publisher of both books was Walter Burre, brother-in-law of Henry Middleton, who appears to have replaced William Aspley as the company's publisher. Burre's first book on the East Indies, *The last East Indian voyage* is an anonymous journal 'begun by one of the voyage; since continued out of the faithful observations of them that are come home.'[12] Like its predecessors, it is a straightforward journal of events at sea and in the harbors where the *Dragon* anchored. It is without introductory material, other than a brief note by the publisher, and appears to have had little intention of arousing a national interest in the East Indies. It has more literary merit than the 1603 publications following Lancaster's voyage, although it contains wide gaps: for example, missing are the days from August 14 to December 19 during which the fleet sailed from Table Bay to Sumatra; and from August 16, 1605 to February 1, 1606, on the return voyage, only eight entries were made. It does, nevertheless, give an almost daily account of the sailings of the *Dragon* among the East Indian islands and is most detailed in its account of negotiations for trade and the difficulties with the Dutch and Portuguese there. The anonymous author was obviously more interested in these commerical, diplomatic and military affairs than in the peoples of these islands, for he wrote but little of their customs, dress, and religions—topics that frequently caused extensive comment among travelers to the East.

The most important feature of the book consists of three letters from the kings of Ternate, Tidore, and Bantam. The first of these monarchs invited the English to trade with his people, even though he had given promise of a monopoly to the Dutch in exchange for Dutch help against the Portuguese, whom he portrayed as his greatest enemies. The King of Tidore, however, invited the English to come to his aid against the

Dutch and the Ternatians who had done his people great harm. The ruler of Bantam rejoiced, 'Now England and Bantam are both as one.'[13] These letters gave evidence of England's new strategic position as a potential ally of native peoples against her European competitors, and with the narrative of the voyage, they confirmed England's opportunity for commercial expansion into islands hitherto in the preserve of the Portuguese and the Dutch.

In his brief note to the reader, publisher Burre had promised that if his book found public favor he would shortly issue an 'exact and large discourse, written by Maister Scott, chiefe factor at Bantam ever since the first voyage.'[14] Apparently he was satisfied with reader response, for later the same year he published *An exact discourse of... the East Indians*, which is easily the best of these early accounts of the East Indies based on English experience. Like the others, however, it is devoid of any imperialistic fervor. Edmund Scott, who had been left in charge of the English factory at Bantam by Lancaster, did not see himself as a pioneer of empire, but as a merchant concerned with securing goods for the East India Company and with protecting these goods against the uncommon proclivities toward thievery among the Javanese. Much of his narrative is taken up with methods used to foil the thieves, whose favorite stratagem was to start a fire in the factory, or near it, and when the factors' attention was diverted, to make off with the goods. Scott's descriptions of dealings with Chinese merchants resident in Bantam, relations with the Dutch factors there, and internal problems within the English factory give a good picture of the problems and responsibilities of this little band of Englishmen who watched anxiously for the sails of an English ship, only to find upon the arrival of Middleton that the crew was in the worst possible physical condition, and 'Bantam is not a place to recover men that are sicke, but rather to kill men that come thither in health.'[15]

In the final section of the book, Scott described Java, particularly Bantam, in great detail, noting the types of people, their customs, religions, locations of markets, warehouses, etc. Altogether, he presented England with an excellent and frequently exciting picture of the meeting of civilizations—Dutch, English, Javanese, Malayan, Chinese, and Portuguese—in one market town. His total impression of Bantam was not entirely favorable, yet he felt that Englishmen should not be frightened by it, for he believed it would be more agreeable to them as they became better known and made friends there.

These reactions of a man of business, the first Englishman to have prolonged commercial contact with the long-sought East Indies, apparently did not create sufficient interest to induce publishers to seek out returning merchants, factors, or sailors in the following years, for to the end of the period of the 'separate voyages' only one more narrative of English mercantile activity in the East Indies was published. It is obvious that the clamor made for reaching the riches of the East at the time of Frobisher had no wide public participation, for during the years between 1603 and 1613, when the 'separate voyages' ended, English merchants and sailors discovered the true intricacies of the eastern trade, but publishers apparently saw little opportunity for profit in reporting the events of these voyages.

There was much more to the East Indian trade than rounding the Cape of Good Hope and buying spices at Bantam and the islands to the east. After the first two voyages, the company called for penetration into new markets, for the spice trade was somewhat disillusioning. Actually, the area into which the company's ships were venturing was one with a well-developed inter-island and inter-regional economy in which the Portuguese had early discovered that the greatest actual earning power was to be found, not in the return of spices to Europe, but in supplanting native shipping in the carrying trade between the important entrepôts of the East. The Dutch had quickly understood this situation, and the English acquired the same information from their visits to the spice centers.

What had to be learned was that India, chiefly the Coromandel coast, supplied to the East Indian islands cloth of the various cities on the coast—foremost among them Negapatnam, Pulicat, and Masulipatam—and each had its own specialties in color, design, and quality which were the particular choice of the individual island markets. The means of placing orders with artisans, of supplying them with cash in advance and of placating local political authorities—all of these must be learned if the really lucrative inter-regional trade was to be exploited en route to the spice markets. Not only were the Indian cities and the East Indian islands involved in this commerce but other Asiatic traders as well, for Chinese merchants came to the major ports to sell silk, porcelain and other goods, taking back pepper in return, and between China and the islands were such important ports of call as Patani, Malacca, and Tenasserim on the Malay Peninsula, Bangkok in Siam, and Pegu on the southern extremity of Burma. From these ports came lead, tin, hides, gums, wood, and rice. Even distant Japan was, for a time, linked with the outside world through Siam.[16]

By the time William Keeling, in charge of the company's third voyage, departed in April, 1607, some of these facts had been impressed on Company officials through the two previous voyages, and Keeling cast his net wider than his predecessors had done. He stopped at Mozambique and bought aloes, then sailed on to Priaman, where he saw the wisdom of dealing in cloth 'especially blue Callicoes, white Callicoes, blue striped and checkered Stuffes.'[17] In Bantam he learned from the Siamese ambassador that in Siam he could sell a thousand red cloths in two days in exchange for gold and precious stones. After a visit to Banda he called at Macassar on Celebes Island. Meanwhile, one of his captains, William Hawkins, took the *Hector* to Surat, where a thriving business was done until the Portuguese took his ship, leaving him stranded. He proceeded overland to Agra, where he arrived in April, 1609, and was well received. In May, 1610, Keeling was back in England, but no account of his voyage was published at that time.

During Keeling's absence William Barret made an effort to capitalize on the current interest in the East Indies when on May 21, 1608, he registered with the Stationers' Company a translation of the account of Dutch actions against the Portuguese in the East Indies by Cornelis Matelief. *An historicall and true discourse of a voyage made... into the East Indies* was published as a version of a letter from Matelief, presumably to the States General, giving details of the naval engagements around Malacca in which seven Portuguese ships were destroyed.[18] There is little in the narrative except descriptions of these engagements, which took place between August and December of 1606.

Barret's publication was not a propaganda piece to solicit wider interest in the undertakings of the East India Company. It was entirely without introductory matter to relate it to England's interest in the East Indies, and it made no mention of the departure of Alexander Sharpey with two ships, the *Ascension* and the *Union,* comprising the company's fourth voyage. Sharpey, like Keeling, sought out new commercial opportunities as he called at Pemba Island near Zanzibar, at Melindi on the east African coast just below the equator, at Aden and Mocha on the Red Sea, and at Socotra Island before sailing across the Indian ocean to Surat. This was the route of the *Ascension,* which was separated from the *Union* in a storm on the outward voyage; the latter vessel proceeded directly to Bantam, but on its return voyage was broken up on the rocks of Brittany. And misfortune ultimately befell the *Ascension* also as it was wrecked at Cambaya, with a complete loss of its cargo. The crew members went to Surat, and most of them went

from there to Agra with Captain Sharpey. Among these was Robert
Coverte, who was to write an outstanding account of India and Persia
upon his ultimate return to England.[19]

This voyage marks the lowest depth to which the company's misfortunes sank in its early years, for the loss of the two ships nearly ruined
it financially, and in 1609 only 13,700 pounds could be raised and only
one ship was sent out.[20] This ship, the *Consent*, was commanded by
David Middleton, who had been in the East Indies with his brother
Sir Henry. This was a conservative voyage, as Middleton made straight
for Bantam upon leaving Saldanha Bay. From Bantam he did undertake
new explorations as he visited the islands of Buton and Banggai before
going to the more familiar Banda group. He returned to England in
1611, discovering at Saldanha that his brother had recently stopped
there on his way east with three ships.

The return of Keeling, the departure of Sir Henry Middleton, and
the return of the *Consent*, all within a little more than one year, brought
forth no literature on the new lands and markets English merchants
and sailors were finding. Interest in the East was apparently quite
closely confined to the members of the company, who did not make any
effort to spread the news of their eastern enterprises to a wider public.
This was not due to any policy of secrecy, nor was it born of complacency, for the company was not prosperous and was constantly seeking
ways of making its trade more profitable. It was especially anxious to
make something of the area of the Indian Ocean and Red Sea, and
Sir Henry Middleton spent nearly two adventure-filled years trading
and negotiating with Arabs, Turks, Indians, and Portuguese in Socotra,
Aden, Mocha, and Zenan before sailing down the Indian coast, past
Ceylon to Sumatra. He finally returned to England in 1613. Here was
a voyage of sufficient adventure to make several books of potentially
popular reading. The situations overcome, the people encountered, the
trade carried on—all were spectacular and frequently thrilling. Yet no
account of this voyage was published until it was included in *Purchas
his pilgrimes* in 1625.[21]

If the general public was not interested in the East Indies, the East
India Company felt a continuing need for more information on the
commerce of that area. Just as Dutch narratives in translation had
stimulated English interest in the islands and seas beyond the Cape of
Good Hope, so also did many of the details of the eastern commerce
come from contact with the Dutch. The most striking example of this
relationship was the offer in November, 1609, of two Dutchmen known

generally as Peter Floris and Lucas Antheunis to take a ship to India's Coromandel coast for the company.[22] Floris had been there as early as 1603, having been a factor at Masulipatam, and Antheunis had held a similar position at Petepoli. In offering their services, they were making available to English merchants the intricate details of the trade of that part of India. The company accepted and placed Anthony Hippon in charge of the venture, which consisted of only one ship, the *Globe*.

Departing from England on January 15, 1611, the *Globe* made its first call in India at Pulicat, but with little success. Farther north at Petepoli and Mesulipatam a more favorable reception awaited the Englishmen and their Dutch guides. With a cargo of cloth they proceeded to Bantam, but market conditions were not favorable, so they turned north to Patani on the Malay Peninsula, where they enjoyed a profitable stop. A visit to Bangkok, another call at Masulipatam, another at Bantam, and the eastern itinerary was completed. The entire voyage required four years, but it exposed English merchants to the intricacies of a trade they had not participated in before. Nevertheless, this seventh voyage of the company, like its predecessor, went unpublished for another decade.

The remainder of the separate voyages had a similar bibliographic outcome. The eighth voyage, also departing in 1611, sent John Saris to Japan where he established an English factory. The farthest possible eastward extension of English trade had been reached.[23] The following year, four ships were dispatched to the East by the company; between them they made three voyages—the ninth, tenth and eleventh of the company. Edmund Marlowe took the *James* to Priaman, Bantam, Pulicat, Musalipatam, and Petepoli. Meanwhile the *Dragon* and *Hosiander*, under Thomas Best, sailed to Surat and Bantam, after which the *Hosiander* proceeded via Borneo to Japan.[24] The *Solomon*, departing February 1, 1611, has left no record of its voyage, but it is unlikely that it went beyond Bantam, since it was back at Ascension Island by June 10, 1613. The twelfth and last of the separate voyages was that of Christopher Newport, whose mission was not entirely commercial. He sailed into the Persian Gulf to return Sir Robert Sherley to Persia. Sherley was now the Persian ambassador to Europe. Following this stop, Newport went to Bantam, and thence back to England, arriving July 10, 1614.

During these years of unprecedented English travel and trade into the East there was a great dearth of literature describing the voyages of the East India Company's ships. Between 1608 and 1614 only one book appeared which described England's new-found commerce, and this was not closely related to the places actually visited by English merchants. The journey on foot by Robert Coverte, which he reported in his *True and almost incredible report* had the characteristics of a private, rather than a corporate or national enterprise, although, as a servant of the East India Company, Coverte did show a natural concern for what English goods might find sale in the cities he visited.[25]

Coverte sailed as steward on the *Ascension* under Captain Sharpey, and when the ship was wrecked near Cambay, he escaped with the rest of the crew, going first to Surat and then inland to Agra, seat of the court of the Great Mogul. From Agra, Coverte traveled northeast through Afghanistan, Persia, and Mesopotamia to Aleppo, and from there back to England, where he arrived at the end of April, 1611. In recounting his journey, Coverte did not forget the hardship of it, for his dedication to the Earl of Salisbury and the note to the reader contain little else than the reminder that this was a hard and tedious adventure. He made no claim to having performed a great service for England or her merchants, but only to personal inconveniences. The outward voyage is described in terms of trade, difficulties with the native peoples encountered, and worry over Portuguese interference. There is a general description of watering places and ports of call along the way to Aden. In the Red Sea area, the chief city of interest to Coverte was Mocha, which he described as 'a City of great trading for our Commodities: as Tynne, Iron, Lead, Cloth, Sword blades, and all English commodities. It hath a great Bussart or Market every day in the weeke. There is a great store of fruit, as Apricocks, Quinces, Dates, Grapes abundance, Peaches, Limmons, and Plantins great store...[26]

Coverte's record of his overland travels contains innumerable observations of a similar type. He described Sabay, enroute to Agra, as 'a Towne, only consisting of Spinners and Weavers, and there is much Calicoe made.'[27] At Bramport (Burhampur) he was much impressed that the city was 'farre bigger then London, and great trade of all sorts of merchandise therein.'[28] He considered it an excellent potential market for English cloths. In Agra he met William Hawkins of the third voyage who introduced him to the Great Mogul. Coverte described the Mogul's court and also the goods passing through the market at Agra, which he and Hawkins agreed would be a good market for English silks and velvets.

With four other Englishmen, Coverte departed for England, noting the towns they passed through in India and the heavy traffic in goods from China and India that moved through Afghanistan. Many of the entries in this journal are extremely brief but never unduly so when an important market town was to be described. Altogether Coverte's picture of the regions he visited is enlightening, and sometimes enthusiastic. It is not as precise as Federici's description of the eastern cities translated by Thomas Hickock in 1588, but it is surely excellent proof of the ability of Englishmen to record their travels in an interesting way, despite their apparent reluctance to do so. The fact that Coverte's book was published again in 1614 indicates also that there was a public appreciation of this particular account.[29]

By the end of 1614 English voyages to the East Indies had firmly established the English commercial interests in the islands which were so much sought by a few enthusiasts for overseas trade in Elizabeth's reign. Yet this new eastern trade produced only five books based upon English experience there, and of these only one was of sufficient public interest to call for a reprinting. Nor did the use of the Cape of Good Hope route shake the English interest in the Levant trade, for its prosperity continued even though it was based on goods from the farther east. Thomas Mun estimated that the Levant trade increased by one third in the first two decades of the seventeenth century.[30] The Levant trade was very agreeable to the English public for it took large quantities of woolens and did not require the export of money as did the East Indian commerce. Where money was needed, as at Zante where currants were bought and there was no cloth market, the money was provided by Spanish and Portuguese purchasers of English goods from eastbound ships.[31]

The English Levant trade grew at the expense of French and Venetian commerce there. It invited competition from the Dutch, but during the first half of the seventeenth century the Dutch were easily outdistanced in this area. The chief worry to the Levant merchants was the ever-present hostility between the Turks and the Persians which caused the latter periodically to consider sending their merchandise out via the rivers of Russia, and in 1615 the appearance of East India Company merchants from Surat in the Persian Gulf offered another means of exporting without sending goods through lands controlled by the Turks. For the most part, however, the Levant trade was settled and comfortable, and the Levant Company had little need to propagandize and little inclination to expand. It was not a trade calculated to stir adventurers to action or publishers to describe the sailings of its ships. Consequently, none of the books describing the Levant which

were published between 1603 and 1620 were directly related to the
Levant Company or any of its merchants.

The most popular accounts of travels in the Near East appear to
have been those relating to the Sherley brothers, an adventurous group
whose activities have already been touched upon. In addition to Anthony Sherley, whose mission to Persia has already been described,
there was Robert, who ultimately became Persian ambassador to Europe, and Thomas, who was less distinguished, being merely a buccaneer
in the eastern Mediterranean.[32] The first book to describe the activities
of the Sherley brothers was Anthony Nixon's *The three English brothers*
which borrows heavily from Parry's *Discourse*, is wanting in accuracy,
and contains little to enlighten the reader about the eastern Mediterranean, except in matters of government, diplomacy, and war.[33] Hap-
hazardly put together, *The three English brothers* was an attempt at
popular patriotic literature reminiscent of the works of Henry Roberts,
'divulging the memorable Acts of such worthy personages whose Noble
Spirits... have drawne other Nations into admiration of their valours,
and emulation of their virtues.'[34] It was issued twice in 1607 with no
alteration in the text but with different title pages, the second issue
being titled *The travels of three English brothers*. In general this book
conforms to other publications of Anthony Nixon which were of contemporary news interest.

Sir Anthony Sherley's travels took him from Persia to Russia, Germany, Italy, Morocco and Spain, but he never returned to England.
Nevertheless, he was well publicized there, for in 1613 another narrative of his Persian adventure was published. This *Relation of his travels
into Persia* appears to have been based upon a manuscript returned to
England by Sir Robert Sherley, and is for the most part a tedious narrative of diplomacy and war, showing great understanding of eastern
politics, but with little concern for the Persian or Turkish peoples.
Yet, in Sir Anthony's view this was not just a private adventure, for
he looked upon his mission for the Earl of Essex as a service to 'first,
the glory of God,' and 'the perticular good of our Country.'[35] Nor was
he unmindful of the specific manner in which England might be served
by eastern travels: '... answering to her Majesties Merchants trades in
Turky, and Muscovy; and besides, being not unlikely but some parts
might have bene found fit for the Indian Navigation, then principated
in Holland and muttered of in England.'[36] Despite the breadth of
purpose with which he set forth in 1599, Sir Anthony's narrative is
essentially a diplomat's view of a local situation involving the rivalry

between Turkey and Persia, and he despaired of finding any lasting solution to that problem.

Between Nixon's and Sherley's books there appeared another description of the Levant, the *Travels* of William Biddulph, which was sufficiently popular to require two editions within four years.[37] This account of English travels in the Near East was brought into print by one Theophilus Lavender who had spoken with Belaziel Biddulph about letters he had received from his brothers William and Peter who appear to have been in the service of the Levant Company. These letters describe the travels of William Biddulph, Jeffrey Kirbie, Edward Abbot, John Elkin and Jasper Tyson in the Levant, and Lavender decided that the descriptions of eastern regions contained in these letters must be published even without the authors' consent. His purpose was less to stimulate interest in travel abroad than to confirm in English hearts a love for their homeland. 'Heereby hearers may learne to love and reverence their Pastors,... wives may learne to love their husbands, ... servants may be taught to be faithful and dutifull, ... rich men may learn to be thankfull to God.'[38]

With these lessons in mind, Lavender merged the letters to Biddulph so as to make them appear to recount the events of a continuous trip, describing chiefly the Greek Islands, Constantinople, and the Levantine cities of Tyre, Sidon, Antioch, and Scanderone, with one letter devoted to Jerusalem. Included in these descriptions are accounts of the laws and religion of the Mohammedans and the Jews, mention of several varieties of Christians encountered in Jerusalem, the Turks' treatment of their servants and descriptions of Turkish food and drink, including 'sherbet made of water and Sugar, or hony, with snow therein to make it coole.'[39] Altogether there is little that is new in Biddulph's letters. They add up to a mixture of classical and religious lore which could as easily have been compiled a century earlier.

A similar work is *A relation of a journey* by George Sandys, who divided his account of eastern travels into four books describing Greece and Turkey, Egypt, the Holy Land, and the Mediterranean Islands. This is a painfully detailed picture of the eastern Mediterranean area, laden with Biblical and classical history, but despite this orientation it does contain from time to time evidence of the author's awareness of the contemporary relationship of the Levant to England's existence. For example, after a long discourse on Greece and Turkey, the author added: 'The principall commodities that our Merchants fetch from hence, are Turkie carpets, chamolets, and grogerams... also some quantitie of raw silke, and carpets of Persia...' [40] In the same way, after a description of the Holy Land which was dominated by Biblical lore he noted the trade of the French at Rama.

Books such as these by Biddulph and Sandys indicate that English interest in the Levant was still much more closely related to the classical interests of the intelligentsia and the general interest in religion than it was to the English commercial enterprises being carried on there. The appeal of accounts of the Holy Land to Protestant England should not be underestimated, for in the years when the East India Company and the Virginia settlers were establishing the beginnings of empire in two hemispheres, a medieval-type pilgrimage book was being reprinted repeatedly. Henry Timberlake's *A true and strange discourse of the travailes of two English pilgrimes*, a booklet of twenty-six pages given largely to description of Jerusalem and its environs, was published in eight editions between 1603 and 1620, a performance unequaled by any travel book in English until that time.[41] In its general content and attitudes it was not unlike pilgrimage literature of the previous century, in which strange happenings are recorded, distances from city to city noted, and information available in the late Middle Ages is retailed once more. That such a book should be popular in Stuart England is testimony to the essentially medieval outlook of many Englishmen at that time. What is more difficult to account for is the absence of similar pilgrimage books, for Timberlake's book stands as the lone example of this type of literature in the first two decades of the seventeenth century.

The lucrative trade of the Levant Company and the English interest in the lands of Biblical and classical association were not sufficient to hold some of the more adventurous of England's merchants and travellers from using the Levant as a gateway to the farther East. Among these were John Mildenal and John Cartwright, free-lance merchant and preacher respectively. Together they set out from Aleppo on July 7, 1600, traveling northeastwardly to the Caspian ports of Derbend and Shemakha, thence southward into Persia where they separated, Mildenal going to Agra and Cartwright to Ispahan.

While Mildenal negotiated trading privileges in Agra, Cartwright made his way back to England via Arabia and Aleppo, and in 1611 he published an account of his journey. In his book, which he titled *The preachers travels*, he cited two reasons for writing it: 'I have not yet seene any that hath made full description of these parts,' and 'I doe verily perswade my selfe, that this discourse will breede much delight unto any indifferent Reader, when hee shall understand how mighty are the forces of the Persian King...'[42]

Cartwright's traveling abroad had begun with his enlistment as chaplain of Captain Weymouth's fleet which sought the northwest passage in 1602. While he found no reason to describe the northern regions he had visited, Cartwright found much to interest him in the East. He showed an equal concern for the civil government of the regions he visited, the religion of the Armenians, the courses of rivers, the potentialities of the Caspian Sea as a connecting point of Persian, Russian and Tartarian trade, the commodities of the bazaars, and the opportunities he sensed for English commerce. Like the writings of Biddulph and Sandys, Cartwright's book shows a great interest in Biblical and classical allusions, and indeed, these interests overshadowed his descriptions of contemporary situations in the lands he visited.

This emphasis on the ancient history of the Levant disturbed one Englishman who anonymously translated from the manuscript an account of the Near East and the East Indies by Henri de Feynes, Monsieur de Monfart, which he published as *An exact and curious survey of all the East Indies*. Before he undertook the translation of Monfart's manuscript, the translator tells us, he 'was careful both to recover and persue all such Bookes and Pamphlets, as are to be found in English, concerning Asia-Travailes, which in all doe not amount to five or sixe. And finding the most part speakes of nothing els then of Graecia, Arabia, Syria, with some stale tales of Jerusalem, so contrary to one another, and so much beaten, and beaten againe, as it is both shame and losse that such toyes should be uttered... I thought this Author could not but prove profitable and welcome.'[43] This impatient translator gave to English readers a book only half again as long as that of Timberlake, but in content it was not unlike the excellent survey of the Near and Middle East by Federici. Indeed, it was even more inclusive in that it extended its view all the way to Canton.

With no great pretense to modesty, the translator claimed to be also 'the Fashioner of this work as well as the translator,' for he stated that the author, a French gentleman, was low on writing ability, noting, '... it is onely for a Gentleman to ride, not to reade, and rather handle a bad sword then a good boke, but a Pen least of all.'[44] The title page indicates more than the usual scholarly and Biblical interest as it refers to the recent embassy of Sir Thomas Roe to India, and throughout the narrative, the book shows a steady interest in the material aspects of the East.

M. de Monfart's travels appear to have been undertaken in 1608, as a means of 'leaving behinde olde displeasures,' and they took him first to Aleppo, 'one of the fairest and greatest Mart-Citties in all the world.'[45] In a caravan of about 10,000 men he crossed the desert, arriving in Nana, 'a good towne, full of bad people,'[46] and went on to Baghdad, which he believed to be twice as big as Paris, and to Ispahan which seemed to him one of the great cities of the world. Throughout Persia he was impressed with the abundance and variety of riches that he saw and the opportunities for trade. From Persia he went to Cambaya where he was interested in the jewel and cloth trade, the use of elephants in war, the customs of the people, and the vegetation of the region. All along the Indian coast he noted the products in the important market cities, and in Sumatra and Malacca the spice trade impressed him. Macao he saw as a place of no great importance, but Canton was the ultimate in richness as well as the farthest point in his journey, for 'what rarities soever there be throughout all China, are to be had in this citty... to wit great store of cloth of gold and silk, cabinets, wrought vessels, Venus shells, Massive gold, and many other things.'[47] His return trip via Macao, Pegu, Cambodia, Siam, India, Mozambique, Sofala, and Lisbon is described more briefly than the outward trip, but he added a conclusion, 'Certain generall observations touching the Indies,'[48] which chiefly concerned the products of the East.

This little book of forty-five pages could not have been expensive. It was full of contemporary information of use to merchants and it contained other interesting material as well. It described areas where Englishmen were sailing and merchandising at the time of its publication, but it knew only one English edition, whereas Timberlake's pilgrimage book had eight printings, and Biddulph's *Travels* had two. The Biblical and the classical orientation among English readers of geography was still strong, and the new geography made progress slowly in the bookstalls of London.

### NOTES TO CHAPTER X

[1] William L. McElwee, *England's precedence* (London: Hodder and Stoughton, Ltd., 1956), p. 26.
[2] *A true and perfect relation of the newes sent from Amsterdam, the 21. of February, 1603* (London: Thomas Archer, 1603), p.1.

3 *Ibid.*, p. 8.
4 Sir William Foster (ed.), *The voyage of Sir Henry Middleton to the Moluccas, 1604–1606* (London: The Hakluyt Society, 1943), pp. xi–xiv.
5 Foster, *Lancaster*, p. xxxiii.
6 *A true and large discourse of the voyage of the whole fleete of ships set forth the 20. of April 1601* (London: Thomas Thorpe, to be sold by William Aspley, 1603), p. [1].
7 *Ibid.*
8 *Ibid.*, p. 2.
9 *Ibid.*, p. 15.
10 *A letter written to the right worshipfull the governours and assistants of the East Indian marchants in London* (London: Thomas Thorpe to be sold by William Aspley, 1603), p. 8.
11 Foster, *Middleton*, pp. xv–xvii.
12 *The last East Indian voyage* (London: T. P. for Walter Burre, 1606), title page.
13 *Ibid.*, fol. K4 verso.
14 *Ibid.*, fol. B1 verso.
15 Edmund Scott, *An exact discourse of the subtilties, fashishions [sic], pollicies, religion, and ceremonies of the East Indians* (London: W. W. for Walter Burre, 1606), fol. K1 recto.
16 W. H. Moreland (ed.), *Peter Floris, his voyage to the East Indies in the 'Globe', 1611–1615* (London: The Hakluyt Society, 1934), pp. xix–xxv.
17 Samuel Purchas, *Hakluytus posthumus or Purchas his pilgrimes* (20 vols.; Glasgow: James MacLehose and Sons, 1905–1907), II, 519.
18 *An historicall and true discourse of a voyage made... into the East Indies* (London: For William Barret, 1608). First published as *Historiale ende ware beschrijvinge van de reyse des Admiraels Cornelis Matelief de jonge* (Rotterdam: Jan Janssz, 1608).
19 See pp. 183–84 above.
20 Boies Penrose (ed.), *The travels of Captain Robert Coverte* (Philadelphia: Wm. F. Bell Company for Boies Penrose, 1931). pp. 4–5.
21 Samuel Purchas, *Purchas his pilgrimes* (4 vols.; London: W. Stansby, 1625).
22 For a full study of the identity of these two Dutchmen, see Moreland, (ed.), pp. xxxvi–liiii.
23 Sir Ernest M. Satow (ed.), *The voyage of Captain John Saris to Japan, 1613* (London: The Hakluyt Society, 1900), *passim.*
24 Sir William Foster (ed.), *The voyage of Thomas Best to the East Indies, 1612–14* (London: The Hakluyt Society, 1934), p. xxxix.
25 Robert Coverte, *A true and almost incredible report of an Englishman, that... travelled by land through many unknowne kingdomes, and great cities* (London: William Hall for Thomas Archer and Richard Redmer, 1612).
26 *Ibid.*, p. 22.
27 *Ibid.*, p. 25.
28 *Ibid.*, p. 29.
29 The second edition was printed by N. O. for Thomas Archer. It was entirely reset, although page endings are the same throughout.
30 Wood, *A history of the Levant Company*, p. 42.
31 *Ibid.*, pp. 42–43.
32 A. H. Bullen (ed.), *The works of John Day* (London: The Chiswisk Press, 1881), pp. iv–vii, introductory to Day's *The travailes of the three English brothers*, a drama which cannot be counted as travel literature for purposes of this study, but which testifies to the popular interest in these adventurers.
33 Anthony Nixon, *The three English brothers* (London: John Hodgets, 1607).
34 *Ibid.*, fol. B1 recto.
35 Sir Anthony Sherley, *Sir Anthony Sherley his relation of his travels into Persia* (London: For Nathaniel Butter and Joseph Bagfet, 1613), pp. 4, 5.

[36] *Ibid.*, p. 4.
[37] William Biddulph, *The travels of certaine Englishmen into Africa, Asia, Troy, Bythnia, Thracia, and the Black Sea* (London: Th. Haveland for W. Aspley, 1609); The second edition is *The travels of foure Englishmen and a preacher into Africa...* (London: Felix Kingston for William Aspley, 1612).
[38] Biddulph (1609 ed.), fol. A2 recto.
[39] *Ibid.*, pp. 65–66.
[40] George Sandys, *A relation of a journey begun An: Dom: 1610* (London: For W. Barrett, 1615), p. 86.
[41] Henry Timberlake, *A true and strange discourse of the travailes of two English pilgrimes* (London: For Thomas Archer, 1603). Subsequent editions were published in 1608, 1609, 1611, 1612, 1616, and 1620.
[42] John Cartwright, *The preachers travels* (London: For Thomas Thorppe, 1611), pp. 2–3.
[43] Henri de Feynes, *An exact and curious survey of all the East Indies, even to Canton, the chiefe cittie of China* (London: Thomas Dawson for William Arondell, 1615), fol. B1 verso.
[44] *Ibid.*, fol. B1 recto.
[45] *Ibid.*, pp. 2–3.
[46] *Ibid.*, p. 6.
[47] *Ibid.*, pp. 30–31.
[48] *Ibid.*, p. 38.

# Chapter XI

## PREACHERS AND PLANTERS

Englishmen who established the foundations of an empire in the East Indies went about their work like the businessmen they were, building a profitable enterprise for themselves. The Atlantic Ocean touched deeper emotions. This was the area of England's traditional interest to which the successors of John Rastell had called their countrymen to effort in the name of religion, social welfare, the national honor, and 'the commodity of our country.' Here, too, Spain had frustrated English hopes as she gave her religion to the natives and hauled out their gold. Spanish power, however, had not prevented privateering in Caribbean waters from becoming a favorite maritime profession, and as Elizabeth's reign came to an end the truth of Lawrence Kemys' observation that preying upon Spanish shipping was no longer a rewarding occupation became more apparent. Spanish ships were being driven from the seas, and money hitherto finding good returns in privateering now turned to new forms of overseas investment. From the Amazon River to Hudson Bay, projects were undertaken to provide outlets for investment and for satisfaction of religious enthusiasm and emotional nationalism as well. The wilderness of America called for Englishmen to settle there with their families, their institutions, and their religion. Sailors, merchants, and miners did not suffice for this undertaking. Persons of many crafts and professions were required, and this gave a potentially broader interest to colonial enterprise than had any previous English venture. To satisfy and to increase this interest, publishers and promoters provided a steady flow of literature on the New World between 1603 and 1620.

It is not surprising that as privateering along the Spanish Main declined, a clandestine trade should take its place. Sir John Hawkins had demonstrated the willingness of the Spaniards to trade when they were not too closely watched by their officials. English goods were traded for Spanish or native commodities, and before the end of the sixteenth century an active salt trade was being developed at Punta Araya on the Venezuela coast.[1] In concluding peace with Spain in August, 1604, James I agreed to keep English ships out of this Spanish sphere

*References, p. 214–216*

of empire, but he was not able to do so. The Spaniards could not enforce that provision of the treaty either, and an illicit commerce in tobacco and other products quickly developed.

Even before the treaty was signed, plans were under way to improve the organization of this Guiana trade, as it was called, by establishing a trading colony on the Wiapoco River. Captain Charles Leigh had been out to Guiana in 1602, and his interest in the area prompted his brother, Sir Oliph Leigh, and others to advance funds to get the colony started. On May 22, 1604, forty-six men and boys arrived there from England.[2] The privateering urge had not gone out of Englishmen, however, and dissension was soon created among the colonists by those who preferred raiding to settled commerce. Native hostility and the climate weakened the colony, and the arrival of thirty additional colonists in the autumn of 1604 was offset by the death of Charles Leigh and by the loss of a supply ship which went astray the following year, ending up at St. Lucia. The stranded Wiapoco colonists were finally picked up by French and Dutch ships which regularly frequented these shores, and this brief chapter of American colonization was ended by May, 1606.[3]

The promoters of the Leigh colony, which was purely a commercial undertaking, apparently saw no need to attempt to interest the public in their enterprise, for unlike Raleigh they issued no glowing accounts of Guiana. The only publication relating to this colony appears to have resulted from the accidental adventures of John Nicholl and his companions aboard the supply ship *Oliph Branch* which missed Guiana and came to St. Lucia. *An houre glasse of Indian newes*, published in 1607, is an exciting story of their fights with the natives of various islands and the arrival of five survivors on the mainland near Cartagena where they were picked up by Spaniards and ultimately taken to Spain, whence the author took ship for England.[4] In addition to the adventures told there, Nicholl's book gave readers the only history of the Leigh colony published in England at that time. It also presented some description of the natives and products of the Caribbean area.

Far to the north, on the New England coast, the desire to establish a plantation was frustrated during these early years of James's reign by similar circumstances. The commercial possibilities of this area, called Norumbega, had become apparent to informed persons such as Richard Hakluyt and a group of Bristol merchants who in 1603 sent out Martin Pring with two ships laden with utensils and trinkets to trade with the natives. Their chief objective was to lade sassafras, and in this they were successful, returning with a cargo in midsummer. Two years later Sir Ferdinando Gorges, the Earl of Southampton, and Lord Arundell of Wardour combined to send out George Weymouth, who came to anchor at Monhegan Island off the coast of Maine, and then explored the St. George River.[5] Upon the return of this expedition to England, James Rosier, who had also been to America with Gosnold in 1602, wrote an account of the voyage called *A true relation of the most prosperous voyage made this present year 1605*. Rosier had been employed by Lord Arundell to make observations and to report on the voyage, and when the patron's interest in the enterprise was diverted, the publication of the book was taken up by 'some honourable Gentlemen of good worth and qualitie, and Merchants of good sufficiency and judgement.'[6] These patrons were also undertaking to plant a colony in Norumbega.

Rosier's book was clearly a vehicle for propaganda on behalf of this enterprise, and it performed that function well. The productivity of the region was quickly made known, for gooseberries, strawberries, wild peas, cod and haddock came into the narrative shortly after the report of sighting land. Excellent clay for brick and tile was discovered, peas and barley that were planted 'in sixteen days grew eight inches above the ground,'[7] and among ten varieties of wood listed were fir trees yielding turpentine and gum. Mussels were found containing pearls. Tobacco and furs were considered likely items for a profitable commerce. The climate was agreeable to Englishmen, the natives 'seemed all very civill and merrie: shewing tokens of much thankfulnesse, for those things we gave them.'[8] The St. George River was compared favorably with the Orinoco, the Seine, and the Loire. 'From ech banke of this river are divers branching streams into the maine,' he reported, 'wherby is afforded an unspeakable profit by the convenience of transportation from place to place.'[9]

This description of Norumbega was unusual in that it made no mention of the possibility of finding gold and no reference to the likelihood of a northwest passage in the near vicinity, indicating that a merchant group was finally accepting North America as a region of commercial potential, and advertising it as such. Rosier's report apparently was effective, for the following year Sir Ferdinando Gorges, a prominent figure in Plymouth, and Sir John Popham, chief justice of the king's bench, secured a patent for colonizing the region Weymouth had explored, and in 1607 they sent out two ships under the command of George Popham, brother of Sir John Popham, and Raleigh Gilbert, son of Sir Humphrey. A settlement was erected near the

mouth of the St. George, and ships returning to England carried glowing accounts of it. But the following winter was a harsh one, the death
of George Popham deprived the group of a leader, and by the following
spring the colonists were ready to give up the attempt.[10]

The mercantile urge that gave life briefly to the Guiana and Maine
colonies gave rise at the same time to the beginnings of another venture
that was destined to have longer life, although a precarious one in its
early years. The Virginia Company had its beginnings in a charter
issued by James I on April 10, 1606. He granted to two groups, from
London and Plymouth, the lands lying between 34 and 45 degrees on
the North American coast. The grant was divided equally between the
two groups, and islands within 100 miles of the coast were also included.
The charter recognized the intent to colonize, and it provided for
governing councils in America and noted that the law and church of
England should go there with the colonists. The primarily mercantile
interest of the adventurers was recognized in the company's right to
collect revenues from ships trading to its ports. The right to prospect
for and mine precious metals which was granted to the company was
an indication of the tenacity of the motive that had so largely dominated the thinking of overseas adventurers in the previous century.
The prestige of the Virginia Company is apparent from the willingness
of Sir Thomas Smith, governor of the East India Company, to become
its treasurer.

On January 1, 1607, three ships carrying 143 persons departed for
America under the command of Christopher Newport, to establish a
colony for the Virginia Company. The following May 13 they anchored
in a river they called the James, and while most of the colonists set
about building a fort, Newport, John Smith, and a band of twenty-
three men ascended the river. On June 22, Newport sailed for England
with samples of American products. Hard work, disease, and native
hostility soon disillusioned the colonists; by September fifty of them
had died, provisions were low, and there was dissension among the
leaders of the colony. Smith succeeded in negotiating for some supplies
from the Indians, and upon Newport's return in April, 1608, with more
settlers, he and Smith carried on further negotiations for grain to keep
the colonists alive. A group of seventy reinforcements came later in the
spring of 1608, and when these supply ships returned to England they
carried back cargoes of sassafras, walnut boards, cedar posts, and iron
ore.[11] With the return of the *Phoenix*, a supply ship, also went the first
account of the Virginia colony from the hand of John Smith, to be

published as *A true relation of such occurrences and accidents of noate as hath hapned in Virginia* by William Welby, whose imprint was to become familiar to readers of news from Virginia.

It was the London promoters of the colony rather than the author or the publisher that took the initiative in bringing this report on Virginia to the attention of the public, for the editor, 'J. H.' stated that 'induced thereunto by divers well willers of the action... I thought good to publish it.'[12] In his note to the reader, the editor conveyed the impression that the worst of the colony's hardships were over, the first settlers 'having indured the heate of the day, whereby those that shall succeede may at ease labour for their profit, in the most sweete, coole, and temperate shade.'[13] He also disclosed that he had learned from returning seamen and others 'that the Country is excellent & pleasant, the clime temperate and health full, the ground fertill and good, the commodities to be expected (if well followed) many.'[14] Yet he implied that something greater than profit enticed Englishmen to this land, 'to the high glory of God, to the erecting of true religion among Infidells... to the winning of many thousands of wandering sheepe unto Christs fold... yea, I say the Action... will tend to the everlasting renowne of our Nation.'[15]

The impressions intended by the 'well willers' and some of the information reported by John Smith were not altogether compatible. He did little to conceal the hardships experienced in the settlement, relating 'we had no houses to cover us, our Tents were rotten, our Cabbins worse then nought... our chiefest men either sicke or discontented, the rest being in such dispaire, as they would rather starve and rot with idlenes, then be perswaded to do any thing for their owne reliefe without constraint.'[16] For all his hardiness, Smith's morale apparently suffered from the alleged hoarding of spirits by the leaders of the colony, and he was distressed by the tendency to thievery among the natives. But his complaints were against men rather than nature, and he concluded with praise for the land, 'we doubt not but by God's gracious assistance, and the adventurers willing minds, and speedie furtherance to so honorable an action in after times, to see our Nation to enjoy a Country,... very profitable for commerce in generall...'[17]

Smith's enthusiasm for Virginia was not matched in London, where an air of pessimism and desperation among the adventurers found expression in the instructions given to Captain Newport on his return to Virginia in the autumn of 1608. He pledged not to return to England without a lump of gold, news of a northwest passage, or the rescue of

Raleigh's lost colony; he was also obligated to return with a cargo worth 2,000 pounds. If he failed in these pledges, the company was going to abandon the colony. Actually, the colony was capable of less rather than more, and it became obvious that, if it was to survive, a new and more favorable charter must be obtained. This was granted on May 23, 1609, and provided for a governor with absolute civil and military authority in the colony. Thomas West, Lord De La Warr, was given this position, and new plans were made for revitalizing Virginia.[18]

More than political reorganization was needed to revitalize Virginia. A sense of purpose, an enthusiasm for something other than immediate profits was required if the settlers in Virginia were to survive the early years of trial and error in a type of enterprise where England had no experience. The lack of this emotional ingredient among the nobility, the merchants, scholars, and members of the court had been expressed in books of overseas interest since the *Interlude* of John Rastell. In 1609 a real enthusiasm for empire was apparent, and the nine ships that departed for Virginia on June 1, 1609, left an England that was being stirred by a series of pamphlets, four of them issued that year, calling Englishmen to empire in a spirit unknown to earlier English literature of expansion. It was an aggressive, missionary spirit, borne upon a wave of idealistic and purposeful religious intent. England gave way briefly to God, and the surplus and needy people of the homeland came after the American natives in the thoughts of colonial promoters who went into print with their ideas.

Many of the books which have been described carried a perfunctory reference to 'the glory of God' as a motive for overseas expansion, but by 1609 the expression had taken on a meaning requiring action by some of England's churchmen and citizens. These were from among the Puritan element within the Church of England, a restless group of visionaries that brought the emotional potential of religion into expressions of imperialistic ambition. In Virginia they thought they saw an opportunity to develop a system of government in line with that of Geneva, which, according to Sir Edwin Sandys, was 'made in heaven.'[19]

The Puritans began their rousing even before the new Virginia charter was granted. On April 25 William Symonds preached a sermon to a group of future Virginia colonists, and it quickly found its way to the printer, appearing as *Virginia. A sermon preached at White-Chappel*. The lesson was from Genesis 12: 1–3, 'For the Lord had said unto Abram, get thee out of thy Countrey, and from thy kindred, and from thy fathers house, unto the land that I will show thee. And I will make thee a great nation...' [20] There was no element of doubt in the message for 'the Lord that called Abraham into another Countrey, doeth also by the same holy hand, call you to goe and carry the Gospel to a Nation that never heard of Christ.' [21] While he spoke positively of colonization and of spreading Christianity, Symonds spoke also to the objectors who apparently were still numerous in England, and much of his sermon was defensive in tone. He referred to those who objected to colonization as an invasion of the lands of peaceful peoples, and stated that such objectors had 'come dropping out of some Anabaptist Spicery' or were 'hatched of some popish egge.' [22] Not all opponents were so easily identified with outlandish sects, for he concluded his sermon with the admonition to 'go on couragiously, and notwithstanding the snorting idleness of the ministry, suspect not the blessing of God.' [23]

Symonds' appeal went beyond the purely religious, however, as he noted the economic condition of England, where populations of whole townships were reduced 'to a shepheard and his dog,' [24] and the sad condition of the metal worker who 'worketh his bones out.' [25] The answer was obvious. '... The strong olde bees doe beate out the younger, to swarme & hive themselves elsewhere. Take the opportunity, good honest labourers which indeede bring all the hony to the hive, God may so blesse you, that the proverbe may be true of you, that a May swarme, is worth a kings ransome.' [26] This was not an appeal to the Crown or the Privy Council to send people abroad, but an invitation to workers, merchants, and Christians to go abroad into a land of abundance.

Equally optimistic and religion-centered was *Nova Britannia*, brought to the press by Robert Johnson. This he described as 'the summe of a private speech or discourse, touching our plantation in Virginia, uttered not long since in London, where some few adventurers... being met together touching their intended project, one among the rest stood up and began to relate (in effect) as followeth.' [27] After defending England's right to Virginia, the speaker gave out the general purpose of his oration, 'I wish and intreat all well affected subjects, some in their persons, others in their purses, cheerfully to adventure, and joyntly take in hand this high and acceptable worke, tending to advance... the Kingdome of God, ... among so many millions of men and women, Savage and blind, that never yet saw the true light shine before their eyes, to enlighten their minds and comfort their soules...' [28] He also added that the adventurers would be honoring their king, enlarging the kingdom, and aiding the colonists already in Virginia. Something

of the change in emphasis in English attitudes toward America is indicated in the author's treatment of the earlier Virginia colony of
Raleigh, which he said failed because those who were to supply it were
'Tainted with that common corruption of time, turned their head
another way, and with greedie minds betooke themselves wholly to
hunt after Pillage upon the Spanish Coast.' [29] Gold was no longer first
in the thoughts of these Englishmen looking toward America. He admitted that there was a profit to be made in America, 'but look it not
be chiefe in your thoughts.' [30] Again, he went against the ideas of colonization advanced by Elizabethans who merely wanted to rid England of undesirables, for he cautioned against sending out beggars and
criminals, calling instead for honest and ambitious men, of whom he
said there was an abundance in England.

The picture he gave of Virginia was one of a land of plenty awaiting
only the hands of industrious planters, 'bee they never so poore, so
they bee honest, and painefull, the place will make them rich.' [31] Link-
ing good government to religion, the speaker felt Virginia would pros-
per best if papists and corrupt officials were kept out, but the primary
purpose of both government and planting was to establish and maintain a colony which would carry religion to the American Indian. The
second purpose was to create an English empire and the third to gain
wealth for the homeland. Despite his own confidence that the colony
could achieve these ends, the author felt it necessary to scold 'the blind
diffidence of our English natures, which laugh to scorne the name of
Virginia, and all other new projects, be they never so probable.' [32]
Like Symonds' sermon, this discourse was a call to action by individuals, not an attempt to influence government or to induce official action.

Those who spoke on behalf of Virginia in 1609 did not have a convinced audience. The opposition referred to by Johnson was even more
clearly identified in a sermon preached on May 28 at Paul's Cross by
Daniel Price of Exeter College, Oxford. In print the sermon bore the
title, *Sauls prohibition staide*, and while it was a chastisement of all sorts
of evil-doers it specifically called attention to 'those that traduce the
Honourable Plantation of Virginia' in a subtitle.[33] The message was
hardly subtle, for Price gathered up papists, swearers, drunkards, and
others of whom he disapproved, and likened them all to Saul as perse-
cutors of Christ. So also were those who stood in the way of good works,
such as the Virginia enterprise, where there was opportunity to make
'a Savadge country to become a sanctifyed country' and where 'you
will enlarge the boundes of this Kingdome, nay the bounds of heaven.' [34]

The preacher defended Virginia as one of the most fertile and fruitful places on earth; yet he kept his emphasis on the thousands of souls waiting to be saved, and asked 'Shall Scepticall Humorists bee a meanes to keep such an honour from us, such a blessing from them?' [35]

Another call to Englishmen to betake themselves to Virginia was a sermon of Robert Gray, *A good speed to Virginia*, which was less pointedly religious in appeal than those of Symonds, Johnson, and Price, but it paid more attention to the social and economic realities of England which made emigration necessary and beneficial. Gray set the tone of his message with a reading of Joshua 17:14, 'If thou beest much people, get thee up to the wood, and cut trees for thy selfe in the land of Perizzites, & of the Giants, if mount Ephraim be too narrow for thee.' [36] He excused past lethargy toward colonization among Englishmen by the sense of comfort and sufficiency that the nation had enjoyed in earlier times. But now this had changed, and 'we are a great people, and the lande is too narrow for us.' [37] The solution to this problem was obvious, for it was now possible to participate in an adventure that would advance the glory of God, enlarge the territories of England, employ people who were idle, increase the customs revenues, and spread the fame of England to all the world. These ambitions eclipsed the earlier ones of finding gold, locating a passage to the Pacific, and countering the strength of Spain in the New World; the old motives were replaced not only by a new interest in America, but also by a new spirit in which religion and social concern for England's poor were united. The Reverend Richard Hakluyt had shown concern for men hanged in England for petty crimes when they could have been sent abroad as colonists, but he had little to say about the causes of the poverty which made criminals of good men. He, and Thomas Churchyard as well, thought of colonies as a means of ridding England of these undesirables, but for the benefit of England rather than for the good of these people, or the good they might do among the natives of America. Gray had pity for those who could find no work, but only harsh words for the wealthy class that 'finde delaies and devise shifts, either to save their purses or their persons, from such honourable and profitable designments' as the Virginia colony. He saw a duty beyond that of helping one's countrymen, as he held it the duty of every Christian to travel abroad 'to bring the barbarous savage people to a civill and Christian kinde of government.' [38]

Recognizing the existence of opposition to colonization, Gray blasted the arguments of his opponents who lamented the invasion by Englishmen of the peaceful land of the American Indian, or who cited the examples of failure in the past and who were impatient of the time required for the colony to produce results. Instead of excuses and delays, he urged action in setting up this colony for which he advised a stable and honest government and good ministers of religion, 'Policie thus establishing religion, and religion guiding policie.' [39] This was the voice of Puritanism, giving English colonization literature a strong, clear purpose in an appeal made directly to the people. Although the Virginia Company was by no means an exclusively Puritan enterprise, they were making the most of it as a vehicle for carrying their faith to the New World.

Although he was not of the Puritan persuasion, Richard Hakluyt participated in the enthusiasm of 1609, and two books published that year resulted from his interest. He was quick to acquire a copy of Lescarbot's *Histoire de la Nouvelle France*, and to suggest to Pierre Erondelle, a French Huguenot living in London, that portions of this work, which is of considerable literary merit, be translated as an aid and encouragement to colonists intending to go to Virginia. [40] The dedication, addressed to Prince Henry by Erondelle, contained some of the same enthusiasm noted in the Puritan pamphlets. He considered the French edition as religious propaganda, 'to the end that it might stirre them the more to prosecute the populating of lands heerein described, to bring the Naturals thereof... to civilitie and right knowledge of God.' [41] He praised the royal interest in colonization as an aid in spreading religion abroad as he wrote: 'Alexander would have runne in the Olympian games if kings had runne there; now Kings doe run; now Princes doe worke in the Lords harvest, to spread that name which must gather the elect from the utmost endes of the world... with their authoritie and meanes.' [42]

It is clear from Erondelle's selection of only those portions of Lescarbot's work which relate to areas bordering on Virginia that this was colonial propaganda, designed to encourage 'that generous and godly action' which would in turn be to 'the generall benefit of this land, too much pestred with over many people.' [43] The book told of French experience in settling, fishing, and planting in Canada, and gave extensive descriptions of the natives' religion, dress, language, diet, dances, marriage customs, methods of hunting, fishing, waging war, etc. It was, therefore, reasonably pertinent to the Virginia colony.

Far less pertinent, despite its title was Hakluyt's *Virginia richly valued*, a translation from the Portuguese of a narrative of De Soto's expedition into Florida.[44] In his dedication to the 'Councellors for the advancement of that Christian and noble plantation in Virginia,' Hakluyt expounded at length on the likelihood of finding gold in Virginia. He also mentioned the probability of finding there a passage to the South Sea. These concerns show a considerably more materialistic and traditional attitude toward America than the Puritan pamphlets which were driving the Virginia enterprise forward. His view of the natives as untrustworthy savages who may need strong treatment was perhaps more realistic than that held by other preachers who wrote about Virginia, but it was hardly calculated to enlist civilian settlers for Virginia. While Hakluyt listed products to be found in nearby areas, he could have done much better with a new edition of Hariot's description of Virginia from 1588.

On June 1, 1609, nine ships under the command of Captain Newport departed from Plymouth, carrying colonists and supplies for Virginia. But the new charter granted to the Virginia Company and the emotional drive to plant Christianity in the New World were not sufficient to assure success at once. The three highest ranking officers of the colony—Newport, Sir Thomas Gates, and Sir George Somers—sailed in the same ship, the *Sea Venture*, and when a hurricane separated the fleet, their ship was cast up on Bermuda, an uninhabited and little-frequented island. With the arrival of the other ships in Virginia there was an absence of authority, for the new government was to supersede that of Captain John Smith, but with the officers and instructions for the new government missing in the *Sea Venture*, Smith refused to relinquish control, and he was able to secure consent to continue as chief officer of the colony until the *Sea Venture* should appear. An injury to Smith made it possible to remove him, however, and he departed for England in September. With him undoubtedly went complaints against the management of Virginia, for on December 14, 1609, a tract defending the purposes of the enterprise and explaining its difficulties was entered in the *Stationers' register*.

This *True and sincere declaration* was issued by the Virginia Council in London, and it set out to 'redeeme our selves and so Noble an action, from the imputations and aspersions, with which ignorant rumor, virulent envy, or impious subtilty, daily callumniateth our industries, and the success of it.'[45] Again the motives for the undertaking were outlined —with preaching, baptizing and spreading the Gospel ranked first, the honor and prestige of the King and his realm second, and finally the 'private commodity to the particular undertakers ...'[46] The brief history of the colony which followed attributed its difficulties to the loss of the *Sea Venture*, and the council promised to send out Lord De La Warr to restore good order. Not entirely defensive, the tract concluded with an appeal for thirty-four different types of workmen needed in Virginia, admitting no doubt as to the ultimate success of the colony.

While seeking to counteract the aspersions cast upon Virginia by critics, the company found among its Puritan allies a more rigorous attitude toward critics and recalcitrants. William Crashaw, an outspoken Puritan, voiced an intolerant opinion of those that did not come forward with help for Virginia in *A sermon preached in London before the...Lord Lawarre*, published in 1610. The reason he gave for the general reluctance to participate was simply that most men 'are unconverted and unsanctified men, and seeke meerely the world and themselves, and no further.' [47] Of the profit-hungry investors he said, 'Tell them of getting XX. in the C. oh how they bite at it, oh how it stirres them! But tell them of planting a Church, of converting 10000. soules to God, they are senseless as stones.' [48] Puritan dogmatism regarding duty to the non-Christian was summed up coldly: 'either we are not converted, or they are not our brethren, or els that we being converted must labour their conversion.' [49]

Stepping outside the bounds of religious concerns, Crashaw answered the recurring legal objection that Englishmen had no right to trespass on Indian lands in America by affirming that Englishmen would only take in trade what the natives had in abundance, and would give, in exchange, goods, civilization and Christianity. The arguments advanced against the colony by its detractors such as distance, climate, smallness of the settlement, and unruly colonists were readily refuted. Hardship he viewed as a good thing for the English people, referring to the founding fathers of England and asking, 'What was there ever excellent in the world that was not difficult?' [50] As for want of profits, Crashaw saw in this no legitimate objection to the colony. 'If there be any that came in only or principally for profit, or any that would so come in, I wish the latter may never bee in, and the former out againe,' he wrote, adding that if spreading Christianity was not inducement enough 'it is a pitie they be in at all.' [51] To the greedy and the unsanctified he added several other elements, whom he considered more active opponents of the Virginia effort. These were the Devil, papists, and players, the latter 'because wee resolve to suffer no Idle persons in Virginea, which course if it were taken in England, they would know they might turne to new occupations.' [52] Against these forces, however,

Crashaw relied on the steady favor of God and right-minded English-men to bring Virginia to fruition, both religious and economic.

The hand of God was clearly seen working on behalf of the Virginia colony by its proponents in 1610, for on May 23 two boats built on Bermuda arrived there bearing the survivors of the *Sea Venture*, all of whom had been given up for lost by their compatriots. But in Virginia the newcomers found hardship so intense that their leader, Sir Thomas Gates, made ready to abandon the colony. As he prepared to sail, a ship arrived from England, bringing Lord De La Warr who persuaded Gates to remain.

One of the three books printed in 1610 which celebrated these evidences of the favor of Providence owed much to the earthly opposition confronting the enterprise. *A true declaration of the estate of the colonie in Virginia* announced in its title that it was 'a confutation of such scandalous reports as have tended to disgrace so worthy an enterprise.' The motives of the Virginia colonization were again recited and may be summarized thus: 'By way of marchandizing and trade [we] doe buy of them the pearles of earth, and sell to them the pearles of heaven.'[53] To the 'Romish boasters' who criticized the colony, the anonymous author of the *True declaration* showed evidence of the fruitfulness of Virginia which assured its success. And now to these known riches was added the remarkable deliverance of the *Sea Venture's* people, leading to the conclusion, 'Doubt ye not but God hath determined... that he will raise our state, and build his Church in that excellent climate, if the action be seconded with resolution and Religion.'[54]

The *Sea Venture* episode did indeed give the preachers impressive evidence of God's blessing on the colony, and a poet named Richard Rich who had sailed with the 1609 fleet used it in his *Newes from Virginia* to celebrate this assurance and to berate those

> *That wish the worke should not goe on,*
> *with words doe seeme to kill.*[55]

He related the survival on Bermuda in a doggerel style reminiscent of Henry Roberts, and if he did not enumerate the motives for colonization in the manner of other writers, they came through in his verses.

> *To glorifie the Lord tis done,*
> *and to no other end:*
> *He that would crosse so good a worke,*
> *to God can be no friend.*[56]

*Let England knowe our willingnesse,*
  *for that our worke is good,*
*Wee hope to plant a Nation,*
  *where none before hath stood.*[57]

*In mannaging so good a worke,*
  *two gallant ships: by name*
*The* Blessing *and the* Hercules,
  *well fraught, and in the same*
*Two ships, are these commodities:*
  *Furres, Sturgeon, Caviare,*
*Black-walnut-tree, and some deale-boards:*
  *with such they laden are:*
*Some pearle, some Wainscot and clapboards,*
  *with some Sassafras wood:*
*And Iron promist, for tis true,*
  *their Mynes are very good.*[58]

The story of shipwreck and survival on Bermuda appears to have had a considerable appeal to readers in England. The general belief that Bermuda was bewitched added to the excitement of the seemingly miraculous deliverance of those who sailed in the *Sea Venture* from the fury of the Atlantic storm. Along with Richard Rich's poetic narrative of 1610 came an account of the same events by Silvester Jourdain entitled *A discovery of the Barmudas.* Jourdain reported this much-despised island to be 'in truth the richest, healthfullest, and pleasing land... and meerely naturall as ever man set foote upon.'[59] Fish, fowl, hogs, turtles, fruit, pearl, ambergris, whales, and other commodities made survival easy, and the absence of rats and mice added to Bermuda's healthfulness. Its relative inaccessibility to the uninitiated made it easily defended against the natural enemy, Spain.

All of these factors made Bermuda an excellent base for supplying Virginia, and the absence of any native population removed the missionary motive from the consideration of a group of London merchants who began making plans in 1611 for the establishment of a permanent colony on Bermuda.

Meanwhile, Virginia was surviving, but survival was achieved only with great effort. The missionary zeal largely disappeared from the Company's propaganda after 1609; there was sufficient question about the survival of the colony to keep the proponents of the enterprise steadily on the defensive. When poor health forced Lord De La Warr to return to England in 1611, he published a *Relation* which was first issued to the general assembly of the Virginia Company and which he assured his readers that he was publishing 'because I perceive, that since my coming into England, such a coldnesse and irresolution is bred, in many of the Adventurers, that some of them seeke to withdraw those paiments, which they have subscribed...'[60] He explained that his return was not due to the condition of Virginia, but to successive bouts with ague, flux, cramps, gout, and scurvy. While God, the nation, and trade were again listed as the concerns of the colony, the governor made no report on missionary progress but did include a statement in some detail on the soil of Virginia, the grain trade with the Indians, the state of the cattle, etc. These were of first concern to the investors.

Further evidence that monetary return was taking the attention of Englishmen away from the missionary motive was the appearance in 1611 of another issue of Hakluyt's translation of the account of De Soto's expedition, in the introduction to which commodities received far more attention than religion.[61] The only one of the six Virginia books issued in 1609 to be reprinted, it continued to recognize motives of the Elizabethan age—gold and the western passage.

While Virginia was being doubted and defended in London, her people were arriving at a higher degree of stability and prosperity under the rigorous discipline of Captain Thomas Dale, who went out to the colony early in 1611 as deputy for Lord De La Warr. He moved the settlement about fifty miles up the river from Jamestown, where he believed disease would be less likely, and cultivation increased quickly with the improved health of the colonists. A code of laws issued by Dale left no doubt that he intended to allow no weakness to appear in the colony for want of authority. To give encouragement to producers of agricultural goods, he allowed private plots of three acres each to replace in part the communal agriculture of the previous years. There is no evidence that Dale took in hand any project for converting the natives to Christianity.

Although complaining continued, the colony began to take on the appearance of permanence, and by the end of 1611 there were 700 people settled there, living under a set of *Laws divine, morall and martiall* which William Strachey edited for all prospective colonists to read in 1612. This code was an embodiment of a military type of rule familiar to Captain Dale, the spirit of the laws being summed up at the outset: 'And forasmuch as no good service can be performed, or warre managed, where militarie discipline... cannot be kept, where the rules or

chiefe parts thereof be not certainely set downe, and generally knowne,
I ... doe now publish them to all persons in the Colonie, that they may
as well take knowledge of the Lawes themselves, as of the penaltie and
punishment, which without partialitie shall be inflicted upon all break-
ers of the same.'[62] This stern code called for the death penalty for
impious speech against the Trinity or the Articles of Religion, independent trading with the Indians, misappropriation of the company's
supplies, and blasphemy on the third offense. Disrespect for ministers
of religion was punished by whipping. Administered by Captain Dale,
the spirit of the laws was no less harsh than the words, and he quickly
convinced the Virginia settlers that he meant to enforce the new regulations when he ordered eight insubordinate colonists put to death for
failure to apply themselves properly to building the new community.

It is not to be wondered at that complaining continued, but the
malcontents drew counter-fire from such stalwart defenders of Virginia
as Robert Johnson and William Symonds, who had launched the fleet
of 1609 with books in praise of this enterprise devoted to spreading
God's word. In 1612 Johnson supplemented his *Nova Britannia* with *The
new life of Virginea*, an official publication of the Virginia Company
which recognized that 'not only the ignorant and simple minded are
much discouraged, but the malitious and looser sort... have whet their
tongues with scornfull taunts against the action it self,'[63] to the extent
that Virginia was under more criticism than any other topic in English
conversation at that time. The purpose of Johnson's book was 'to free
the name [Virginia] it selfe from the injurious scoffer.'[64] But despite
the complaints, which were instrumental in turning two-thirds of the
original investors away from Virginia, Johnson reported that the colony was doing well, with 'seven hundred men at least, of sundrie arts
and professions... they stand in health, and few sicke.'[65] He urged more
men to emigrate to Virginia with Captain Argall, who was then
ready to leave London with two ships.

While still religiously motivated, *The new life* was less aggressively so
than *Nova Britannia*. The conversion of the natives remained the key to
the solution of other problems in Johnson's view, but he spent more of
his Puritanical zeal hammering away at the need for a good example
to be set in America, for if idleness, swearing, unchastity and 'unbridled
appetite' took the place of virtue, he predicted 'miserie and confusion
will be the end of this.'[66] He advanced no plan for organizing and im-
plementing the missionary program so actively advocated in his publication of three years earlier.

The declining state of the religious motive among those who had been in Virginia is also shown in Captain John Smith's *Map of Virginia*, also published in 1612. Smith did not ignore the Indian and his religion, since he gave four pages to the natives' beliefs and customs, and he mentioned that efforts were made to interest them in Christianity, but he noted no success, nor did he call for intensified effort. Their religion was described in the same matter-of-fact manner that he used to describe rivers, products, climate, and other aspects of Virginia. His account of the crafty and malicious nature of the natives was not likely to convince missionaries that their task would be easy. Altogether, Smith's description was favorable to Virginia, and it was published to counter 'the clamors and the ignorance of false informers... and our ingenious verbalists who were no lesse plague to us in Virginia, than the Locusts to the Egyptians.'[67] The map which was included was the first cartographic portrayal of the colony to be published in England.

Not only was Virginia defended, but the actions of Smith as well, in a tract titled *The proceedings of the English colonie in Virginia*, edited by William Symonds and published together with Smith's *Map of Virginia*. A collection of reports ostensibly by several people who had returned from Virginia, it is primarily a history of the colony from 1606 to 1609, uniformly presenting a point of view favorable to Smith's actions there. One of the 'contributors', T. Abby, wrote, 'If any can resolve this doubt it is those who have lived residents in the land: not salers, or passengers, or such mercenary contemplators, that only bedeck themselves with others plumes.'[68] In the final pages, where Symonds rounded out the history of Virginia with a few pages covering the 1609–12 period, he described the way in which Smith was missed as a procurer of supplies after he had returned to England. The fact that these tracts by Smith and Symonds were published in Oxford is not evidence that colonial enthusiasm was spreading to that city. Rather, this lone instance of Oxford's participation in imperialistic propaganda is generally explained by hostility toward Smith within the Virginia Company, and since many members of the Stationers' Company were also Virginia investors, it was impossible for Smith's point of view to be made known through the London printers.[69]

As the Virginia colonists held on precariously and the promoters and critics of the enterprise railed at each other, a final word of encouragement and advice came from Michael Lok, now eighty-one years old, and still in debt due to his heavy investment in Frobisher's voyages. He translated the *Decades* of Peter Martyr in 1612, stating that his purpose was to call attention to the industry and resoluteness of the Spaniards in planting abroad, 'All which, may bee exemplary unto us, to performe the like in our Virginea, whiche beeing once throughly [sic] planted, and inhabited with our people may returne... greate benefite to our Nation... for although it yeeld not gold, yet is it a fruitfull pleasant countrey.'[70] It is probable that Richard Hakluyt was instrumental in having this translation made and published, for it is in his pattern of emphasizing Spanish imperialism as an example to the English; but whoever was responsible for its publication, his methods and interests were those of the Elizabethan age, not at all a part of the recent Puritan drive for an empire to propagate religion, and the book was of only slight relevance to the Virginia enterprise.

While Johnson, Smith, and Symonds disdained preaching in favor of defending the colony or its governors, the Reverend Alexander Whitaker was not willing to give over the offensive to the baser motives. In his *Good newes from Virginia* the missionary fire flamed again as he chastised not only scoffers but also those who hoped for nothing but wealth from Virginia. He opened with a challenge: 'Be bould my Hearers to contemne riches, and frame your selves to walke worthie of God; for none other be worthie of God, but those that lightly esteeme of riches.'[71] In his effort to put some idealism into the Virginia Company, Whitaker had the assistance of William Crashaw who introduced the book with a twenty-three-page Epistle Dedicatory which adds up to a scolding of doubters who questioned the wisdom of the Virginia project when 'assuredly God himselfe is the founder, and favourer of this Plantation.'[72] He presented Whitaker as a clear contradiction to the charges of critics who contended that only those who were unsuccessful in England went to America, for Whitaker was one of Virginia's foremost clergymen, and was 'a Scholler, a Graduate, a Preacher, well borne and friended in England, not in debt nor disgrace... not in want, but (for a schollar, and as these dayes be) rich in possession.'[73]

Whitaker's message was based upon service in Virginia, for he had gone to the colony in 1611 and was to remain there until his death in 1617. Many of Virginia's troubles he attributed to the lack of faith in God and the 'miserable covetous men' among the adventurers. He recognized the need for profits to sustain interest on the part of the investors, and he promised a quicker return than was to be had from ventures with the East India Company. Yet he could not countenance interest in quick gain ahead of concern for 'the glory of God... & good of your Countrey.'[74] In his final eight pages Whitaker described Virginia as a commodious, pleasant, healthful land, lamenting only, 'I would to God our soules were no sicker than our bodies.'[75] The hope he saw for the new colony lay in a continued and vigorous missionary activity there, and the fact that it was published by Welby and dedicated to Sir Thomas Smith suggests that it found favor with the higher authorities within the Virginia Company.

By the time Whitaker's book was published, his colony had competition in America, for while the charter of 1612 incorporated Bermuda into the jurisdiction of the Virginia Company, the island in fact became the colony of eighteen investors, and in its management and products it offered an alternative to Virginia, as was noted in the second edition of Silvester Jourdain's account of Bermuda, published in 1613, with a new title, *A plaine description of the Barmudas*.[76] Following the narrative of the *Sea Venture's* voyage, this edition added an account of the second expedition to Bermuda, which arrived there on July 11, 1612, with sixty settlers under the command of Richard Moore. The new arrivals marveled at finding alive and well the three men who had been left behind when the rest of the *Sea Venture's* people departed for Virginia. This and subsequent accounts of the abundance of natural products found on the island proved the ease with which civilized people could survive there. Virginia had not so good a record. The island's fine weather and the fact that there was little sickness there was stressed, and those who were skeptical of Virginia were offered Bermuda as a ready substitute for their interest.

In a similar manner Lewis Hughes wrote to England from Bermuda, stressing the productiveness of the island. His *Letter sent into England from the Summer Ilands* predicted that tobacco would be the main crop, but he held high hopes for indigo, silk culture, and fruits as well. He reported that livestock brought from England had been well sustained on Bermuda and that children who came there with their parents were healthy and vigorous. Hughes was clearly propagandizing for the colony on Bermuda, and he warned his countrymen that this was a new settlement, lacking some of the comforts of England. Also, there were tools and household utensils to be brought, and he enumerated these. While he could not tell Englishmen of the soules they would rescue, as did his clerical colleagues in Virginia, he did speak out, urging good people to come to Bermuda to make a good life for themselves. 'Above all,' he advised, 'have a care to leave their sins behinde them, and come hither as it were into a new world, to lead a new life.'[77]

Colonists did indeed continue to settle in Bermuda, and despite the strife that developed over the deposits of ambergris found on the island, miracles continued to sustain the settlers. In 1614 Governor Moore and a small band of defenders stood off two Spanish ships, and the following year, with starvation stalking the island, an English sailor, Daniel Elfrith, arrived with a ship full of meal taken from the Spaniards. In 1615 a new charter was granted, acknowledging the Bermuda adventurers to be a distinct group: the Governor and Company of the City of London for the Plantacon of the Somer Islands. While the leadership of the colony was distinguished, some of the settlers were below the standards Lewis Hughes had set. Many of them were needy, criminal, or depressed people, picked up in the streets of London. By 1615 there were five hundred inhabitants on Bermuda, but they aroused no great public interest in England, for the next five years saw nothing published concerning the Bermuda settlement.

Virginia was also losing some of its publicity value. Whitaker alone defended it in 1613, no news of the colony was published the following year, and in 1615 the only book to appear was Ralph Hamor's *A true discourse on the present estate of Virginia*. Here the author, who had returned to England after four years in Virginia, admitted the lack of public interest in his subject, lamenting, 'it were hard to say whether one of so many thousands as abound in England, might be thereby moved to... become a harty and devoted furtherer of an action so noble, as this is...'[78] He attempted, nevertheless, to stimulate interest in both settling and investing. His first appeal was a call to missionary effort as he urged that 'now is the appointed time to descend in mercie, to lighten them that sit in darkness, and in the shadow of death, and to direct their feete in the waies of peace.'[79] As in earlier books making this appeal, no actual plans were put forward as to how missionary work was to be accomplished in Virginia. Hamor also appealed to nationalistic sentiments as he asked 'What [is] more honourable... then to reduce a farre disjoyned forraigne nation, under the due obedience of our dread Sovereigne.'[80] The heart of the book, however, was an appeal to England's oppressed people to come to Virginia, where each family would receive twelve acres, provisions to get started in a new life, tools, poultry, 'and if he deserve it, a Goate or two,' at the company's charge.[81]

Hamor's book makes it clear that in Virginia it was settlers and investment which were considered most essential to the colony's progress, and that an appeal to the unfortunate of England was believed to hold more promise than continued appeals for missionary work. It was ap-

parent also in Virginia that the missionary appeals had not had satisfactory results, for Hamor appended a letter from Alexander Whitaker
to his book, along with letters from John Rolfe and Thomas Dale, in
which the preacher complained that so few of his colleagues among the
Puritan ministry had come to America. 'Be there not any amongst them
of Moses his minde, and of the Apostles, that forsooke all to follow
Christ?'[82] With such pleading and admission of little interest in Virginia, it is not surprising that Hamor's book, like so many others of its
type was published by William Welby, indicating company sponsor-
ship.

The much-lamented lethargy and opposition, however, were not
sufficient to stifle the life of the Virginia colony. By 1616 the Council
for Virginia was able to announce the division of land, fifty acres per
man, or per investment of twelve pounds ten shillings, as had been
promised seven years before. A triumphant note was sounded in the
council's *A briefe declaration of the present state of things in Virginia* published
that year, which reviewed the history of the colony from its beginnings
when 'it was a thing seeming strange and doubtfull in the eye of the
world,'[83] to the time of this publication when the colonists were 'able
to maintaine themselves with food, they are also prepared... to set upon
the minerals, whereof there are many sorts.'[84] This was, it is true, an
appeal for more funds, but it showed confidence in the future of Virginia, as did a broadside issued probably the same year in which it was
announced that there was no lack of food in Virginia and that the
council would not attempt to restrain anyone in the colony who might
wish to return to England.[85]

With the achievement of this modest degree of success, the pleading
ended, and subsequent publications were able to announce developments in Virginia with less apology and more assurance than heretofore. No publications on behalf of Virginia were issued in 1617 or 1618,
but in 1619 and 1620 two leaflets were published which told of the
growth of the population. The first of these stated that Virginia had
2,400 settlers, and the 1620 leaflet noted that 1,000 more people were
sent out that year. They also listed ships that sailed to Virginia, and
gifts that had been made for the construction of schools and churches
there. These were obviously official announcements issued by the Council for Virginia.[86]

In 1620 the directors of the colony also issued *A declaration of the state
of the colonie and affaires in Virginia,* a collection of five tracts which
summed up the history of the settlement and reviewed its general

condition. The reader was not allowed to overlook the early hardships endured by the colonists, not the least of which were the harsh things said against it by critics in England. But now 'wee have assuredly found, those Letters and Rumours to have been false and malicious... and Virginia is proved to be abounding in all Gods naturall blessings.'[87] This tract for the first time related Virginia's blessings to England's total commercial situation. The furs and cordage which England had bought in Russia could be found in Virginia. The masts, naval stores, hemp and flax that were received from Scandinavia, Poland, and Germany were available in Virginia also. Iron was abundant, and there was wood to smelt it. The wines, fruit, and salt of France and Spain, the silk of Italy and Persia, these too could be produced in Virginia. To these were added woods, berries, dyes, oils, gums, cotton, sugar, grain and fish. In short, Virginia was 'a countrey, which nothing but ignorance can think ill of, and which no man but of a corrupt minde and ill purpose can defame.'[88]

Not only was the country good, but good men were going there, 'most of them choise men, borne and bred up to labour and industry,'[89] including farmers from Devon, Warwick, and Staffordshire, iron workers from Sussex and others from various parts of the homeland who had left England for Virginia where they now lived a cheerful life under good government and in the care of the Church.

This progress report was also an advertisement for further investment, but it carried a confident tone. It made no mention of plans for large-scale missionary efforts, nor did it dwell on the probability of finding gold mines or a passage to the Pacific. The motivations of the Elizabethan age had given way to an English interest in America sufficiently mature to see in Virginia an opportunity for investment and colonization. Yet this view of Virginia was not universally held throughout England. The pleas of the most ardent champions of the enterprise suggest considerable opposition to the colony for the first decade of its existence, calling into question Wertenbaker's statements that 'it was really the English nation that had decided to second their king in gaining a foothold in America,' and that 'James I and his people were agreed as to the necessity of extending the English nation to America.'[90] The decline in the number of publications relating to Virginia after its establishment indicates that whatever amount of support the people of England gave to the colony, it was not a subject for which booksellers found a large and waiting audience.

## NOTES TO CHAPTER XI

1 A. P. Newton, *The colonising activities of the English Puritans* (New Haven: Yale University Press, 1914), p. 14.

2 James A. Williamson, *English colonies in Guiana and on the Amazon, 1604–1668* (Oxford: Clarendon Press, 1923), p. 31.

3 *Ibid.*, pp. 35–39.

4 John Nicholl, *An houre glasse of Indian newes* (London: [E. Allde] for Nathaniell Butter, 1607).

5 Parks, *Hakluyt*, pp. 302–4; Charles Knowles Bolton, *The real founders of New England* (Boston: F. W. Faxon Company, 1929), pp. 21–22.

6 James Rosier, *A true relation of the most prosperous voyage made this present yeere 1605, by Captaine George Waymouth...* (London: George Bishop, 1605), fol. A2 recto.

7 *Ibid.*, fol. B2 recto.

8 *Ibid.*, fol. B3 verso.

9 *Ibid.*, fol. D4 recto–verso.

10 Benjamin F. De Costa, 'Norumbega and its English explorers,' *Narrative and critical history of America*, ed. Justin Winsor, III, 175–177.

11 Robert A. Brock, 'Virginia, 1606–1689,' *Narrative and critical history of America*, ed. Justin Winsor, III, 127–29.

12 John Smith, *A true relation of such occurrences and accidents of noate as hath hapned in Virginia since the first planting of that collony* (London: J. Tappe, sold by W. W[elby], 1608), 2nd preliminary leaf, recto.

13 *Ibid.*, verso.

14 *Ibid.*

15 *Ibid.*, 2nd preliminary leaf, verso and following leaf, recto.

16 *Ibid.*, fol. B1 recto.

17 *Ibid.*, fol. E4 verso.

18 Brock, pp. 132–33.

19 George M. Brydon, *Virginia's mother church* (2 vols.; Richmond: Virginia Historical Society, 1947), I, 8.

20 William Symonds, *Virginia. A sermon preached at White-Chappel, in the presence of many... planters for Virginia* (London: I. Windet for Eleazar Edgar and William Welby, 1609), p. 1.

21 *Ibid.*, p. 9.

22 *Ibid.*, pp. 3–4.

23 *Ibid.*, p. 54.

24 *Ibid.*, p. 20.

25 *Ibid.*, p. 21.

26 *Ibid.*, p. 22.

27 Robert Johnson, *Nova Britannia. Offering most excellent fruites by planting in Virginia* (London: Samuel Macham, 1609), fol. A3 verso.

28 *Ibid.*, fol. B1 recto.

29 *Ibid.*, fols. B2 verso–B3 recto.

30 *Ibid.*, fol. C1 recto.

31 *Ibid.*, fol. D3 recto.

32 *Ibid.*, fol. B3 verso.

33 Daniel Price, *Sauls prohibition staide* (London: For Matthew Law, 1609).

34 *Ibid.*, fol. F3 recto.

35 *Ibid.*

36 Robert Gray, *A good speed to Virginia* (London: Felix Kyngston for William Welbie, 1609), fol. B1 recto.

37 *Ibid.*, fol. B2 verso.

38 *Ibid.*, fol. C2 recto.
39 *Ibid.*, fol. D3 recto.
40 Marc Lescarbot, *Nova Francia: or the description of that part of New France, which is one continent with Virginia*, trans. Pierre Erondelle (London: George Bishop, 1609). Another issue of this translation from Lescarbot was published by Andrew Hebb in 1609. The first French edition was published in Paris by Jean Milot in 1609.
41 *Ibid.*, fol. ¶¶1 recto.
42 *Ibid.*, fol. ¶¶1 verso.
43 *Ibid.*, fol. ¶¶2 recto.
44 Ferdinand de Soto, *Virginia richly valued, by the description of the maine land of Florida, her next neighbour*, trans. Richard Hakluyt (London: Felix Kyngston for Matthew Lownes, 1609). First published in Evora by Andre de Burgos as *Relaçam verdadeira dos trabalhos que ho governador Don Fernando d'Souto* in 1557.
45 *A true and sincere declaration of the purpose and ends of the plantation begun in Virginia* (London: For J. Stepneth, 1610), p. 2. *STC* 24832a notes another issue with the imprint 'for J. Stepney.'
46 *Ibid.*, p. 4.
47 William Crashaw, *A sermon preached in London before the... Lord Lawarre* (London: William Welby, 1610), fol. C2 recto.
48 *Ibid.*
49 *Ibid.*, fol. C3 recto.
50 *Ibid.*, fol. F4 recto.
51 *Ibid.*, fol. G2 verso.
52 *Ibid.*, fol. H4 recto. Critics of the colony who spoke from the stage in such plays as *Eastward Ho!* written by John Marston and others in 1605 annoyed the Virginia adventurers, and the actors were fair game for Puritan preachers on other grounds as well.
53 *A true declaration of the estate of the colonie in Virginia* (London: For William Barret, 1610), p. 9.
54 *Ibid.*, p. 68.
55 Richard Rich, *Newes from Virginia. The lost flocke triumphant* (London: Edward Allde, to be sold by John Wright, 1610), fol. B2 verso.
56 *Ibid.*, fol. B2 recto.
57 *Ibid.*
58 *Ibid.*, fol. B2 verso.
59 Silvester Jourdain, *A discovery of the Barmudas, otherwise called the Ile of Divels* (London: John Windet, sold by Roger Barnes, 1610), p. 10.
60 Thomas West, Lord De La Warr, *The relation of the Right Honourable the Lord De-La-Warre, lord governor and captaine generall of the colonie, planted in Virginea* (London: William Hall for William Welbie, 1611), fol. A3 verso.
61 This issue bore the title *The worthye and famous history of the travailes, discovery and conquest, of that great continent, Terra Florida*. The printer and publisher were the same as for the 1609 edition.
62 William Strachey (ed.) *For the colony in Virginea Britannia. Lawes divine, morall and martiall, etc.* (London: For Walter Burre, 1612), pp. 1–2.
63 Robert Johnson, *The new life of Virginea... being the second part of 'Nova Britannia'* (London: Felix Kyngston for William Welby, 1612), fol. A3 verso.
64 *Ibid.*
65 *Ibid.*, fol. D1 verso.
66 *Ibid.*, fol. E2 recto.
67 John Smith, *A map of Virginia* (Oxford: Joseph Barnes, 1612), p. 39.
68 William Symonds, *The proceedings of the English colonie in Virginia* (Oxford: Joseph Barnes, 1612), fol. A2 recto.

69 George Wotson Cole, *A catalogue of books relating to the discovery and early history of North and South America forming a part of the library of E. D. Church* (5 vols.; New York: Dodd, Mead and Co., 1907), note to item 359.

70 Pietro Martire d'Anghiera, *De Novo Orbe, or the historie of the West Indies*, trans. Michael Lok (London: For Thomas Adams, 1612), fol. B1 verso.

71 Alexander Whitaker, *Good newes from Virginia* (London: Felix Kyngston for William Welby, 1613), p. 1.

72 *Ibid.*, fol. A4 verso.

73 *Ibid.*, fol. A4 recto.

74 *Ibid.*, p. 33.

75 *Ibid.*, p. 39.

76 Silvester Jourdain, *A plaine description of the Barmudas, now called Sommer Ilands* (London: W. Stansby for W. Welby, 1613).

77 Lewis Hughes, *A letter sent into England from the Summer Ilands* (London: I. B. for William Welby, 1615), fol. b3 verso.

78 Ralph Hamor, *A true discourse of the present estate of Virginia* (London: John Beale for William Welby, 1615), fol. A2 recto–verso. Two issues of this work appeared in 1615.

79 *Ibid.*, fol. A4 recto.

80 *Ibid.*, p. 48.

81 *Ibid.*, pp. 19–20.

82 *Ibid.*, p. 60.

83 This tract has no title page, but begins, *By His Majesties counseil for Virginia. A briefe declaration of the present state of things in Virginia*. The quotation is from p. 1.

84 *Ibid.*, p. 4.

85 This broadside bears the heading, *By His Majesties councell for Virginia*.

86 The titles of these leaflets are as follows: *A note of the shipping, men, and provisions, sent to Virginia, by the treasurer and company, in the yeere 1619;* and *A note of the shipping, men, and provisions, sent and provided for Virginia, by the Right Honorable, the Earle of Southampton, and the company, this yeare, 1620*.

87 *A declaration of the state of the colonie and affaires in Virginia* (London: T. S[nodham], 1620), p. 2. This is a collection of tracts with individual paginations which were almost certainly issued at one time, for in the second issue, also of 1620, they were paged consecutively.

88 *Ibid.*, p. 5.

89 *Ibid.*

90 Thomas J. Wertenbaker, *Virginia under the Stuarts, 1607–1688* (Princeton: Princeton University Press, 1914), p. 32.

## Chapter XII

# EMPIRE AND WORLD VIEW

English interest in America was not by any means devoted entirely to Virginia and Bermuda. There were those who still dreamed of a tropical empire in Guiana and others who insisted that the northwest passage to Asia was worth further exploration. The fact that one of Captain Newport's obligations of 1608 was to find such a passage within the latitudes of Virginia shows that even among the promoters of the colony the dream of Frobisher and Davis still made an appeal. Weymouth's failure in 1602 was followed four years later by the abortive attempt of John Knight who landed on the coast of Labrador and disappeared, apparently captured by natives. The Muscovy Company kept alive an interest in northern passages, for competition with the Dutch in Russian waters was reducing its trade, and the hope of finding a passage across the North Pole induced it to send out Henry Hudson in April, 1607.

With his son and ten crew members, Hudson probed the east coast of Greenland, moved east to Spitzbergen, and finding no open water to the north, returned to England in August, 1607. Not discouraged, the Muscovy Company then sent him to try the northeast passage the following year, but he failed to get beyond Novaya Zemlya. Leaving England for service with the Dutch, Hudson tried the northeast route again, but mutiny forced him to go westward, and he followed the North American coast as far south as Virginia and then northward again into the Hudson River. When he stopped at Dartmouth on his return, the English refused him permission to go to the Netherlands, some believing that he had found the long-sought passage through North America.[1]

The Hudson voyages to the northeast aroused Richard Hakluyt to bring before the English public Gerrit de Veer's accounts of the three voyages in that direction undertaken by the Dutchman Willem Barents in 1594, 1595 and 1596. Again it was William Phillip who translated from the Dutch, and he wrote of being 'interested by some of my Friends, and principally by M. Richard Hakluyt' to make this translation.[2] Once more Hakluyt failed to see to it that the translation was accompanied by some commentary or preface to make it clear to the reader that the northeast passage was important to England. The dedication by Phillip to Sir Thomas Smith, governor of the Muscovy Company, ignored Hudson's efforts toward the northeast, and the failures of Barents were not closely related to English interest, as Phillip stated rather casually, 'If any of our nation be employed that way in time to come, here they have a great part of their Voiage layd open.'[3]

For the enthusiasm requisite to a northern voyage, a reader in 1609 might have turned instead to Anthony Linton's *Newes of the complement of the art of navigation*, which was an extraordinary mixture of imperialism, fumbling science, and religion. Linton was a Sussex parson who praised navigation, 'for without it the nations of the world dwelling farre asunder, neither should nor could ever at any hand by traffique or commerce be partakers of others, commodities, manners, learning, policies or religion.'[4] He also believed in imperialism, urging that nations learned in navigation would be able to protect their liberties and extend their rule over others. He cited Spain, Portugal and Holland as examples.

Linton's 'complement' was a secret theory which he promised to reveal in a forthcoming book, which never appeared. It was to contain a new method of determining longitude, a problem navigators had not yet solved.[5] He tied his secret to the northeast passage by including in his book ten statements regarding China and the means of getting there, the most significant of which was 'That there is greater hope than ever was heretofore, of a free and safe passage by sea, Northerly from Europe to Cataia,'[6] hardly a revelation of consequence. The combination of scientist and clergyman in Linton gave the northeast passage a religious appeal for the first time, as he sought for England 'the benefits of planting the Gospell amongst those Ethnique and Idolatrous nations of Cataia, and others by the way.'[7] He also noted the usual economic values of the passage.

The efforts of these literary advocates of the northeast passage fell between the peaks of enthusiasm for northern exploration that produced the Hudson voyages. By 1610 the northeast route was pushed into the background as interest mounted in a new attempt being made to the northwest. With the backing of Sir Thomas Smith of the Muscovy, East India, and Virginia companies, as well as the support of Prince Henry and others, Hudson set sail on his last voyage in April, 1610. He found the entrance into Hudson Bay, followed the east coast of the bay southward into James Bay, and froze in there for the winter. In the spring a mutinous crew put Hudson, his son, and seven sailors in a boat and abandoned them.

When the eight surviving mutineers returned to England and exhibited their chart of the great bay extending to the south, with no western shore, there was little difficulty in finding 288 subscribers to fit out two ships for a company called the Discoverors of the North-West Passage. With greater optimism than even Frobisher had known, Thomas Button sailed westward for Asia in 1612. In the spirit of assured success, Sir Dudley Digges, who had been a backer of Hudson in his final voyage and was a partner in this one, wrote a brief treatise to disprove the arguments of those who were sceptical of northwestward navigation. His book, *Of the circumference of the earth*, replied to maps that 'either shew no passage, or else so high into the North, and long into the West, that Cold and Ice, and Fogges, and so foorth make it of no use,'[8] by calling attention to the monstrous errors frequently found on maps. Working from errors in Ptolemy's theory of the size of the earth through the evidence gained from Spanish exploration in the Pacific Ocean, he concluded that North America 'is nothing broad, how ever it be painted.'[9] He felt certain that some three hundred miles westward from the Virginia coast was the Pacific shore, tending in a northeastwardly direction. This sort of wishful thinking was dashed when Captain Button came up against the western side of Hudson Bay. Though the attempts to find a western passage continued year after year, no more books promising its existence appeared until after 1620.[10]

Failure in the far north during these years was matched by failure on the Guiana coast where further attempts were made to build the empire Raleigh had envisioned in the 1590s. Just as the Virginia colony was being revitalized in 1609, a new plan for settling colonists in Guiana was put forward by Robert Harcourt, of gentle birth and Oxford education. With a group of associates he received a license to sail for Guiana on February 13, 1609, and arrived at the mouth of the Wiapoco River some three months later. With him were sixty men whom he intended to leave there as colonists and factors in several settlements through which English goods would be exchanged for South American products. After exploring the Guiana coast for likely factory sites Harcourt returned to England, leaving the colony in the care of his brother Michael. In England, beset by legal difficulties, he was not able to send the necessary aid to his people in Guiana, and they appear to have given up and returned to England in 1612 or 1613.[11]

With the life of the colony ebbing, Harcourt determined to make another try and a new grant was obtained, assigning to Harcourt land between the Amazon and Essequibo rivers. To arouse interest in his colony, Harcourt wrote *A relation of a voyage to Guiana*, a book that is wonderful in its optimism, considering the steady decline in the colony since its beginnings. Harcourt described how Guiana could provide employment and satisfaction for all occupations, and noted 'that from Guiana, without any great labour, there may be returned within the yeare good store of Fethers, all kindes of rich Woods, Balsamums, Jasper, and Porpherie stone, waxe, Honey, and Tobacco, and so every yeare may we pay the transportation, untill we encrease in people to make Sugars, and discover Mines.'[12] While Harcourt was striving to make his colony appear profitable to investors, he was also, as an English nationalist, charmed with the idea of empire. He praised Raleigh's ventures on behalf of his country's honor and asserted that the failure of Spain to settle successfully in Guiana was proof that 'God doth worke for us in this behalfe; and hath reserved the execution of this action to the honour of our nation.'[13]

Harcourt was aware that his colony was a competitor to Virginia, and he yielded nothing to that enterprise, stating 'if Virginia had not a sharpe winter, which Guiana hath not... and that it had that store of victuals which Guiana hath, it would in a short time grow to be a most profitable place.'[14] In his account of his travels in Guiana Harcourt showed a similar confidence in the country: the natives were friendly, food was abundant, exports were readily available, and there was a ready market among the Indians for metal tools and ornaments. The use of gold ornaments by the natives kept all of his company convinced that there was gold in the vicinity.

Harcourt's book was an appeal in the traditions of Rastell, Eden, Hakluyt, Churchyard, and Raleigh. It spoke emotionally of empire and appealingly of the opportunities for profit while making a nod to the religious motive. It gave a large play to the employment abroad of 'all young Gentlemen, Souldiers, and others that live at home in idleness, and want employment,'[15] and in addressing his work to Prince Charles, Harcourt was calling for support from the Crown, as his predecessors had done. He made little appeal to the people who would have to constitute the population of his colony. But the appeals of private gain and national honor had not founded an empire in Elizabeth's reign, and Harcourt's use of them seems to have been equally ineffective, for no voyage in Harcourt's interest followed this confident advertisement of Guiana.

There were others who saw reason to believe that Guiana offered prospects for successful colonization. In 1610 Sir Thomas Roe sailed up the Amazon, to its confluence with the Topojoz River and along the Guiana coast to Trinidad. The following year he appears to have sent two more expeditions to Guiana, but from these three voyages the only known result was a settlement of twenty colonists at the mouth of the Amazon. It is not surprising that five of these colonists were reported to have arrived in Holland in 1617, for in these years there was considerable cooperation between the Dutch and English in probing the Guiana coast for likely sites' for settlement. In 1614 Captain Edward Harvey, who had sailed with Harcourt, appears to have commanded an Anglo-Dutch project for settlement in Nicaragua, and in 1617 he probably took another group of settlers to the Wiapoco River region. It also seems quite certain that in 1616 an Anglo-Dutch enterprise was undertaken on the Amazon. Departing from Flushing, the expedition appears to have settled 130 men and fourteen women on the northern bank of the river near its confluence with the Parú where the settlers traded in tobacco, dyestuffs and wood.[16] Surely England received a continuous flow of information about Guiana from these adventurers, but it was not until the spectacular Sir Walter Raleigh returned to the scene in 1618 that Guiana come to the public notice by way of a printed book.

It is remarkable that Raleigh, who had explored with merchantable products in mind to a greater extent than any of his sixteenth century contemporaries, should close out his career with a desperate gold-hunting affair in Guiana which produced one last publication portraying the mirage of El Dorado. From his position of high favor in the last years of Elizabeth's reign, Raleigh was quickly reduced to a prisoner in the first year after James's accession. For his conviction of having been involved in a plot to have Arabella Stuart succeed to Elizabeth's throne, and for accusations of secret dealings with Spain he spent more than twelve years in the Tower.[17]

Raleigh's one hope for freedom lay in the need James had for money and in his knowledge of and belief in Guiana. By proposing to lead an expedition there to reveal a gold mine which he claimed to have knowledge of he secured his release in 1616. During the next fifteen months a fleet of fourteen ships was made ready, a thousand men recruited, and an investment of 30,000 pounds raised.[18] On pain of his life Raleigh was ordered not to molest any Spanish garrison in America. Departing in August, 1617, Raleigh's fleet arrived in Guiana on November 11, and six days later one of the fleet who merely signed himself 'R.M.' wrote *Newes of Sr. Walter Rauleigh. With the true description of Guiana.* It was published in 1618. Since the book was written so shortly after the arrival of the fleet, it could not contain much in the way of new observations of Guiana. It relied, rather, on earlier experiences there and on mere hearsay. It is a strongly partisan book, opening with a condemnation of selfish men whose positions were built upon the ruin of others. The author attempted to establish an air of optimism by reviewing some of the accounts of the riches of the Inca and by describing the earlier voyage Raleigh had made to Guiana, when a native chief 'shewed him a wonderfull great Myne of Gold in a manner of a Rock or hard golden stones, which without especiall strong engines... was not to be pierst,'[19] and also a mountain which he was assured contained diamonds and other precious stones. In Guiana, according to the author, 'the Souldier may fight for Gold, and pay himself instead of pence with plates of gold a foot broad,' for he announced: 'The graves have not been opened for Gold, the Mines not broken with sledge or pickaxe, nor their Images puld downe out of their Temples.'[20]

Despite this evidence of gold-hunger, precious metal was not emphasized at the expense of other possibilities in Guiana. We read again of the good hunting, excellent air, abundance of brazil wood, cotton, silk, pepper, and of soil ideal for growing sugar and ginger. Quoting Raleigh, the author promised that Guiana would 'satisfie any industrious judgement whatsoever... [being] eyther rich in Gold or in other Marchandise.'[21]

Raleigh found no gold in Guiana. His men fought with the Spaniards, and his own son was killed in the conflict. His trusted aid, Lawrence Kemys, committed suicide in disappointment at the failure of the expedition. Raleigh, now old and frequently ill, saw his fleet disintegrate as the various ships went off on pursuits of piracy, and mutineers on his own ship prevented him from trying to reach Newfoundland. He returned to England where pressure from the Spanish ambassador forced James to have him executed on the basis of the 1603 conviction for treason. Yet even after his death the Crown felt it necessary to review the Guiana adventure once more to justify its action against Raleigh. This was done in *A declaration of the demeanor and cariage of Sir Walter Raleigh*, published in 1618, which contained Raleigh's charter and an account of his last voyage.[22] It sought to prove that he was not intent upon developing a gold mine but merely in finding enough ore to prove that a mine existed, thus justifying further confidence in him which would enable him to enrich himself at the expense of Spanish shipping and settlements in the New World.

Raleigh's failure and death removed Guiana from serious consideration as a competitor to Virginia, but there was one more region in the Western hemisphere where English interest persisted. This was the Norumbega and Newfoundland area where the failure of the Popham-Gorges colony of 1608 had not discouraged other Englishmen from trying their fortunes as free-lance traders and fishermen. This was a natural area for English fishermen, and although competition was intense, good profits were possible. It is not surprising to find Captain John Smith, who had seen the value of Virginia ahead of most of his contemporaries, setting out in March, 1614, for the region he named 'New England.' He went there to fish and to study and map the shores, for he had a long-range fishing plan in mind. Upon returning to England he secured the backing of some west-country investors and sailed again for New England, only to be frustrated by weather and French privateers. When he returned to England in 1616 he published *A description of New England* in which he began by anticipating the doubters, and by scolding the idle as he wrote. 'Little hony hath that hive, where there are more Drones than Bees.' [23]

He left no doubt about his motives in New England, for 'our plot was there to take Whales and make tryalls of a Myne of Gold and Copper.' [24] Failing in these, Smith and his company took to fishing, buying furs from the Indians, and exploring the coast. In his description of the shore from Penobscot to Cape Cod he noted economic opportunities in furs, stone, slate, iron, timber, etc. He summed up his impressions in his typically bold style. 'Could I have but meanes to transport a Colonie, I would rather live here then any where: and if it did not maintaine it selfe, were we but once indifferently well fitted, let us starve.' [25] Throughout his description of the region and his plea for the planting of a colony there, he returned again and again to fishing as the foundation of a future wealth in New England. While paying passing respect to the religious motive, Smith asserted: 'I am not so simple, to thinke, that ever any other motive then wealth, will ever erect a Commonweale.' [26]

His appraisal of motivation seems to have been sound, for his book brought six ships to New England in 1616, and fishing was their goal. From Monhegan Island they explored the coast and came generally to a favorable view of New England as a place to settle a colony. Yet, despite the going and coming of ships, nothing appeared in print to praise the area until Smith published his *New Englands trials* in 1620. The arguments Smith presented on behalf of New England in this tract had been used in 1618 when he tried to induce Francis Bacon, Lord High Chancellor of England, to become interested in New England. The first copies of the book carried a dedication 'To the Right Honorable and Worthy adventurers to all discoveries and Plantaitions, espetially to New England,' while others were dedicated to the Company of Fish-Mongers. Its message was assuredly directed to people interested in fishing. Smith argued that with bases in New England where wood for ship-building, salt for curing, and food for supplying ships were all plentiful, England could gain a great advantage over her competitors in the North Atlantic. He cited his own experience in making 1,500 pounds gross profit in fish and furs in less than five months, and attacked those who delayed his development of the New England fishery by withholding funds 'in such a penurious and miserable maner, as if I had gone a begging to builde an University.' [27] Confident of New England's merits, and bitter at delays, he assured his readers, 'the fishing will go forward if you plant it or no.' [28]

Smith's two books on New England had greater effect than his books describing Virginia. His *Description of New England* must have reached the attention of a group of English dissenters at Leyden who were beginning to consider the possibility of emigrating to New England. A thousand copies of his *New Englands trials* were presented 'to thirty of the Chiefe Companies in London at their Halls' as Smith sought to arouse enthusiasm for his New England colony. [29] Notably low on religious appeal, Smith's books were based on his belief that profits were the chief concern of investors and that there was no altering that fact. He also gave less notice to the greater glory of England than most writers of colonization literature; he was only concerned that England get actively into the New England fishing trade. No books were more forthright in their appeal for overseas interest, and none were more successful, for they influenced both investors and religiously motivated colonists. Some seventy merchants put up money that made possible the emigration of 102 persons to New England from their religious exile in Leyden.

By 1620 English enterprise in America had returned to the point of its beginnings, the Newfoundland region, where John Cabot had first claimed the continent for England. Now English concern with this northern area which had excited Rastell and had frequently been referred to as the most natural area for English interest, called forth two books in 1620 in support of a colony that had been started in New-foundland. In 1612, just after the grant of the second Virginia charter, King James had granted a charter to a group of Bristol and London merchants to start a settlement on Newfoundland—which was beyond the northern borders of Virginia—and settlement was begun that year.[30]

One of the chief figures in Newfoundland during the first decade of the settlement was John Mason, who became governor in 1615, suc-ceeding John Guy of Bristol. When Mason wrote his friend, John Scott, in Edinburgh in 1620, he described the potentialities of Newfoundland, and added, 'if you thinke it may doe good by incouraging any of your Countrie to the interprise, I am willing you publish it.'[31] *A briefe dis-course of the New-found-land* appeared in print shortly, containing a note to the reader by Mason indicating that he was more than casually interested in the publication of his letter. Here he gave an admirable impression of honesty, blaming equally those who misrepresented New-foundland, 'some too much extolling it, some too much debasing it.'[32] He recognized Virginia as his chief competitor for settlers, and made a comparison of the two areas, admitting the superiority of Virginia's soil and climate, but reminding the reader that Newfoundland was only about half as far from England as Virginia. He also pointed out that Newfoundland already had a well-developed trade, that costs of transporting a man to Newfoundland were about one-tenth those in-volved in moving to Virginia, and that there was greater security from enemies, both foreign and native, on Newfoundland. While he exag-gerated the agricultural potentialities of the island, he recognized that of all Newfoundland's advantages 'the most admirable is the Sea, so diversified with severall sorts of Fishes abounding therein.'[33]

Mason's knowledge was based on five years' residence in Newfound-land. He was far surpassed in experience by Richard Whitbourne, who first went there in 1580, and who was on hand when Gilbert took possession of the island for England. Several times during the next forty years, Whitbourne had returned to Newfoundland and during that time must have acquired an air of authority there, for in 1615 he was sent out to restore order among some unruly fishermen. In 1620 he wrote *A discourse and discovery of New-found-land*, which he dedicated to the King, acknowledging that his purpose was 'to beget a disposition in all your Majesties Subjects, for a Plantation in the New-found-land.'[34]

As promotional literature, Whitbourne's book is very similar to Smith's *New Englands trials*. He admitted 'that it is an hard matter to perswade people to adventure into strange Countries.'[35] He made a bow to the spreading of England's religion in America, and to the expansion of England's empire, but his real plan for Newfoundland centered around fishing. He advocated that one of every five men leaving England for the Newfoundland fishery should remain on the island to maintain a secure base, to provide drying facilities, and during the winter to lay up a supply of provisions.[36] Whitbourne, like Smith, was a practical, profit-motivated expansionist.

After a century of awareness of North America, the means of putting the New World to the service of England began to take form. Whitbourne's book came after forty years of sailing to and from Newfoundland, and it represented the maturing of ideas that had first been hinted at in the writings of Gilbert and Churchyard. The opportunities for profits on the fishing banks off Newfoundland, the overpopulation of England, and the need to convince people to go to the New World, rather than to persuade the government to send them, had all come together in the comparative absence of purely emotional expansionism and dreams of great stores of gold which had dominated imperialist thought from the beginning.

The success of English colonial undertakings between 1603 and 1620 had the effect of bringing English literature of overseas interest into narrower focus, but special pleading for one project or another did not drive travel and geography books of broad scope and little pertinence to empire from the market. Publishers continued to see as much hope for profit in a book describing Asia or Africa as in a Virginia tract, although travel was not a popular subject, considering the number of Englishmen who were going abroad in this period. It might be noted also that much of what was written by English travelers and geographers was of a rather tedious content.

For example, Nathaniel Butter published *Sir Thomas Smithes voiage and entertainment in Rushia* in 1605, describing Smith's embassy of the previous year, and despite all of the commercial activity that had developed between England and Russia since Richard Eden's attempts to get information on the country from Muscovy merchants, Butter's book was far inferior to Eden's account.[37] It did not approach that of Giles Fletcher in balance or completeness, being essentially a description of personal experiences and observations on Russian officialdom, even though Smith had a long and personal interest in the Muscovy Company. Similarly, *A true historicall discourse of Muley Hamets rising to the three kingdomes of Moruecos, Fes and Sus* emphasized politico-military maneuverings at the expense of information on the regions he ruled, although the late chapters present some interesting observations on the religion and customs of the people, the gold trade to the Senegal River, and an account of the grasshoppers that plagued Morocco.[38]

While England sent out travelers to trade, to convert Indians to Christianity, and to deal with foreign governments, she also had others who traveled for the sheer love of seeing distant and interesting places. In this category were William Lithgow and Thomas Coryate. Lithgow's book, *A most delectable, and true discourse, of an admired and painefull peregrination from Scotland, to the most famous kingdomes in Europe, Asia and Affricke,* had much of the personal and the curious to report, but little to relate to England's interests in these areas.[39] It was a traditional type of travel that Lithgow undertook, relating chiefly to places of classical and Biblical interest, yet it was sufficiently well received to call for a second edition in 1616, two years after the first printing.[40] Coryate, on the other hand was England's most unusual traveler during this period. He was something of a court jester whose odd appearance and ready wit provided amusement among the aristocrocy. It was said that 'The word Travaile affects him in a Waine oxe-, or Packe-horse... The meere Superscription of a letter from Zurich settes him up like a top: Basil or Heidelberg makes him spinne. And at seeing the word Frankford, or Venice, though but on the title of a booke, he is readie to break doublet, crackle elbowes, and overflow the roome with his murmure.'[41] The enthusiasm of this 'legge stretcher' took him out to India in 1612, and in his *Greeting from the court of the Great Mogul,* 1616, he boasted of having walked all the way from Jerusalem to Asmere in India, 'with divers paire of shooes,' so proud was he of his 'agilitie of footmanship.'[42] His narrative was primarily one of personal experiences and observations during his travels and his visit to the Mogul's court, and it took the form of letters to his friends and his mother, relating not at all to England's interests in India.

In 1618 another letter from Coryate to his mother was published under the title *Mr. Thomas Coriat to his friends in England sendeth greeting,* and here again the prowess of the author as a traveler was celebrated, this time in verse:

> *Virginia of thy worth doth onely heare,*
> *And longs the weight of thy foot-steps to beare.*[43]

Coryate told of staying at the court of the Mogul to learn languages, and of living with English merchants and 'not spending one little peece of mony either for diet, washing, lodging, or any other thing.' [44] This free-loader gave little information beyond events relating to his personal affairs, but he filled much of his book with a Persian oration to the Mogul, and a speech on Mohammedanism delivered in Italian.

English views of the outer world were but little colored by translations of foreign publications in the decade prior to 1620. A new edition of the earlier translation of *A geographical historie of Africa* by Leo Africanus in 1617 kept that work available[45], and a translation of a Jesuit letter from Japan, published in France in 1619 gave Englishmen their first complete book describing those islands. This translation from the Spanish was titled *A briefe relation of the persecution lately made against the Catholike Christians in the kingdome of Japonia*, and was much given to descriptions of burnings and banishings in a tone sympathetic to the victims.[46] Indeed, it was dedicated to all Catholics who suffered persecution for their faith in England. This is the only book of its kind to be published in English to this time, and it points up the loss England suffered by not publishing more of the Jesuit letters which were so common on the Continent; for while it was wanting in accuracy and was heavily concerned with religious affairs, it did give useful descriptions of the people, products and government of the island. This book announced itself to be the first of two parts, but the second part is not known to have been published.

A more significant translation published in 1617 was the petition which Pedro Fernandes de Quiros addressed to the King of Spain in 1610, requesting permission to explore the supposed 'Terra Australis Incognita.' This pamphlet had enjoyed wide popularity on the Continent, and its translation into English as *Terra Australia Incognita, or a new southerne discoverie, containing a fifth part of the world* gave Englishmen their first description of this phantom continent which they were to pursue for a century and a half.[47] It was presented as a region swarming with inhabitants, plentifully supplied with food and good harbors, an ideal entrepôt lying between South America and the East Indies.

Two years later William Phillip dedicated to Sir Thomas Smith another work related to the South Pacific area. This was Willem Schouten's *The relation of a wonderful voiage*, which had also had immense popularity on the Continent, in part because of the fact that Schouten's voyage disclosed a route to the south of the Strait of Magellan, around Cape Horn, thereby making unnecessary the troublesome voyage through the Strait. But more important, it broke the monopoly of the Dutch East India Company upon trade to the East Indies, for that company had been granted exclusive rights in East Indian trade via the Cape of Good Hope and the Strait of Magellan. Phillip saw the possible implications for English trade to the East Indies, and he presented his translation to Smith, 'wishing it a meanes to further and advance your trade to India.'[48] The text is a straight translation of the journal of Schouten's voyage around the world, beginning from the Netherlands in 1615, proceeding around Cape Horn and returning by way of the Cape of Good Hope in 1618. The English edition did not include a map showing Schouten's route as did the contemporary editions published on the Continent, but the title page did contain a map showing the track of the fleet around Cape Horn.

England's new position in the reign of James as an emerging imperial power did not excite any large segment of the English population, and even among those interested in travel abroad there was a conservatism that attempted to hold Englishmen to patterns of interest and conduct that were traditional and secure. This is made apparent in Sir Thomas Palmer's *An essay of the meanes how to make our travailes... the more profitable and honorable*, published in 1606, in which all types of travel were examined in a systematic way.[49] The emphasis was clearly upon European travel, how it should be planned, conducted and reported. But Palmer did show a knowledge of peoples of Asia, Africa, and America, though he was able to discuss them hurriedly without showing any interest in exploration, colonization or imperial effort of any kind. In considering 'voluntary' travelers, such as ambassadors and others in the peaceful service of their country, colonists and explorers seem to have entirely escaped Palmer's legalistic mind which categorized travelers in an arbitrary way. Bishop Joseph Hall went beyond ignoring explorers and colonists, and actively opposed distant travel abroad for any reason, except for an admission that merchants must venture abroad. Yet in his book *Quo Vadis? A just censure of travell as it is commonly undertaken by the gentlemen of our nation*, 1617, he warned the traveling merchant, 'Onely let our Merchants take heed, least they go so farre, that they leave God behind them.'[50] In travel he saw only temptation, being convinced that the soul will 'gather no mosse in this rolling, but suffers the best graces it hath, to molder away insensibly in such unnecessary agitation.'[51] This attitude on the part of a churchman, the author of some fifty books, gives credence to the complaints of lethargy and hostility to travel that had frequently been noted since the earliest writings of Richard Eden.

Bishop Hall wrote to a nation that had not yet become accustomed to its position as the mother of an empire. While the outside world had made irremovable inroads on the English mentality, and travel and travel literature were to increase with expanding opportunities for overseas trade, England still had much of the medieval mentality that found excitement in travel literature of an earlier time. The *Travels* of Sir John Mandeville were re-issued in 1612 and 1618 without commentary to relate Mandeville's tales to seventeenth century knowledge.[52] The acceptance of Mandeville as a great traveler by Samuel Purchas, who had probably read more travel literature than any man in England in 1620, confirms the persistence of medieval interest and attitudes with respect to geographical literature after the beginnings of empire had been established. The popularity of the chap-book type of travel-adventure story is further confirmed by the publication in 1614 of *A true relation of the travailes and most miserable captivitie of William Davies*, which was not Mandevillian in the fabulist sense, but like Mandeville's *Travels* was travel literature with no purpose but to entertain.[53] Davies' book was for the most part not an account of a captivity, but a description of twelve places he claims to have visited, including Algiers, Tunis, the Amazon River, Cyprus, and Morria, an island of women in the Amazon. His emphasis was on cruelties, unusual customs, tortures, conversion methods used by the Mohammedans, etc., but he does give considerable other information about the places he visited. His account of the Amazon River is supposedly based on a ten week stay there, although he does not indicate the time of his visit or its purpose, throwing doubt on the authenticity of his information.

The conservatism apparent in the continued publication of such chap-books as these is also obvious in the persistence of earlier geographical information, unmodified, in works of navigational interest published during this period. Blundeville's *Exercises* were published again in 1606 and 1613, substantially unchanged in their treatment of the voyages of Drake and Cavendish, Mercator's globe and the map of Petrus Plancius.[54] Although John Davis died in 1605, *The seaman's secrets* appeared again in 1607 with the same dedication to Lord Howard dated August 20, 1594, in which Davis had insisted on the existence of a northwest passage.[55] Similarly, the *Tractatus de globis* of Robert Hues was reprinted in 1611, without alteration.[56] When in 1616 Robert Tanner wrote *A brief treatise on the use of the globe celestiall and terrestriall*, which was issued a second time in 1620, his geographical information was elementary, contributing little more than the location of various points on the earth by position of latitude and longitude.[57]

*References, p. 237–241*

Considering the small number of original or up-to-date books of geography and travel which appeared in England in the 1600–1620 period, it is hardly surprising that world geographies published in these years should also be of a mediocre quality, generally. Two small works of this type which enjoyed some success were the *Epitome of the theater of the Worlde* of Abraham Ortelius and Robert Stafforde's *A geographicall and anthologicall description of all the empires and kingdomes... of this terrestriall globe*. The former is a small atlas with maps and one-page descriptions of European countries and some Asiatic and African regions. It contains no descriptions of North or South America, but its popularity was sufficient to justify English editions of 1603 and 1610.[58] Stafforde called his book 'a poore Survey... not of my travels, but reading,' and gave it the halting recommendation, 'the briefnesse of it cannot loose thee much time.'[59] This little handbook, first issued in 1607, could have been culled from any atlas or world geography, but its descriptions are too brief to have been of any use to any but the most elementary reader of geography. So complex a subject as the people of India, for example, is handled as follows: 'The inhabitants are a mixt sort of people, being Persians, Scythians, Arabians, Hebrews, and some Christians. They are commonly ingenious, much inclined to al Sciences. They adore one sole God, which they paint with three heads, but cannot give a reason for it.'[60] After noting the discovery of Virginia by Raleigh, Stafforde referred his readers to the writings of Hariot and Hakluyt, which he spelled 'Hackaut'. Yet Stafforde's book appeared again under two imprints in 1618.[61]

Several geographies much better than these were available early in the seventeenth century, and one of the best of them was *The naturall and morall historie of the East and West Indies*, 1604, a translation by Edward Grimstone, an English scholar of considerable reputation, from the Spanish Jesuit, José de Acosta.[62] Unlike most geographical works published in England during this period, Grimstone's translation went beyond mere descriptive geography, and took its English reader into philosophical discussion of such problems as the possibility of pre-Columbian knowledge of America, the means by which the New World became inhabited, the location of Ophir, the lands and seas in the polar regions, reasons for the existence of volcanoes, and other unsolved questions, as well as such overworked topics as the roundness of the earth. Acosta did not, however, omit the usual information on the soil, climate, natives and minerals of the New World which was his chief interest, despite the title of the book. This is a book that would surely have excited Richard Eden or John Frampton. It had been very well received on the Continent; no less a person than Jan Huygen van Linschoten translated it into the language of his people.[63] Yet in England it had only one edition.

The same was true of the greatest atlas of this period, the *Theatrum orbis terrarum* of Abraham Ortelius which came into the English language in 1606.[64] This magnificent volume containing 155 maps was dedicated by the printer John Norton to James I just as the East India Company made its claim to a portion of the spice trade and the Virginia enterprise was being formulated in London. Yet James and his subjects found not a single comment in this volume pertinent to England's interests abroad. This first English world atlas took its maps from the 1595 Antwerp edition, without altering the Latin cartouche inscriptions, although the text accompanying the maps was in English. There was no translator's message to the English reader, but a translation of Ortelius' note to the reader, written in 1570 and hardly pertinent to an English edition. The high quality of both maps and text did not sufficiently impress English book-buyers into calling for another printing of this atlas, nor did the example of it stimulate the publication of others, for it was not until 1627 that John Speed published the first general atlas originating in England.[65]

In the meantime, George Abbot's *A briefe description of the whole worlde* continued to find readers in abundance. The editions of 1599 and 1600 already mentioned were followed in 1605 by a considerably enlarged edition, the number of leaves being increased from thirty-two to eighty-four, and, with slight extensions of text, Abbot's book was issued again in 1608, 1617, and 1620.[66] While slightly more modern than the 1599 and 1600 editions, the augmented versions of this geography were still heavily oriented toward classical and Biblical sources, and only slightly concerned with England's new position in the world. Abbot's description of India made no mention of Dutch or English presence there, and America was described primarily from the standpoint of Spanish activity. He gave no hope to potential Virginia colonists as he reported briefly on the first Raleigh colony there, 'not finding any sustenaunce in the Countrie... they had like to have perished for famine.'[67]

Another general geography that found wide acceptance among English readers was *The travellers breviat* by Giovanni Botero, the later editions of which appeared with other titles. This translation by Robert Johnson which was first published in 1601 was steadily enlarged and altered as it appeared in editions of 1603, 1608, 1611, and 1616.[68]

It has a more modern tone than Abbot's book, and it contains information on areas in which England was showing an imperialistic interest; yet the major additions to the text related to Europe. The 1603 printing added eighty-one pages to the 1601 edition through the inclusion of 'another relation of the state of Spain,' and additions to the descriptions of central Europe and Italy. In 1608 six pages pertaining to America were added, but the remainder of the text is unchanged. In the 1611 edition, the work was divided into six books, with a section of 'observations' added at the beginning, and when the 1616 edition appeared, Book Six was further divided into descriptions of 'America' and 'America Magellannica' and was reorganized and somewhat augmented. Yet for all of these alterations, by 1616 the book still did not contain a word about Virginia, Newfoundland, or Norumbega in the section on America.

The reasons for the persistence and popularity of outmoded geographies, when Virginia or the East Indies might have been expected to find a ready audience, must lie in the conservatism of the great majority of Englishmen who bought books. We should not expect most of them to be aware that an empire was being born, and we should not look for sudden departures from established reading tastes which were based on the Church and the classics as pillars of authority and style. Dionysius Periegetes had described the world in verse in the first or second century, and Richard Zouch's *The dove: or passages of cosmography*, published in 1613, was admittedly patterned somewhat on the classical geographer's work. Although the author claims 'I ever admired then professed Poetry'[69] he managed to put together 147 stanzas of six lines in which he described Asia, Africa and Europe. An implied excuse for his omission of the New World may be contained in his statement, 'I have not touched all, because I would be short, and have used shortnes, as unwilling to sweat, and make a labor of my sport.'[70] The verses suggest that their author was less interested in geography than in constructing rhymes, but nevertheless, he retailed information which was not entirely common in England, such as this sample from his description of Asia.

> *Bord'ring on China Northward lies Cathay,*
> *Rul'd by her Emperour, the mighty Cham,*
> *To whom great Tartarie doth tribute pay:*
> *Great Tartary whose farre distended name,*
> *Twixt auncient India, and the Icy Sea,*
> *Possesseth all to Westerne Muscovy.*[71]

Ancient authority was not only accepted and copied, it was defended against the claims of recent authors. When a complete translation of the *Omnium gentium mores* of Johann Boemus was published in 1611, E. Aston, the translator, backed his outmoded authority against contemporary writers, contending, 'there is no reason that a multitude of Mandivels [*sic*] that wander abroad in this pamphletting age in the habits of sincere Historiographers... should... cancel and deface... opinions so authenticke and anciently received.'[72] Yet he recognized the need for a spirit of adventure in England which would enable her sons to learn more of the distant lands, and regretted the 'many rubbes, and impediments, to hinder and deterre us from travell, as it is, in a manner utterly neglected.'[73] This conflict between acceptance of authority and searching for new information is apparent in the additions Aston made to Boemus' work. He added 'The manners of divers nations, collected out of the workes of Nicholas Damascen,' which was a collection of curiosities mostly pertaining to the obscure customs of various peoples.[74] This was followed by a translation of Jean de Lery's description of Brazil,[75] and, finally, a portrayal of 'The faith, religion and manners of the Aethiopians' from Damião de Goes.[76] The travels of Englishmen in Aston's own time went unnoticed. Edward Grimstone revealed a similar reluctance to associate modern voyages with the geography of antiquity, for in his translation of Pierre d'Avity's massive world geography under the title of *The estates, empires and principallities of the world* he gave England more than twelve hundred pages of geography in which the countries of Europe, Asia, and Africa were described in great detail, but primarily those areas known to antiquity.[77] America was included as a part of Spain, and there was no mention of New France, indicating that this section of the French original was based on some early sixteenth century source. Grimstone added nothing which would relate this geography to England's current interests, provided no analysis or commentary on the text, but at great length presented information which he must have known was out of date.

In view of the persistence of religion as a major topic in public and private affairs, it is not surprising that one of the most popular geographies of the second decade of the seventeenth century was *Purchas his pilgrimage* which was published four times between 1613 and 1617.[78] Purchas was a theologian who in 1614 became chaplain to George Abbot, then Archbishop of Canterbury. Not unlike Abbot's work in that it relied heavily on classical and religious sources in its presentation of 'relations of the world and the religions observed in all ages', Purchas's volume listed some 750 authorities on which its information was based. He divided his book into 'Relations and Theologicall discoverie of Asia, Africa, and America', yet he did not rule out the possibility that his book might be of some value to geographers as well as theologians, stating 'The studious of Geographie may somewhat be helped... not that wee intend an exact Geographie... but yet limiting everie Countrie in his true situation and bounds; and performing happily more then some, which take upon them the title of Geographers.'[79]

Purchas wrote only of Asia, Africa, and America, expecting to describe Europe in a later volume. About two thirds of the book was given over to Asia's religions, from sources ancient, modern, and Biblical, but the description of America, which comprises Book Eight, is more general, containing a description of the Virginia colony, its history and a survey of the plants, animals, and geography of this part of the New World. Here again Purchas is eclectic, drawing upon Spanish, German, English and French sources. Having established himself with this book as Hakluyt's successor, Purchas found willing helpers in his expansion of the America section of his book. The second edition, published in 1614, contained material provided by Hakluyt himself, who by this time appears to have given up any thought of further publication, and others close to England's imperialistic enterprises came forth with information, among them Sir Walter Raleigh, Sir Dudley Digges, and Sir Thomas Smith. This additional information enabled Purchas to extend the America material from 149 pages in the first edition to 201 pages in the second, which was issued twice in 1614, the later issue bearing a new title page. By the time the third edition appeared in 1617, Hakluyt had died without turning over any additional material to Purchas, so this edition had few significant additions of geographical material.

It seems unlikely that the inclusion by Purchas of descriptions of English enterprise in Guiana, Virginia, and Hudson Bay had any notable influence on the popularity of the book, for other accounts of these regions, equally descriptive, and much less expensive had not fared so well. Nor was the wide acceptance of the *Pilgrimage* due to any reputation the author enjoyed, for he called his book 'my first looking and leaping out of the dungeon Obscuritie.'[80] Comparable in size to Hakluyt's *Principal navigations* of 1589, and considerably larger than the English edition of Linschoten's *Itinerario*, it overshadowed them in public acceptance, probably because of its religious theme.

While *Purchas his pilgrimage* was enjoying its popularity Robert

Brerewood, brought to the press a manuscript of Edward Brerewood, his lately deceased uncle, a writer of religious works, and published it as *Enquiries touching the diversity of languages, and religions through the chiefe parts of the world.*[81] The book is dedicated to George Abbot. The first portion of the text is more a history of the development of languages than a linguistic gazetteer, although the major linguistic groups are divided geographically. With Chapter Ten the author gets to a discussion of those parts of the world where Christianity prevails, and he shows good information on recent missionary advances in Japan, New Spain, and Virginia. His list of sources here as elsewhere shows a good knowledge of geographical literature, including the writings of Oviedo, Benzoni, Linschoten and others. In discussing the parts of the world inhabited by Mohammedans and idolaters he refers to Marco Polo, Leo Africanus, Nicolo de Conti and others as his sources. His discussion of the location of the Jews and Tatars, leads on to a discussion of the possible relationship between Tatars and American Indians. A concern for the comparative advantage enjoyed by Christians, Mohammedans, and idolaters results in conjecture as to the extent of Terra Australes Incognita. With religion as his major concern, therefore, the elder Brerewood under his nephew's editorship does provide a substantial amount of information on the world and its inhabitants.

By 1620 England had placed the cornerstones of empire in both the eastern and western hemispheres, and by that date there was little doubt about the survival of these overseas ventures. It is apparent, however, that this novel experience had not sufficiently excited the general reading public to create a demand for descriptions of New World colonies, or of the East Indies that would induce publishers to invest frequently in this type of publication. Nor had the first two decades of settled trade, colonization, and missionary activity abroad lured the scholars far from their traditional classical and Biblical orientation in their view of the world's geography. The popularity of their works compared to that of travel and geographical literature based upon recent exploration and colonization efforts testifies to the still medieval mentality of most Englishmen in the reign of James. But there was a difference in the appeal that accompanied descriptions of the New World from what had been used in the time of Elizabeth. No longer were the promoters writing with Eden's 'small and obscure members of the common wealth' in mind, nor were they hoping with Hakluyt that a book might stir the royal heart to an interest in overseas enterprise. Rather, the appeal was now being made to the people, fulfilling the beliefs of Christopher Carleill who had predicted that the time would come when the common people of England could be made to see the benefits that would come to them through emigration. He had seen this as the final stage of colonial planning. This realistic appraisal of the economic value of North America, built upon the emotional nationalism of the Elizabethan promoters and the religious enthusiasm of the Puritans joined to equip the English nation to go abroad as a colonizer. Books describing the intended areas of settlement were the essential vehicles for bringing these appeals to the public. Since colonists were not needed in the East Indies, no such popular appeal was necessary, and none was made. From William Caxton to John Smith, publishers, authors, translators, and promoters had offered the English public a literature of geography and travel, bringing into print knowledge of the ancient scholars, medieval interpreters of the world, and founders of modern empires. Aware that a knowledge of geography was essential to empire, the imperialists used it as a means of breaching England's medieval world view, yet these were a small minority of Englishmen, and their use of the press was counterbalanced by publishers of the more popular traditional types of geographical book, leaving England in 1620 toiling toward the future but weighted down with the authority of the past.

## NOTES TO CHAPTER XII

1 Llewelyn Powys, *Henry Hudson* (London: John Lane, the Bodley Head, Ltd., 1927) pp. 24–38, 45–49, 84–119.

2 Gerrit de Veer, *The true and perfect description of three voyages... by the ships of Holland and Zeland*, trans. William Phillip (London: T. Pauier, 1609), fol. A2 recto. A popular book on the Continent, de Veer's narrative was translated from the original Dutch edition of 1598 into French, Latin, and German the same year, and into Italian in 1599. The *Stationers' register* contains an entry of this work under a different title to John Wolfe, June 13, 1598, but apparently it did not come into print at that time. Of these early editions, the English is the only one not to contain the interesting engravings depicting the events of Barents' voyages.

3 *Ibid.*, fol. A2 recto.

4 Anthony Linton, *Newes of the complement of the art of navigation, and of the mightie empire of Cataia* (London: Felix Kingston, 1609), p. 3.

5 The relationship of Linton's science to the theories of his contemporaries is treated briefly in E. G. R. Taylor's *Late Tudor and early Stuart geography, 1583–1650* (London: Methuen & Co., Ltd., 1934), pp. 71–2.

6 Linton, p. 22.

7 *Ibid.*, p. 25.

8 Sir Dudley Digges, *Of the circumference of the earth: or, a treatise of the northeast passage* (London: W. W[hite] for J. Barnes, 1612), p. 2. Despite the title, this book is given entirely to the northwest passage.

9 *Ibid.*, p. 25.

10 For a history of the early mapping of Hudson Bay see Ernst C. Abbe, and Frank J. Gillis, 'Henry Hudson and the early exploration and mapping of Hudson Bay', *Merchants ad scholars*, ed. John Parker.

11 Williamson, *English colonies in Guiana*, pp. 42–47

12 Robert Harcourt, *A relation of a voyage to Guiana* (London: John Beale for W. Welby, 1613), fol. B4 verso.

13 *Ibid.*, fol. B3 verso.

14 *Ibid.*, fol. B4 verso.

15 *Ibid.*, p. 62.

16 Williamson, *English colonies in Guiana*, pp. 52–59, 64–65, 71.

17 Quinn, *Raleigh and the British Empire*, pp. 174–76.

18 V. T. Harlow, *Raleigh's last voyage* (London: The Argonaut Press, 1932) p. 24 notes that about half the total investment came from Raleigh, his estates, and his family.

19 *Newes of Sir Walter Rauleigh. With the true description of Guiana* (London: H. G[osson] and are to be sold by J. Wright, 1618), p. 36.

20 *Ibid.*, pp. 38–39, 41.

21 *Ibid.*, p. 38.

22 *A declaration of the demeanor and cariage of Sir Walter Raleigh, knight, as well in his voyage, as in, and sithence his returne* (London: Bonham Norton and John Bill, 1618).

23 John Smith, *A description of New England* (London: Humphrey Lownes for Robert Clerke, 1616), fol. ʒ4 recto.

24 *Ibid.*, p. 1.

25 *Ibid.*, p. 10.

26 *Ibid.*, p. 37.

27 John Smith, *New Englands trials. Declaring the successe of 26 ships employed thither within these sixe years* (London: William Jones, 1620), fol. C1 recto.

28 *Ibid.*, fol. C1 verso.

29 E. Keble Chatterton, *Captain John Smith* (London: John Lane, the Bodley Head, Ltd., 1937), p. 275.

30 John Ward Dean, *Capt. John Mason, the founder of New Hampshire* (Boston: The Prince Society, 1887), p. 11.

31 John Mason, *A briefe discourse of the New-found-land* (Edinburgh: Andro Hart, 1620), fol. [A2] recto.

32 *Ibid.*, fol. [A2] verso.

33 *Ibid.*, fol. [A4] verso.

34 Richard Whitbourne, *A discourse and discovery of New-found-land* (London: Felix Kyngston for William Barret, 1620), fol. A3 verso.

35 *Ibid.*, fol. B3 recto.

36 *Ibid.*, p. 23.

37 *Sir Thomas Smithes voiage and entertainment in Rushia* (London: Nathaniel Butter, 1605). STC identifies Smith as the author, but this seems improbable since it is written in the first person with frequent references to 'the ambassador.'

38 *A true historicall discourse of Muley Hamets rising to the three kingdomes of Moruecos, Fes and Sus* (London: Thomas Purfoot for Clement Knight, 1609).

39 William Lithgow, *A most delectable, and true discourse, of an admired and painefull peregrination from Scotland, to the most famous kingdomes in Europe, Asia and Affricke* (London: Nicholas Okes, to be sold by Thomas Archer, 1614).

40 This edition, printed in black letter, was also printed by Okes for Acher.

⁴¹ Quoted in an introductory section 'The character of the famous Odcombian' in Coryate's *The Odcombian banquet* (London: Thomas Thorp, 1611), fol. B1 verso.

⁴² Thomas Coryate, *Thomas Coriate traveller for the English wits: Greeting from the court of the Great Mogul* (London: W. Jaggard and Henry Featherstone, 1616). pp. 4, 19.

⁴³ Thomas Coryate, *Mr. Thomas Coriat to his friends in England sendeth greeting* (London: J. B[eale], 1618), fol. A2 recto.

⁴⁴ *Ibid.*, fol. B1 verso–B2 recto.

⁴⁵ Johannes Leo Africanus, *A geographicall history of Africa* (London: I. L. for A. H., and part of the impression made over to be vented for the benefit of the children of John Minsheu deceased, [ca. 1617]).

⁴⁶ *A briefe relation of the persecution lately made against the Catholike Christians in the kingdome of Japonia*, trans. W. W[right] ([St. Omer]: 1619). William Wright was a member of the Jesuit Society. The title page notes that this was first printed in Spanish in Mexico, 1616.

⁴⁷ Pedro Fernandes de Quiros, *Terra Australis Incognita, or a new southerne discoverie, containing a fifth part of the world* (London: For John Hodgetts, 1617). This edition was first published in an edition of two leaves, folio, Seville, 1610. Another edition was published that year in Pamplona. A German edition appeared in Augsburg, 1611; a Dutch and two Latin editions in Amsterdam, 1612; and two French editions in Paris, 1617.

⁴⁸ Willem Schouten, *The relation of a wonderful voiage... shewing how south from the Straights of Magelan... he found and discovered a newe passage through the great South Sea*, trans. William Phillip (London: T. D[awson] for Nathanaell Newberry, 1619), second preliminary leaf. Three Dutch, two French and one German edition of this book appeared in the Netherlands in 1618. A Paris edition was also published in 1618. At least six editions were published on the Continent in 1619.

⁴⁹ Sir Thomas Palmer, *An essay of the meanes how to make our travailes, into forraine countries the more profitable and honourable* (London: H. Lownes for M. Lownes, 1606), p. 4.

⁵⁰ Joseph Hall, *Quo Vadis? A just censure of travell as it is commonly undertaken by the gentlemen of our nation* (London: Edward Griffin for Nathaniel Butter, 1617), p. 4.

⁵¹ *Ibid.*, fol. A4 recto.

⁵² Sir John Mandeville, *The voyages and travailes...* (London: Thomas Snodham, 1612) and (London: T. S[nodham], 1618). The widow of Thomas East, publisher of the editions of 1568 and 1582, assigned her copyrights to Snodham on June 17, 1609. These editions closely resemble the 1582 printing by East. See J. W. Bennett, *Mandeville*, pp. 349–50.

⁵³ William Davies, *A true relation of the travailes and most miserable captivitie of William Davies.* (London: For Nicholas Bourne, 1614).

⁵⁴ Thomas Blundeville, *M. Blundeville his exercises, containing eight treatises* (London: John Windet, 1606); the 1613 edition had the same title but was published by William Stansby.

⁵⁵ John Davis, *The seaman's secrets* (London: Thomas Dawson, 1607).

⁵⁶ Robert Hues, *Tractatus de globis, coelesti et terrestri ac eorum usu* (London: Officina Nortoniana, 1611).

⁵⁷ Robert Tanner, *A brief treatise on the use of the globe celestiall and terrestriall* (London: Felix Kyngston for Thomas Man, 1616). The 1620 edition was published by Richard Field for Thomas Man.

⁵⁸ Abraham Ortelius, *Abraham Ortelius his epitome of the theater of the worlde* (London: For Jeames Shawe, 1603). The 1610 edition was published by John Norton. The earliest edition of this atlas was the *Epitome du theatre du monde*, containing 94 maps, published by Christophe Plantin for Philippe Gallé in Antwerp, 1588. A Latin edition by Plantin for Gallé followed in 1589. The number of maps in the Latin

edition of 1601 had been increased to 123, and a French edition of the following year had a like number. An Italian edition was published in Brescia, 1598.

59 Robert Stafforde, *A geographicall and anthologicall description of all the empires and kingdomes... of this terrestriall globe* (London: T. C. for Simon Waterson, 1607), fol. A3 recto.

60 *Ibid.*, p. 54.

61 One of the 1618 editions was printed by Nicholas Okes for John Parker, the other he printed for Simon Waterson.

62 José de Acosta, *The naturall and morall historie of the East and West Indies* trans. E. Grimstone (London: Valentine Sims for Edward Blount and William Aspley, 1604).

63 The first two parts of Acosta's book, in Latin, were published in Salamanca in 1589. A complete edition appeared in Seville in 1590. Spanish editions were published in Barcelona, 1591; Madrid, 1608 and 1610. An Italian translation appeared in Venice in 1596, the Dutch edition was published at Enckhuysen in 1598, and French editions were published in Paris in 1597 and 1600. De Bry issued a German edition in 1601, and Latin editions in 1602 and 1603.

64 Abraham Ortelius, *The theatre of the whole world* (London: John Norton, 1606). Norton was at that time printer to the king. He does not identify the translator. The first edition of this atlas was published by C. Diesth in Antwerp, 1570.

65 R. V. Tooley, *Maps and map-makers* (London: B. T. Batsford Ltd., 1952), p. 52.

66 George Abbot, *A briefe description of the whole worlde* (London: For J. Browne, 1605). The 1608 edition contains no notable additions to that of 1605. The 1617 edition extends the collation from A–V4 to A–Y4, and like the previous editions was published by John Browne. In 1620 John Marriott issued an edition identical to that of 1617.

67 Abbot, 1605 ed., fol. S3 verso.

68 All of these editions were published by John Jaggard. The 1603 edition was titled *An historicall description of the most famous kingdomes and common-weales in the worlde*; the later editions bore the title *Relations, of the most famous kingdoms and commonweales thorough the world*.

69 Richard Zouch, *The dove: or passages of cosmography* (London: For George Norton, 1613), fol. E4 recto.

70 *Ibid.*, fol. E7 verso.

71 *Ibid.*, fol. B3 verso.

72 Johann Boemus, *The manners, lawes and customs of all nations*, trans. E. Aston (London: G. Eld, 1611), fol. ſ 3 verso. The original edition was published in Augsburg in 1520, and it was from subsequent editions of this work that William Prat and William Waterman translated parts of this works in 1554 and 1555, respectively.

73 Boemus, fol. ſ3 recto.

74 Nicolaus Damascenus, *Universal historia seu moribus gentium* ([Heidelberg]: Petrum Santandreanum, 1593).

75 Jean de Lery, *Histoire d'un voyage fait en la terre du Bresil* (La Rochelle: A. Chuppin, 1578).

76 Damião de Goes, *Fides, religio, moresque Aethiopum...* (Louvain: R. Rescii, 1540).

77 Pierre d'Avity, *The estates, empires and principallities of the world*, trans. E. Grimstone (London: Adam Islip for Mathewe Lownes and John Bill, 1615). The original edition was published by Charles Boscard in St. Omer, 1614.

78 Samuel Purchas, *Purchas his pilgrimage. Or relations of the world and the religions observed in all ages* (London: William Stansby for Henry Fetherstone, 1613). A new edition appeared in 1614 and went through two issues, a third edition was published in 1617. All were printed by William Stansby for Henry Fetherstone.

79 *Ibid.*, fol. 54 verso.
80 *Ibid.*, fol. 52 recto.
81 Edward Brerewood, *Enquiries touching the diversity of languages, and religions through the chiefe parts of the world* (London: For John Bill, 1614).

# BIBLIOGRAPHY

The following list contains items mentioned in the foregoing text and notes, arranged chronologically. Collations are given by signatures, since this seems to be the most useful type of collation for books containing numerous errors in pagination. In instances where more detailed collations or collations differently expressed are available in the more easily attainable bibliographic sources, these bibliographies are cited. They are as follows: E. Gordon Duff, *Fifteenth century English books* (Oxford, 1917); George Watson Cole, *A catalogue of books relating to the discovery and early history of North and South America forming a part of the library of E. D. Church* (New York 1907); and *Catalogue of the John Carter Brown Library* (Providence, 1919). Numbers from A. W. Pollard and G. R. Redgrave, *A short-title catalogue of books printed in England, Scotland, & Ireland... 1475–1640* are supplied to facilitate the location of exemplars of books cited. When books are not listed in the *Short-title catalogue*, locations are supplied.

1481 Gautier of Metz. *Mirrour of the world.* [Westminster, William Caxton, 1481]. a–m$^8$, n$^4$; illustrations in the text. Duff, 401.
STC 24762.

1482 Higden, Ranulf. *Polichronicon.* [Westminster] William Caxton [1482]. a–b$^8$, c$^4$, 1–28$^8$, []$^2$, 29–48$^8$, 49$^4$, 50$^8$, 52–55$^8$. Duff, 172.
STC 13439.

1490 Gautier of Metz. *Mirrour of the world.* [Westminster] William Caxton [1490]. a–l$^8$; illustrations in the text. Duff, 402.
STC 24763.

1495 Bartholomaeus Anglicus. *De proprietatibus rerum.* [Westminster: Wynkyn de Worde, 1495].
A–B$^6$, C$^2$, b$^6$, c–e$^8$, l$^7$, m$^7$, n–q$^8$, r$^9$, s–z$^8$, &$^8$, ʒ$^8$, A–G$^8$, H$^6$, I–S$^8$, T$^7$, V$^8$, X–Z$^6$, aa–cc$^8$, dd$^7$, ee–gg$^6$, hh–mm$^8$, nn$^4$, oo$^6$. Duff, 40.
STC 1536.

1495 Higden, Ranulf. *Policronicon.* Westminster: Wynkyn de Worde, 1495. aa$^8$, bb–gg$^6$, hh$^5$, a–y$^8$, z$^6$, A–S$^8$, T$^6$, V$^8$, X$^8$. Duff, 173.
STC 13439.

1496 Mandeville, Sir John. [*Travels*]. [London: Richard Pynson, 1496]. a–g$^8$, h$^6$, i$^6$, k$^4$. Duff, 285.
STC 17246

1498 *Informacon for pylgrymes unto the Holy Londe.* [Westiminster] Wynkyn de Worde [1498?].
a–e$^6$. Duff, 225.
STC 14081.

1499 Mandeville, Sir John. *Here begynneth a lytell treatyse or booke named Johan Maundevyll knight... & speketh of the wayes of the holy londe towarde Jherusalem & of marveyles of Ynde & of other dyverse countries.*
A–S$^6$; illustrations in the text. Duff 286.
STC 17247.

1501  Mandeville, Sir John. [*Travels*]. [London? 1501?].
Only two leaves are known to exist from this edition.
STC 17248.

1503  Arnold, Richard. [*Chronicle of London*]. [Antwerp: Adrian van Berghen, 1503?].
A⁴, A⁸, B⁴, C–E⁸, F–Q⁶, R⁸, S–T⁶, V⁵.
STC 782.

1503  Mandeville, Sir John. [*Travels*]. [Westminster: Wynkyn de Worde, 1503].
The only copy known is imperfect, containing thirty leaves; illustrations in the text.
STC 14294.

1509  Brant, Sebastian. *This present book named the shyp of folys of the world...* London:
Richard Pynson, 1509.
+⁴, a⁸, b–p⁶, q⁷, r–z⁶, &⁶, A–Q⁶, R⁵, S–X⁶, Y⁵; illustrations in the text.
STC 3545.

1509  Brant, Sebastian. *The shyppe of fooles.* London: Wynkyn de Worde, 1509.
A⁸, A–C⁴, D⁸, E⁴, F⁸, G⁴, H⁸, I⁴, K⁸, L⁴, M⁸, N⁴, O⁸, P⁴, Q⁸, R⁴, S⁸, T⁴, U⁸,
Aa⁴, Bb⁸, Cc⁴, Dd⁸, Ee⁴, Ff⁸, Gg⁷. Illustrations in the text.
STC 3547.

1510  *Of the newe landes and of ye people founde by the messengers of the Kynge of Portyngale
named Emanuel.* [Antwerp: Jan van Doesborch, ca. 1510–15].
A⁶, B⁴, C⁴, D⁶, E⁴.
STC 7677.

1511  *This is the begynnynge and contynuance of the pylgrymage of Sir Richarde Guylforde
knyght, and controuler unto our late soveraygne lorde Kynge Henry VII.* London: Richard
Pynson, 1511.
A–K⁶.
STC 12549.

1515  *The way to the Holy Lande.* London: Wynkyn de Worde, 1515.
A⁸, B⁴, C⁸.
STC 14082.

1517  Brant, Sebastian. *The shyppe of fooles.* London: Wynkyn de Worde, 1517.
a⁸, A⁴, B⁸, C⁴, D⁸, E⁴, F⁸, G⁴, H⁸, I⁴, K⁸, L⁴, M⁸, N⁴, O⁸, P⁴, Q⁸, R⁴, S⁸, T⁴,
U⁸, Aa⁴, Bb⁸, Cc⁴, Dd⁸, Ee⁴, FF⁸, GG⁶; illustrations in the text.
STC 3547a.

1517  Rastell, John. *A new interlude and a mery of the nature of the iiii elements.* [London:
John Rastell, ca. 1517].
A–C⁸, E⁸, (D signature wanting in only copy extant).
STC 20722.

1520  Hethum, Prince of Korghos. *Here begynneth a lytell cronycle...* London: Richard
Pynson, [1520?].
A–E⁶, F⁴, G³, H⁶, I³. Woodcut on title page.
STC 13256.

1521  Arnold, Richard. *In this boke is conteined ye names of the baylyfs custose mayrs and
sherefs of ye cyte of London.* [Southwark, Peter Treveris, 1521].
A⁴, B⁸, C⁴, B⁴, C–E⁸, F–Q⁶, R⁸, S–T⁶, V⁵.
STC 783.

1522  Langton, Robert. *The pylgrimage of M. Robert Langton.* London: Robert Copland, 1522.
[A]², B⁴, C⁴.
STC 15206.

1524 *The way to the Holy Lande.* London: Wynkyn de Worde, 1524.
A⁸, B⁴, C⁸.
STC 14083.

1527 Gautier of Metz. *The myrrour: & dyscrypcyon of the worlde.* London: Laurence Andrewe [1527–29].
b–f⁴, +⁴, g–y⁴. Illustrations in the text.
STC 24764.

1527 Higden, Ranulf. *Polycronycon.* Southwark: Peter Treveris, 1527.
aa⁸, bb–gg⁶, hh⁵, a–y⁸, z⁶, A–S⁸, T⁶, V⁸, X⁸.
STC 13440.

1532 Ptolemy, Claudius. *Here begynneth the compost of Ptholomeus.* London: Robert Wyer, [1532?].
a–r⁴.
STC 20480.

1533 Goes, Damião de. *The legacye or embassate of the great emperour of Inde Prester John unto Emanuell Kynge of Portyngale in the yere of our Lorde MVCXIII.* London: William Rastell, 1533.
A–E⁴, E⁴, F⁴, G².
STC 11966.

1535 Bartholomaeus Anglicus. *De proprietatibus rerum.* Thomas Berthelet, 1535.
ꝝ⁸, A–Z⁶, Aa–Zz⁶, a–s⁶, t⁴.
STC 1537.

1535 *Mappa mundi, otherwise called the compasse and cyrcuet of the worlde.* London: Robert Wyer [1535].
A–C⁴.
STC 17297.

1535 Ptolemy, Claudius. *The compost of Ptholomeus.* London: Robert Wyer, [*ca.* 1535].
A–S⁴.
STC 20480a.

1540 Ptolemy, Claudius. *The compost of Ptholomeus.* London: Robert Wyer, [*ca.* 1540].
A–S⁴.
STC 20481.

1551 More, Sir Thomas. *A fruteful and pleasaunt worke of the beste state of a publyque weale, and of the newe yle called Utopia.* London: Abraham Vele, 1551.
+⁸, A⁴, B–R⁸, S⁴. JCB I, 165.
STC 18094.

1552 Ascham, Anthony. *A lytel treatyse of astronomy.* London: William Powell, 1552˙
A–C⁸, D⁴.
STC 857a.

1553 Münster, Sebastian. *A treatyse of the newe India, with other new founde landes and ilandes, as well eastward as westwarde.* London: Edward Sutton, 1553.
aa⁸, A–L⁸, M⁶. JCB I, 177.
STC 18244.

1554 Boemus, Johann. *The discription of the countrey of Aphrique.* London: William Powell, 1554.
A–K⁸, L⁷.
STC 191.

1555 Boemus, Johann. *The fardle of facions.* London: John Kingstone and Henry
Sutton, 1555.
*3, A–Y8, Z3.
STC 3197.

1555 Eden, Richard. *The decades of the Newe Worlde or West India.* London: William
Powell, 1555.
[ ]4, b4, a–d4, A–Z4, Aa–Zz4, AAa–ZZz4, AAAa–ZZZz4, AAAAa6; two maps.
Church, 102.
STC 645–648.

1556 More, Sir Thomas. *A fruteful pleasaunt, & wittie worke, of the beste state of a
publique weale, and of the newe yle, called Utopia.* London: Abraham Velle, [1556].
A–S8. JCB I, 193.
STC 18095.

1556 Record, Robert. *The castle of knowledge.* London: Reginalde Wolfe, 1556.
a8, A–Z6, &6. Illustrations in the text.
STC 20796.

1557 Record, Robert. *The whetstone of witte.* London: John Kyngstone, 1557.
a–b4, A–C4, F–Q4, S–Z4, Aa–Rr4. Diagrams and tables in the text.
STC 20820.

1559 Cuningham, William. *The cosmographical glasse, conteinyng the pleasant principles
of cosmographie, geographie, hydrographie, or navigation.* London: John Day, 1559.
A–S6, T3. Illustrations in the text; two folding views. JCB I, 204.
STC 6119.

1561 Cortés, Martín. *The arte of navigation.* London: Richard Jugge, 1561.
¶4, ¶¶4, A–K8, L4, M2. Illustrations in the text. JCB I, 211.
STC 5798.

1563 Ribaut, Jean. *The whole and true discoverye of Terra Florida.* London: Rouland
Hall for Thomas Hacket, 1563.
[ ]3, A2–8, B8, C7.
STC 20970.

1563 Seall, Robert. *A commendation of the adventerus viage of the wurthy capatin M. Thomas
Stutely... towards the land called Terra Florida.* London: John Alde [1563].
broadside.
STC 22139.

1566 Le Challeux, Nicolas. *A true and perfect description, of the last voyage or navigation,
attempted by Capitaine John Rybaut,... into Terra Florida.* London: Henry Denham
for Thomas Hacket [1566].
A4, B–D8.
STC 15347.

1566 Plinius Secundus, Caius. *A summarie of the antiquities, and wonders of the worlde.*
London: Henry Denham for Thomas Hacket [1566].
A–H8.
STC 20031.

1568 Mandeville, Sir John. *The voiage and travayle, of Syr John Maundevile knight, which
treateth of the way toward Hierusalem, and of marvayles of Inde with other ilands and
countryes.* London: Thomas East, 1568.
A4, B–E8, F7, G–M8, N2. Illustrations in the text.
STC 17250.

1568 Thevet, André. *The new found worlde, or Antarctike.* London: Henrie Bynneman for Thomas Hacket, 1568.
\*4, A4, B–S8, T4. JCB I, 238; Church 113.
STC 23950.

1569 Hawkins, Sir John. *A true declaration of the troublesome voyadge... to the parties of Guynea and the West Indies.* London: Thomas Purfoote for Lucas Harrison, 1569.
A8, B7. Church 113A.
STC 12961.

1572 Cortés, Martín. *The arte of navigation.* London: Richard Jugge, 1572.
℃–℃℃4, A–K8, L4, M2. Illustrations in the text; one folding map.
STC 5799.

1572 Dionysius Periegetes. *The surveye of the world, or situation of the earth, so muche as is inhabited.* London: Henrie Bynneman, 1572.
\*4, A–E8, F3.
STC 6901.

1572 Münster, Sebastian. *A briefe collection and compendious extract of straunge and memorable thinges gathered oute of the Cosmographye of Sebastian Munster.* London: Thomas Marshe, 1572.
\*3, B–N8, O3 (imperfect). Only copy known in British Museum.
STC 18242.

1574 Bourne, William. *A regiment for the sea.* London: Thomas Hacket [1574].
A–C4, A–Q4; diagrams and tables in the text.
STC 3422.

1574 Münster, Sebastian. *A briefe collection and compendious extract of straunge and memorable thinges, gathered out of the Cosmographye of Sebastian Munster.* London: Thomas Marshe, 1574.
A–N8.
STC 18243.

1576 Gilbert, Sir Humphrey. *A discourse of a discoverie for a new passage to Cataia.* London: Henry Middleton for Richarde Jhones, 1576.
¶–¶¶¶4, ¶¶¶¶2, B–H4, I2; one folding map. Church, 117; JCB I, 261.
STC 11881.

1577 Dee, John. *General and rare memorials pertayning to the perfect arte of navigation.* London: John Day, 1577.
△4, \*4, \*\*4, A–K4, [L2]; woodcut on title page.
STC 6459.

1577 Eden, Richard. *The history of travayle in the West and East Indies.* London: Richard Jugge, 1577.
(.)4, ⁊6, A–B4, C–Z8, Aa–Zz8, Aaa–Ooo8. Church, 119; JCB I, 266.
STC 649.

1577 Monardes, Nicolás. *The three bookes written in the Spanish tongue.* London: Willyam Norton, 1577.
\*4, A–Z4, Aa–Dd4, Ee2.
STC 18005.

1577 Monardes, Nicolás. *Joyfull newes out of the newe founde worlde.* London: Willyam Norton, 1577.
\*4, A–Z4, Aa–Dd4, Ee2. JCB I, 266.
STC 18005a.

1577 Settle, Dionyse. *A true reporte of the laste voyage into the west and northwest regions...
by Capteine Frobisher.* London: Henrie Middleton, 1577.
First edition: A⁴, B–C⁸, D⁴. Church, 119A; JCB I, 267.
Second edition: A–C⁸.
STC 22265, 22266.

1577 *The strange and marveilous newes lately come from the great kingdome of Chyna.* London: Thomas Gardyner and Thomas Dawson, [1577].
A²⁻⁷.
STC 5141.

1578 Best, George. *A true discourse of the late voyages of discoverie, for the finding of a
passage to Cathaya, by the northweast.* London: Henry Bynneman, 1578.
a–h⁴, i², A–N⁴, O²; two folding maps. Church, 122; JCB I, 268.
STC 1972.

1578 Bourne, William. *A booke called the treasure for travelers.* London: For Thomas Woodcocke, 1578.
*-**⁴, ***³, A–G⁴, H¹, H⁵, Aa–Ff⁴, Gg², Aaa–Fff⁴, Aaaa–Ffff⁴, Bbbbb-Eeeee⁴; diagrams and tables in the text.
STC 3432.

1578 Churchyard, Thomas. *A discourse of the Queenes Majesties entertainement in Suffolk
and Norffolk... whereunto is adjoyned a commendation of Sir Humphrey Gilberts ventrous
journey.* London: Henry Bynneman, [1578].
A–L⁴ (K⁴ blank). Church 120B.
STC 5226.

1578 Churchyard, Thomas. *A prayse and reporte of Maister Martyne Forboishers voyage
to Meta Incognita.* London: Andrew Maunsell, [1578].
A–C⁸. Church, 120A.
STC 5251.

1578 Ellis, Thomas. *A true report of the third and last voyage into Meta Incognita.* London: Thomas Dawson, 1578.
A–B⁸, C⁴; one folding leaf of illustrations. Church, 120C.
STC 7607.

1578 Fernández de Enciso, Martín. *A briefe description of the portes, creekes, bayes, and
havens, of the Weast India.* London: Henry Bynneman, 1578.
A–D⁴, E¹.
STC 10823.

1578 Guevara, Antonio de. *A booke of the invention of the art of navigation.* London: Ralph Newberrie, 1578.
[]⁶, B–F⁴, G³.
STC 12425.

1578 López de Gómara, Francisco. *The pleasant historie of the conquest of Weast India,
now called New Spayne.* London: Henry Bynneman, 1578.
a⁴, b², B–Z⁴, Aa–Zz⁴, Aaa–Fff⁴. Church, 123; JCB I, 271.
STC 16807.

1579 Cortés, Martín. *The arte of navigation.* London: Widow of Richard Jugge, 1579.

¶⁸, A–K⁸, L⁴; diagrams and illustrations in the text; one folding map.
STC 5800.

1579 Escalante, Bernardino de. *A discourse of the navigation which the Portugales doe make to the realmes and provinces of the east partes of the worlde.* London: Thomas Dawson, 1579.
A–M⁴.
STC 10529.

1579 Polo, Marco. *The most noble and famous travels of Marcus Paulus.* London: Ralph Newbery, 1579.
*–***⁴, *****², A–X⁴.
STC 20092.

1580 Bourne, William. *A regiment for the sea.* London: T. East for John Wight, 1580.
¶A–¶C⁴, A–V⁴, []¹; diagrams and illustrations in the text.
STC 3425.

1580 Cartier, Jacques. *A shorte and briefe narration of the two navigations and discoveries to the northweast partes called Newe Fraunce.* London: Henry Bynneman, 1580.
A–B², C–M⁴. Church, 125; JCB I, 278.
STC 4699.

1580 Monardes, Nicolás. *Joyful newes out of the newe founde worlde.* London: William Norton, 1580.
*⁴, A–Z⁴, Aa–Rr⁴, Ss⁵, Xx⁵, Tt⁴, Xx¹, Yy⁴, Zz². JCB I, 281.
STC 18006.

1580 Támara, Francisco de. *A discoverie of the countries of Tartaria, Scithia, & Cataya, by the north-east.* London: Thomas Dawson, 1580.
¶⁴ (first leaf blank), A–E⁸.
STC 11255.

1581 Zárate, Augustín de. *The discoverie and conquest of the provinces of Peru.* London: Richard Jhones, 1581.
A⁴, ¶⁴, B–Z⁴, Aa⁴. JCB I, 287.
STC 26123.

1582 Hakluyt, Richard. *Divers voyages touching the discoverie of America, and the ilands adjacent unto the same.* London: For Thomas Woodcocke, 1582.
[]², ¶⁴, A–D⁴, A–G⁴, H², I–K⁴; two folding maps. Church, 128; JCB I, 292.
STC 12624.

1582 Lopes de Castanheda, Fernão. *The first booke of the historie of the discoverie and conquest of the East Indias, enterprised by the Portingales.* London: Thomas East, 1582.
A², A–Z⁴, Aa-Tt⁴.
STC 16806.

1582 Parmenius, Stephanus. *De navigatione… Humfredi Gilberti, ad deducendam in novum orbem coloniam susceptâ, carmen.* London: Thomam Purfutium, 1582.
A², B⁴, C². Church, 127.
STC 19308.

1583 Carleill, Christopher. *A discourse upon the entended voyage to the hethermoste partes of America.* n.p.n.d. [ca. 1583].
A–B⁴. JCB I, 283.
Not in STC. John Carter Brown Library.

1583 Carleill, Christopher. *A breef and sommarie discourse upon the entended voyage to the hethermoste partes of America.*
n.p. n.d. [ca. 1583].
A–B4.
Not in STC. Westminster Abbey Library.

1583 Las Casas, Bartolomé de. *The Spanish colonie, or briefe chronicle of the acts and gestes of the Spaniardes in the West Indies*. London: Thomas Dawson for William Brome, 1583.
¶–¶¶⁴, A–Q⁴, R². Church, 130; JCB I, 295.
STC 4739.

1583 Mandeville, Sir John. *The voyages and travailes of Sir John Mandevile knight*. London: Thomas Este [1583?].
A–T⁴, U³; Illustrations in the text.
STC 17251.

1583 [Nicholas, Thomas]. *A pleasant description of the Fortunate Ilandes called the Ilands of Canaria, with their straunge fruits and commodities*. London: Thomas East, 1583.
A², B–C⁴, D².
STC 4557.

1583 Peckham, Sir George. *A true reporte, of the late discoveries, and possession, taken in the right of the Crowne of Englande, of the New-found Landes*. London: J₍ohn₎ C₍harlewood₎ for John Hinde, 1583.
[]⁴, §⁵, B–G⁴, H¹, I³.
STC 19523.

1584 Cortes, Martin. *The arte of navigation*. London: Johan Jugge, wydowe, 1584.
¶⁸, A–K⁸, L⁴; illustrations in the text; one folding map.
STC 5801.

1585 Mela, Pomponius. *The worke of Pomponius Mela the cosmographer, concerning the situation of the world*. London: For Thomas Hacket, 1585.
[]³, C–O⁴.
STC 17785.

1585 Nicolay, Nicholas de. *The navigations, peregrinations and voyages made into Turkie*. London: Thomas Dawson, 1585.
¶⁴, A⁴, B–X⁸, Y²; sixty full-page illustrations.
STC 18574.

1585 Plinius Secundus, Caius. *The secrets and wonders of the world*. London: For Thomas Hacket, 1585.
[]², B–H⁴, I¹.
STC 20032.

1585 Roberts, Henry. *A most friendly farewell... to the right worshipful Sir Frauncis Drake*. London: Walter Mantell and Thomas Lawe [1585].
A–B⁴.
STC 21084.

1587 Bourne, William. *A regiment for the sea*. London: Thomas East for John Wight, 1587.
A–C⁴, A–U⁴; diagrams and illustrations in the text.
STC 3426.

1587 Espejo, Antonio de. *New Mexico. Otherwise the voyage of Anthony of Espejo*. London: Thomas Cadman, 1587.
A–B⁸.
Not in STC. Henry E. Huntington Library.

1587 Greepe, Thomas. *The true and perfecte newes of the woorthy and valiaunt exploytes, performed and doone by... Syr Frauncis Drake*. London: John Charlewood for Thomas Hackett, 1587.
A–C⁴.
STC 12343.

1587  Laudonnière, René Goulaine de. *A notable historie containing foure voyages made by certayne French captaynes unto Florida.* London: Thomas Dawson, 1587. []⁴, A–R⁴. Church, 132. STC 15316.

1587  Plinius Secundus, Caius. *The secrets and wonders of the worlde.* London: Thomas Hacket, 1587. A², B–H⁴, I¹. STC 20033.

1587  Saunders, Thomas. *A true discription and breefe discourse, of a most lamentable voiage, made latelie to Tripolie in Barbarie.* London: Richard Jones for Edward White, 1587. A–C⁴. STC 21778.

1587  Solinus, Caius Julius. *The excellent and pleasant worke of Julius Solinus Polyhistor.* London: J. Charlewood for Thomas Hacket, 1587. A–Y⁴, Aa–Ff⁴, Gg². STC 22896.

1587  Tanner, Robert. *A mirror for mathematiques.* London: J. C[harlewood] to be sold by Richard Watkins, 1587. A–O⁴; diagrams and illustrations in the text. STC 23674.

1588  Federici, Cesare. *The voyage and travaile: of M. Caesar Frederick, merchant of Venice, into the East India, the Indies, and beyond the Indies.* London: Richard Jones and Edward White, 1588. A–L⁴. STC 10746.

1588  González de Mendoza, Juan. *The historie of the great and mightie kingdome of China.* London: J. Wolfe for Edward White, 1588. ¶⁴, A–Z⁸, Aa–Bb⁸, Cc⁶. Church, 134. STC 12003.

1588  Hariot, Thomas. *A briefe and true report of the new found land of Virginia.* London: [Robert Robinson] 1588. A–F⁴. Church, 135. STC 12785.

1589  Blundeville, Thomas. *A briefe description of universal mappes and cardes, and of their use.* London: Roger Ward for Thomas Cadman, 1589. A–E⁴, F²; one diagram. Church, 137. STC 3145.

1589  Bigges, Walter. *A summarie and true discourse of Sir Frances Drakes West Indian voyage.* London: Richard Field, 1589. []², B–G⁴, H²; four folding maps. Church, 136. STC 3056 [two issues].

1589  Bigges, Walter. *A summarie and true discourse of Sir Frances Drakes West Indian voyage.* London: Roger Ward, 1589. A³, B–E⁴, F³. The four folding maps apparently were not included. STC 3057.

1589 Boazio, Baptisto. *The famouse West Indian voyadge made by the English fleete of 23 shippes and barkes... from Plimmouth in the moneth of September 1585 and ended at Portesmouth in Julie 1586.* n.p., ca. 1589.
Map, 417 × 536 mm.
Not in STC. James Ford Bell Collection.

1589 Cortes, Martin. *The arte of navigation.* London: [Abell Jeffes] for Richard Watkins, 1589.
¶8, A–K8, L4; illustrations in the text; one folding map. JCB I, 316.
STC 5802.

1589 Hakluyt, Richard. *The principall navigations, voiages and discoveries of the English nation.* London: George Bishop and Ralph Newberie, 1589.
*8, A–T6, V–X4, Aa–Vv6, Xx4, Yy6, Aaa–Mmm6, []6, Nnn–Yyy6, Aaaa–Eeee6, F3; one folding map. Church, 139; JCB I, 317.
STC 12625.

1589 Meierus, Albertus. *Certaine briefe, and speciall instructions for gentlemen, merchants, souldiers, marriners, etc. employed in services abrode.* London: John Wolfe, 1589.
A–C4, D3.
STC 17784.

1590 Mela, Pomponius. *The rare and singuler worke of... wherunto is added that... of Julius Solinus.* London: For Thomas Hacket, 1590.
A–R4, S2; A–Y4, Aa–Ff4, Gg2.
STC 17786.

1590 Webbe, Edward. *The rare and most wonderful things which Edward Webbe... hath seene and passed in his troublesome travailes in the cities of Jerusalem, Damasko, Bethlehem and Galely...* London: Ralph Blower for Thomas Pavier, [1590].
A–B4, C2.
STC 25154.

1590 Webbe, Edward. *The rare and most wonderfull things which Edward Webbe... hath seene and passed in his troublesome travailes in the cities of Jerusalem, Damasko, Bethlem and Galely...* London: A. I. for William Barley [1590].
A–D4; illustrations in the text.
STC 25153

1590 Webbe, Edward. *The rare and most wonderfull things which Edw. Webbe... hath seene and passed in his troublesome travailes, in the cities of Jerusalem, Damasko, Bethlehem and Galely...* London: For William Wright, 1590.
A–C4, D3; illustrations in the text.
STC 2152.

1591 Fletcher, Giles. *Of the Russe common wealth.* London: T. D. for Thomas Charde, 1591.
A2-4, B–P8, Q4.
STC 11056.

1591 Hortop, Job. *The rare travailes of Job Hortop, an Englishman, who was not heard of in three and twentie yeeres space.* London: William Wright, 1591.
A–C4.
Not in STC. British Museum.

1591 Hortop, Job. *The travailes of an Englishman.* London: [T. Scarlet] for William Wright, 1591.
A–D4.
STC 13828.

1592 Bourne, William. *A regiment for the sea.* London: T[homas] Est for Thomas Wight, [1592].
A², ¶B–¶C⁴, A–V⁴, X², A–E⁴, F²; tables and diagrams in the text.
STC 3427.

1592 Lipsius, Justus. *A direction for travailers… enlarged for the behoofe of the… Earle of Bedford.* London: R. B[lower] for Cuthbert Burbie, 1592.
A–C⁴, D².
STC 15696.

1592 Roberts, Henry. *Our Ladys retorne to England.* London: A. I. for William Barley, 1592.
*⁴.
Not in STC. Henry E. Huntington Library.

1594 Blundeville, Thomas. *M. Blundeville his exercises, containing sixe treatises.* London: John Windet, 1594.
A–Z⁸, Aa–Xx⁸, Yy⁶; five folding tables and diagrams; charts, tables, diagrams in the text.
STC 3146.

1594 Hues, Robert. *Tractatus de globis et eorum usu.* London: Thomas Dawson, 1594.
¶⁴, ¶¶⁴, A–Y⁴; one folding table.
STC 13906.

1594 Roberts, Henry. *Newes from the Levan[t]e seas.* London: William Wright, 1594.
A–C⁴.
STC 20572.

1595 Adrichem, Christian van. *A briefe description of Hierusalem and of the suburbs thereof.* London: Peter Short for Thomas Wight, 1595.
¶⁴, A–P⁴, Q²; one folding map.
STC 152.

1595 Davis, John. *The seamans secrets.* London: Thomas Dawson, 1595.
¶⁴, A–C⁴, D², E⁴, F², G⁴, []², H–L⁴, M²; diagrams and illustrations in the text.
Not in STC. British Museum.

1595 Davis, John. *The worldes hydrographical discription.* London: Thomas Dawson, 1595
A–C⁸. Church, 249.
STC 6372.

1595 Minadoi, Giovanni Tommaso. *The history of the warres betweene the Turkes and the Persians.* London: John Wolfe, 1595.
A–R⁴, S⁵, T–Z⁴, Aa–Zz⁴, Aaa–Ggg⁴, HHh–IIi⁴; one folding map.
STC 17943.

1595 Hasleton, Richard. *Strange and wonderfull things happened to Richard Hasleton… in his ten yeares travailes in many forraine countries.* London: A.I. for William Barley, 1595.
A²⁻⁴, B–D⁴, E³.
STC 12925.

1595 Roberts, Henry. *Lancaster his allarums, honorable assaultes, and supprising of the block-houses and store-houses belonging to Fernand Bucke in Brasill.* London: A.I. for William Barley [1595].
A–C⁴, []¹. JCB I, 337.
STC 21083.

1595 Roberts, Henry. *The trumpet of fame: or Sir Frauncis Drakes and Sir John Hawkins farewell.* London: Thomas Creede to be sold by William Barley, 1595.
A⁴, B³.
STC 21088.

1596 Bigges, Walter. *A summarie and true discourse of Sir Frances Drakes West Indian voyage*. London: For William Ponsonby, 1596.
A², B–G⁴, H²; four folding maps.
Not in STC. New York Public Library.

1596 Blagrave, John. *Astrolabium uranicum generale*. London: T. Purfoot for W. Watts, 1596.
A–H⁴, I²; one folding map.
STC 3117.

1596 Bourne, William. *A regiment for the sea*. London: Thomas Este for Thomas Wight, 1596.
A², ¶B⁴, ¶C⁴, A–U⁴, X²; diagrams and tables in the text.
STC 3428.

1596 Kemys, Lawrence. *A relation of the second voyage to Guiana*. London: Thomas Dawson, 1596.
A⁴, A–G⁴. Church, 250.
STC 14947.

1596 López de Gómara, Francisco. *The pleasant historie of the conquest of Weast India, now called New Spaine*. London: Thomas Creede, 1596.
a⁴, b², B–Z⁴, Aa–Zz⁴, Aaa–Fff⁴. JCB I, 346.
STC 16808.

1596 Monardes, Nicolás. *Joyfull newes out of the new-found worlde*. London: E. Allde by the assigne of Bonham Norton, 1596.
A⁴, A–Z⁴, Aa–Yy⁴. Church, 253; JCB I, 346.
STC 18007.

1596 Raleigh, Sir Walter. *The discoverie of the large, rich and bewtiful empire of Guiana*. London: Robert Robinson, 1596.
A⁴, ¶⁴, B–P⁴. Church 254; JCB I, 349. The three editions collate identically.
STC 20634, 20635, 20636, 20636a.

1596 Record, Robert. *The castle of knowledge*. London: Valentine Sims, assigned by Bonham Norton, 1596.
B⁶, C–Y⁴, Aa–Ii⁴. Illustrations in the text.
STC 20797.

1597 Blundeville, Thomas. *M. Blundeville his exercises, containing eight treatises*. London: John Windet, 1597.
A–Z⁸, Aa–Zz⁸, Aaa–Ddd⁸; one folding map, four folding diagrams and tables; tables charts, diagrams in the text. JCB I, 351.
STC 3147.

1597 Lopes, Duarte. *A reporte of the kingdome of Congo, a region of Africa*. London: John Wolfe, 1597.
❧⁴, *⁴, **¹, A–Z⁴, Aa–Ee⁴; three folding maps, nine illustrations.
STC 16805.

1597 More, Sir Thomas. *A most pleasant, fruitfull, and wittie worke, of the best state of a publique weale, and of the new yle called Utopia*. London: Thomas Creede, 1597.
A–B², C–T⁴.
STC 18096.

1598 Geraldson, Cornelius. *An addition to the sea journal or navigation of the Hollanders unto Java*. London: John Wolfe, 1598.
A–E⁴; one map; silhouette maps in the text.
STC 11747.

1598–1600 Hakluyt, Richard. *The principal navigations, voyages, traffiques, and discoveries of the English nation.* London: George Bishop, Ralph Newberie and Robert Barker, 1598–1600.
(3 vols. Vol. I is found in issues of both 1598 and 1599.
Vol. II was published in 1599, and Vol. III in 1600).
Vol. I: *–**⁶, A–Z⁶, Aa–Zz⁶, Aaa–Eee⁶, Fff⁴.
Vol. II: *⁸, A–Z⁶, Aa–Cc⁶, Aaa–Rrr⁶.
Vol. III: (A)⁸, A–I⁶, K⁸, L–Z⁶, Aaa–Ccc⁶. Church, 322; JCB I, 360, 372.
STC 12626.

1598 Langenes, Bernardt. *The description of a voyage made by certaine ships of Holland into the East Indies.* London: John Wolfe, 1598.
A–L⁴; six full-page maps.
STC 15193.

1598 Linschoten, Jan Huygen van. *John Huighen van Linschoten. his discours of voyages into ye Easte & West Indies.* London: John Wolfe, 1598.
A⁴, B–Q⁶, R⁸, *S², S–Z⁶, Aa⁶, Bb–Cc⁴, Dd–Pp⁶, Q⁷; maps in the text, three folding plates, thirteen folding maps. Church 321; JCB I, 362.
STC 15691.

1599 Abbot, George. *A briefe description of the whole world.* London, T. Judson for John Browne, 1599.
A–D⁸, E².
STC 24.

1599 *A true report of the gainefull, prosperous and speedy voiage to Java in the East Indies.* London: P. S[hort] for W. Aspley, [1599].
A²⁻⁴, B–C⁴, D³.
STC 14478.

1600 Abbot, George. *A briefe description of the whole worlde.* London: R. B. for J. Browne, 1600.
A–H⁴.
STC 25.

1600 Africanus, Johannes Leo. *A geographical historie of Africa.* London: George Bishop, 1600.
[]⁴, a–e⁶, A–O⁶, Q–Z⁶, Aa–Nn⁶; one folding map.
STC 15481.

1600 Tatton, Gabriel. *Maris Pacifici quod vulgo Mar del Zur.* Engraved by Benjamin Wright [London: 1600].
Map, 585 × 484 mm. John Carter Brown Library.

1600 Tatton, Gabriel. *Nova et rece terraum et regnorum Californiae, Nova Hispaniae, Mexicanae, et Peruviae...* Engraved by Benjamin Wright [London: 1600].
Map, 534 × 410 mm. John Carter Brown Library.

1600 *A true report of Sir Anthony Shierlie's journey overland to Venice from thence by sea to Antioch, Aleppo and Babilon.* London: R. B[lore] for J. J[aggard], 1600.
A⁴, B².
STC 22425.

1601 Botero, Giovanni. *The travellers breviat, or an historicall description of the most famous kingdomes in the world.* London: Edm. Bollifant for John Jaggard, 1601.
[]², B–Z⁴, Aa².
STC 3398.

1601 Botero, Giovanni. *The worlde, or an historicall description of the most famous king-domes and common-weales therein.* London: Edm. Bollifant for John Jaggard, 1601.
[]², B–Z⁴, Aa–Ee⁴, Ff³. JCB II, 10.
STC 3399.

1601 Galvão, Antonio. *The discoveries of the world from their first originall unto the yeere of our lord 1555.* London: George Bishop, 1601.
A–N⁴, O³. Church, 323.
STC 11543.

1601 Neck, Jacob Corneliszoon van. *The journall, or dayly register, contayning a true manifestation, and historicall declaration of the voyage... under the conduct of Jacob Corneliszen Neck... which sayled from Amsterdam the first day of March, 1598.* London: For Cuthbert Burby and John Flasket, 1601.
¶², A²⁻⁴, B–P⁴, Q³.
STC 18417.

1601 Parry, William. *A new and large discourse of the travels of Sir Anthony Sherley... to the Persian Empire.* London: Valentine Simmes for Felix Norton, 1601.
A–E⁴, F³.
STC 19343.

1602 Brereton, John. *A briefe and true relation of the discoverie of the north part of Virginia.* London: George Bishop, 1602.
First Issue: A–C⁴. Church, 325; JCB II, 15.
Second Issue: A–F⁴. Church, 326; JCB II, 15.
STC 3610, 3611.

1603 Botero, Giovanni. *An historicall description of the most famous kingdomes and common-weales in the worlde.* London: For John Jaggard, 1603.
[]², B–Z⁴, Aa–Ll⁴, Mm².
STC 3400.

1603 *A letter written to the right worshipfull the governours and assistants of the East Indian marchants in London.* London: Thomas Thorpe, to be sold by William Aspley, 1603.
A⁴, B³.
STC 7448.

1603 Ortelius, Abraham. *Abraham Ortelius his epitome of the theater of the worlde.* London: Jeames Shawe, 1603.
[]¹, +⁸, A–P⁸, Q⁶; 124 maps. JCB I, 21.
STC 18856.

1603 Timberlake, Henry. *A true and strange discourse of the travailes of two English pilgrimes.* London: For Thomas Archer, 1603.
A–C⁴, D².
STC 24079.

1603 *A true and large discourse of the voyage of the whole fleete of ships set forth the 20. of Aprill 1601.* London: Thomas Thorpe to be sold by William Aspley, 1603.
A–E⁴.
Not in STC. British Museum.

1603 *A true and perfect relation of the newes sent from Amsterdam, the 21. of February, 1603.* London: T. C. for Thomas Archer, 1603.
[]⁴.
Not in STC. British Museum.

1604 Acosta, José de. *The naturall and morall historie of the East and West Indies*. London: Valentine Sims for Edward Blount and William Aspley, 1604.
A⁴, a–b⁴, B–Z⁸, Aa–Pp⁸. JCB II, 24.
STC 94.

1605 Abbot, George. *A briefe description of the whole worlde*. London: For J[ohn] Browne, 1605.
A–V⁴, X².
STC 25.

1605 Rosier, James. *A true relation of the most prosperous voyage made this present yeere 1605, by Captaine George Waymouth, in the discovery of the land of Virginia*. London: George Bishop, 1605.
A–E⁴. Church, 341; JCB II, 35.
STC 21322.

1605 *Sir Thomas Smithes voiage and entertainment in Rushia*. London: Nathanyell Butter, 1605.
A–B², C–M⁴, M³ (repeated); one portrait.
STC 22869.

1606 Blundeville, Thomas. *M. Blundeville his exercises, containing eight treatises*. London: John Windet, 1606.
A–Z⁸, Aa–Zz⁸, Aaa–Ddd⁸; one folding map, four folding diagrams and tables; tables, charts, diagrams in the text.
STC 3148.

1606 *The last East-Indian voyage*. London: T[homas] P[urfoot] for Walter Burre, 1606.
[]², B–K⁴. JCB II, 41.
STC 7456.

1606 Ortelius, Abraham. *The theatre of the whole world*. London: John Norton, 1606.
[221] pp. text, 155 double-page maps, five double-page views, four ornamental engravings, one portrait. JCB II, 41.
STC 18855.

1606 Palmer, Sir Thomas. *An essay of the meanes how to make our travailes, into forraine countries the more profitable and honourable*. H. L[ownes] for Matthew Lownes, 1606.
A–R⁴, S²; four folding diagrams. JCB II, 41.
STC 19156.

1606 Scott, Edmund *An exact discourse of the subtilties, fashishions, [sic] pollicies, religion, and ceremonies of the East Indians*. London: W. W[hite] for Walter Burre, 1606.
A–N⁴.
STC 22061.

1607 Davis, John. *The seaman's secrets*. London: Thomas Dawson, 1607.
A–L⁴, M².
STC 6369.

1607 Nicholl, John. *An houre glasse of Indian newes*. London: [E. Allde] for Nathaniell Butter, 1607.
A–E⁴, F². JCB II, 47.
STC 18532.

1607 Nixon, Anthony. *The three English brothers*. London: John Hodgets, 1607.
A–K⁴.
STC 18592.

1607 Nixon, Anthony. *The travels of three English brothers.* London: John Hodgets, 1607.
A–K⁴, woodcut of ship on A¹ verso.
STC 18593.

1607 Stafforde, Robert. *A geographicall and anthologicall description of all the empires and kingdomes, both of continent and ilands of this terestriall globe.* London: T[homas] C[reed] for Simon Waterson, 1607.
A–K⁴.
STC 23135.

1608 Abbot, George. *A briefe description of the whole worlde.* London: For John Browne, 1608.
A–V⁴. JCB II, 49.
STC 26.

1608 Botero, Giovanni. *Relations, of the most famous kingdoms and common-weales thorough the world.* London: For John Jaggard, 1608.
[]², B–Z⁴, Aa–Tt⁴, Vv¹.
STC 3401.

1608 Matelief, Cornelis. *An historicall and true discourse of a voyage made... into the East Indies.* London: For William Barret, 1608.
A–C⁴, D³.
STC 17651.

1608 Smith, John. *A true relation of such occurrences and accidents of noate as hath hapned in Virginia since the first planting of that collony.* London: For John Tappe, sold by W. W[elby], 1608.
[]³, A³⁻⁴, B–E⁴. Church, 333; JCB II, 55.
STC 22795.

1608 Timberlake, Henry. *A true and strange discourse of the travailes of two English pilgrimes.* London: For Thomas Archer, 1608.
A–E⁴, F².
STC 24080.

1609 Biddulph, William. *The travels of certaine Englishmen into Africa, Asia, Troy, Bythnia, Thracia, and to the Blacke Sea.* London: Th. Haveland for W. Aspley, 1609.
¶⁴, A–X⁴.
STC 3051.

1609 Gray, Robert. *A good speed to Virginia.* London: Felix Kyngston for William Welbie, 1609.
A–D⁴. Church, 336; JCB II, 59.
STC 12204.

1609 Johnson, Robert. *Nova Britannia. Offering most excellent fruites by planting in Virginia.* London: Samuel Macham, 1609.
A–D⁴, E². Church, 338; JCB II, 60.
STC 14699.

1609 Lescarbot, Marc. *Nova Francia: or the description of that part of New France, which is one continent with Virginia.* London: George Bishop, 1609.
[]², ¶¶–¶¶¶¶⁴, A–Z⁴, Aa–Pp⁴, Qq². Church, 341.
STC 15491.

1609 Lescarbot, Marc. *Nova Francia: or the description of that part of New France, which is one continent with Virginia.* London: Andrew Hebb [1609].
[]², ¶¶–¶¶¶⁴, A–Z⁴, Aa–Pp⁴, Qq². Church, 341; JCB II, 62.
STC 15492.

1609 Linton, Anthony. *Newes of the complement of the art of navigation, and of the mightie empire of Cataia.* London: Felix Kyngston, 1609.
A–F⁴. Church, 343; JCB II, 63.
STC 15692.

1609 Price, Daniel. *Sauls prohibition staide.* London: For Matthew Law, 1609.
A–F⁴. JCB II, 66.
STC 20302.

1609 Soto, Ferdinand de. *Virginia richly valued, by the description of the maine land of Florida, her next neighbour.* London: Felix Kyngston for Matthew Lownes, 1609.
A–Z⁴, Aa². Church 337; JCB II, 68.
STC 22938.

1609 Symonds, William. *Virginia. A sermon preached at White-Chappel, in the presence of many... adventurers and planters for Virginia.* London: J. Windet for Eleazar Edgar and William Welby, 1609.
A–H⁴. Church, 344; JCB II, 66.
STC 23594.

1609 Timberlake, Henry. *A true and strange discourse of the travailes of two English pilgrimes.* London: For Thomas Archer, 1609.
A–D⁴, E³.
STC 24081.

1609 *A true historicall discourse of Muley Hamets rising to the three kingdomes of Moruecos. Fes and Sus.* London: Thomas Purfoot for Clement Knight, 1609.
A–K⁴, L¹.
STC 4300.

1609 Veer, Gerrit de. *The true and perfect description of three voyages... by the ships of Holland and Zeland.* London: T. Pavier, 1609.
A², B–U⁴, X³. JCB II, 67.
STC 24628.

1610 Crashaw, William. *A sermon preached in London before the... Lord Lawarre.* London: William Welby, 1610.
A–L⁴. Church, 345; JCB II, 69.
STC 6029.

1610 Jourdain, Silvester. *A discovery of the Barmudas, otherwise called the Ile of Divels.* London: John Windet, sold by Roger Barnes, 1610.
A³, B–C⁴, D².
STC 14816.

1610 Ortelius, Abraham. *An epitome of Ortelius his theatre of the world.* London: John Norton, [1610].
A⁴, B–R⁸; 125 maps.
STC 18857.

1610 Rich, Richard. *Newes from Virginia. The lost flocke triumphant.* London: Edward Allde, to be solde by John Wright, 1610.
A⁴, B³. Church, 346; JCB II, 71.
STC 21005.

1610  *A true and sincere declaration of the purpose and ends of the plantation begun in Virginia.* London: For J. Stepneth, 1610.
A–C⁴, D³. Church 347; JCB II, 72.
STC 24832, 24832a (with imprint 'For J. Stepney').

1610  *A true declaration of the estate of the colonie in Virginia.* London: For William Barret, 1610.
A–F⁴, F⁴, H–I⁴. (G omitted). Church, 348; JCB II, 73.
STC 24833.

1611  Boemus, Joannes. *The manners, lawes and customes of all nations.* London: George Eld, 1611.
¶³, A–B⁴, C–Z⁸, Aa–Nn⁸. JCB II, 73.
STC 3198.

1611  Cartwright, John. *The preachers travels.* London: For Thomas Thorppe, to be sold by Walter Burre, 1611.
A³, B–O⁴, P³.
STC 4705.

1611  Hues, Robert. *Tractatus de globis, caelesti et terrestri ac eorum usu.* London: Officina Nortoniana, 1611.
A–O¹², P¹¹; two folding tables.
STC 13906a.

1611  Soto, Ferdinand de. *The worthye and famous history of the travailes, discovery and conquest, of that great continent, Terra Florida.* London: [Felix Kyngston] for Matthew Lownes, 1611.
A–Z⁴, Aa².
STC 22939.

1611  Timberlake, Henry. *A true and strange discourse of the travailes of two English pilgrimes.* London: For Thomas Archer, 1611.
A–D⁴, E³.
STC 24082.

1611  Timberlake, Henry. *A relation of the travells of two English pilgrimes.* London: I. N. for Hugh Perry, 1611.
A–D⁴, E³.
Not in STC. British Museum.

1611  West, Thomas, Lord De La Warr. *The relation of the Right Honourable the Lord De-La-Warr, Lord Governor and Captaine Generall of the colonie, planted in Virginea.* London: William Hall for William Welbie, 1611.
A–B⁴, C². Church, 349.
STC 25266.

1612  Anghiera, Pietro Martire d'. *De novo orbe, or the historie of the West Indies.* London: For Thomas Adams, 1612.
A–Z⁸, Aa–Ss⁸. Church, 358; JCB II, 86.
STC 650.

1612  Biddulph, William. *The travels of foure Englishmen and a preacher into Africa, Asia Troy, Bythnia, Thracia, and to the Blacke Sea.* London: Felix Kyngston for William Aspley, 1612.
A²⁻⁴, B–R⁴, S².
STC 3052.

1612 Coverte, Robert. *A true and almost incredible report of an Englishman, that... travelled by land through many unknowne kingdomes, and great cities.* London: William Hall for Thomas Archer and Richard Redmer, 1612.
A²⁻⁴, B–J⁴, K³.
STC 5895.

1612 Digges, Sir Dudley. *Of the circumference of the earth: or, a treatise of the northeast passage.* London: W. W[hite] for J. Barnes, 1612.
A⁸, B⁷.
STC 6847.

1612 Johnson, Robert. *The new life of Virginea... being the second part of 'Nova Britannia.'* London: Felix Kyngston for William Welby, 1612.
A–G⁴. Church, 355; JCB II, 85.
STC 14700.

1612 Mandeville, Sir John. *The voyages and travailes of Sir John Mandevile knight.* London: Thomas Snodham, 1612.
A–U⁴; illustrations in the text.
Not in STC. Library of Congress.

1612 Smith, John. *A map of Virginia.* Oxford: Joseph Barnes, 1612.
*⁴, A–E⁴. One folding map. Church, 359; JCB II, 88.
STC 22791.

1612 Strachey, William (ed.) *For the colony in Virginea Britannia. Laws divine, morall and martiall, etc.* London: For Walter Burre, 1612.
A–N⁴. JCB II, 90.
STC 23350.

1612 Symonds, William. *The proceedings of the English colonie in Virginia.* Oxford: Joseph Barnes, 1612.
A–O⁴, P². Church, 359; JCB II, 88.
Included in STC 22791, above.

1612 Timberlake, Henry. *A true and strange discourse of the travailes of two English pilgrimes.* London: For Thomas Archer, 1612.
A–D⁴, E³.
STC 24083.

1613 Blundeville, Thomas. *M. Blundeville his exercises, containing eight treatises.* London: William Stansby, 1613.
A–Z⁸, Aa–Zz⁸, Aaa–Eee⁸; four folding tables and diagrams; tables, charts, diagrams in the text.
STC 3149.

1613 Harcourt, Robert. *A relation of a voyage to Guiana.* London: John Beale for W. Welby, 1613.
A–L⁴. Church, 361; JCB II, 95.
STC 12754.

1613 Jourdain, Silvester. *A plaine description of the Barmudas, now called Sommer Ilands.* London: W. Stansby for William Welby, 1613.
A–F⁴, G². Church, 362; JCB II, 96.
STC 14817.

1613 Purchas, Samuel. *Purchas his pilgrimage. Or relations of the world and the religions observed in all places discovered, from the creation unto the present.* London: William Stansby for Henrie Fetherstone, 1613.
¶⁶, A⁸, B⁴, C–Z⁶, Aa–Zz⁶, Aaa–Ttt⁶, U⁵. JCB II, 98.
STC 20505.

1613 Sherley, Sir Anthony. *Sir Anthony Sherley his relation of his travels into Persia.*
London: For Nathaniell Butter and Joseph Bagfet, 1613.
A–S⁴, T².
STC 22424.

1613 Whitaker, Alexander. *Good newes from Virginia.* London: Felix Kyngston for
William Welby, 1613.
A–I⁴. Church, 364; JCB II, 100.
STC 25354.

1613 Zouch, Richard. *The dove: or passages of cosmography.* London: For George
Norton, 1613.
A⁴, B–E⁸.
STC 26130.

1614 Brerewood, Edward. *Enquiries touching the diversity of languages, and religions
through the chiefe parts of the world.* London: [William Stansby] for John Bill,
1614.
*², A[¹], ¶⁴, ¶¶⁴, A¹, B–Z⁴, Aa–Bb⁴, Cc³.
STC 3618.

1614 Coverte, Robert. *A true and almost incredible report of an Englishman, that... trav-
elled by land through many unknowne kingdomes, and great cities.* London: N[icholas]
O[kes] for Thomas Archer, 1614.
A²⁻⁴, B–J⁴, K².
STC 5896.

1614 Davies, William. *A true relation of the travailes and most miserable captivitie of Wil-
liam Davies.* London: For Nicholas Bourne, 1614.
A–E⁴. JCB II, 101.
STC 6365.

1614 Lithgow, William. *A most delectable, and true discourse, of an admired and paineful
peregrination from Scotland, to the most famous kingdomes in Europe, Asia and Affricke.*
London: Nicholas Okes, to be sold by Thomas Archer, 1614.
A³, a², B–S⁴, T².
STC 15710.

1614 Purchas, Samuel. *Purchas his pilgrimage. Or relations of the world and the religions
observed in all ages and places discovered, from the creation unto the present.* London:
William Stansby for Henrie Fetherstone, 1614.
¶⁶, A⁸, B–Z⁶, Aa–Zz⁶, Aaa–Zzz⁶, Aaaa–Kkkk⁶. JCB II, 105.
STC 20506.

1615 Avity, Pierre d'. *The estates, empires and principallities of the world.* London: Adam
Islip for Mathewe Lownes and John Bill, 1615.
[]³, A–B⁶, C⁴, D⁸, E–Z⁶, Aa–Zz⁶, Aaa–Zzz⁶, Aaaa–Zzzz⁶, Aaaaa-Lllll⁶,
Mmmmm⁵.
STC 988.

1615 Feynes, Henri de. *An exact and curious survey of all the East Indies, even to Canton,
the chiefe cittie of China.* London: Thomas Dawson for William Arondell, 1615.
A², B–F⁴, G³.
STC 10840.

1615 Hamor, Ralph. *A true discourse of the present estate of Virginia.* London: John
Beale for William Welby, 1615.
A–I⁴, K³. Church, 365; JCB II, 107.
STC 12736.

1615 Hughes, Lewis. *A letter sent into England from the Summer Ilands*. London: I. B[eale] for William Welby, 1615.
A⁶, B⁴. Church 367A.
STC 13919.

1615 Sandys, George. *A relation of a journey begun An: Dom: 1610*. London: For W. Barrett, 1615.
[]², B–Z⁶, Aa–Dd⁵; one map, one view; maps and illustrations in the text.
STC 21726.

1616 Botero, Giovanni. *Relations, of the most famous kingdoms and commonweales thorough the world*. London: For John Jaggard, 1616.
A², B–Z⁸, Aa–Ee⁸, Ff⁵. JCB II, 112.
STC 3403.

1616 *By His Majesties counseil for Virginia. A briefe declaration of the present state of the things in Virginia*. n.p.n.d. [London: Thomas Snodham, ca. 1616].
A⁴. JCB II, 115.
STC 24834.

1616 *By His Majesties councell for Virginia. Whereas upon the returne of Sir Thomas Dale...*
[London?, ca. 1616].
broadside.
STC 24839.

1616 Coryate, Thomas. *Thomas Coriate traveller for the English wits: Greeting from the court of the Great Mogul*. London: W. Jaggard and Henry Featherstone, 1616.
A–H⁴.
STC 5811, 5812.

1616 Lithgow, William. *A most delectable, and true discourse, of an admired an painefull peregrination from Scotland, to the most famous kingdomes in Europe, Asia and Affricke*. London: Nicholas Okes, to be sold by Thomas Archer, 1616.
A–Q⁴, R³.
STC 15711.

1616 Smith, John. *A description of New England*. London: Humphrey Lownes for Robert Clerke, 1616.
¶⁴, A–I⁴. Church, 369; JCB II, 113.
STC 22788.

1616 Tanner, Robert. *A brief treatise on the use of the globe celestiall and terrestriall*. London: Felix Kyngston for Thomas Man, 1616.
A²⁻⁸, B–C⁸, D⁷.
STC 23672.

1616 Timberlake, Henry. *A true and strange discourse of the travailes of two English pilgrimes*. London: Nicholas Okes for Thomas Archer, 1616.
A–D⁴, E³.
STC 24084.

1617 Abbot, George. *A briefe description of the whole worlde*. London: [Thomas Snodham] for John Browne, 1617.
A–Y⁴. Church, 369A.
STC 28.

1617 Africanus, Johannes Leo. *A geographicall history of Africa*. London: I. L. for A. H., and part of the impression made over to be vented for the benefit of the children of John Minsheu deceased, [ca. 1617].
a–e⁶, A–Z⁶, Aa–Nn⁶; one folding map.
Not in STC. Frank Hammond, bookseller.

1617 Hall, Joseph. *Quo vadis? A just censure of travell as it is commonly undertaken by the gentlemen of our nation.* London: Edward Griffin for Nathaniel Butter, 1617. A–G⁸. Another edition, A–F⁸, G⁴.
STC 12075, 12075a, 12075b.

1617 Purchas, Samuel. *Purchas his pilgrimage. Or relations of the world and the religions observed in all ages and places discovered from the creation unto the present.* London: William Stansby for Henrie Fetherstone, 1617.
¶⁶, ¶⁶, A⁸, B–Z⁶, Aa–Zz⁶, Aaa–Zzz⁶, Aaaa–Zzzz⁶, Aaaaa–Ccccc⁶, Ddddd⁴.
JCB II, 120.
STC 20507.

1617 Queiros, Pedro Fernandes de. *Terra Australis Incognita, or a new southerne discoverie, containing a fifth part of the world.* London: For John Hodgetts, 1617.
A²⁻⁴, B–D⁴. JCB II, 117.
STC 10822.

1618 Coryate, Thomas. *Mr. Thomas Coriat to his friends in England sendeth greeting.* London: J. B[eale?] 1618.
¶³, A⁵, a⁴, B–E⁴.
STC 5809.

1618 *A declaration of the demeanor and cariage of Sir Walter Raleigh, knight, aswell in his voyage, as in, and sithence his returne.* London: Bonham Norton and John Bill, 1618.
[]², A–H⁴, I². Another edition, []², A–H⁴. JCB II, 123.
STC 20653, 20653a, 20654, 20654a.

1618 Mandeville, Sir John. *The voyages and travailes of Sir John Mandevile knight.* London: T[homas] S[nodham], 1618.
A–U⁴; illustrations in the text.
STC 17252.

1618 *Newes of Sr. Walter Rauleigh. With the true description of Guiana.* London: H. G[ossen] and are to be sold by J. Wright, 1618.
[]¹, B–F⁴, G³. JCB II, 128.
STC 17148.

1618 Stafforde, Robert. *A geographicall and anthologicall description of all the empires and kingdomes... of this terrestriall globe.* London: Nicholas Okes for S[imon] W[aterson], 1618.
A–K⁴. JCB II, 130.
STC 23136.

1618 Stafforde, Robert. *A geographicall and anthologicall description of all the empires and kingdomes... of this terrestriall globe.* London: N[icholas] O[kes] for John Parker, 1618.
[A]–K⁴.
STC 23136a.

1619 *A briefe relation of the persecution lately made against the Catholike Christians in the kingdome of Japonia.* [St. Omer], 1619.
A–Y⁸.
STC 14527.

1619 *A note of the shipping, men and provisions, sent to Virginia, by the treasurer and company, in the yeere 1619.* [London, 1619].
A².
STC 24842.

1619 Schouten, Willem. *The relation of a wonderfull voiage... shewing how south from the Straights of Magelan... he found and discovered a newe passage through the great South Sea.* London: T. D[awson] for Nathanaell Newbery, 1619.
[ ]², A–L⁴; map on title page, repeated in the text. Church, 337; JCB II, 142.
STC 21828.

1620 Abbot, George. *A briefe description of the whole worlde.* London: For John Marriott, 1620.
A–Y⁴.
STC 29.

1620 *A declaration of the state of the colonie and affaires in Virginia.* London: T[homas] S[nodham], 1620.
First edition: A–B⁴, *⁴, C⁴, A², C–F⁴, A–E⁴. Church, 381; JCB II, 150.
Second edition: A–N⁴. Church, 382; JCB II, 151.
STC 24835, 24836.

1620 Mason, John. *A briefe discourse of the New-found-land* Edinburgh: Andro Hart, 1620.
[ ]⁴, B³. Church, 379; JCB II, 148.
STC 17616.

1620 *A note of the shipping, men, and provisions, sent and provided for Virginia, by the Right Honorable, the Earle of Southampton, and the company, this yeare, 1620.* [London: 1620].
[ ]².
STC 24842a.

1620 Smith, John. *New Englands trials. Declaring the successe of 26 ships employed thither within these sixe years.* London: William Jones, 1620.
[ ]², B–C⁴. JCB II, 149.
STC 22792.

1620 Tanner, Robert. *A brief treatise of the use of the globe celestiall and terrestriall.* London: Richard Field for Thomas Man, 1620.
A²⁻⁸, B–C⁸, D⁷.
STC 23673.

1620 Timberlake, Henry. *A true and strange discourse of the travailes of two English pilgrimes.* London: Nicholas Okes for Thomas Archer, 1620.
A–D⁴, E³.
STC 24085.

1620 Whitbourne, Richard. *A discourse and discovery of New-found-land.* London: Felix Kyngston for William Barret, 1620.
A–B⁴, C², D–M⁴, N². JCB II, 151.
STC 25372.

# SECONDARY SOURCES

Abbe, Ernst C. and Frank J. Gillis. 'The exploration and mapping of Hudson Bay, 1610–1631,' *Merchants and scholars*. Edited by John Parker. Minneapolis: University of Minnesota Press, 1965.

Adamson, J. W. 'The extent of literacy in England in the fifteenth and sixteenth centuries,' *The library*, 4th series, X (September, 1929), 163–93.

Arber, Edward. *The first three English books on America*. Westminster: Archibald Constable and Co., 1895.

—— (ed.). *A transcript of the registers of the Company of Stationers of London*. 5 vols London, Birmingham: Privately printed, 1874–94.

Barlow, Roger, *A brief summe of geographie*. Edited by E. G. R. Taylor. London: The Hakluyt Society, 1932.

Bearwood, Alice. 'Alien merchants and the English crown in the later fourteenth century,' *Economic history review*, II (January, 1930), 229–60.

Bennett, H. S. *English books and readers 1475–1557*. Cambridge: Cambridge University Press, 1952.

——. 'Science and information in English writings of the fifteenth century,' *Modern language review*, XXXIX (January, 1944), 1–8.

Bennett, Josephine W. *The rediscovery of Sir John Mandeville*. New York: The Modern Language Association, 1954.

Biggar, H. P. 'Jean Ribaut's discoverye of Terra Florida,' *The English historical review*, XXXII (April, 1917), 253–70.

Bindoff, S. T. *Tudor England*. Harmondsworth, Middlesex: Penguin Books, Ltd., 1958.

Bolton, Charles Knowles. *The real founders of New England*. Boston: F. W. Faxon Co., 1929.

Bond, Edward A. *Russia at the close of the sixteenth century*. London: The Hakluyt Society, 1856.

Borish, M. E. 'Sources and intention of *The four elements*,' *Studies in philology*, XXXV (April, 1938), 149–63.

Boxer, C. R. *The Christian century in Japan*. Berkeley: University of California Press, 1951.

Brant, Sebastian. *The ship of fools*. 2 vols. Edited by T. H. Jamieson. Edinburgh, William Paterson, 1874.

Brebner, John B. *The explorers of North America*. Garden City: Doubleday Anchor, 1955.

Brooks, Eric St. John. *Sir Christopher Hatton*. London: Jonathan Cape, 1947.

Brock, Robert A. 'Virginia, 1606–1689,' *Narrative and critical history of America*. 8 vols. Edited by Justin Winsor. Boston: Houghton, Mifflin and Co., 1889.

Bullen, A. H. (ed.). *The works of John Day*. London: The Chiswick Press, 1881.

Burwash, Dorothy. *English merchant shipping, 1460–1540*. Toronto: University of Toronto Press, 1947.

Cooper, Ernest R. 'The Dunwich Iceland ships,' *The mariner's mirror*, XV (April, 1939), 170–177.

Coote, S. H. *The voyage from Lisbon to India, 1505–6*. London: B. F. Stevens, 1894.

Chatterton, E. Keble. *Captain John Smith*. London: John Lane, the Bodley Head, Ltd., 1937.

Carus-Wilson, E. M. 'The Iceland trade,' *Studies in English trade in the fifteenth century.* Edited by Eileen Power and M. M. Postan. London: George Routledge and Sons, Ltd., 1933.

——. 'The overseas trade of Bristol,' *Studies in English trade in the fifteenth century.* Edited by Eileen Power and M. M. Postan. London: George Routledge and Sons, Ltd., 1933.

—. *The overseas trade of Bristol in the later Middle Ages.* n.p.: For the Bristol Record —Society, 1937.

Dean, John Ward. *Capt. John Mason, the founder of New Hampshire.* Boston: The Prince Society, 1887.

De Costa, Benjamin F. 'Norumbega and its English explorers.' *Narrative and critical history of America.* 8 vols. Edited by Justin Winsor. Boston: Houghton, Mifflin and Co., 1889.

Duff, E. Gordon. *A century of the English book trade.* London: The Bibliographical Society, 1905.

—— (ed.). *Information for pilgrims unto the Holy Land.* London: Lawrence and Bullen, 1893.

Ellis, George Edward. 'Las Casas, and the relations of the Spaniards to the Indians,' *Narrative and critical history of America.* 8 vols. Edited by Justin Winsor. Boston: Houghton, Mifflin and Co., 1889.

Ellis, Sir Henry. *The pylgrymage of Sir Richard Guylforde to the Holy Land, A. D. 1506.* London: For the Camden Society, 1851.

Elton, G. R. *England under the Tudors.* London: Methuen & Co. Ltd., 1959.

Fisher, F. J. 'Commercial trends and policy in sixteenth century England,' *Economic history review,* X (November, 1940), 95–117.

Foster, Sir William. *England's quest for eastern trade.* London: A. & C. Black, Ltd., 1933.

—— (ed.). *The voyage of Sir Henry Middleton to the Moluccas, 1604–1606.* London: The Hakluyt Society, 1943.

—— (ed.). *The voyage of Thomas Best to the East Indies, 1612–14.* London: The Hakluyt Society, 1934.

Gates, Frances A. *John Florio.* Cambridge: Cambridge University Press, 1934.

Gosling, William G. *The life of Sir Humphrey Gilbert.* London: Constable and Co., 1911.

Gould, J. D. 'The crisis in the export trade, 1586–87,' *The English historical review,* LXXI (April, 1956), 212–222.

Guerra, F. *Nicolas Bautista Monardes, su vida y su obra.* Mexico City: Compañia Fundidora de Fierro y Acero de Monterrey, 1961.

Hanke, Lewis. *Aristotle and the American Indians.* London: Hollis and Carter, 1959.

Harlow, V. T. *Raleigh's last voyage.* London: The Argonaut Press, 1932.

Harrison, W. E. C. 'An early voyage of discovery,' *The mariner's mirror,* XVI (April, 1930), 198–99.

Harrisse, Henry. *Americus Vespuccius.* London: B. F. Stevens, 1895.

Harte, W. J. 'Some recent views on Drake's voyage around the world,' *History,* new series, XX (March, 1936), 348–53.

Hues, Robert. *Tractatus de globis et eorum usu.* Edited by Clements R. Markham. London: The Hakluty Society, 1889.

Jusserand, J. J. *English wayfaring life in the Middle Ages.* London: T. Fisher Unwin, 1889.

——. *A literary history of the English people.* 3 vols. London: T. Fisher Unwin, 1895.

Kingsford, Charles L. 'The beginnings of English maritime enterprise,' *History*, XIII (October, 1928), 193–98.

——. *English history in contemporary poetry*, Vol. II: *Lancaster and York*. London: For the Historical Association by George Bell and Sons, Ltd., 1913.

——. *Prejudice and promise in XVth century England*. Oxford: Clarendon Press, 1925.

Kronenberg, M. E. 'Notes on English printing in the Low Countries,' *The library*, 4th series, IX (September, 1928), 139–63.

Lenhart, J. M. 'Pre-Reformation printers and their services to the Church,' *Ecclesiastical review*, LXXXI (August, 1929), 154–66.

Letts, Malcolm. *Sir John Mandeville, the man and his book*. London: Batchworth Press, 1949.

——. 'The source of the woodcuts in Wynkyn de Worde's edition of Mandeville's *Travels*, 1499,' *The library*, 5th series, VI (June, 1951), 154–61.

Lipson, Ephraim. *The history of the woolen and worsted industries*. London: A. & C. Black, Ltd., 1921.

McElwee, William L. *England's precedence*. London: Hodder and Stoughton, Ltd., 1956.

McFee, William. *Sir Martin Frobisher*. London: John Lane, the Bodley Head, Ltd., 1928.

Marcus, G. J. 'The first English voyages to Iceland,' *The mariner's mirror*, XLII (1956), 313–18.

Markham, Albert Hastings (ed.). *The voyages and works of John Davis the navigator*. London: The Hakluyt Society, 1880.

Markham, Clements R. *A life of John Davis*. London: George Philip and Son, 1889.

—— (ed.). *The voyages of Sir James Lancaster, Kt. to the East Indies*. London: The Hakluyt Society, 1877.

Miller, Edwin H. *The professional writer in Elizabethan England*. Cambridge, Mass.: Harvard University Press, 1959.

Moreland, W. H. (ed.). *Peter Floris, his voyage to the East Indies in the 'Globe', 1611–1615*. London: The Hakluyt Society, 1934.

Myers, A. R. *England in the late Middle Ages*. Harmondsworth, Middlesex: Penguin Books, Ltd., 1956.

Newton, Arthur Percival. *The colonising activities of the English Puritans*. New Haven: Yale University Press, 1914.

Nugent, E. M. 'Sources of John Rastell's *The nature of the four elements*', *PMLA*, LVII (March, 1942), 74–88.

Parks, George B. *The contents and sources of Ramusio's 'Navigationi'*. New York: The New York Public Library, 1955.

——. *The English traveler to Italy*. Stanford: Stanford University Press, [1954].

——. 'The geography of *The interlude of the four elements*,' *Philological quarterly*, XVII (July, 1938), 251–62.

——. 'George Peele and his friends as 'ghost poets',' *The journal of English and German philology*, XLI (October, 1942), 527–36.

——. *Richard Hakluyt and the English voyages*. New York: American Geographical Society, 1928.

Parr, Johnstone. 'More sources of Rastell's *Interlude of the four elements*,' *PMLA*, XL (March, 1945), 48–58.

Penrose, Boies (ed.). *The travels of Captain Robert Coverte*. Philadelphia: Wm. F. Bell Company for Boise Penrose, 1931.

Plomer, Henry R. 'The importation of books into England in the 15th and 16th centuries,' *The library*, 4th series, IV (September, 1923), 146–50.

——. 'The importation of Low Country and French books into England, 1480 and 1502–3,' *The library*, 4th series, IX (September, 1928), 164–68.

————. *Wynkyn de Worde and his contemporaries*. London: Grafton and Company, 1925.

Pompen, Aurelius. *The English versions of the ship of fools*. London: Longmans Green and Co., 1925.

Powys, Llewelyn. *Henry Hudson*. London: John Lane, the Bodley Head, Ltd., 1927.

Purchas, Samuel. *Hakluytus posthumus or Purchas his pilgrimes*. 20 vols. Glasgow: James MacLehose and Sons, 1905.

Quinn, David B. 'The argument for the English discovery of America between 1480 and 1494,' *The geographical journal*, CXXVII (September, 1961), 277–85.

————. 'Edward IV and exploration,' *The mariner's mirror*, XXI (July 1935), 275–84.

————. 'England and the St. Lawrence, 1577–1602,' *Merchants and scholars*. Edited by John Parker. Minneapolis: University of Minnesota Press, 1965.

————. *Raleigh and the British Empire*. New York: Collier Books, 1962.

————. *The Roanoke voyages*. 2 vols. London: The Hakluyt Society, 1955.

————. *The voyages and colonising enterprises of Sir Humphrey Gilbert*. 2 vols. London: The Hakluyt Society, 1940.

Ramsay, G. D. *English overseas trade during the centuries of emergence*. London: Macmillan, 1957.

Reed, Arthur W. *Early Tudor drama*. London: Methuen & Co. Ltd., 1921.

————. 'John Rastell's voyage in the year 1517,' *The mariner's mirror*, IX (May, 1923), 137–47.

Read, Conyers. *The Tudors*. New York: Henry Holt and Co., 1936.

Rogers, Francis M. *The quest for eastern Christians*. Minneapolis: University of Minnesota Press, 1962.

Ross, Sir E. Denison. *Sir Anthony Sherley and his Persian adventure*. London: George Routledge & Sons, Ltd., 1933.

Routh, E. M. G. *Sir Thomas More and his friends*. London: Oxford University Press, 1934.

Rowland, Albert Lindsay. 'England and Turkey: The rise of diplomatic and commercial relations,' *Studies in English commerce and exploration in the reign of Elizabeth*. Philadelphia: University of Pennsylvania Press, 1924.

Rowse, A. L. *The expansion of Elizabethan England*. London: Macmillan, 1955.

————. *Sir Richard Grenville*. London: Jonathan Cape, Ltd., 1937.

Ruddock, Alwyn A. 'Alien merchants in Southampton in the later Middle Ages,' *The English historical review*, LXI (January, 1946), 1–17.

————. *Italian merchants and shipping in Southampton*. Southampton: University College, 1951.

————. 'The method of handling cargoes of medieval merchant galleys,' *Bulletin of the Institute of Historical Research*, XIX (1942), 140–48.

Salter, F. R. 'The Hanse, Cologne and the crisis of 1468,' *Economic history review*, III (January, 1931), 93–101.

Sargent, Ralph M. *At the court of Queen Elizabeth; the life and lyrics of Sir Edward Dyer*. London: Oxford University Press, 1935.

Satow, Sir Ernest M. (ed.). *The voyage of Captain John Saris to Japan, 1613*. London: The Hakluyt Society, 1900.

Schulze, Franz. (ed.). *Balthasar Springers Indienfahrt, 1505–06*. Strassburg: J. H. Heitz, 1902.

Scott, William R. *The constitution and finance of English, Scottish and Irish joint stock companies to 1720*. 3 vols. Cambridge: Cambridge University Press, 1912.

Shea, John Gilmary. 'Ancient Florida,' *Narrative and critical history of America*. 8 vols. Edited by Justin Winsor. Boston: Houghton, Mifflin and Co., 1889.

Sheavyn, Phoebe. 'Writers and the publishing trade, circa 1600,' *The library*, 2nd series, VII (October, 1906), 337–65.

Slafter, Carlos, *Sir Humphrey Gylberte and his enterprise of colonization in America*. Boston: The Prince Society, 1903.

Smith, Goldwin Albert. *A history of England*. New York: Charles Scribner's Sons, 1949.

Smith, H. Maynard. *Pre-Reformation England*. London: Macmillan & Co., Ltd., 1938.

Stefansson, Vilhjalmur (ed.). *The three voyages of Martin Frobisher*. 2 vols. London: The Argonaut Press, 1938.

Taylor, E. G. R. *Late Tudor and early Stuart geography, 1583–1650*. London: Methuen & Co., Ltd., 1934.

——. *The mathematical practitioners of Tudor and Stuart England*. Cambridge: Cambridge University Press, 1954.

—— (ed.). *A regiment for the sea and other writings in navigation by William Bourne*. Cambridge: For the Hakluyt Society, 1963.

—— (ed.). *The troublesome voyage of Captain Edward Fenton*. Cambridge: For the Hakluyt Society, 1959.

——. *Tudor geography*. London: Methuen & Co. Ltd., 1930.

Thomson, P. 'The patronage of letters under Elizabeth and James I,' *English*, VII (1949), 278–82.

Tooley, R. V. *Maps and map-makers*. London: B. T. Batsford Ltd., 1952.

Vaughn, Earnest V. 'English trading expeditions into Asia under the authority of the Muscovy Company (1557–1581),' *Studies in the history of English commerce in the Tudor period*. New York: D. Appleton and Co., 1912.

Wagner, Henry R. *Sir Francis Drake's voyage around the world*. San Francisco: John Howell, 1926.

Warner, Sir George (ed.). *The libelle of Englyshe polycye*. Oxford: Clarendon Press, 1926.

Waters, David W. *The art of navigation in England in Elizabethan and early Stuart times*. London: Hollis and Carter, 1958.

Watson, Foster. *The beginnings of the teaching of modern subjects in England*. London: Sir Isaac Pitman & Sons, Ltd., 1909.

Webb, John. 'The Van Deutecum map of Russia and Tartary,' *Merchants and scholars*. Edited by John Parker. Minneapolis: University of Minnesota Press, 1965.

Weiner, A. 'Early commercial intercourse between England and Germany,' *Economica*, II (June, 1922), 127–48.

Weiss, R. *Humanism in England during the fifteenth century*. Oxford: Basil Blackwell, 1957.

Wertenbaker, Thomas J. *Virginia under the Stuarts, 1607–1688*. Princeton: Princeton University Press, 1914.

Wey, William. *The itineraries of William Wey*. London: The Roxburgh Club, 1857.

Wieder, Frederick C. *Monumenta cartographica*. 5 vols. The Hague: Martinus Nijhoff, 1925–33.

Willan, T. S. *The Muscovy merchants of 1555*. (Manchester: Manchester University Press, 1953.

——. 'Trade between England and Russia in the second half of the sixteenth century,' *English historical review*, LXIII (July, 1948), 307–21.

Williams, Franklin B. *Index of dedications and commendatory verses in English books before 1641*. London: The Bibliographical Society, 1962.

Williamson, James A. *The Cabot voyages and Bristol discovery under Henry VII*. Cambridge: For the Hakluyt Society, 1962.

——. *English colonies in Guiana and on the Amazon, 1604–1668*. Oxford: Clarendon Press, 1923.

——. *Hawkins of Plymouth*. London: Adam and Charles Black, 1949.

——. *Maritime enterprise*. Oxford: Clarendon Press, 1913.

——. *The voyages of John and Sebastian Cabot.* London: For the Historical Association, 1937.

——. *The voyages of the Cabots and the English discovery of America under Henry VII and Henry VIII.* London: The Argonaut Press, 1929.

Wood, Alfred C. *A history of the Levant Company.* London: Oxford University Press, 1935.

Wright, Louis B. 'The Elizabethan middle class taste for history,' *The journal of modern history*, III (June, 1931), 175–97.

——. *Middle class culture in Elizabethan England.* Chapel Hill: University of North Carolina Press, 1935.

——. *Religion and empire.* Chapel Hill: University of North Carolina Press, 1943.

# INDEX